Memory

and Cultural

Politics

Memory
and Cultural
Politics

New Approaches

to American

Ethnic Literatures

E D I T E D   B Y   *Amritjit Singh, Joseph T. Skerrett, Jr., Robert E. Hogan*

Northeastern University Press   ·   Boston

Northeastern University Press
Copyright 1996 by Northeastern University Press

Library of Congress Cataloging-in-Publication Data

Memory and cultural politics : new approaches to American ethnic
   literatures / edited by Amritjit Singh, Joseph T. Skerrett, Jr.,
Robert E. Hogan.
      p. cm.
   Includes bibliographical references and index.
   ISBN 1–55553–234–9 (cloth) — ISBN 1-55553-254-3 (pbk)
   1. American literature—Minority authors—History and criticism.
   2. Politics and literature—United States—History.   3. Ethnic
   relations in literature.   4. Ethnic groups in literature.
   5. Minorities in literature.   6. Memory in literature.   I. Singh,
   Amritjit.   II. Skerrett, Joseph T.   III. Hogan, Robert E.
   PS153.M56M45   1996
   810.9'920693—dc20   95–10351

Designed by David Ford
Printed and bound by Edwards Brothers, Inc., in Ann Arbor, Michigan.
The paper is Glatfelter, an acid-free sheet.

MANUFACTURED IN THE UNITED STATES OF AMERICA
99 98 97 96 95   5 4 3 2 1

FTW

AHW 9376

In memory of

Charles Twitchell Davis

and for

Bal Krishna Kalia

and

Joel M. Porte

teachers who taught and remembered

Contents

Contents

Contents

Preface

The capacious idea of memory and cultural politics, one sounded in our time with urgency and anguish, provides the controlling rubric for this volume. As immigration, the Emancipation, and industrialization exerted growing pressures on the traditional Anglo-American construction of American identity around the turn of the century, cultural historians such as Van Wyck Brooks searched for a usable past to restore that identity. However, such attempts by young intellectuals in a provincial and self-conscious America were faced with many challenges: a general disillusionment that followed World War I; a sense of American cultural thinness that drove artists into European exile; and new patterns of urbanization and internal migration. Since then, several historical factors such as the Great Depression, World War II, the Nazi Holocaust, the cold war, the Civil Rights movement, the Vietnam War, the women's liberation movement, and the growing presence of non-European immigrants have altered forever the landscape of memory that Van Wyck Brooks had mapped out in *America's Coming-of-Age* (1915) and that modernists such as T. S. Eliot had evoked in their writings.

Emerging from this new cultural landscape, American ethnic writers have provided arresting images of the modern predicament and postmodernist settings. Self-reliant individualism is the favored American sense of self, but it is a weak form of social legitimation. The overwhelming hunger for a cultural identity (expressed in the nostalgia for the lost relation, in the re-creation of the cultural connection, and in the need for an affirmation of the long-denied allegiance) drives much of cultural politics. Ethnic writing explores the human relationship to countervailing forces—mythic knowledge, community, kinship, and family—in ways that are reminiscent of Eliot's "roots that clutch."

The fifteen previously unpublished essays we have collected in this volume address the work of writers across the spectrum of American literatures, including Chicano/a, Chinese American, African American, Jewish American, Arab American, Native American, Japanese Canadian,

and Caribbean American. They cover a wide range of topics and pay special attention to the generation and/or maintenance of cultural identity.
Together, they reflect the range and complexity of issues surrounding
memory and cultural politics: real and imagined pasts; personal, generational, and collective histories; remembered pain, nostalgia, and yearning; region and folklore; work, identity, and authenticity; storytelling
and postmodernism; the politics of remembering and forgetting.

Each essay establishes the contours of one critical approach to the
complex subject of memory and culture, among a broad array of theoretical and historical methods represented in this volume. These essays
offer a spectrum of perspectives on memory and its challenges, interrogating the dominant American narrative already fissured by race and
gender. Although some essays deal with a single text / ethnic literature
and others engage multiple texts / ethnic traditions, all of them aim at
articulating the issues and paradigms that involve our responses to all
ethnic literatures. The discussion of these essays in our Introduction—
consciously different from their sequence in the Contents—highlights
how each of them situates its project in relation to the specific histories
and material conditions of relevant ethnic communities, even as it illuminates the myriad forms that textual memory and the act of remembering itself take in American writing and culture. The essays speak to one
another in many ways and together represent a significant conversation
on the sources and possibilities of American multiculturalism. We hope
that the thematic focus in this volume on memory and cultural politics
will open the possibility of moving teaching and scholarship in American ethnic writing and cultural studies beyond the introductory levels at
which they exist today on most campuses.

Our work on this two-volume project has taken us well over four years
to complete. No such project can ever be completed without the generous help of families, friends, and colleagues. We want to acknowledge
the cheerful and energetic participation of many of our contributors in
all aspects of our research and editing. We also commend them all for
their patience and understanding. As in the case of *Memory, Narrative,
and Identity* (1994), we have profited immensely from excellent sugges-
tions made by many colleagues, including Wendy Barker, Betty Berg-
land, William Boelhower, J. Birje-Patil, Jules Chametzky, G. Thomas
Couser, Arlene Elder, Robert Elliot Fox, Pauline Kaldas, A. Robert Lee,
Lisa Majaj, James Robert Payne, Marco Portales, Maureen Reddy, Werner
Sollors, Eric Sundquist, and Stan Yogi. Others who have been helpful in
many ways include Joseph Conforti, Linda Dowling, Lee Finkle, Gurleen

Grewal, Meradith McMunn, Seiwoong Oh, David and Judy Ray, Arlene Robertson, Marjorie Roemer, Prem and Reshma Singh, Joseph Urgo, and James White. We also owe thanks to Barbara Silliman and David Wright, who served as research assistants at different stages of this project, to Ann Flaherty and Kurt Hemmer, who prepared the index, and to the library staffs at the University of Massachusetts at Amherst and Rhode Island College for their unfailing courtesy.

Memory

and Cultural

Politics

Introduction

Those who are alive receive a mandate from those who are silent forever. They can fulfil their duties only by trying to reconstruct precisely things as they were, and by wresting the past from fictions and legends.

—Czeslaw Milosz, Nobel Prize speech, December 8, 1980

Inside the doorway are
torn-out pictures—a memory
like something left over,

a dark negative, finally developed
on the day I leave—

the memory is that part of the present
which exposes the future.

—Bo Carpelan, "Memory"

Uncle Hansen's Children: Are They?

What the son wishes to forget the grandson wishes to remember." This formulation, from the pioneering essay "The Problem of the Third Generation Immigrant" (1938), by Marcus Lee Hansen, served for several decades as a useful framework for certain discourses on American ethnic and immigrant history. In formulating his famous thesis, Hansen sought "to codify the laws of history" in emulation of his teacher Frederick Jackson Turner. Hansen's Law inscribes the differences between successive generations of immigrants to America in terms of memory. Hansen's exemplary "son," the second-generation immigrant, forgets the cultural past in the process of becoming an American, whereas the third-generation grandson, in quest of a new identity shaped partly by disillusionment with the promises of American democracy, attempts to recover the ethnic past.

Hansen's thesis remains useful when approaching the experience of European immigrants during the nineteenth and early twentieth centuries. For example, Irish immigrants to America, beginning with those who came around the time of the 1840s famine, overcame nativist resistance to their presence, assimilating more fully into the general population with each successive generation. Their memory of the Old Country—a memory of hunger, political impotence, and despair—was repressed or forgotten by the early Irish immigrants, and a countermemory of rural idylls, quaint folklore, and cultural homogeneity was put in its place. The later generations of Irish immigrants, remembering the Irish past, or the Irish American past, wrested from erasure what their predecessors did not want to remember: Paddy jokes and No Irish Need Apply signs; the political struggle for jobs and other opportunities; and tenement poverty, as recorded in fictional works such as Stephen Crane's *Maggie: A Girl of the Streets* and James Sullivan's *Tenement Tales of New York*.

Serious complications arise, however, when Hansen's Law is applied to the experience of such diverse groups as immigrant women from Europe, Native Americans, African Americans, Japanese Americans, and new immigrants of color. The Native American memory and experience both precede the national memory and conflict with it. For native peoples, this is the Old Country, and they refuse to forget it or their original relation to it. They have resisted efforts to make them assimilate, to make them strangers in their own land at a heavy price, which their writing explores. African Americans, brought hither in chains from their homes across the Atlantic, have struggled to remember a past from which they were cut off by the Middle Passage and by slavery. As with Native Americans, this feat of memory could not be undertaken without conflict with the dominant national narrative, which denied any value to the African American past and its cultural products. But these nonimmigrant groups do not pose the only challenge to the rubric laid down by Hansen. Not all immigrants come with the same cultural baggage or face the same hurdles in their progress toward Americanization. Some, like post–World War I Armenians and post–World War II Jews, live with a knowledge of betrayal and genocide that makes them wary of assimilation and commitment. Others experience America as an extended exile, an estrangement from a homeland (Cuba, South Africa, Russia) that they wish more to transform than to forget. Thus, memory and countermemory, nostalgia and forgetting, serve a variety of functions outside the loop of assimilation.

The case of Japanese Americans is only one example of how memory enters the realm of cultural politics in ways entirely unanticipated by

Hansen's formulation. Until 1941 Japanese Americans enjoyed a rich relationship with their Asian past. Religion, language, folkways, music, and literature were alive in the memory of families, who also did not question their American identity. After Pearl Harbor, however, this bifocal cultural self-definition broke down because of the decision to remove Japanese Americans in large numbers to "relocation centers," ostensibly as part of the national security effort. Stripped of economic and social standing, forbidden or afraid to express their ethnic culture in music and language, insulted and injured in their self-esteem, many Japanese Americans suffered cultural shock. They did not forget their Japanese heritage, which, they realized more clearly than ever, was emblazoned on their faces. Instead they responded with pain, bewilderment, and silence to the memory of their American oppression. Their descendants struggle to remember, to recover the meaning of "American" as complicated in their parents' lives by racism, war, and denial. Hansen's confidence in the assimilation of the second-generation immigrant is unqualified; he did not consider race and color as issues affecting the immigrant experience. Many Japanese American writers, more than their Euro-American counterparts, distrust the assimilated/acculturated American identity because it exposed them to the betrayal of the camps. And because whole families were interned, the second generation's experience—oppression and rejection—collapsed into that of the first.

Similarly, the work of recent historians and novelists in reconfiguring the experience of American slavery highlights the risks inherent in mythologizing collective memory to serve nationalistic ideologies. As Antonio Gramsci's concept of hegemony indicates, the ruling classes need to turn constantly to both coercion and persuasion in order to maintain power and authority. The dominant group in any nation-state often resorts to nostalgia, to mental or cultural ellipses, and to general forgetfulness in search of meanings and definitions that serve its own ideological needs of the moment. The reluctance of contemporary Japan to deal openly with its histories in China and Korea and the *völkisch* strategies Nazi Germany used in the 1930s to serve its genocidal ends are two very different examples of the ways in which collective memory can be distorted by those in power to shape nationalist goals in a given period of history. As Ernest Renan argued toward the end of the nineteenth century, "forgetting" and "historical error" are essential factors "in the creation of a nation and that is why the advance of historical studies is often a danger for the nationality." Ethnic memory, as reflected in the many ethnic literatures of the United States—no less than the work of the revisionist historians with reference to women, Native Americans, African Americans, and other neglected groups—represents a real challenge to hegemonic constructions of nation, culture, and history. As part of the ongoing argument between history and memory, marginalized groups often attempt to maintain at the center of national memory what the dominant group would often like to forget. The process results in a collective memory always in flux: not one memory but multiple memories constantly battling for attention in cultural space, as seen in the controversies surrounding Lynne Cheney's recent attacks on new guidelines for teaching American history in secondary schools. (See Karen J. Winkler, "Who Owns History?" *Chronicle of Higher Education,* January 20, 1995.)

Since the Civil Rights movement, a growing sensitivity to issues of race, ethnicity, region, and gender has transformed the very meaning of memory in American culture. The process has been aided by feminist and postcolonial critiques of traditional models of immigrant history with which we now associate Hansen's Law, rooted in turn in a vision of the melting pot as a possible ideal and contingent upon an unquestioning acceptance of America as white and "democratic." For most new Americans, for example, ethnicity or national origin is no longer a matter of shame or stigma. Although class has become a more significant factor within each immigrant community, the self-consciousness of new immigrants is no longer invested so heavily in what distinguishes them from second- or third-generation Americans in how they talk, eat, or dress. The shaming rituals associated with turn-of-the-century immigration and often directed at ethnic clothing, food, or speech, for instance, have assumed a less threatening form. (Coincidentally, that earlier immigrant experience is now subject to a benign revisionist reading evident in the transformation of Ellis Island into a national shrine, at the same time as the golden door is being shut in the face of the tired and the poor from such places as Haiti.) Immigrants no longer have the compelling need to disown the language and speech they bring with them. It is more possible now to straddle two national identities without being torn asunder, as evidenced in the growing practice of maintaining dual citizenship. Recent immigrants can assume double nationalities, even double identities, more easily than could their earlier counterparts.

One could say the same now with some credence about W. E. B. Du Bois's notion of "double consciousness" for African Americans. Many Americans of African descent might see their double consciousness today as a useful bifocal lens, and not as the crippling diplopia of the past. Yet

6

a disorder of vision in which two images of a single object are seen because of unequal action of the eye muscles.

Introduction

African Americans have often been forced to remember the distinctiveness of their identity and of their history by the behavior of others toward them—250 years of slavery and another century of Jim Crow. And unlike some new immigrants from Europe and Asia, African Americans have, since the 1950s, dealt with a distinctive pattern of adjustment and assimilation in which success is often confused with compromise, so that being middle class and black is seen in many quarters as a contradiction in terms. In Louis Patterson's *Take a Giant Step* (1953) and Lorraine Hansberry's *A Raisin in the Sun* (1959), we see sixth- and seventh-generation black American "freedmen" and "freedwomen" caught in a process of generational change that has been prolonged far beyond what Hansen's Law envisioned. One might argue that many African Americans—stuck, as it were, at the second-generation stage of Hansen's Law—have worked assiduously to embrace their American identity, with their efforts to establish their Americanness extending to special enlistment campaigns in wars throughout American history. At the same time, many younger African Americans—growing up in integrated middle-class communities, or born to racially mixed couples, or socialized by their experiences at white colleges—are like the third generation of Hansen's Law, having consciously to work toward acquiring the meaning of their African ancestry, however defined.

Yet since the 1960s, this search for African roots (ending, for some, no farther back than the American South) has altered the nature of African American remembering by focusing on positive ways of constructing a new identity, even out of the painful experiences of the past. This process, which Toni Morrison names "re-memory," has had a life of its own since historians, literary scholars, poets, and novelists began to reorient our sense of history by reclaiming slave narratives. One popular cultural manifestation of this process can be seen today in "Malcolmania." Indeed, the entire African American scene—literary, cultural, and academic—seems to have embraced the blues aesthetic, where, in Ralph Ellison's memorable words, one keeps "the painful details and episodes of a brutal experience alive in one's aching consciousness, to finger its jagged grain, and to transcend it." Two prominent examples of this phenomenon are George Rawick's bringing to light, in the 1960s, the nineteen volumes of the WPA narratives and the republication, under Henry Louis Gates's supervision in the 1980s, of the fifty or so nearly forgotten texts that now comprise the Schomburg Library of Black Nineteenth-Century Women Writers.

Memory and Cultural Studies

Nineteenth-century women writers and their literary descendants in this century have shaped many new perspectives on nostalgia and memory, homeland heritage and American participation. In recent decades, many postcolonial writers and scholars—themselves turned American ethnics—have explored their palimpsest memories as new Americans and/ or alerted us to the dangers of nostalgia. Although they have sometimes viewed the United States as a postcolonial nation in a world of transnational realities, they have also taken note of American participation since World War II in neocolonial ventures around the world. In reminding us that our understandings of cultural production and its impact must necessarily derive from a vast variety of popular resources, and not just high art, scholars in cultural studies—like the practitioners of feminist and postcolonial discourses—have sharpened our sense of the intricate nature of power relations and the immense possibilities of hybrid identities.

The development of cultural studies has interrogated the familiar models of assimilation and ethnic identity rooted in a male, Eurocentric tradition. In the tradition of cultural studies, "culture is understood both as a way of life—encompassing ideas, attitudes, languages, practices, institutions and structures of power—and a whole range of cultural practices," including literature (Nelson, 5). Cultural studies make us aware of how these discourses and their play of power change over time, responding to the forces of history, and in the process alter our consciousness of our individuality, gender, and class. In paying attention to nontraditional sources of knowledge and understanding, such as film and folklore, graffiti and advertising, cultural critics remind us that memory, like other constructions of culture, stands in a complex, reciprocal relationship with its bearers. Not only do we create and maintain the memories we need to survive and prevail, but those collective memories in turn both shape and constrain us. In Toni Morrison's *Song of Solomon*, for example, Milkman seeks his personal destiny, which he at first believes to be a fortune, only to discover later that it is instead the decoding of the riddle of history. Morrison's text presents history as riddle, a blues song to be learned by the newborn singer, a cultural artifact that must be subjectively understood by Milkman if he is to locate his place in the family, group, and nation.

Projects such as Recovering the Hispanic Heritage—the enormous compilation and projected publication of Hispanic and Chicano/a texts by Arte Público Press—as well as research into Chicano/a journalistic and autobiographical writings by scholars such as Genaro Padilla in the Bancroft Library, represent the cultural studies impulse to empower the disenfranchised or silenced voices of marginalized cultural groups. These projects will direct the attention of scholars to texts that are not only, in many cases, written by nontraditional authors but also, in as many cases, written in nontraditional genres.

From a cultural studies point of view, ethnic writers and scholars also exemplify the notion of engaged participation in the transformative nature of cultural production. Cultural studies permit us to view ideologically diverse ethnic writers and scholars as cultural workers, making it possible for us to see how the oppositional pairing in mainstream culture of ethnic writers of similar backgrounds is governed by the exaggerated value assigned to ideologies associated with each of them. We know now the understandable "anxiety of influence" that often shapes the work of contemporaneous writers—consider, for example, the mutually shaping aesthetics and worldviews of Emerson and Hawthorne or of Hemingway and Faulkner. However, a similar "anxiety" among ethnic writers has often been viewed as a kind of "battle royal" for the limited cultural space assigned to them. Ethnic scholarship has begun to come to terms now with the many ways in which ethnic writers have been pitted against each other in American cultural history—for example, Richard Wright and Zora Neale Hurston (or James Baldwin or Ralph Ellison), Frank Chin and Maxine Hong Kingston, Gerald Vizenor and Leslie Silko, Ishmael Reed and Amiri Baraka, Cynthia Ozick and Philip Roth.

Granddaughters Remember

Just as Hansen's thesis does not define the generational paradigm of cultural memory for non-European ethnic and immigrant groups, feminist criticism—recognizing that women's experience of American life is qualitatively different from that of men—notes that the language of Hansen's historical formulation is obviously patriarchal. Parallel to the process by which revisionist versions of the frontier thesis have emerged since the 1970s, the scientism apparent in Hansen's Law has now given way, in both literary and historical scholarship, to an acknowledgment of individual and collective subjectivities. We now recognize that what granddaughters might remember is often very different from what grandsons remember.

If granddaughters remember differently from grandsons, the powerful impulse of nostalgia "is by no means gender specific" (Greene, 295). Ethnic women writers, like women writers in general, feel the necessity to "differentiate nostalgia from more productive forms of memory." There are reasons for women not to have much to be nostalgic about, "for the good old days when the grass was greener and young people knew their place was also the time when women knew their place, and it is not a place to which most women want to return" (Greene, 296). For example, immigrant women may expend much less nostalgia than immigrant men on homeland memories, which often include painful recollections of sexist behavior and patriarchal attitudes, customs, and conventions. In Mary Gordon's novel *The Other Side* (1989), Ellen MacNamara feels no sentimental nostalgia for her Irish homeland and no stereotypical religious sympathies. Discussing how memory is engendered in Arab American writing, Lisa Suhair Majaj, in her contribution to this volume, demonstrates how the emphasis on mythologizing the past becomes a trap for women, "within which attempts to alter traditional roles are often taken as attempts to subvert ethnicity itself." Majaj notes how, in D. H. Melhem's *Rest in Love* (1978), "the nurturing but constraining domestic labor of [the protagonist's] mother and grandmother provides a useful counterpoint to male nostalgia."

So, while immigrant women of color in real life—like their fictional counterparts—have generally complained about being orientalized, stereotyped, and racialized, they have also sometimes expressed a sense of liberation in their new American lives from old-world gender roles, welcoming spaces and opportunities to redefine themselves. Yet for women, critiquing the past does not mean rejecting cultural history any more than it amounts to valorizing the present. As Gayle Greene notes, "Women especially need to remember because forgetting is a major obstacle to change" (298). Lacking outlets in the present, many women "live more in the past, which is why they are the keepers of diaries, journals, family records, and photographic albums" (296). Aunt Emily in Joy Kogawa's *Obasan*, for example, is almost obsessive in her compilation of such records. For Chicana writer Gloria Anzaldúa, the self she constructs in her writing is an act of "kneading, of uniting and joining," which recalls individual and collective memory in the service of cultural pluralism.

Postcolonial Voices

If feminist studies have highlighted the patriarchal bias of cultural for-
mulations such as Hansen's Law, postcolonial studies, too, have questioned linear conceptions of American identity and immigrant memory.
Postcolonial discourses in relation to the study of American ethnicity
have projected America itself as a postcolonial nation. We remember in
Fourth of July rituals and in other celebrations of the American Revolution our own postcolonial moment. But postcolonial discourses compel
us to remember America also as an imperialist nation—that is, to remember the conquest of Mexico, the annexation of Hawaii, the "splendid
little war," the acquisition of Puerto Rico and the Philippines, the invasion of Haiti, and the political engineering of the Panama Canal. Two
major applications of the postcolonial discourse that crystallize the pervasive mythology of "whiteness" include the colonial treatment of Native Americans in the settling of the American continent and the colonization of slaves in the South. Many postcolonial and Marxist critics view
the United States' support of dictatorships since World War II—
rationalized in terms of its anti-Communist goals during the cold
war—as an extension of the colonial mind-set. In contrast to the understandings of ethnic assimilation developed by literary historians such as
Werner Sollors, postcolonial theory argues that the unchanging status of
African Americans and Native Americans in American society might best
be explained in terms of their treatment as internal colonial subjects. If
we think about the Irish as colonized by the British, and the Finns by the
Swedes, we can see the value of postcolonial studies illuminating patterns of colonization among the Europeans, making it difficult to view
all Europeans or Euro-Americans as one cohesive group. In addition,
postcolonial approaches to hybrid and transnational identity allow us to
understand how the context and assumptions of new immigrants differ
in significant ways from their counterparts who arrived around the turn
of the century. Instead of denying their ethnicity and national origin,
most of these new immigrants struggle to maintain a "double citizenship" through contact with homeland cultures—or by otherwise viewing
themselves as sojourners.

Yet some postcolonial writers in their American ethnic incarnations
have also found it necessary to warn us against the excesses of nostalgia,
or against the glorification of exile and expatriation. For instance, in her
short story "Nostalgia," Bharati Mukherjee shows how a psychiatrist of

East Indian background living in culturally diverse New York City discovers the emptiness of his nostalgia through his unpleasant encounter with a fellow South Asian immigrant more ruthlessly "American" than himself. As Frederick Buell notes, in this story a mug of Horlicks, a British export to India, "undercuts nostalgia for a separate, bounded, cultural universe just as strongly as the similarly nostalgic memory" (199) of a drink of Hershey's chocolate does in Oscar Hijuelos's *Our House in the Last World* (1983).

Postcolonial discourses have extended and complicated our understandings of how changing patterns of racial formulation and immigration are affecting the emergence of a new American identity. Making a strong case for its inclusion in any study of postcolonial discourse, Arjun Appadurai sees the contemporary United States as a meeting ground of diverse diasporic and transnational populations. The existing images of American "complexity-in-diversity" such as the "mosaic," the "rainbow," and the "quilt" are, as Appadurai has noted, "growing rapidly threadbare" under the assault of transnational communities that are an increasing presence in the United States. "Safe from the depredations of their home-states, [these] diasporic communities become doubly loyal to their nations of origin, thus ambivalent about their loyalties to America" (Appadurai, 803). As Appadurai notes, "No existing conception of Americanness can contain this large variety of trans-nations." Thus, the hyphenated American might have to be twice hyphenated (for example, Asian-American-Japanese or African-American-Jamaican), or "perhaps the sides of the hyphen will have to be reversed and we become a federation of diasporas, American-Italians, American-Haitians, American-Irish, American-Africans" (804). Seen from this perspective, Appadurai predicts, "America may yet construct another narrative of enduring significance, a narrative about the uses of loyalty after the end of the nation-state. In this narrative, bounded territories could give way to diasporic networks, nations to trans-nations, and patriotism itself could become plural, serial, contextual and mobile" (806). Although postcolonial commentators such as Appadurai might be right about the ways in which the presence of global diasporas resists traditional definitions of patriotism and subverts any conceptions of melting-pot assimilation, we also need to remind ourselves that *each* diasporic community is shaped by its own specific histories of class, religion, language, race, and region and to remain alert to the dangers of totalizing tendencies inherent in some postcolonial discourses.

*　　*　　*　　*　　*

A major consequence of these intersections among cultural, feminist, and postcolonial studies in relation to memory and history is our recognition of the plural self, shaped by the ongoing dialogue between the ethnic individual and mainstream culture as well as by such factors as class, religion, and sexual orientation. In Ralph Ellison's *Invisible Man*, one of the ways in which the young protagonist interrogates issues of identity and strategy is by recalling his English teacher's analysis of Joyce's *Portrait of the Artist as a Young Man*. Woodridge, who influences the nameless protagonist during his college years at a segregated school in the South, makes the assertion that Stephen Dedalus's problem was "not actually one of creating the uncreated conscience of his race, but of creating *the uncreated features of his face*." Woodridge goes on to remind his students that "the conscience of a race is the gift of its individuals who see, evaluate, record," and who create not only a race but also a culture. In recent years, Gloria Anzaldúa has talked about her *mestiza* heritage and the selective process by which she must choose from among the cultural models she has inherited to create a new culture. She sees herself living in the borderlands between cultures as both a necessity and a responsibility:

> What I want is an accounting with all three cultures—white, Mexican, Indian. I want the freedom to carve and chisel my own face, to staunch the bleeding with ashes, to fashion my own gods out of my entrails. And if going home is denied me then I will have to stand and claim my space, making a new culture—*una cultura mestiza*—with my own lumber, my own bricks and mortar and my own feminist architecture.

This dialogue between the ethnic self and the dominant culture is a significant part of the process by which both the individual and the group confront the sociopolitical challenges of American life.

The Essays

Our essays are primarily concerned with the role of memory in the construction of ethnic identity, and the relationship between memory and writing—in the multiplicity of ways, for instance, in which individual memory rises out of, contradicts, selectively erases, and ultimately revises collective memory. They explore the many literary strategies that ethnic writers employ in response to the repression or erasure of their communal history.

One group of essays may be seen as showing the ways in which ethnic and racial memory proves to be a powerful insurgent force against a dominant historiography that fails to represent the whole picture. In "Yearning for the Past: The Dynamics of Memory in Sansei Internment Poetry," Stan Yogi explores the poetic response of third-generation, Japanese Americans to the suppressed memory of their parents regarding the World War II internment. Yogi shows how three Japanese American poets—Lawson Inada, Janice Mirikitani, and David Mura—have in their own distinctive ways created memory out of history, silences, fragments, documentation, hints, and denials. David Palumbo-Liu, in "The Politics of Memory: Remembering History in Alice Walker and Joy Kogawa," explores the contention among conflicting versions of history, focusing particularly on ethnic memory's ability to destabilize history. Using Walker's "Elethia" and Kogawa's *Obasan,* he goes on to point out the problematics of epistemology and politics which inform that destabilization. Toby C. S. Langen's essay, "Nostalgia and Ambiguity in Martha Lamont's 'Crow and Her Seagull Slaves,' " looks at a Lushootseed traditional story as told by the same person twice, with ten years separating the tellings. Langen offers many lines of inquiry and speculation to suggest that tribal or collective memory is relative, as well as regenerative. She shows that the links among memory, recitation, and creativity are psychologically and culturally complex. Sandra G. Shannon's essay, "The Role of Memory in August Wilson's Four-Hundred-Year Autobiography," treats Wilson's proposed ten-play cycle as an epic of memory, personal and collective. Wilson's imagination, informed by the blues, transforms memory into a universally accessible theater experience.

How personal memory shapes and is woven into group memory in American ethnic writing today is often apparent in the choices writers make—what they select for inclusion, as well as the linguistic and narrative strategies that sometimes subvert the hegemonic narrative of historical events or otherwise enrich the collective memory. A second group of essays explores some of these choices and strategies. In her essay, "Telling History: Inventing Identity in American Jewish Fiction," Victoria Aarons focuses on how narrators/authors in Gilbert Rogin's short story "What Happens Next?" and Art Spiegelman's *MAUS* search for identity by juxtaposing their own brief histories with a father's larger history and with the still larger context of ethnic history. Aarons also discusses the problems such narrators face: deciding what to include or exclude; distinguishing between facts and understanding; and grasping the relationships among past, present, and future possibilities. Similar relations between history and ethnicity are explored in Yiorgos Kalogeras's

"Producing History and Telling Stories: Maxine Hong Kingston's *China Men* and Zeese Papanikolas's *Buried Unsung*." Kalogeras demonstrates how the narrators of these texts attempt to juxtapose their ethnicity with the official historiography. Each book sets an "oral, fragmentary, largely undocumented" heritage beside the hegemonic and assimilationist mainstream history, in a complex act of recovery and cultural memory, foregrounding and reprivileging the oral and the legendary. In *"Chicanismo* as Memory: The Fictions of Rudolfo Anaya, Nash Candelaria, Sandra Cisneros, and Ron Arias," A. Robert Lee develops a comparison of four leading Chicano/a storytellers' deployment of different forms of "memory": in Anaya the historic blends into the mythic; in Candelaria memory serves as counterhegemonic chronicle, an imagined "other" history; in Cisneros a Chicana world of intimacy and womanism is invoked; and in Arias memory functions as dream fantasy. Thus all four use history and memory to create a past at once collective and specific, shared and yet idiosyncratic.

A third group of essays turns to disruptions of psyche, memory, and identity through displacement, colonization, and slavery. These essays indicate the ways in which the reliving of these disruptions of the past can be liberating, marking a profound contemporary reckoning with race, memory, and ethnic history. Gurleen Grewal, in her essay, "Memory and the Matrix of History: The Poetics of Loss and Recovery in Joy Kogawa's *Obasan* and Toni Morrison's *Beloved*," discusses the ways in which the two historical novels explore, from a women-centered perspective, "the elisions, the repressions, and the silences" of conventional historiography in an effort to confront and heal the violent ruptures of the past. Both narratives aim to register the far-reaching consequences of familial ties wrenched in the past and to articulate the traumatic memories held in silence in their own communities. In her essay, "Beyond Mimicry: The Poetics of Memory and Authenticity in Derek Walcott's *Another Life*," Sandra Pouchet Paquet examines Derek Walcott's writings as an attempt to create at once a song of the individual and the collective Caribbean. Drawing on both personal memory and the collective memory embodied in folk songs, tales, and rituals, Walcott's work ultimately erases the boundary between personal experience and myth.

Another set of essays focuses our attention on the politics of remembering and forgetting. William Boelhower, in "Ethnographic Politics: The Uses of Memory in Ethnic Fiction," examines works by Frank Lloyd Wright, Jean Toomer, Louise Erdrich, Zora Neale Hurston, Amy Tan, and

John Edgar Wideman, among others, to illustrate the complex connection between semiotics and memory, and between ethnic identity and citizenship in the United States—to map, in other words, "the function of ethnic semiosis in American literature." As an ethnographic scrutiny of our culture reveals, America is a land of many peoples, many different pasts, and an incredible variety of cultural sites. Boelhower views all these as archaeographically mixed in our big cities, making us cultural sleuths who track down the uncanny resonance of our own names. G. Thomas Couser, in "Oppression and Repression: Personal and Collective Memory in Paule Marshall's *Praisesong for the Widow* and Leslie Marmon Silko's *Ceremony*," examines how each novel leads its protagonist through a hallucinatory experience of misperceived or misunderstood personal and racial memories. Reordering the story of their lives proves to be a regenerative process of realigning personal and cultural memory, so that, for Couser, "the two novels do not so much reproduce ethnic customs as they model ethnicity as a cultural production dependent on the creative labor of each generation for its perpetuation." In his essay, "Feathering the Serpent: Chicano Mythic 'Memory,' " Rafael Pérez-Torres foregrounds the current use of "memory" as a counterdiscursive strategy by which twentieth-century Chicano/a poets seek to further projects of empowerment and differentiation. By problematizing their sense of the mythic "memory" as a cultural creation in their poetry, these writers both engage with traditional Chicano/a poetic expression and use it to further expand the borders of Chicano/a cultural identity.

Finally, we have a group of essays that limn the complexities of personal and collective identities as shaped by the strategies of power maintenance and marginalization in America. Jennifer Browdy de Hernandez's essay, "The Plural Self: The Politicization of Memory and Form in Three American Ethnic Autobiographies," argues, *à la* Bakhtin, that "language itself has its own embedded memory" and that the autobiographical writings of Gloria Anzaldúa, N. Scott Momaday, and Audre Lorde engage in a dialogue between individual and collective identities which shapes both theme and form in their works. In focusing on how ethnic texts merge individual with communal conceptions of the self—what she calls "communal 'bio-phonography' "—Browdy de Hernandez offers insights into the cycle of repetition and renewal in ethnic action and memory. Viewing memory and the voices that accompany it as "vehicles of identity," Herman Beavers, in his essay, "Tilling the Soil to Find Ourselves: Labor, Memory, and Identity in Ernest J. Gaines's *Of Love and Dust*," reads Gaines's novel as one in which "the individual must reach a new state of awareness or self-recovery by resisting the collective memory." He emphasizes "breaking out of a repressive paradigm in order to construct a new relationship to the past," a project "as important as using the past to manifest communal ties." Lisa Suhair Majaj argues in "Arab American Literature and the Politics of Memory" that "memory functions on both a cultural and a personal level to establish narratives of origin and belonging." Many earlier Arab American works of literature celebrated "nostalgia for an idealized, patriarchal ethnic past." But more recent works "turn to memory not just for cultural authentication, but to negotiate an ethnic identity that is heterogenous and engaged across cultural borders." Majaj reminds us that "like other modes of knowledge," memory "is mediated and constructed" in the context of history and politics.

As the range of discussions in this volume shows, we have come a long way from the certainty and simplicity of Hansen's Law, which, after all, was articulated in response to the notion of immigrants in a melting pot. Hansen's understanding of the largely European predicament did not take into account the historical conditions affecting the lives of Native Americans, Mexican Americans, and African Americans; nor did Hansen anticipate the racial, ethnic, and gender complexities that affect the lives of new Americans of color. Only with the emergence of the cultural politics of race, ethnicity, and gender identity in the last two decades have we begun to unravel the many complex layers of American immigrant and ethnic experience. In bringing together some of the new scholarship on American ethnic literatures, this volume crystallizes the understandings our contributors share in viewing the writer/scholar as a cultural worker, for whom creativity and social change are mutually inclusive processes. Like the literary texts they explore, these essays together are a step toward our affirmation of ethnic memories and identities which challenge popular conceptions of history and culture and compel us to come to terms with erasures, biases, and distortions. In raising issues and presenting examples that complicate and enrich Hansen's thesis about the role of memory in acculturation and assimilation, coexistence and survival, they challenge and extend Hansen in several directions. The essays in this volume converge, however, in the desire to articulate the reconstruction of memory for all groups. Although the specific histories of oppression and struggle may differ vastly, the need to keep trying to find or to construct a usable past is shared by all of us as Americans.

Works Cited

Appadurai, Arjun. "The Heart of Whiteness." *Callaloo* 16, no. 4 (1993): 796–807.

Buell, Frederick. *National Culture and the New Global System.* Baltimore: Johns Hopkins University Press, 1994.

Greene, Gayle. "Feminist Fiction and the Uses of Memory." *Signs* 16, no. 2 (1991): 290–321.

Nelson, Cary, Paula A. Treichler, and Lawrence Grossberg. "Cultural Studies: An Introduction." In *Cultural Studies,* edited by Lawrence Grossberg, Cary Nelson, and Paula A. Treichler, 1–16. New York: Routledge, 1992.

Ethnographic Politics:

The Uses of Memory in

Ethnic Fiction

WILLIAM BOELHOWER

In the last few decades, the promises of citizenship in our democratic country have come to sound increasingly faint and poorly distributed. Urban poverty, racism, random violence, sexism, lack of social solidarity, all suggest that Herbert Croly's *The Promise of American Life* continues to remain utopian. And yet there is a master text—the Constitution—and a popular form of constitutional "we-speak" that encourage us to sustain our willful illusions in democracy (Rieff, 545). Here is a spirited example of the will to full citizenship from Mary Antin's turn-of-the-century autobiography *The Promised Land:*

> What more could America give a child? Ah, much more! As I read how the patriots planned the Revolution . . . and the rejoicing people set up the Republic, it dawned on me gradually what was meant by *my country.* The people all desiring noble things, and striving for them together . . . all this it was that made my country. It was not a thing that I *understood.* . . . But I knew one could say "my country" and *feel* it, as one felt "God" or "myself." . . . For the Country was for all the Citizens, and *I was a Citizen.* And when we stood up to sing "America," I shouted the words with all my might. (225–26)

In her biography of the people of Minnesota and Wisconsin, *North Star Country,* Meridel Le Sueur is more specific about the values informing the procedural landscape of democracy when she quotes the man with a torn coat and split shoes who declared over his glass of beer, "That's what the Constitution says for a man: life, liberty, and the pursuit of happiness" (264). But today it is more and more difficult for people in tattered clothes—both women and men, Hispanic and African American, Amerindian and Asian American—to believe in such ideal laws.

As the etymon of law (*lex*) implies, it is above all the Constitution that binds our vast republic into the palpable image of a people and nation governed by a shared set of inalienable rights. In her book *On Revolution* Hannah Arendt explains that the word *nomos* (our higher law) originally meant "the notion of a range or province, within which defined power may be legitimately exercised" (186–87). And it is this understanding of "the country as a living presence in the midst of the citizens" that the Constitution alone makes possible (Arendt, 253). For, unlike many other countries, the inhabitants of North America who later became the people of the United States could not count on such unifying factors as one language, one religion, one racial source, one set of customs and traditions. Our democratic ethos was based solely on political premises. Herein lie both the strength and the weakness of our peculiarly modern notion of democratic sovereignty. We have no supportive genealogy like Tacitus's *Germania* to fall back upon.

Indeed, given the exquisitely political nature of the invention of our republican form of government, ethnographic arguments had little or nothing to do with the definition and practice of democratic sovereignty. If we were one people, it was exclusively because there was a will to consensus. As Ernest Renan famously put it in his essay "Qu'est-ce qu'une nation?" published in 1887, if the process of democratic representation was to work, consensus would have to take the form of "a daily plebiscite" (19). We need, according to his argument, a nation of Mary Antins. Without active participation in the process of creating consent, full citizenship and full sovereignty remain an illusion. Let us return to Renan:

> A nation is a spiritual principle, . . . a spiritual family not a group determined by the shape of the earth. We have now seen what things are not adequate for the creation of such a spiritual principle, namely, race, language, material interest, religious affinities, geography, and military necessity. (18–19)

The latter factors, in Renan's opinion, are superfluous. They pertain to an "ethnographic politics" (15) that has little to do with "the kind of moral conscience which we call a nation" (20). To believe in this rather voluntaristic view of nationality, Renan had to have absolute faith in the category of the political, had to believe that by itself the higher law was capable of upholding consensus, in spite of the residual interference of such ethnographic factors as race, language, religion, custom, and traditions. Ultimately, however, Renan presents us with an explanation of the modern democratic process that does not convince. The mere principle of consent—of citizenship—is considered sufficient to protect democracy against de Crèvecoeur's more realistic view that "the man will get the better of the citizen" (Arendt, 140).

I quote what is perhaps the most famous remark from Renan's essay on the nation: "Forgetting, I would even go so far as to say historical error, is a crucial factor in the creation of a nation, which is why progress in historical studies often constitutes a danger for [the principle of] nationality" (11). When in his *Letters from an American Farmer* de Crèvecoeur asks, "What is the American?" the answer he provides centers above all on the act of forgetting (letter 3). Those who come to this country in the hope of starting over leave their past behind them, he informs us. This is what Benjamin Franklin did when he set out to begin life in Philadelphia. Thanks in no small part to him, the new nation's ideal enlightenment city became a physio-political image of the type of procedural landscape the entire national territory had to become if republican democracy was to work.

Later, Walt Whitman gained his reputation as national poet by celebrating the road, movement, progress, and the democratic present. He rarely expressed any nostalgia for what was forgotten or left behind. Only at the end of his career, in *Specimen Days,* did he return to the tombs of his grandparents and parents and loosen the tears this belated autobiographical turn occasioned. And yet, as national poet he suffered a great deal over the ineffective implementation of democratic ideals and voiced his acutest *cri de coeur* in *Democratic Vistas.* If we look closely, we can observe the poet frequently imploding the procedural landscape of political democracy, which he celebrates by taking his songs north, south, east, and west (arguably the dominant trope of *Leaves*), in order to raise the ghosts of the past. Thus, while celebrating the horizontal space of the city, he simultaneously calls attention to the archaeomythology that subtends it: "I was asking for something specific and perfect for my city, / Whereupon lo! upsprang the aboriginal name. / Now I see what there is in a name, a word, liquid, sane, unruly, musical, self-sufficient, / I see that the word of my city is that word from of old" (585). And again: "Worth fully and particularly investigating indeed this Paumanok (to give the spot its aboriginal name)" (696).

What Whitman is giving us here is an ethnographic method, an alternative way of reading his *Leaves* not only as a hymn to the country's exalted present but also as a memory theater of a people's foundations. In the foreword to *An American Primer,* he confirms the presence of this countermethod when he suggests, "All the greatness of any land, at any time, lies folded in its names" (31). Ultimately, then, Whitman was trying like no other poet of his day to bridge the gap between his country's ethos and the ethics of Jacksonian democracy. If he soared like a bird over its expansive projects, he was also able to observe, "And I found that every place was a burial-place" (561). Essential to Whitman's ethnographic poetics, in other words, is a politics of memory. And in the twentieth century no poet is cited more frequently as a model for orienting oneself in the new semiocentric world of urban democratic America, where the need for "aboriginal names" would seem utterly superfluous.

Life in Alphabet City: A Story of Initiation

Surely one of the most eloquent, if not exemplary, scenes of entry into the modern city is young Frank Lloyd Wright's as he tells it in his *Autobiography*. An aspiring architect, he spontaneously pays close attention to the kind of cultural space that surrounds him. The time is six o'clock on a late spring evening in 1887; the scene is downtown Chicago. Having gotten on a cable car, Wright finds himself "compelled" to read the "crowding" signs:

> Got on a [cable car] heading north now. . . . Half-resentful because *compelled* to read the signs pressing on the eyes everywhere. They claimed your *eyes* for this, that and everything besides. They lined the car above the windows. They lined the way, *pushing, crowding* and *playing* all manner of tricks on the *victim's eye*. (86, italics mine)

The signs are everywhere. They "play" with him and "push" him, to the point where he becomes their "victim." Once in the car, things begin to accelerate. Surfaces begin to move. The point is, young Frank has precociously crossed over into the multiracial topology of twentieth-century America.

In effect, he is bombarded by signs, signs of all kinds and from every possible direction. Their fine "dust" penetrates everywhere; indeed, they themselves *are* now the only reality. There is nothing *more* to see, let alone wonder at. But, to cut matters short, what is the nature of these signs? Wright's "supersensitive ears and eyes" (86) continue to fill up with the new space: "Compelled again—until the procession of saloons, food shops, barber shops, eating houses, saloons, restaurants, groceries, laundries . . . became chaos in a wilderness of Italian, German, Irish, Polack, Greek, English, Swedish, French, Chinese and Spanish names in letters that began to come off and get about, interlace and stick, climb and swing again" (87). Not a forest of symbols but a chaosmos of signs. What is dawning on young Wright is the fact that he has entered a new cultural order. Indeed, he presents us with the very process of his initiation, which, I suggest, is exemplary. Language liquefies into single letters, and these in turn are free-floating and random. The migrant names, ethnic in origin, are separated from their objects; their etymons become eccentric as they unstick, interlace, "climb and swing again."

As the names transcend their original identity, they enter a space of total possibility. Their combinatory potential is now virtually infinite. The same holds true for the name Frank Lloyd Wright. It is strange, is it not, that young Wright finds himself fighting for his inner sanity and freedom at the very moment he enters the most representative space of citizenship, the city, where American democracy is so fully deployed. Never before had he been so free to consume so much; so free to happen down the endless streets of democratic possibility; so free to enter brave new possible worlds. Already in Ben Franklin's day the city had become the perfect stage for the people to express its sovereignty. Like Philadelphia, Chicago too was ordered, lit up, and set going for this supreme body. In it the crowd held sway, gave itself form, and had all the means it needed to speak. And yet, something was not quite right, as if young Wright had already sensed the appropriateness of Michel de Certeau's definition of the city as "the masterword of an anonymous law, the substitute for all proper names" (108). In fact, at issue in Wright's Chicago are the proper names: the identities they conceal, the origins they are burdened with, the stories they intimate, the questions they raise.

"Compelled" to follow the procession of endless possibilities unfolding before him, Wright is overcome by an uncanny sense that none of all this connects him to himself. Whence, therefore, sovereignty? At one point in his rite of passage, when most bewildered and disheartened, he is, not surprisingly, overcome by a severe attack of homesickness. Is it that Wright is quite literally trying to hang on to his name? As de Certeau argues, the function of the city is to produce a universal and anonymous subject, the city itself (94). In its administrative space Greeks, Italians, Chinese, Swedes, French, Spaniards, and other ethnics become part of the world of signs and hieroglyphs; their names, emblems of a subjective residue, are swept aside as semantic dross. They are indeed citizens of the city and can properly say, in the words of Umberto Eco, "We are, as subjects, that which the form of the world produced by signs makes us" (Eco 1984, 54). Wright now joins this multicultural "we."

To live in extravagant Chicago, Wright must become nomadic. Signs freed of their referents determine the modern order and its new pathos.

When names explode into letters, then language itself takes on the appearance of ruins. Young Wright suffers the city, misses the material bond of signs, sees enigmas everywhere, and longs for what now appears to be unrepresentable. In his own words:

> Got to bed at the Brigg's House north on Randalph Street, wrapped a sheet around myself—it seemed awfully like a winding sheet as I caught sight of it in the mirror—and slept. A human item—insignificant but big with interior faith and a great hope. In what? I could not have told you. Asleep in Chicago. Chicago murderously actual. (87)

Finally alone and completely still, he goes to bed and wraps himself up in what becomes a winding sheet. By putting himself so to rest, he is slyly encouraging us to imagine that from now on the former Frank Lloyd Wright, a Welsh American from Spring Green, Wisconsin, is posthumous, one of T. S. Eliot's living dead. In the modernist habitat of the city the self as internal sign finds itself expelled. If Wright has become posthumous, it is because he is now fully one of the crowd, not to mention a more fully sovereign citizen. At any rate, he is the *same* as they.

In the city human subjectivity is dealt with in much the same way as Wright describes. His entrance into the city traces his emergence as an individual self, a citizen, a future worker and consumer. In short, by joining the Chicago crowd as it pours over the Wells Street Bridge, he also goes through the experience of being imprinted with the social ideology of American liberal democracy. As he lies in bed in Brigg's House after having completed his initiation experience, he realizes for the first time that he has become that strange thing, a fully liberated American citizen.

The Sovereign Self: An Impossible Subjectivity

Young Wright, however, rightly sees his own initiation as part of the contractual terms of democracy: he must surrender his personal sovereignty. He must consent to his new condition. This process of substitution, which Wright dramatizes so well, also comprehends the conversion of goods into exchange value and culture into electronic bits of information. The lights of Chicago, a substitute for Wright's hometown of Spring Green, represent a total change. Everything is indeed flowing: the cars, the crowd, the signs, the names. But even such a spectacle is cause for tears. Rights are not evenly distributed, many people are not well enough off, even more are downright poor, and, on top of this, it remains far from obvious what a truly acculturated American is. Due to a host of only half-understood reasons, people continue to withdraw their consent, retreat into silence, resort to violence instead of political representation, or simply refuse to participate in the daily throes of democracy. All these practices exceed the structural conditions of democratic life.

In a deeper sense, the very advantages of freedom, consumption, and mobility that Chicago offered Wright ultimately turned him against himself. As he learns quickly enough, the city is an atopic space. The very notion of home is foreign to it. Nor can the urban dweller find philosophical repose in it, since it never sleeps. Above all, the city's dazzling functionalism cancels the mechanisms of memory that once constituted the very raison d'être of the traditional city. All this produces a loss, a sense of amnesia, a tension in absentia.

In his autobiography *Lost in America*, Isaac Bashevis Singer describes his first contact with New York in a way similar to Wright's. The fact that we now have an immigrant perspective produces no difference in the kind of experience described. After they travel by train through the city, are deafened by its roar and dazzled by its lights, Isaac's brother remarks: "Try to describe this! . . . All life in America keeps constantly changing. . . . I get an occasional urge to write about America but how can you describe character when everything around is rootless" (125–26). Later on, when someone asks Isaac how he feels in his new country, he replies, "Confused," which leads to this further comment: "That's how we all felt when we first came. Uprooted, as if we had dropped from some other planet. That feeling has remained with me to this day. I can't seem to become adjusted" (133).

Singer ends up calling America "a mental catastrophe" (107) and closes his autobiography with the climactic announcement, "I am lost in America, lost forever" (257). Like Wright, he too begins to live posthumously. "I fantasized that I was already dead, one of those legendary corpses which . . . leave their graves to reside in the world of chaos," he confesses, adding, "I had described such living dead in my stories, and now in my imagination I had become one of my own protagonists" (15). So much for Singer's way of coping with the enigma of arrival.

The Use of Names in Ethnic Narration

On the way to their posthumous condition, both Singer and Wright describe the self becoming other to itself the moment it enters the semioticized space of the modern metropolis. What is lost is the intimate relation of the self to itself, as belonging to an ethos defined largely by

Renan's retrogressive categories. It is this idiosyncratic self, with its specific genealogy, body, and memory, that becomes irrelevant to the city's major signifying activities, all of which produce an exquisitely contemporary space. Sitting alone and bewildered in the Chicago Opera House, young Wright tries nostalgically to resuscitate this lost self. He tries by means of an extreme act of memory to return to what, for lack of a better term, we might call his ethnic self. Like Singer, he does so by imploding his name, by reintroducing what the city of democracy expels as superfluous. In Wright's Chicago, you will remember, the Irish, Chinese, Italian, Greek, and Spanish names exploded like balloons into a myriad shining letters. In short, their established sense became virtual. By withdrawing himself from the city's one-dimensional spatiality, Wright in effect initiates an interpretive practice that is essential to ethnic narration: namely, the activity of the self in search of its lost intimacy, the very intimacy that the modern self—as citizen of the synchronic space of representative democracy—has desemioticized.

According to Charles Sanders Peirce, a sign is that which opens us to something else, which makes us know something more. It is a relation of referral (Eco 1984, 52 ff.). As for names, they are in a sense reified verbs (Eco 1979, 37). As Nanapush says of Fleur, a Chippewa conjure woman, in the opening story of Louise Erdrich's novel *Tracks,* "She was too young and had no stories or depth of life to rely upon. All she had was raw power, and the names of the dead that filled her" (7). As the novel unfolds, she gets in touch with those names. By imploding his or her name, the ethnic subject mines its signifying potential. "And now I'm going to tell you why I decided to go to my native village first" (1–2), Zora Neale Hurston writes at the beginning of *Mules and Men:* because there "I was just Lucy Hurston's daughter, Zora" (2). This means that "here in Eatonville I knew everybody was going to help me" (3). In Gloria Naylor's novel *Mama Day,* as soon as Ophelia sets foot on the island of Willow Springs, she is known by another name. She mentally addresses her husband, George: "And I wondered how you would take the transformation, beginning with something as basic as my name" (176). The change is far from trivial: "I became a child again in this house" (177), she says. And earlier, "The rest of me—the whole of me—was here" (176).

As if he instinctively sensed the restorative potential of imploding his name, Wright, in his moment of crisis, approaches it as an intimate sign of his virtual, now extrasemiotic self. Even more to the point, his intention is to reintroduce a cultural logic of relatives in much the same fashion as Naylor's Ophelia and Erdrich's Fleur do. By evoking through memory an image of home and of his mother, he is in effect claiming, "I, Frank Lloyd Wright, am the son of—." It is an interesting coincidence that Peirce, Eco, and before them John Poinsot use the example of sonship to explain the very activity of semiosis. For Poinsot, "Near or far, a son is in the same way the son of his father" (Deely, 45; Eco 1979, 36). And he might have added, as Deely does (45), that one remains a son or a daughter regardless of whether one's parents are dead or alive, to the extent that one thinks about it.

This form of thirdness, in which "the patterns of knowability" (Deely, 88) are made to depend on the revelatory power of imploding one's name, opens the modern democratic self to a radically temporal space with genealogical (or ethnic) parameters. Such a recursive practice becomes the manifest means by which the subject (as ethnic) uses its virtual otherness to construct and reconstruct its own injured sovereignty. I should add here that the achievement of full economic, political, and cultural representation within American democracy always and above all involves a power struggle over representation (Bourdieu, 109 f.). By practicing ethnic semiosis, the modern subject seeks to possess that which is systematically promised on the level of democratic expression but which is absent on the level of empirical content. As such, ethnicity often (but not only) functions as a constructive heuristic for the underrepresented self to redefine the status quo semantics of political representation. More fundamentally, the categories that Renan thought discardable cannot so easily be dismissed.

In order to regain one's lost sovereignty—in order to win one's political rights, the condition of economic well-being, and a sense of cultural belonging—the citizen *manqué* inaugurates an intimate relation between the suppressed origin of its subjectivity and the offended, conflicted self already present on the battlefield of democratic representation. By originating an archaeology of the self, the ethnic subject poses the problem of democracy's ontologically weak foundations in the very act of reproposing its own virtual threshold for interpreting political practice. Where this form of subjectivity has been transformed into an enigma, the subject as ethnic other is compelled to ponder over his or her origin, his or her own engendering name. As Michel de Certeau notes, "In the spaces brutally lit by an alien reason, proper names carve out pockets of hidden and familiar meanings" (104).

The Topological Turn in Ethnic Narration

It is due to a sense of diminution that Jean Toomer's Northern protagonists in *Cane* are drawn back to Georgia. More than a physical journey by train, their return conjures up an elusive transindividual ethos. This witnessing is signaled by the repetition of a set of archaeomythological signs, which leads Toomer's protagonists to the scene of a cultural inside. The canebrake in particular delineates a place where those "inside" it can get in touch with their ancestral deities and themselves. For those capable of being inspired, the wind that whispers through the cane is more than wind. If the author says right off that cane is "deep-rooted" (title page), it is because he wishes to stress that knowing is also remembering. Thus the narrator of the sketch "Carma" intimates, "The Dixie Pike has grown from a goat path in Africa" (10), which means this road/path is culturally reversible. By plunging into a canebrake, Carma potentially crosses an archaeomythological threshold: "Time and space have no meaning in a canefield" (11), the narrator says.

By walking down the pike and going with Fern through a canebrake, the narrator of the sketch "Fern" is finally relieved of the burden of his diminished urban self; finally he feels "strange" enough to experience all that he subtracted by going north. Indeed, he says, "When one is on the soil of one's ancestors, most anything can come to one . . ." (17). The insinuating end punctuation here—the three dots—is used not to lead us on, but to take us back. For it is on this soil, if only momentarily, that the male narrator enters Fern's eyes and the inner space of his lost ethos: "Her eyes, unusually weird and open, held me" (17). An interesting word, "weird." As a noun, it can mean soothsayer, charm, spell, or, even better for the kind of narrative we have here, a supernatural tale. At any rate, there is enough enchantment in *Cane* to make us ponder over one of the adjective's major possibilities: "relating to witchcraft or to the supernatural . . . unearthly, mysterious" (*Webster's International Dictionary*). The landscape, God, and the narrator all flow into Fern's eyes, which momentarily become the folk source for an act of return and recovery. Anybody who has seen the film *Rosemary's Baby* knows that the following passage is about a scene of possession:

> She [Fern] sprang up. Rushed some distance from me. Fell to her knees, and began swaying, swaying. Her body was tortured with something it could not let out. Like boiling sap it flooded arms and fingers till she shook them as if they burned her. It found her throat, and spattered inarticulately in plaintive, convulsive sounds, mingled with calls to Jesus Christ. And then she sang, brokenly. . . . A child's voice, uncertain, or an old man's. (17)

The wind in the cane, a voice embodied in song, the "thin wraith [meaning ghost?] of smoke" (6) above the pines at dusk, are all signposts of a cultural inside, which *Cane*'s Northern questers learn to connect along the journey of their return. To understand this lesson in how to graph a people's archaeomythology, the reader must attend closely to the topological cues to which Toomer alludes on the book's title page. Of major note, the title itself is derived from the name of a plant that has a hollow stalk like bamboo. By saying that cane is "oracular," the author gives it a symbolic import that makes it not unlike Pascal's thinking reed. But perhaps the author would not have wanted us to go so far afield. If we want to get at the book's meaning *through* its central conduit, we might try chewing it; for, as Toomer specifies, it is "redolent of fermenting syrup." "You know how to eat sugar cane, Mattie?" (18), Butch asks Mattie Michael in the opening story of Gloria Naylor's collection *The Women of Brewster Place.* "You see, eating cane is like living life" (18), he instructs. And then the narrator takes over:

> He finally looked her straight in the face, and Mattie found herself floating far away in the brown sea of his irises, where the words, shoreline and anchor, became like gibberish in some foreign tongue.
> "Here," he said, holding out a piece of the cane wedge to her, "try it the way I told you."
> And she did. (18)

Although Naylor—I think nonchalantly—reverses the gender roles that Toomer inscribed in the scene of possession in "Fern," both she and Toomer intend primarily to offer the reader a lesson in seduction. At the same time, however, they seem intent on making instruction itself a paramount issue, so that while the characters are learning about possession, we as readers learn about how the story—through narrative enchantment—is possessing us. At first sight, Naylor's scene appears to be a cautionary tale for innocent young women, Toomer's an exercise in overcoming the unbearable condition of solitude.

But in a deeper, archaeomythological sense both Toomer and Naylor use cane to promote what Pierre Macherey in *Pour une théorie de la production littéraire* calls "le thème original" (227), the ancestral theme. Thus cane takes on for them the same ethnographic significance that Maryse Condé attributes to it in her novel *I, Tituba, Black Witch of Salem.* After spending most of her life as a slave in New England, Tituba finally succeeds in returning to her West Indian island. Here is how she describes the scene of her homecoming:

> We left the town and suddenly, as is often the case in our islands, the rain stopped and the sun started to shine again, brushing the contours of the hills with light. The sugarcane was in flower, like a purple cloud above the fields. The shining green leaves of the yams were mounting an attack on their poles.

A feeling of lightness drove out my previous thoughts. How could I have believed that nobody was waiting for me when the whole island was there for me to behold lovingly? (143)

When Toomer fixes the words "Purple of the dusk, / Deep-rooted cane" to the title page of his text, he is in effect establishing an *axis mundi.* Thus cane becomes a conduit for plotting an act of cultural return. At the "deep-rooted" etymological level this return also resuscitates the lost splendor of the very notion of ethos. In one sense, *ethos,* like the Latin word *mos,* refers to a people's habits, customs, and traditional behavior. It usually has the force of an unwritten law.

But the word *ethos* has a still older sense that it derives from the Greek word *ethos,* meaning *sedes, domicilium,* or dwelling place. Taken in this sense the word also refers to the spirit of place, as when we say a person's face reads like a map of his or her origin; the implication is that the place one comes from actually adds character to one's name. (For that matter, only in political democracies do people constantly move from one place to another all their lives without ever dwelling in any of them.) In other words, the spirit of place enters those who dwell there, and it was traditionally the word *daimon* that mediated between place and personality (Mancini, 26–36). The very notion of ethics derives from the meaning of *ethos* as dwelling place. It is, in fact, this originary dimension that John Edgar Wideman tries to capture in his collection of short stories *Damballah,* where the urban neighborhood of Homewood is genealogically investigated from the starting point of an archaeomythology.

Instead of cane the central conduit now becomes the voodoo name for the "good serpent of the sky," Damballah. As the opening ethnographic note to the collection explains, "One song invoking Damballah requests that he 'Gather up the Family.' " The first story, entitled "Damballah," foregrounds the theme of transmitting an archaeomythological force or power residing in the word *Damballah.* Orion, a slave from Africa who still practices voodoo, transmits his power to a young slave before being killed by his white master for heathen practices. "This boy could learn the story and tell it again" (18), Orion says. The act of empowerment, which gives the story its inaugural function, describes a pedagogical trope or turning that is repeated again and again in different ways throughout the collection. As in *Cane,* this pedagogical moment is represented as a scene of origin and return. Since we are once again confronted with a cultural inside, the originating force is transmitted through an act of possession:

> Not so much a matter of seeing Orion move as it was feeling the man's eyes
> inside him, hooking him before he could crouch lower in the weeds. Orion's
> eyes on him and through him boring a hole in his chest and thrusting into
> that space one word *Damballah*. Then the hooded eyes were gone. (19–20)

A little farther on in the story the narrator adds to this scene of posses-
sion/instruction without, however, reducing the aura of mystery: "Orion
wasn't speaking but sounds came from inside him the boy had never
heard before, strange words, clicks, whistles and grunts" (21). And then,
to suggest the semiotic threshold of a cultural inside, "Damballah a place
the boy could enter, a familiar sound he began to anticipate, a sound
outside him which slowly forced its way inside" (21).

If the events of the first story antedate the prefatory "Begat Chart" and
"Family Tree," which impose a chronological order on the other stories,
it is because the primal power they convey has been abandoned to itself.
The pedagogical habitus, in other words, has to be recovered story by
story if the urban neighborhood of Homewood is to regain a sense of its
originary ethos. To mention just one more example of an archaeomythological scene, in the last story, "The Beginning of Homewood," it is Sybela Owens (the family tree's great ancestor) who embodies the figure
of power leading directly to Wideman's own legitimation as author of
Damballah. (In the story "Tommy" Tommy addresses his brother as
John, and in the last story there are further indications to suggest that
the writer-narrator is Wideman himself.) Here is the scene of archaeomythological transport:

> May was staring at the tall, straight trees behind the house when she felt eyes
> on her, eyes which had burrowed right down into the place where she was
> daydreaming. May let her own eyes slowly find the ones watching her. Cau-
> tiously she lowered her gaze . . . stopping finally at the old woman who sat
> dark and closed as a fist. Sybela Owens's ancient eyes blinked in the bright
> sunlight but did not waver. . . . She [May] quieted everything inside herself
> as the old eyes shushed her and patted her and said her name in a way she
> had never heard it said before. *May*. The eyes never left her, but after an
> instant which seemed forever, May was released. (200–201)

As a result of this scene of empowerment through possession, Aunt May
and then Mother Bess (that is, Elizabeth, the narrator-author's mother)
become witnesses in much the same way as Toomer's narrator does in
"Fern." As the narrator explains, quoting Mother Bess, "And changed
my life. Yes she [Aunt May] did. Told me to live free all this time and be
a witness all this time. And told me come a day her generations fill this
city and need to know the truth" (202).

What Orion and then Sybela Owens, Aunt May, Mother Bess, and finally the narrator of the last story transmit is a habitus, a disposition,
by which members of the extended family can hold the blighted urban
neighborhood of Homewood in some kind of genealogical focus. This is
no small acquisition, for it is in exercising such a habitus that these people also have a ghost of a chance to reintroduce meaning into their present surroundings. Already through the initial decision to implode their
names, they begin topologically to reconstruct what was once both a
family tree and a neighborhood community. And behind both, the author implies, lies Damballah, "at once the ancient past and the assurance
of the future" (preface, "Damballah"). It is this archaeomythological
confidence that must have led Wideman to include these further words
from Maya Deren's *Divine Horsemen: The Voodoo Gods of Haiti*: "To invoke
them [divinities like Damballah] today is to stretch one's hand back to
that time and to gather up all history into a solid, contemporary ground
beneath one's feet" (preface, "Damballah"). Indeed, so many contemporary narratives choose to invest in, if not reenact, scenes of origin—from
Wilson Harris's *Palace of the Peacock* and Maryse Condé's *I, Tituba, Black
Witch of Salem* to William Melvin Kelley's *A Different Drummer*, Toni Morrison's *Song of Solomon*, Charles Johnson's *Middle Passage*, Gloria Naylor's
Mama Day, and Louise Erdrich's *Tracks*—that archaeomythologies seem
to have become the most readily available evidence of the sovereign
democratic self's impossibility.

Re-sourcing America

As narrative signs, names are virtual stories, and stories are none other
than the expansion of names (Proni, 92). The American metropolis of
Frank Lloyd Wright's Chicago, Toomer's Washington, D.C., Wideman's
Homewood, and Morrison's Detroit is a haunted space where the names-
become-signs flutter about like ghosts, there to be seen or invoked if one
cares to turn to them. "The walls of the stations the train rushes by are
graffitied with names, dates, and epitaphs," the narrator of Stuart Dybek's story "Nighthawks" says (109). And in "Hot Ice," a later story in
the same collection (entitled *The Coast of Chicago*), the narrator observes:

> Things were gone they couldn't remember but missed. . . . At times, walking
> past the gaps, they felt as if they were no longer quite there themselves, half-
> lost despite familiar street signs, shadows of themselves superimposed on
> the present, except there was no present—everything either rubbled past or

promised future—and they were walking as if floating, getting nowhere as if they'd smoked too much grass. (131)

As for the equally desolate area of Chicago mapped out in Dybek's story "Blight,"

> It wasn't until we became Blighters [the name of their neighborhood band] that we began to recognize the obscurity that surrounded us. . . . As Blighters, just walking the streets we became suddenly aware of familiar things we didn't have names for. (55)

By attending to names, the Blighters begin to throw light on an area of the city left in hopeless darkness.

In Danny Santiago's story "The Somebody" another ethnic angel by the name of Chato describes his own local wasteland in Los Angeles as follows:

> They came in with their wrecking bars and their bulldozers. You could hear those houses scream when they ripped them down. So now Shamrock Street is just front walks that lead to a hole in the ground, and piles of busted cement. (215)

Chato's family alone refuses to move. "So I cruised on down to Main Street like a ghost in a graveyard," Chato remarks, adding, "Just to prove I'm alive I wrote my name on the fence at the corner" (216). Liking what he sees, he begins to make an art out of it and strolls down Main "writing all the way" (216). Then he invades the territory of the Sierra Street gang, leaving "a fine little trail of Chato de Shamrock in eight colors" (217). At this point he construes the act of writing his name as a way of repossessing his own local territory. "You know how you put your name on something and that proves it belongs to you?" he explains (217).

From now on he begins to use his signature to create ethnic passages and emblems wherever he goes. When it finally gets dark out, he goes over to Broadway and Bailey not only because a lot of people pass by there but also because it is well lit. "Under the street lamp my name shone like solid gold. I stood to one side and checked the people as they walked past and inspected it," he recounts (220). This tactic in ethnic geography then leads him to a culminating vision that counters his initial description of Shamrock Street. After establishing the story's donnée as the existential experience of worldlessness, Chato now invests his name in the blighted cityscape of Los Angeles in an attempt to make it livable. Here are the final words of the story:

> L.A. is a big city, man, but give me a couple of months and I'll be famous all over town. Of course they'll try to stop me. . . . But I'll be like a ghost, man.

I'll be real mysterious, and all they'll know is just my name . . . CHATO DE SHAMROCK with rays shooting out like from the Holy Cross. (221)

The names disseminate ghosts, turn urban terrain into a phantomized territory. Envisioning a nomadic condition, Chato falls back upon the future tense of dreaming to survive. Being nowhere, he plans to go everywhere, as a ghost. Los Angeles and Chicago are haunted cities. In de Certeau's words, "What can be seen designates what is no longer there" (108). The names become "inward-turning histories, pasts that others are not allowed to read, accumulated times that can be unfolded but like stories held in reserve" (Certeau, 108).

Armed with its "inward-turning stories," the ethnic self relativizes the ritual images that our culture employs to announce its own idealized representation of democratic self-sufficiency. This work of ethnic semiosis involves multiplying as well as realigning the *topological sources* available for building cultural identity and coherence. In his novel *Philadelphia Fire*, for example, John Edgar Wideman circles around the events that converted an African American commune into a disaster area. He sets out to unfold the stories held in reserve, learning to see what is no longer there. The date is 13 May 1985. The place is "Philadelphia. West Philly. Osage Avenue" (10), where a bomb dropped by the police on a besieged row house ended up destroying more than fifty-three houses, a whole neighborhood.

By means of ethnic-semiotic procedure, Philadelphia becomes "infinitely deep" and its narrativization "a way of surviving" (109). For Cudjoe, the novel's narrator and protagonist, the names of the victims remain hopelessly heavy ("Why didn't words rise and fly like balloons?" [198]), but he also realizes, "Names bound those elements, twisted around them, held them close, breathed life into their combinations. Binding. Pulling" (198). Ultimately, though, it is a more intimate story of names that enables him to conclude that he himself is a worthy witness to the events that have shocked him out of his own sense of alienation. Asking himself whether he can ever use his narrative—Cudjoe is a writer—to shore up his own footloose worldlessness, he spontaneously comes up with the words "The son's father. Father's son" (110) and decides to test their healing potential.

This central configuration of an act of return pervades the entire novel and helps to track the narrator's restless initiation into the perspectivism of ethnic semiosis. As Cudjoe himself puts it, "Did I have to ask the right questions in order to free the name? . . . Memory speaking only if addressed in a language it understands" (124). Access to this cultural inside finally leads him to reconsider his relationship with his son all the while he continues, futilely, to seek the only child who has survived the bombed commune. Here is his own version of the logic of relatives:

> Say the word "father." Now say "son." Now think of the space between "father" and "son," as they are words, as they are indications of time and the possibility of salvation, redemption, continuity. . . . The mystery of their connection is that either word will do. (103)

Cudjoe learns to use the "mystery of their connection" to resemioticize his own embattled identity in an ethnic key. The only way to establish the interpretant of the self as ethnic sign, in fact, is to resort to an ethnic sign relation. Cudjoe re-sources his own depleted sense of self by positioning himself in the biographical space between father and son and the communal space between self and ethnic neighborhood. Both connections are below the semiotic threshold of democratic representation in Philadelphia.

Wideman's novel is ultimately about reassuming the habitus of ethnic semiosis. This disposition, as I have suggested earlier, consists in dramatizing scenes of genealogical recovery. Cudjoe is deeply moved after revisiting the now blighted Osage Avenue neighborhood, which stirs in him communal fortitude. Narrative pedagogy once again takes the form of a politics of remembering. The novel chooses as its final scene Philadelphia's central square and closes with this semiotic triumph:

> Cudjoe hears footsteps behind him. A mob howling his name. . . . Words come to him. . . . He'd known them all his life. *Never again*. . . . He turns to face whatever it is rumbling over the stones of Independence Square. (199)

The words that enchant him flow irresistibly from his rediscovered sense of allegiance. Invisible signs, the words are still real enough to spin him about—without visible cause—in Independence Square. The effect is as brilliant as it is visionary, and its special power comes from Cudjoe's having successfully recovered a sense of his community's lost ethos. A novel about doing research on a novel, *Philadelphia Fire* dramatizes the reawakening of the narrator's sense of the uncanny. Relying on story, on the detective work of connecting people, place, and events, Cudjoe finally becomes a possessed person.

In Gloria Naylor's novel *Mama Day*, "before [Cocoa] the child of Grace lives up to her name" (310), she too—like Wideman's Cudjoe—must learn how to listen. As Mama Day says to Cocoa's husband, George, now buried in the family cemetery of Willow Springs, "One day she'll hear you, like you're hearing me" (308). In fact, the novel's closure provides the reader with a scene of instruction in which Cocoa has learned to talk to George: "And I still don't have a photograph of you. It's a lot better this way, because you change as I change. And each time I go back over what happened, there's some new development, some forgotten corner that puts you in a slightly different light" (310). Both Naylor and Wideman not only engage in a politics of memory to construct their archaeomythologies, but also give us a *stratified* vision of history. In other words, they implicitly opt for an archaeological approach to American culture. "And I found every place was a burial place," Whitman, our national poet, writes (561).

Again and again, ethnic semiosis takes the form of mining sites, as if its specific ethical mandate was to recover the original etymological sense of ethos as *domicilium,* or dwelling place, as if the birth or confirmation or recovery of character literally involved returning to places like Zora Neale Hurston's Eatonville. "I was a Southerner, and had the map of Dixie on my tongue" (1985, 135) is her not-too-metaphorical way of putting it. The point is, the normative celebration of scenes of origin in ethnic narratives reveals what is perhaps a peculiar—if not crucial—maneuver of ethnic semiosis. Its spatial optics, that is, depends not so much on a temporal as on a *topological hermeneutics,* which ethnic protagonists themselves learn to use through repeated scenes of instruction. Borrowing from Pierre Bourdieu (Bourdieu and Wacquant, 128–40), I have suggested that such instruction results in a habitus dear to ethnic semiosis. In the opening words of the first chapter of her autobiography *Dust Tracks on the Road,* significantly entitled "My Birthplace," Zora Neale Hurston writes: "Like the dead-seeming, cold rocks, I have memories within that came out of the material that went to make me. Time and place have had their say" (3). It is interesting that she chooses to evoke the notion of geological stratification to explain the relation between the origin of herself and her place of birth, so that access to her past requires nothing less than an act of cultural archaeology.

This hermeneutic principle—mining memories as if they were sites—is then brought to bear on a type of space that is actually below the cartographic surface of political representation. In short, such sites as Toomer's canebrake, Erdrich's lake Matchimanitou, Harris's palace of the peacock, Wideman's Homewood, and Naylor's Willow Springs are archaeomythological in nature. As Mama Day explains in the first pages of Naylor's homonymous novel, "Willow Springs ain't in no state" (4). In fact, when Cocoa's enterprising husband tries to decide what clothes to take along on their vacation at the Springs, he is forced to conclude,

"It's hard to know what to expect from a place when you can't find it on the map" (174). Later he realizes, "I was entering another world" (175). Cocoa again confirms the special status of this cultural inside when she says, "And I sensed that knowledge dawning on you from the moment we crossed over the bridge: you were entering a part of my existence that you were powerless in. Your maps were no good here" (177). As the days on the island of Willow Springs pass, George is increasingly caught up in events that have nothing to do with "the front part of the mind" (111); or, as Mama Day herself at one point puts it, "We ain't talking about this world at all" (268).

Cocoa's and the island's genealogy (Naylor provides us with a graph of Cocoa's family tree and a map of Willow Springs) reaches all the way back to an African-born conjure woman named Sapphira Wade. Here Naylor's treatment of the ancestral theme cannot but remind us of Toni Morrison's previous handling of it in *Song of Solomon*. Morrison's protagonist Milkman, for example, learns that the place he has been seeking, the same as the novel's scene of origin, is not on regular road maps. By discovering the meaning of Shalimar, the town's mysterious name, he also unravels the enigma of his own identity. All this knowledge is contained in a children's folk song that tells of his ancestor who lived in the town before flying back to Africa. It slowly dawns on Milkman that he too belongs to the tribe of flying Africans: "Guitar, my great-granddaddy could flyyyyy and the whole damn town is named after him" (332). Returning now to Naylor's novel, we are better prepared to identify her narrative strategy. When the people of Willow Springs celebrate the annual festivity of Candle Walk, Cocoa explains:

> They'd hum some lost and ancient song. . . . They'd all raise them candles, facing east, and say, "Lead on with light, Great Mother. Lead on with light." Say you'd hear talk then of a slave woman who came to Willow Springs, and when she left, she left in a ball of fire to journey back home east over the ocean. (111)

Like Morrison in *Song of Solomon*, Naylor gives her scene of origin a mythological agency. And thanks to this dimension and the successful evocation of a cultural inside, the Cocoas and Milkmans and Fleur Pillagers and Cudjoes are able to lay down the burden of their impossible subjectivity by dissolving it in a transindividual ethos.

By choosing to mine the place-name Sutton according to the topological procedure defined earlier, William Melvin Kelley, in his novel *A Different Drummer*, succeeds in displaying the past in such a way that it no longer flows. Namely, he spatializes it, so that a character like Bobby-Joe is compelled to ask, "How the hell can something what happened a hundred fifty years ago—if it happened at all—how can that have something to do with what happened this week?" (192). It is Tucker Caliban, direct descendant of a legendary African chief brought to America as a slave, who provides the answer when he explains to his white employer, David Willson, why he wants to buy a certain plot of land and no other: " 'Something special there,' he answered, 'something my grandpa told me was out there' " (183). But perhaps there is no better direct answer than Nanapush's in Erdrich's novel *Tracks:* "We felt the spirits of the dead so near that at length we just stopped talking" (6). When it comes to the originary ethos of a people's dwelling place, time does not pass away but leaves its traces inscribed for all to see. "A hundred fifty years" are like a day, or, as we learn from one of Naylor's witness figures, "Living in a place like Willow Springs, it's sorta easy to forget about time" (160). Tucker Caliban's seven acres become the locus of a scene of origin. They also provide us with this ancestral theme: "And Caliban, whose Christian name got to be First after he got a family and there was more than just one Caliban, was John Caliban's father, and John Caliban's grandson is Tucker Caliban and the African's blood is running in Tucker Caliban's veins" (25).

Ethnic semiosis takes the territory of the United States and converts it into a memory theater. As a book of names, the national map provides us with a synoptic view of the country's founding deeds, its first intentions, its scenes of origin. Taken together, these names exhibit a comprehensive cultural topology and an encyclopedic inventory of the topoi of American literature. Each place-name is both a temporal and a spatial matrix in which the past is displayed as an archaeological site. By imploding these names as stratified digs, ethnic semiosis above all exposes the spatial dimension of time. In other words, the nation's corpus—its Chicagos, Detroits, and Los Angeleses—is examined not as history but as metahistory; not as the procedural landscape of political democracy but as the topology of a people's dwelling. It is at the topological level, in fact, that the exclusively temporal horizon of hermeneutics gives way to the archaeological operations of the local mind. In Wilson Harris's novel *The Palace of the Peacock,* Donne brings us back to the semiotic threshold that the local mind succeeds in crossing when he notes, "Every boundary line is a myth" (22). Once Donne steps through the cartographic lines of colonial empire, he cannot but meet "the eternal folk" (58). Toomer, Kelley, Morrison, Wideman, Erdrich, Naylor, and many other contemporary writers employ a local mind as they set about haunting American democracy. Through their archaeomythologies the nation's resources have become myriad.

Works Cited

Antin, Mary. *The Promised Land.* Boston: Houghton, 1912.

Arendt, Hannah. *On Revolution.* London: Penguin, 1988.

Bourdieu, Pierre. *La parola e il potere.* Translated by Silvana Massari. Naples: Guida, 1988.

————, and Loic J. D. Wacquant. *An Invitation to Reflexive Sociology.* Chicago: University of Chicago Press, 1992.

Certeau, Michel de. *The Practice of Everyday Life.* Translated by Steven Rendall. Berkeley: University of California Press, 1988.

Condé, Maryse. *I, Tituba, Black Witch of Salem.* Translated by Richard Philcox. Charlottesville: University Press of Virginia, 1992.

Crèvecoeur, J. Hector St. John de. *Letters from an American Farmer.* New York: E. P. Dutton, 1957.

Deely, John. *Basics of Semiotics.* Bloomington: Indiana University Press, 1990.

Dybek, Stuart. *The Coast of Chicago.* New York: Alfred A. Knopf, 1990.

Eco, Umberto. *Lector in fabula.* Milan: Bompiani, 1979.

————. *Semiotica e filosofia del linguaggio.* Turin: Einaudi, 1984.

Erdrich, Louise. *Tracks.* London: Picador, Pan Books, 1989.

Harris, Wilson. *The Palace of the Peacock.* London: Faber and Faber, 1988.

Hurston, Zora Neale. *Dust Tracks on a Road.* Urbana: University of Illinois Press, 1985.

————. *Mules and Men.* New York: Harper & Row, 1990.

————. *Their Eyes Were Watching God.* New York: Harper & Row, 1990.

Johnson, Charles. *Middle Passage.* New York: New American Library, 1991.

Kelley, William Melvin. *A Different Drummer.* New York: Doubleday, 1989.

Le Sueur, Meridel. *North Star Country.* Lincoln: University of Nebraska Press, 1984.

Macherey, Pierre. *Pour une théorie de la production littéraire.* Paris: François Maspero, 1974.

Mancini, Italo. *L'ethos dell'Occidente.* Genoa: Marietti, 1990.

Morrison, Toni. *Song of Solomon.* New York: New American Library, 1978.

Naylor, Gloria. *Mama Day.* New York: Vintage Books, 1989.

————. *The Women of Brewster Place.* London: Minerva, 1990.

Proni, Giampaolo. "L'influenza di Peirce sulla teoria dell'interpretazione di Umberto Eco." In *Semiotica: Storia, teoria, interpretazione,* edited by Patrizia Magli, Giovanni Manetti, and Patrizia Violi, 89–98. Milan: Bompiani, 1992.

Renan, Ernest. "Qu'est-ce qu'une nation?" Sorbonne, Paris, 11 March 1882. Reprinted as "What Is a Nation?" In *Nation and Narration,* translated by Martin Thom and edited by Homi K. Bhabha, 8–22. London: Routledge, 1990.

Rieff, David. "Immigration and the Transformation of the US," *Times Literary Supplement,* 25–31 May 1990, 545.

Santiago, Danny (Daniel James). "The Somebody." In *North of the Rio Grande: The Mexican-American Experience in Short Fiction,* edited by Edward Simmen. New York: Mentor Books, 1992.

Singer, Isaac Bashevis. *Lost in America.* Garden City, N.Y.: Doubleday, 1981.

Toomer, Jean. *Cane.* New York: Liveright, 1975.

Whitman, Walt. *An American Primer.* Edited by Horace Traubel. 1904. Reprint, San Francisco: City Lights, 1970.

———. *Walt Whitman.* New York: Library of America, 1982.

Wideman, John Edgar. *Damballah.* New York: Random House, 1988.

———. *Philadelphia Fire.* New York: Random House, 1991.

Wright, Frank Lloyd. *An Autobiography.* New York: Horizon Press, 1977.

The Plural Self:

The Politicization of Memory and Form

in Three American Ethnic Autobiographies

JENNIFER BROWDY DE HERNANDEZ

Ethnicity and autobiography are inherently linked in their emphasis on memory: R. A. Schermerhorn defines an ethnic group as "a collectivity within a larger society having real or putative common ancestry [and] memories of a shared historical past."[1] This emphasis on ancestry, memory, and history is shared by the literary genre of autobiography—the difference being that autobiography traditionally focuses on the *autos*, on documenting the development of the *individual* identity and life, whereas ethnic groups use memory to trace their *collective* development as a people.

In the three American ethnic autobiographies discussed here—N. Scott Momaday's *The Names,* Gloria Anzaldúa's *Borderlands/La frontera,* and Audre Lorde's *Zami: A New Spelling of My Name*—individual memory and collective memory are fused into what Mikhail Bakhtin would call "double-voiced discourse," which represents "a concentrated dialogue of two voices, two world views, two languages."[2] For Bakhtin, language has its own embedded memory:

> Language has been completely taken over, shot through with intentions and accents. . . . All words have the "taste" of a profession, a genre, a tendency, a party, a particular work, a particular person, a generation, an age group, day and hour. Each word tastes of the context and contexts in which it has lived its socially charged life; all words and forms are populated by intentions. (Bakhtin, 293)

In ethnic autobiographies, the very form of the autobiography is already "shot through with intentions." Autobiography as a genre is traditionally considered a highly Western form, linked to the bourgeois European emphasis on individuality,[3] and this history lives on in both form and substance in the ethnic autobiography. Also present, however, in a kind of Bakhtinian internal dialogue, are the traditional forms of the ethnic group to which the autobiographer professes affiliation. Momaday, Anzaldúa, and Lorde all draw on ethnic heritages (Native American, Chicano, and Caribbean/African American, respectively) in which the individual identity is subordinate to the collective identity, and this emphasis appears in their autobiographies, which fuse the Western autobiographical "I" with the ethnic "we." Also figuring strongly in these three autobiographies is a non-Western oral tradition, as well as various ritualistic acts that, inscribed autobiographically, link the individual to the collectivity, the present to the past. The autobiographies of Momaday, Anzaldúa, and Lorde thus enact a dialogue between their particular ethnic group and dominant American culture,[4] between the collective, typically ethnic use of memory and the individual, typically Western use of memory.

The Collective Singular: Communo-Biography

In an essay on preliterate Native American autobiography, Hertha D. Wong contrasts the Native American and Western conceptions of self:

> Generally, Native Americans, although individuals, tend to see themselves first as family, clan, and tribal *members,* and second as discrete individuals. . . . It seems . . . that a Westerner *writes* his/her autobiography to set himself/herself *apart from* . . . his/her society, while an early Native American *speaks* his/her self-expressions to become more fully *accepted into* . . . his/her tribe.[5]

For Wong, the term *autobiography* does not adequately describe preliterate Native American personal narratives, which are oral, dramatic, and artistic in form; she suggests the term "communo-bio-oratory" as being more accurately reflective of "the communal and oral nature of early American autobiographical expressions" (22).

A term such as *communo-biography* might indeed be more reflective of the autobiographies of Audre Lorde, N. Scott Momaday, and Gloria Anzaldúa, all of which place great importance on the memories and experiences of the ethnic group to which they belong. Lorde, who considers herself a part of the lesbian subgroup within the larger Caribbean/African American ethnicities, has in fact called her autobiography a "biomythography," indicating her interest in using her own life story to create a larger myth, or model, for other black lesbians. Since all African Americans were forcibly severed from their ethnic heritage by the brutal passage through slavery, their collective ancestral memories are often unavailable to later generations. For Lorde and other black lesbians, this problem is compounded by the alienation they often feel even from their own black American communities. For black lesbians of Lorde's generation, she says, "there were no mothers, no sisters, no heroes. We had to do it alone."[6]

For Lorde, "doing it alone" means constructing not only a self, but also a mythos to guide that self, and this is the process that is documented in *Zami: A New Spelling of My Name*. Reaching back into the past, Lorde begins by remembering her Grenadian mother, a "powerful" woman, in whom Lorde sees the source of her own lesbianism.

> As a child, I always knew my mother was different from the other women I knew. . . . *Different how?* I never knew. But that is why to this day I believe that there have always been Black dykes around—in the sense of powerful and women-oriented women—who would rather have died than use that name for themselves. And that includes my momma. (15)

Through her mother's memories of Grenada, Lorde creates a home, as well as a mythic place of origin, for herself: "Once *home* was a far way off, a place I had never been to but knew well out of my mother's mouth" (13). Specifically, "home" is the little Grenadian island of Carriacou, where Lorde, building on her mother's memories, imagines her maternal forebears as part of an ideal community of women.

> Here Aunt Anni lived among the other women who saw their men off on the sailing vessels, then tended the goats and groundnuts, planted grain and poured rum upon the earth to strengthen the corn's growing, built their women's houses and the rainwater catchments, harvested the limes, wove their lives and the lives of their children together. Women who survived the absence of their sea-faring men easily, because they came to love each other, past the men's returning. (13–14)

These women are called *Zami*, "a Carriacou name for women who work together as friends and lovers" (255); the word comes from the French patois for "les amies," lesbians. By giving herself the "new name" of Zami in her autobiography, Lorde links her individual identity with the plurality of black lesbians in general, and with her ancestral forebears in particular "My life," she says, has "become increasingly a bridge and field of women. *Zami*" (255). The individual becomes the collective: in the epilogue to *Zami*, Lorde lists "the women who helped give me substance," a hybrid group of friends, family, lovers, and African goddesses: "Ma-Liz, DeLois, Louise Briscoe, Aunt Anni, Linda, and Genevieve; MawuLisa, thunder, sky, sun, the great mother of us all; and Afrekete, her youngest daughter, the mischievous linguist, trickster, best-beloved, whom we must all become" (255). These women, Lorde says, "feed me like corn before labor. I live each of them as a piece of me" (256). For Lorde, the self is plural; as Claudine Raynaud points out, in Lorde's "lesbian utopia, a plurality of identities (black, female, lesbian), a line of women (her ancestors, her mothers, her lovers) coalesce into one name. The autobiographical 'I' becomes a collective 'we,' "[7] and the autobiography becomes a biomythography.

A similar process of communo-biography is evident in N. Scott Momaday's *The Names*. As in his earlier autobiographical text *The Way to Rainy Mountain*, in *The Names* Momaday combines Kiowa mythology, American history, and personal reminiscences, telling his own story by locating himself within the collective story of his family and tribe. Momaday describes his method in these texts as an appeal to "the whole memory, that experience of the mind which is legendary as well as historical, personal as well as cultural."[8] For Momaday, past and present, individual and tribe merge in the individual self: "Notions of the past and future are essentially notions of the present," he writes in *The Names*. "In the same way an idea of one's ancestry and posterity is really an idea of the self."[9]

This collective sense of the self is enacted in a crucial scene in *The Names*, in which Momaday remembers himself as a small child looking at his reflection in a glass and beginning to draw the outlines of the reflection on paper—a primal scene of self-portraiture that foreshadows his later interest in autobiography.

> I see into the green, transparent base of a kerosene lamp; there is a still circle within it, the surface of a deeper transparency. . . . Something of me has just now moved upon the metal throat of the lamp, some distortion of myself, nonetheless recognizable. . . . I look for my image then in the globe, rising a little in my chair, but I see nothing but my ghost, another transparency. . . . I take up a pencil and set the point against a sheet of paper and define the head of a boy. (93)

When he labels the picture, a strange doubling occurs: Momaday gives his self-portrait the name of his Kiowa grandfather, whom he never knew. "I write, in my child's hand, beneath the drawing, 'This is someone. Maybe this is Mammedaty. This is Mammedaty when he was a boy' " (93). Tellingly, this first act of self-portraiture leads straight back to Momaday's ancestry; the picture of himself turns into a picture of his grandfather, just as his adult autobiographical texts will focus as much

on his ancestry as on himself. To Momaday, there is no distinction between the two—past and present merge, to the extent that sometimes,
Momaday says, "I . . . imagine that I am my ancestors. That as I write I
am speaking what my ancestors spoke or would speak through me. . . . I
think sometimes that my voice is the reincarnation of a voice from my
ancestral past."[10]

Unlike Momaday, who wholeheartedly embraces his Kiowa heritage,
Gloria Anzaldúa, in turning to her ethnic heritage as a source of identity
in *Borderlands/La frontera,* is faced with certain aspects of Chicano culture
that she cannot accept. "I abhor some of my culture's ways, how it crip-
ples its women, *como burras,*" she writes. "I abhor how my culture makes
macho caricatures of its men. No, I do not buy all the myths of the tribe
into which I was born."[11] For Anzaldúa, the process of remembering is
inseparable from the process of selection: she must pick and choose from
among the cultural models she has inherited in order to reconstruct her
own identity.

As a Chicana, Anzaldúa is a mixed breed, the product of the repeated
mixing of the native Indians with the Spanish, and of the resulting Mexicans with the northern Anglos. Her cultural heritage is therefore complex and full of contradictions: "Being trilingual, monolingual, bilingual
or multilingual, speaking a patois, and in a state of perpetual transition,
the *mestiza* faces the dilemma of the mixed breed: which collectivity
does the daughter of a darkskinned mother listen to?" (78).

Being lesbian does not make this dilemma any simpler. Women are
already "at the bottom of the ladder" of power in Mexican and Chicano
culture, writes Anzaldúa; the lesbian woman is even lower, as "the Chicano, mexicano, and some Indian cultures have no tolerance for devi-
ance" (18). Like Lorde, Anzaldúa sees the lesbian of color as "alienated
from her mother culture," as well as " 'alien' in the dominant culture."
She is "caught between *los intersticios,* the spaces between the different
worlds she inhabits" (20).

Anzaldúa's response to living in the borderlands between cultures is
one of synthesis rather than division; she demands the right to draw on
all of her cultural roots for sustenance, rather than being forced to
choose between them.

> What I want is an accounting with all three cultures—white, Mexican, In-
> dian. I want the freedom to carve and chisel my own face, to staunch the
> bleeding with ashes, to fashion my own gods out of my entrails. And if going
> home is denied me then I will have to stand and claim my space, making a

new culture—*una cultura mestiza*—with my own lumber, my own bricks and mortar and my own feminist architecture. (22)

In this process of carving her own face, Anzaldúa has frequent recourse to Chicano history, particularly women's history. Like Lorde and Momaday, she turns to her ancestors for guidance, to the dark-skinned woman, who has "been silenced, gagged, caged, bound into servitude with marriage, bludgeoned for 300 years," and yet still continues "to fight for her own skin and a piece of ground to stand on . . . a homeground where she can plumb the rich ancestral roots into her own ample *mestiza* heart" (22–23). Following these "ancestral roots," Anzaldúa finds herself fascinated by the female goddesses of the mixed Indian, Mexican, and Chicano cultures, especially *Coatlicue,* the powerful Meso-American serpent goddess:

> *Coatlicue* is one of the powerful images, or "archetypes," that inhabits, or passes through, my psyche. For me, *la Coatlicue* is the consuming internal whirlwind, the symbol of the underground aspects of the psyche. . . . Simultaneously . . . she represents: duality in life, a synthesis of duality, and a third perspective—something more than mere duality or a synthesis of duality. (46)

It is this "third perspective" to which Anzaldúa attaches the most importance; only through "a massive uprooting of dualistic thinking in the individual and collective consciousness," she writes, can the Chicano culture arrive at "a new mythos . . . a change in the way we perceive reality, the way we see ourselves, and the ways we behave" (80). Her autobiographical text is a contribution to this "new mythos"; her *mestiza* self-construction, in which she understands herself both as an individual and as part of a collective, is evidenced in the way she switches fluidly from the singular to the plural pronoun in the preface to *Borderlands/La frontera:*

> This book, then, speaks of my existence. My preoccupation with the inner life of the Self, and with the struggle of the Self amidst adversity and violation. . . . We Chicanos no longer feel that we need to beg entrance, that we need always to make the first overture. . . . Today we ask to be met halfway. This book is our invitation to you—from the new *mestizas.*

For "new *mestizas*" such as Lorde, Momaday, and Anzaldúa, the self is plural, a mixing of collective and individual memories where "nothing is thrust out [and] nothing abandoned" (79).

Oral Inscriptions and the Ethnic Self

The importance of local oral traditions to the survival of ethnic selfhood is discussed in the Caribbean context by Martinican writers Jean Bernabé, Patrick Chamoiseau, and Raphaël Confiant; under the onslaught of the French education system, they write, the traditional Creole oral culture was "buried in our collective unconsciousness . . . but not without leaving here and there the scattered fragments of its discontinuous contours."[12] Creole writers, claim Bernabé, Chamoiseau, and Confiant, must unearth and inscribe this submerged orality in order to create a "new writing":

> Taking over oral tradition should not be considered a backward mode of nostalgic stagnation. . . . To return to it, yes, first in order to restore this cultural continuity . . . without which it is difficult for collective identity to take shape. To return to it, yes, in order to enrich our enunciation, to integrate it, and go beyond it. . . . We may then, through the marriage of our trained senses, inseminate Creole in the new writing. In short, *we shall create a literature*, which will obey all the demands of modern writing while taking root in the traditional configurations of our orality. (896)

Like the Creole Caribbean cultures, the Caribbean/African American, Native American, and Chicano cultures traditionally maintained their collective memories orally, through storytelling and songs. Lorde, Momaday, and Anzaldúa all seek to tap into these collective oral roots in order to create new, hybridized forms of ethnic autobiography.

Lorde, in a section of her autobiography *Zami* entitled "How I Became a Poet," links her own writing with her mother's spoken words: "When the strongest words for what I have to offer come out of me sounding like words I remember from my mother's mouth, then I either have to reassess the meaning of everything I have to say now, or re-examine the worth of her old words" (31). Lorde's mother's "old words" come from the Creole language and culture of her Grenadian childhood; they are words that for Lorde are euphemisms full of "picaresque constructions and surreal scenes": "We were never dressed too lightly, but rather 'in next kin to nothing.' *Neck skin to nothing?* Impassable and impossible distances were measured by the distance 'from Hog to Kick 'em Jenny.' *Hog? Kick 'em Jenny?* Who knew . . . that these were two little reefs in the Grenadines, between Grenada and Carriacou" (32). It is this Creole language, writes Lorde, that empowers her written poetry, as well as her sense of self: "I am a reflection of my mother's secret poetry, as well as of her hidden angers" (32).

Zami combines poetry, a traditionally oral medium, with the narrative prose of traditional Western autobiography: Lorde's poems, as well as snatches of song, are inscribed in crucial places in the narrative, giving an oral dimension to the written text. Lorde frequently interrupts the description of events with italicized passages that present poetic images. When her friend Gennie is buried, for example, the writing shifts from narrative prose to italicized prose poetry:

> Gennie was buried in Woodlawn Cemetery on the first day of April. The *Amsterdam News* story about her death announced that she was not pregnant and so no reason for her suicide could be established. Nothing else.
>
> *The sound of dirt clods flying hollow against the white coffin. The sound of birds who knew death as no reason for silence. A black-clad man mouthing words in a foreign tongue. No hallowed ground for suicides. The sound of weeping women. The wind. The forward edge of spring. The sound of grass growing, flowers beginning to blossom, the branching of a far-off tree. Clods against the white coffin. (103)*

The prose poetry describes the event in *sounds;* the visual becomes the aural.[13] This return to the aural/oral occurs in other crucial moments of Lorde's text: during her first lesbian encounter, which takes place to the tune of Fats Domino's "Blueberry Hill"; at her father's death, when her sister

> endlessly played a record which she had just gotten on the phonograph in the parlor. Day and night, over and over, for seven days:
> I get the blues when we dance
> I get the blues in advance
> For I know you'll be gone
> and I'll be here all alone
> So I get the blues in advance. (143–44)

As a long-term, important love affair comes to a painful end, Lorde finds strength in the sudden memory of an old spiritual, a collective voice from her African American past welling up in the midst of her individual suffering. Waiting at a bus stop, immersed in the "heartbreak" of losing her lover, Muriel, Lorde is suddenly "transfixed":

> The bus door opened and I placed my foot upon the step. Quite suddenly, there was music swelling up into my head, as if a choir of angels had boarded the Second Avenue bus directly in front of me. They were singing the last chorus of an old spiritual of hope:
> Gonna die this death
> On Cal-va-ryyyyy

BUT AIN'T GONNA

DIE

NO MORE! . . .

The music was like a surge of strength. It felt rich with hope and a promise of life—more importantly, a new way through or beyond pain. (238–39)

At this moment, linked through the memory of music to an ancestral source of strength, Lorde inscribes the line that will become part of the title of her autobiography: "The physical realities of the dingy bus slid away from me. I suddenly stood upon a hill in the center of an unknown country, hearing the sky fill with a new spelling of my name" (239). Lorde's new name, Zami, is one that in itself signifies her individual sense of connection with the collective memory of her ethnic heritage.

Asked in an interview to describe his "deepest voice," N. Scott Momaday linked his most intimate, personal expression of self to his Native American heritage; his "deepest voice" is "lyrical and reverent and . . . bears close relationship to Indian oral tradition. . . . It proceeds out of an ancient voice. It is anchored in that ancient tradition."[14] Voices are constantly sounding in *The Names;* in setting the scene for his childhood memories, Momaday uses bits of conversations, poems, Kiowa phrases, and songs, interspersed with more writerly narrative descriptions. His earliest memories are laced with voices; as an infant, being rocked in "a little hammock," he hears "the voices of my parents, of my grandmother, of others. Their voices, their words, English and Kiowa—and the silences that lie about them—are already the element of my mind's life" (8).

Also included in *The Names* are the voices of Momaday's ancestors, even those who died before he was born. Filling gaps in his knowledge with imagination, he re-creates a meeting of his great-grandparents, Pohd-lohk and Keah-dine-Keah, their laconic conversation becoming a part of his own memory:

Well Pohd-lohk, it is good to have you here; I am glad that you came.
So, I must go on about my business.
Yes?
It is very important.
Yes?
Oh, yes.
Well, then.

> I am on my way to see your great-grandson.
>
> Eh neh neh neh neh!
>
> She clasped her hands together, laughing. And after a moment she was lost in thought, and again there was a silence between them. (54–55)

The great-grandson in question is of course Momaday himself, and the important business Pohd-lohk must take care of is giving the infant Momaday his Kiowa name, Tsoai-talee.

This scene continues with Keah-dine-Keah remembering the old Kiowa story of Momaday's namesake, Tsoai, the bear-boy. The inclusion of this old story, and others, in Momaday's autobiographical texts is another way in which he inscribes traces of the Kiowa oral tradition. Momaday learned many Kiowa stories orally, from his father, who had learned them from his own father: "I'm sure that he had heard many stories from his father," Momaday recalls of his father in an interview. "So he just continued the process by telling me stories."[15] By writing these inherited stories into his autobiography, Momaday is continuing the oral tradition but merging it with the Western literary tradition of dominant American culture. In fact, Momaday believes that the two traditions are more alike than different: "There is a tendency when you're talking about oral tradition to want to distinguish it as much as you can from written tradition, and of course the distinctions are real, but I think that at some point the two traditions come very close together, and perhaps merge . . . they are more apparently different than really different" (121).

Momaday's combination of the oral and the written traditions in *The Names* results in his own hybrid style of storytelling, which he comments on in a prefatory note: "This is one way to tell a story. In this instance it is my way, and it is the way of my people." The hybridization is apparent at the level of language itself. *The Names* is written in short fragments of text, moving quickly from straightforward narrative prose to more lyrical passages that resemble prose poems. Some passages, like the one that follows, clearly retain the traces of the rhythmic, ritualized patterns of Native American oral storytelling.

> It happened so: I was thirteen years old, and my parents gave me a horse. . . . This my horse and I came to be, in the course of our life together, in good understanding, of one mind, a true story and history of that large landscape in which we made one entity of whole motion, one and the same center of an intricate, pastoral composition, evanescent, ever changing. And to this my horse I gave the name Pecos. (155)

There are also sections that clearly draw from the Western literary tradition, especially the Modernist school of writing, as in a passage where Momaday refers to himself in the third person as "the boy," and then slips into first-person stream of consciousness:

> The boy held the milk up to the lamp and looked through the carnival glass. . . . He felt better, and he was getting sleepy.
>
> Well anyway I have this gun this real-looking gun black and brown smooth and hard a carbine tomorrow I will shoot an Indian down by the creek he will see me but I will see him first and I will wait until he sees me it has to be that way of course he sees me and of course he is surprised his eyes are big and his mouth is open and he is *ugly*. (75)

By mixing traces of the oral tradition with Western literary styles, Momaday's autobiography acts as a performative demonstration of the influence of both traditions on his written construction of identity.

The chapter of *Borderlands/La frontera* that addresses Anzaldúa's process of writing begins with a section on storytelling:

> I was familiar with *cuentos*—my grandmother told stories like the one about her getting on top of the roof while down below rabid coyotes were ravaging the place and wanting to get at her. My father told stories about a phantom giant dog that appeared out of nowhere and sped along the side of the pickup no matter how fast he was driving.
>
> Nudge a Mexican and she or he will break out with a story. So, huddling under the covers, I made up stories for my sister night after night. (65)

Out of this storytelling tradition, writes Anzaldúa, her own writing began, and she still thinks of writing as connected to the oral tradition: "My 'stories' are acts encapsulated in time, 'enacted' every time they are spoken aloud or read silently. I like to think of them as performances and not as inert or 'dead' objects" (67). The writing process itself has much to do with performance for Anzaldúa; she relates writing to film, in which "voices and scenes . . . [are] projected in the inner screen of my mind" (69). Writing is also linked to speaking: "To write, to be a writer, I have to trust and believe in myself as a speaker, as a voice for the images" (73).

The autobiographical text that results from this writing process is filled with traces of the Chicano oral tradition. The narrative is interspersed with Chicano and Mexican sayings, songs, and poetry, some of it Anzaldúa's, some reaching as far back as the Aztecs. In a section subtitled "My Native Tongue," Anzaldúa writes of Mexican films and *norteño* music as being formative of her sense of cultural identity: "Even before I read books by Chicanos or Mexicans, it was the Mexican movies I saw at the drive-in . . . that gave me a sense of belonging. . . . The whole time I was growing up, there was *norteño* music. . . . These folk musicians and folk songs are our chief cultural mythmakers" (61).

The most important way in which Anzaldúa integrates the Chicano oral tradition into her autobiography is by writing in the Chicano language, a "bastard language" (58) that moves "from English to Castilian Spanish to the North Mexican dialect to Tex-Mex to a sprinkling of Nahuatl to a mixture of all of these" (Preface). Until relatively recently, Chicano Spanish was exclusively an oral language; Chicano writers would use either English or Spanish, but not a combination of the two, since this hybridization of languages has traditionally been considered "deficient, a mutilation of Spanish," writes Anzaldúa (55).[16]

For Anzaldúa, deciding to write her autobiography in Chicano Spanish is an act of liberation, an affirmation of the complex cultural heritage to which she can lay claim. "Ethnic identity is twin skin to linguistic identity," she writes. "I am my language. Until I can take pride in my language, I cannot take pride in myself" (59). Part of her call for a "*mestiza consciousness*" involves refusing to accept the culturally enforced duality of speaking *either* Spanish *or* English, claiming instead the freedom to blend the two languages into a new "border tongue."

> Until I am free to write bilingually and to switch codes without having always to translate, while I still have to speak English or Spanish when I would rather speak Spanglish . . . my tongue will be illegitimate.
>
> I will no longer be made to feel ashamed of existing. I will have my voice: Indian, Spanish, white. I will have my serpent's tongue—my woman's voice, my sexual voice, my poet's voice. I will overcome the tradition of silence. (59)

Borderlands/La frontera, with its blending of poetry and prose, Spanish, English, Nahuatl, and dialect, draws on all the cultural memories available in order to speak the self in a pluralistic mode.

Ethnic Acts and Ancestral Memories

Ethnic memory is carried forward not only in words, but also in acts, and these ethnic acts are often inscribed in ethnic autobiographies. The performance of the ethnic act links past and present, individual and collective, in a cycle of repetition and renewal.

One of the most powerful ethnic acts recorded in Audre Lorde's auto-biography is culinary: she recalls making a special Grenadian dish on the first day of her first menstruation, the day she entered fully into woman-hood. The act of "pounding spice," part of a culinary tradition handed down from her maternal forebears, binds her to the collectivity of women in general and lesbians in particular, as well as forming a part of her own individual memory. In the prologue to *Zami,* Lorde describes her desire to be "both man and woman": "I would like to enter a woman the way any man can, and to be entered—to leave and to be left—to be hot and hard and soft all at the same time. . . . I would like to drive forward and at other times to rest or be driven" (7). She uses similar language to describe the process of pounding spice, which she learns to do in her mother's special West Indian mortar. The mortar, "of a foreign fragrant wood" and "carved in an intricate and most enticing manner," fascinates Lorde as a child: "I loved to finger the hard roundness of the carved fruit, and the always surprising termination of the shapes as the carvings stopped at the rim and the bowl sloped abruptly downward, smoothly oval but suddenly businesslike" (71). The pestle, "long and tapering," like "a summer crook-necked squash uncurled and slightly twisted," was "slightly bigger at the grinding end than most pestles, and the widened curved end fitted into the bowl of the mortar easily" (72). Using this instrument on the day of her first menstruation to make the West Indian meal of souse enacts Lorde's fantasy of androgynous, les-bian sexuality, which, like the mortar and pestle and the act of pounding spice, is rooted in the collective memory of her female ancestors in Carri-acou. As she pounds the spices in the mortar, she becomes both mortar and pestle, "hard and soft all at the same time."

> I plunged the pestle into the bowl, feeling the blanket of salt give way, and the broken cloves of garlic underneath. The downward thrust of the wooden pestle slowed upon contact, rotated back and forth slowly, and then gently altered its rhythm to include an up and down beat. . . .
>
> As I continued to pound the spice, a vital connection seemed to establish itself between the muscles of my fingers curved tightly around the smooth pestle in its insistent downward motion, and the molten core of my body whose source emanated from a new ripe fullness just beneath the pit of my stomach. . . .
>
> The tidal basin suspended between my hips shuddered at each repetition of the strokes which now felt like assaults. Without my volition the down-ward the thrusts of the pestle grew gentler and gentler, until its velvety sur-face seemed almost to caress the liquefying mash at the bottom of the mor-tar. (78–79)

The orgasmic act of pounding garlic gives way to a scene of unusual tenderness between Lorde and her mother, who are joined in the gendered repetition of menstruation and the ethnic ritual of pounding spice.

For Scott Momaday, important ethnic memories are bound up in the acts of journeying and naming. Traveling is important to Momaday as an individual, and he relates his love of travel to his ethnic heritage: "I love to travel. Travel is very important. And I think it is natural for me to travel. After all, I'm descended from a nomadic people. The Kiowas have always loved to roam over the earth, and so do I" (Woodard, 49). What Momaday describes in *The Names* as "the first notable event in my life" is "a journey to the Black Hills" (42), the ancestral home of the Kiowas. On this journey, the six-month-old Momaday visits a sacred Kiowa site, meets his Kiowa relatives for the first time, and is given his Indian name by his great-grandfather, Pohd-lohk. Momaday re-creates the scene of his own naming, linking the history of the Kiowa people with his own coming into being through his name:

> In the arbor Pohd-lohk entered among the members of his dead stepson's family and was full of good humor and ease. He took up the child in his hands and held it high, and he cradled it in his arms, singing to it and rocking it to and fro. With the others he passed the time of day, exchanged customary talk. . . . But with the child he was deliberate, intent. And after a time all the other voices fell away, and his own grew up in their wake. It became monotonous and incessant, like a long running of the wind. The whole of the afternoon was caught up in it and carried along. Pohd-lohk spoke, as if telling a story, of the coming-out people, of their long journey. He spoke of how it was that everything began, of Tsoai, and of the stars falling or holding fast in strange patterns on the sky. And in this, at last, Pohd-lohk affirmed the whole life of the child in a name, saying: Now you are, Tsoai-talee. (56–57)

By giving him a name, Pohd-lohk welcomes the infant Momaday as a member of the Kiowa tribe, at the same time passing on the ethnic memories of the tribe to the next generation. Naming is sacred to the Kiowas; Pohd-lohk, says Momaday, "believed that a man's life proceeds from his name, in the way that a river proceeds from its source." Naming is inseparable from existence: "When you name something," writes Momaday, "you confer being upon it at the same time" (Woodard, 88). In a slight but crucial distortion of Cartesian subjectivity, Momaday begins *The Names* by saying: "My name is Tsoai-talee. I am, therefore, Tsoai-talee; therefore I am." Without a name and without a forebear to confer it, the

Kiowa part of Momaday would not exist; identity and existence are linked to the past through the ritual of naming.

In the epilogue of *The Names* Momaday again journeys to meet with his ancestors. This time it is an imagined journey in time as well as space: Momaday imagines that he is riding among the primeval buffalo herd, "so many that I could not see the ground beneath them. . . . And farther on there were tipis, some of them partly dismantled. . . . But there were no people; the people had gone away. And for a long time after that I followed their tracks" (166). The tracks lead to Rainy Mountain, where a crowd of Momaday's ancestors await him: "There were old people in the arbor, and they were all very glad to see me, and they called me by my Indian name. And to each one, face to face, weeping, I spoke his name: Mammedaty, Aho, Pohd-lohk, Keah-dine-keah, Kau-au-ointy" (166).

Momaday continues upon into the Black Hills, past Tsoai, the Rock Tree, after which he is named, and back over the territory his distant ancestors had crossed coming down from the Bering Strait, until he reaches what seems to him like "the top of the world." Here, amid the "slow, rolling spill of the mountain clouds," he finds "the fallen tree, the hollow log" (167) out of which his tribe originally entered the world in the Kiowa myth of origin. In the invocation of this creation story, with which he began his autobiographical text, Momaday's autobiographical journey comes full circle, linking his individual origin with that of the tribe.

For Gloria Anzaldúa, the activity of writing is not only Western—what she calls Anglo—but also a profoundly ethnic act, linked through collective memory to the pre-Colombian practice of shamanistic art:

> In the ethno-poetics and performance of the shaman, my people, the Indians, did not split the artistic from the functional, the sacred from the secular, art from everyday life. The religious, social, and aesthetic purposes of art were all intertwined. . . . The ability of story (prose and poetry) to transform the storyteller and the listener into something or someone else is shamanistic. The writer, as shape-changer, is a *nahual*, a shaman. (66)

In writing *Borderlands/La frontera*, Anzaldúa herself becomes a shaman, tapping into ancient practices of art. Reflexively commenting on her own writing process, she compares her autobiographical text to "a mosaic pattern (Aztec-like)," "a beaded work with several leitmotifs and with a central core" (66). The text is also a manifestation of Coatlicue, the Meso-American goddess: "This female being is angry, sad, joyful, is *Coatlicue*, dove, horse, serpent, cactus. Though it is a flawed thing—a clumsy, complex, groping blind thing—for me it is alive, infused with spirit. I talk to it; it talks to me" (67).

Hybridizing the Western practice of writing with the indigenous practices of her Indian ancestors, Anzaldúa incorporates ancient ethnic rituals into her modern, individual activity as a writer. Before writing, "I make my offerings of incense and cracked corn, light my candle. In my head I sometimes will say a prayer—an affirmation and a voicing of intent" (67). Later, ready to write, she describes herself sitting at the computer, which is at once a tool of writing and an altar to the indigenous, preliterate goddesses: "I sit here before my computer, *Amiguita*, my altar on top of the monitor with the *Virgen de Coatlalopeuh* candle and copal incense burning. My companion, a wooden serpent staff with feathers, is to my right while I ponder the ways metaphor and symbol concretize the spirit and etherealize the body" (75).

The act of writing becomes a complex ethnic act that spans the borderland between the Western and the indigenous. The product, in this case the autobiographical text *Borderlands/La frontera*, is not only a Western-style book, but also "Aztecan blood sacrifices" (75). Writing is an ethnic act for Anzaldúa, saturated with centuries of collective ethnic experience: "When I write," she says, "it feels like I'm carving bone. It feels like I'm creating my own face, my own heart—a Nahuatl concept" (73).

Politicizing Memory

American ethnic autobiographies, like the similarly hybridized novels Bakhtin studied, "are pregnant with potential for new world views, with new 'internal forms' for perceiving the world in words" (Bakhtin, 360). If, as Fredric Jameson insists in *The Political Unconscious*, "the production of aesthetic or narrative form is to be seen as an ideological act in its own right,"[17] then American ethnic autobiography must be read as a politically charged rewriting of the traditional genre of autobiography. Using Dan Aronson's definition of ethnicity as "an ideology of and for value dissensus and disengagement from an inclusive sociopolitical arena" (Aronson, 15), we can say that ethnic autobiography represents the appropriation and modification of a traditionally Western form for use in the service of a nonconforming, resistant ethnic ideology.

The autobiographies of Momaday, Anzaldúa, and Lorde, although drawing on the past, are profoundly future oriented; they enact what bell hooks calls "a politicization of memory that distinguishes nostalgia, that longing for something to be as it once was, a kind of useless act, from that remembering that serves to illuminate and transform the present."[18] They call for, and demonstrate the possibility of, a pluralistic conception of self and society. "What we must do," writes Lorde in the essay "Learning from the '60s," "is commit ourselves to some future that can include each other and to work toward that future with the particular strengths of our individual identities. And in order to do this, we must allow each other our differences at the same time as we recognize our sameness."[19]

Momaday, speaking from the Native American perspective, insists that "the Indian . . . must accommodate himself to what we call the dominant society. That is his future. . . . The question is how. How to do it without sacrificing the valuable parts of one's traditions and heritage" (Woodard, 199). Momaday's autobiographical texts, like those of Lorde and Anzaldúa, attempt to demonstrate how this cultural dialogue can be written into autobiography, and into the self. As Michael M. J. Fischer observes in his essay "Ethnicity and the Post-Modern Arts of Memory," "the process of assuming an ethnic identity is an insistence on a pluralistic, multidimensional concept of self: one can be many different things, and this personal sense can be a crucible for a wider social ethos of pluralism."[20]

Individual and collective memory is put in the service of this "ethos of pluralism" in the autobiographies of Momaday, Anzaldúa, and Lorde. The autobiographical subject becomes, in Anzaldúa's words, "a plural personality" (79). "*Soy un amasamiento*," she writes. "I am an act of kneading, of uniting and joining that not only has produced both a creature of darkness and a creature of light, but also a creature that questions the definitions of light and dark and gives them new meanings" (81). Ethnic autobiography gives "new meanings" and new possibilities to the term *autobiography*. Using "retrospection to gain a vision for the future" (Fischer, 198), ethnic autobiographers create a hybridized, double-voiced form of autobiography in which collective ethnic memory and individual memory are linked in a dialogue that is itself, like Anzaldúa's "*mestiza* consciousness," "greater than the sum of its severed parts" (80).

Notes

1. Richard A. Schermerhorn, *Comparative Ethnic Relations* (New York: Random House, 1970), 12.

2. Mikhail M. Bakhtin, "Discourse in the Novel," in *The Dialogic Imagination,* ed. Michael Holquist, trans. Michael Holquist and Caryl Emerson (Austin: University of Texas Press, 1981), 324–25.

3. For a discussion of the evolution of the concept of individuality in the Western autobiographical tradition, see Karl J. Weintraub, *The Value of the Individual* (Chicago: University of Chicago Press, 1978), and Sidonie Smith, *Identity, Subjectivity, and the Body: Women's Autobiographical Practices in the Twentieth Century* (Bloomington: Indiana University Press, 1993).

4. I am using Dan Aronson's definition of ethnicity as "an ideology of and for value dissensus and disengagement from an inclusive sociopolitical arena" ("Ethnicity as a Cultural System: An Introductory Essay," in *Ethnicity in the Americas,* ed. Frances Henry [The Hague: Mouton Publishers, 1976], p. 15); the idea of a dialogue between ethnic and dominant cultures is thus constitutive of the concept of ethnicity. Aronson's definition not only adds an important political dimension to the idea of ethnicity, but also eliminates the onus of essentialism: "natural" links between ethnicity and race are irrelevant to his understanding of the term.

5. Hertha D. Wong, "Pre-literate Native American Autobiography: Forms of Personal Narrative," *MELUS* 14, no. 1 (1987): 18–19.

6. Audre Lorde, *Zami: A New Spelling of My Name* (Freedom, Calif.: Crossing Press, 1982), 176.

7. Claudine Raynaud, " 'A Nutmeg Nestled Inside Its Covering of Mace': Audre Lorde's *Zami,*" in *Life/Lines,* ed. Bella Brodski and Celeste Schenck (Ithaca: Cornell University Press, 1988), 223.

8. N. Scott Momaday, *The Way to Rainy Mountain* (Albuquerque: University of New Mexico Press, 1969), 4.

9. N. Scott Momaday, *The Names* (Tucson: University of Arizona Press, 1976), 97.

10. Charles L. Woodard, *Ancestral Voice: Conversations with N. Scott Momaday* (Lincoln: University of Nebraska Press, 1989), 112.

11. Gloria Anzaldúa, *Borderlands/La frontera: The New Mestiza* (San Francisco: Spinsters/Aunt Lute, 1987), 21–22.

12. Jean Bernabé, Patrick Chamoiseau, and Raphaël Confiant, "In Praise of Creoleness," trans. Mohamed B. Taleb Khyar, *Callaloo* 13 (1990): 895.

13. I am drawing here on Walter J. Ong's discussion of the visual and the aural/oral as it relates to writing and oral culture in *Orality and Literacy: The Technologizing of the Word* (London: Methuen, 1982), 73–74, 115–23.

14. Woodard, *Ancestral Voice,* epigraph.

15. Woodard, *Ancestral Voice,* 113.

16. For a discussion of the history of Chicano literature and its movement from English to Spanish to bilingual forms, see Raymund A. Paredes, "The Evolution of Chicano Literature," in *Three American Literatures,* ed. Houston A. Baker, Jr. (New York: Modern Language Association, 1982), 33–79.

17. Fredric Jameson, *The Political Unconscious* (Ithaca: Cornell University Press, 1981), 79.

18. bell hooks, "Choosing the Margin as a Space of Radical Openness," in *Yearning: Race, Gender and Cultural Politics* (Boston: South End Press, 1990), 147.

19. Audre Lorde, "Learning from the '60s," in *Sister Outsider* (Trumanburg, N.Y.: Crossing Press, 1984), 142.

20. Michael M. J. Fischer, "Ethnicity and the Post-Modern Arts of Memory," in *Writing Culture,* ed. James Clifford and George Marcus (Berkeley: University of California Press, 1986), 196.

Telling History:

Inventing Identity in

Jewish American Fiction

VICTORIA AARONS

> There is a long time in me between knowing and telling.
> —Grace Paley, "Debts"

There is a long tradition in Jewish literature, indeed since Hebrew Scripture, of bearing witness through the telling of stories. Well before the beginnings of a secular Jewish literature (its founding fathers, the three major Eastern European Yiddish writers, Mendele Mocher Sforim, Sholom Aleichem, and I. L. Peretz),[1] storytelling served Jewish communities as a means of bearing witness to the events of the past and of inculcating precepts and values by which to live. In this way, history is preserved as personal history; history is given shape and meaning through the interpretation of individual lives. And just as history is made up of personal histories, so, too, personal identities are formed in relation to a larger ethical and cultural context. Certainly if one regards the Bible not only as sacred wisdom but as literary genre, we find storytelling to be the governing narrative technique; the transmission of stories identifies and interprets cultural norms and values within the context of personal histories, personal triumphs and failures (Cain's betrayal of Abel, Abraham's willingness to sacrifice Isaac, Jacob's theft of Esau's birthright, Job's validation of God's omniscience). In this way, storytelling serves as a means of establishing an ethical code, of providing guidelines for living in a community, and of balancing personal morality with communal necessity. And just as Abraham's willingness to sacrifice that which he loves most is testimony to a people's unswerving devotion to a just God, so does bearing witness to the ethical choices of a community, those choices which define its "making," thus preserve a kind of cultural ethos within which individual identities may be formed.

So telling stories becomes the artifice for a deeply ingrained history of bearing witness in Jewish literature, the main controlling device in the fictional narratives of Jewish writers, from Sholom Aleichem's Tevye to Philip Roth's Zuckerman to Grace Paley's Faith, characters who, in telling their personal histories, bear witness to the survival—if only in memory—of a community. And, whether the characters tell their own stories or those of someone else in the "community," communities defined by Grace Paley's New York neighborhoods or Sholom Aleichem's shtetls, the drama is in the very act of telling stories, stories that frame and bond communities. For these characters, telling stories becomes a vital necessity, at times a final act of despair, but invariably an affirmation of self possible only within the security of consistently acknowledged communal values, if only as an insistent reminder of them. Since, in bearing witness to history—the disintegration of the shtetls, the devastation of the Holocaust, the dislocation of the immigrant—they are able to place themselves within a communal context defined by Judaism; their very lives speak to a shared suffering and to a shared cultural ethos.

This notion of bearing witness is complicated in Jewish literature; it does not function simply as a set of testimonials that serve to dogmatize a community. Rather, bearing witness is an intimate and often difficult process of validating self in relation to a communal past defined by suffering and to a future without permanence. In making public the events of their lives, their individual sorrows and perceived inequities, the host of characters who people Jewish literature attempt to control and make sense of an otherwise incomprehensible and intolerable universe. In Job's determination to "not hold my peace; / I will speak out in the distress of my mind / and complain in the bitterness of my soul" (7:11), we are witness to what will become the main thematic and structural characteristic in the secular fiction: storytelling as both dramatic pathos and narrative frame.

For in the works of Sholom Aleichem, for example (whose writings mark the beginnings of a tradition of secular Jewish fiction), we find characters who, like Job, are moved to tell their stories, to be heard, and thus to assert for themselves a secure place in an otherwise tenuous and often chaotic universe. " 'I ask you, what do I have out of life?' " demands one of Sholom Aleichem's many character-narrators. " 'What did

I do to deserve such a bitter end? Why has such a lonely old age befallen me? Why and what for?' "[2] Unlike the tragic immediacy of Job's plea to have a hearing with God, Sholom Aleichem's characters relate events with a great deal of comic flourish. However, the comic for Sholom Aleichem always gives way to pathos, since it is in the telling, more often than not, that his characters' suffering is made transparent. Sholom Aleichem's character-narrator Tevye, for example, concludes the story of his daughter's leave-taking with a comic understatement that gives way to the depth of his grief: "Let's talk about something more cheerful. Have you heard any news of the cholera in Odessa?"[3] The articulation of personal sorrow here, as elsewhere in the literature, gives voice to the shape of the community at large, since, in this case, Tevye's daughter's break from tradition and custom reveals the inevitable disintegration of shtetl life.

In the fiction of contemporary Jewish American writers, however, the necessity to tell is rivaled only by the urgency to hear, to know the stories of the past, especially for American-born Jews, a generation for whom America is, as Cynthia Ozick's character Edelshtein puts it, "the empty bride," without dowry, without history, without a past.[4] Although without "the cruel history of Europe,"[5] as one of Grace Paley's characters defines Jewish American history, those American-born characters, seemingly free from the baggage of the ghetto, nevertheless are haunted by it, haunted by a past they never really knew, one that existed only in the memory of parents and grandparents before them.

All the many forces brought to bear on Judaism in the twentieth century—dispersion, genocide, Zionism, immigration, and assimilation—have heightened the existing sense of fragmentation and marginality, which have fast become the concerns of Jewish American literature. And hearing the stories of the past becomes a major preoccupation, especially for those American-born characters, who, in a fundamental sense, have been denied a communal Jewish identity. However, this desire to know one's heritage, as it were, is a double-edged sword for such characters. The past for which they hunger exists in the shadows, colored by persecution, oppression, and denial of the very identity that this generation of American Jews seeks. "Isn't it a terrible thing to grow up in the shadow of another person's sorrow?" asks Paley's haunted character in "The Immigrant Story" (172). Yet more often than not it is a shadow of the character's own making in the fiction that dramatizes the tension between Jewish immigrants and their American-born sons and daughters. We find in such fiction characters who are obsessed, characters for whom knowing the past, imagining lives before them, is fundamental to their ability to define for themselves their own future.

So this fiction at once is designed around characters whose very lives depend upon the telling of stories, all the while calling attention to its own artifice, parodying itself by questioning the authority and legitimacy of the telling voice. The multiplicity of voices—those of author, narrator, and character(s)—and the ease of telling create both intimacy and urgency, since the combining of voices, of points of view, functions collaboratively. The voices are interdependent. Such an exchange of stories, a communal enterprise, is crucial to the lives of these characters. And the stories themselves are about the characters' attempts to create stories, to create fictions by which to live. Nathan Zuckerman, Philip Roth's self-conscious narrator in *The Counterlife*, ruminates on this very point: "The kind of stories that people turn life into, the kind of lives that people turn stories into."[6] There is really no separation, no distinction between the events and experiences of living and our fictional interpretation of them, as Roth himself demonstrates further in his autobiography, *The Facts*, a manuscript ironically framed by letters to and from his returning character, Nathan Zuckerman.

The articulation of experience thus defines the ethical dimensions of the character as well as the texture of his or her narrative. As a result, we are typically told stories in first-person narration, a device that allows the writer to create a duality of voices: the character-narrator's struggle to define and articulate experience and the writer's implicit and thus often ironic judgment of that character. This is a characteristic device in the episodal narratives of Sholom Aleichem and in the short fiction of writers such as Herbert Gold,[7] Grace Paley, Tillie Olsen, Delmore Schwartz, and Philip Roth, where the intermingling of narrative postures gives voice to a range of interpretative possibilities for identifying and validating individual experiences within historical frames. And even in the fiction usually governed by more conventional omniscient narration—I am thinking here particularly of the works of writers such as Isaac Bashevis Singer, Stanley Elkin, and Bernard Malamud—we find that the controlling story, the plot, is often only a container, establishing the linguistic boundaries for other stories.[8]

Typically, then, in the fiction of contemporary Jewish American writers, we find narrators, characters themselves, for whom the very act of telling stories, of narrating events, becomes the central controlling narrative device. Narratives are frames for hearing stories. More often than not, the frame story brackets other narratives; that is, the telling of one story provides the context for another. And these frames both open and protect the "real" story. The initial frame story, that of the narrator's attempt to uncover a story from the past, provides an impetus for the main dramatic tension, the unfolding of the narrator's coming to terms with his or her life in a larger context. Such narrative frames both contain and delimit the stories told. They also, however, allow a fluidity, an openness to the narrative, because they give free reign to an ongoing, unresolved dialogue that creates, in Grace Paley's terms, the "open destiny of life."[9]

Both Gilbert Rogin's short story "What Happens Next?: An Uncompleted Investigation"[10] and Art Spiegelman's remarkable cartoon depiction of the Holocaust, *MAUS: A Survivor's Tale,* parts 1 and 2,[11] are in many ways representative texts, narrated by characters who, dramatized in their own right, attempt to uncover their fathers' pasts. And both do so by approaching their fathers as potential biographers. Although the narrative tone is necessarily distinct in each work, both character-narrators are portrayed as authors, the artifice of storytelling in these works made all the more apparent by the characters' plan to interview their fathers. This "interview technique" for getting information not surprisingly creates a complicated web of humor, ironic self-parody, and pathos, a masterly and somewhat unsettling narrative design. From the outset of each work, the narrator makes clear his intention. Whereas Rogin's narrator is less specific about the nature of his interview—"I tell my father of my intention to write about him, and that I expect him to hold still for an interview" (122)—Spiegelman, who "plays" himself, is more focused but equally single-minded: "I still want to draw that book about you. . . . The one I used to talk to you about. . . . About your life in Poland, and the war" (1:12). In both works, however, the ostensible purpose of the interview gives way to a different outcome. All questions lead finally to the making of character. And the making of character is what this fiction is all about.[12]

In a delightfully comic and warm tone, Rogin's urbane, self-assured narrator, Julian, begins, with some urgency, the interview for the biography of his father. With a comic flourish that only barely disguises the narrator's determination to pursue his father, Julian sets the stage for his own self-disclosure. Although the narrator establishes himself as an interviewer, an objective reporter of the events of his father's life, he continually corrects and amends his father's version of such events. In fact, he reminds his father of incidentals that his father omits in telling his own narrative. For example, in an anecdote describing a childhood experience in Latvia, in which Julian's father tells his son how, as a young boy, he picked the seeds from tall sunflowers growing in his grandfather's garden, Julian breaks into the narrative and demands clarification: " 'If they are tall, how can you reach the seeds?' I ask" (122). Julian, ironically, wants the "facts"; he wants to envision and thus create detailed accuracy, a posture that will allow him to intellectualize and objectify his father's life, thus sparing him the emotional and irrational response that uneasily connects him to his father. But this position, at best, merely provides him with a tenuous mask, a disguise that eventually gives way as the "interview" unfolds. The title is our initial clue to this posturing. As the ironic title suggests, we do not understand life as we do a story, in a kind of linear subsequent unfolding of events, "what happens next." Any such accounting, by necessity, must be "an uncompleted investigation," because one can never know "what happens next."

Such a presumption, as Grace Paley's narrator in "A Conversation with My Father" contends, flies in the face not only of good fiction but of life. When asked by her eighty-six-year-old father, a father to whom she has promised her family to give the "last word," to "write a simple story just once more, . . . the kind de Maupassant wrote, or Chekhov, the kind you used to write. Just recognizable people and then write down what happened to them next," she resists:

> I want to please him, though I don't remember writing that way. I *would* like to try to tell such a story, if he means the kind that begins: "There was a woman . . ." followed by plot, the absolute line between two points which I've always despised. Not for literary reasons, but because it takes all hope away. Everyone, real or invented, deserves the open destiny of life. (161–62)

"The absolute line" demands a kind of closure on life to which neither Paley's nor Rogin's narrator will acquiesce. For to do so is to deny possibilities for an unambiguous reconciliation to their fathers and to their fathers' choices and ethical postures.

The title of Rogin's story—"What Happens Next?"—suggests the subtle complexity illustrated by the choice of tense. "What Happens Next?" paradoxically is the opening for the narrator's attempts to uncover his father's past, all the while really speaking to the future, to what the narrator will make of the events he unearths, to what, in other words, he will make of his own life, a future we can only infer from the text. One cannot, however, with any accuracy predict the future, the acknowledgment of which underscores the narrator's anxiety in this story. Nor can one really envision or make sense of the past, especially a past of which one has not been a part. As a result, the narrator has no option but to fictionalize his father's responses to his questions. In a self-ironically willful exertion of control, Julian acknowledges his own attempts at authorial omniscience. To his father's question, " 'Are you in fact putting down everything I say?' " our narrator responds, " 'I am, but I'm going to change it' " (124); " 'it's not going to be true' " (127). He will make of his father's reminiscences as he will, so that he might create a context out of his father's personal history within which he can envision a place for himself.

Such vision, however, is difficult to come by. Because the narrator recognizes the futility of such attempts to know, with any certainty, the father whose life defines his own ethical choices and postures, recognizes it even while he is in the midst of it, he can begin his interrogation only with questions that address his own not-too-distant past. But these, too, are incomplete. The initial interview question, " 'Do you think we look at all alike?' " (122), is asked with ironic self-absorption, and while humorously serving the narrator as a means of getting the interview under way, speaks to what will later in the interview be his real purpose: to exact from his father the generational link that will both place him in history and allow him to fashion his own future. Although the narrator asks questions designed to investigate his father's life and character, in part in the hope of forming his own, the questions never get at the heart of the kind of men father and son are. They cannot, because such questions merely reveal the narrator's own needs and insecurities. It is, however, the humorous affection with which the dialogue is conducted and what the responses almost inadvertently reveal that demonstrate the quality of the relationship between father and son.

From the outset of the story, the narrator's motives for the interview are clearer to us than they are to him. The narrator is anxious about his father, about his inevitable death, a dying the narrator feels is all the more immediate because of his sense that his father will leave him prematurely, before he knows his father. Of course, such leave-taking is always premature, since the death of a parent inevitably delimits one's own future and, in fact, makes the past finite. Philip Roth, in *The Facts*, suggests that, at least in his particular case, the anxiety attendant upon recognizing such realities is cause for both a reassessment of self and a subsequent self-disclosure.

Though I can't be entirely sure, I wonder if this book was written . . . as a palliative for the loss of a mother who still, in my mind, seems to have died inexplicably—at seventy-seven in 1981—as well as to hearten me as I come closer and closer and closer to an eighty-six-year-old father viewing the end of life as a thing as near to his face as the mirror he shaves in. . . . I wonder if there hasn't been some consolation, particularly while recovering my equilibrium, in remembering that when the events narrated here were happening we all were there, nobody having gone away or been on the brink of going away, never to be seen again for hundreds of thousands of billions of years. I wonder if I haven't drawn considerable consolation from reassigning myself as myself to a point in life when the grief that may issue from the death of parents needn't be contended with, when it is unperceivable and unsuspected, and one's own departure is unconceivable because they are there like a blockade. (8–9)

I have quoted Roth at some length here because he speaks eloquently, I think, to the urgency to write about the past as a way of exorcising one's fears and staving off the inevitable. In some ways, the "blockade" to which Roth refers exists as both resistance to and resilience toward one's memory of the past. The past is incased in and by one's parents. Their demise calls for a shifting in responsibility, an active taking hold of, and to a certain extent reifying, memory and, in it, a recovery of the past. But, as Roth suggests, it is a recovery only after a loss. In this way perhaps loss is a requirement to bearing witness both to the past and to the future. And so, Roth speaks to a fundamental connection between the perception of one's future possibilities in relation to an ongoing dialogue with one's parents. By *dialogue* here I am referring in the broadest sense to interaction and to critical self-awareness and self-assessment. One's parents' impending death intimates one's own.

For Rogin's character-narrator, like Roth's and Paley's, the impending death of his father impels him to write. Unlike Roth's and Paley's fictive fathers, however, Julian's father, while aged, has no intention of dying, a condition that causes a comic misunderstanding in the dialogue between them. In fact, the narrator's father is characterized as an active man, clearly in control of his life. The narrator's irrational fear that his father will elude him before he has reconciled himself to his past and can thereby anticipate a future creates the catalyst for the interview:

> I tell my father of my intention to write about him, and that I expect him to hold still for an interview.
> "You'll have to hurry, Julian," he says.
> Uh-oh, he's back with death again.
> "You're only sixty-nine," I say.

> "Mother and I are going on a cruise the eighteenth instant," he says, delving into his pocket and handing me a carbon of his itinerary. . . .
> I fear he will die at sea and, wrapped in the flag he loves, be tipped over the rail between one illegible island and another. (122)

Although this introductory passage seems to address the narrator's sense of potential loss and anxiety regarding his father, the very tone of the dialogue and of the narrator's musings suggests that the narrator is aware of the humor of the crossing of motives and purposes between his father and him.

From the opening lines of the story, the narrator's self-irony, his own sense of the humorous posture he has created in requesting that his father "hold still for an interview," sets the tone for their interaction. The son's exaggerated journalistic guise, the self-parody with which he calls attention to his posturing—"I ceremoniously open my notebook" (122); "I lounge against the tiles, taking notes. Oh, boy, this is it"; "I've dreamed up some more questions" (127)—saves the narrator from mere bathos. The humor with which he conducts his interview suggests a greater understanding of his own psychology than one would suspect from a fictional character on a quest for identity. Yet the narrator in "What Happens Next?" does not entirely lose sight of his own obsessional neurosis about his father's unlikely but all the more disturbing death at sea, "wrapped in the flag he loves." This final detail establishes the narrator's ethical and experiential distance from his father, the immigrant for whom America symbolized what it never could for the American-born son. Julian perceives their experiences, their individual perceptions of their place and their hopes for and identification with America as vastly different, a difference the son wants to obviate; that is, Julian believes his own experiences to be inferior to those of his father, since they lack, in his perception of a hierarchy of events, historical moment. And so he wants his father's stories to serve as a bridge to bring him to the other side of experience, a reenactment of the past.

The narrator's means for doing so, however, are comic. To interview one's father would seem, at best, to elicit distance, the son so much on the outside that he must formalize and officiate over their dialogue. However, it is this very form that, on the contrary, reinforces the obvious intimacy between father and son, despite the son's efforts at control, because the father in this story is willing to play along. " 'Would you like me to run through my life?' " (122), queries Julian's father just prior to his autobiographical account of place of origin, followed by memories of his childhood in Latvia, and culminating in his immigration to America.

" 'Was that good stuff I gave you? . . . Do you want to go on in the same vein?' " (123), he asks. Conspicuously, this last question is prompted by the father himself. And we find, as the interview continues, that it is, as we've suspected all along, the father who is in control of the unfolding narrative. In answering his son's questions, the father consciously eludes him; he maintains the upper hand despite his son's relentless determination to get answers. Our narrator, undaunted by his father's absence, is never stymied in his invention of yet more questions and continues his interview by letter:

1. Are you obedient to a moral code?
2. Do you dream? If so, how much? Are your dreams disquieting? Do they have any great themes?
3. When was the last time you shed tears?
4. What do you regret?
5. What are the kindest words a stranger ever addressed to you?
6. Eight years ago last December, I am nearly positive I saw you at the bar of the Woodstock in the company of a woman wearing a black suit, whose partly revealed bosom you were steadfastly regarding. Please comment. (125–26)

Such self-consciously and humorously reductive questions serve the narrator as a protective shield against coming to terms with his anxieties. But his cleverness here is a guise. The narrator's father, not to be outwitted by his son, replies to his questions, addressed to him "at sea" (a metaphor suggestive of elusive distance), and meets them head on in a correspondingly formalized response, *"In re* your queries" (126). The narrator's misguided directives to the kinds of biographical material he seeks—" 'Today I would appreciate it if you would tell me how you regard yourself' "—are answered in kind—" 'I am inclined to be roguish" (123); " 'I think I've been a worthwhile member of society' " (124). The narrator's father reminds him of what his rather farcical tone presumes he really knows anyway, that "you don't know me in my extra-parental guise" (123). This statement underscores the controlling irony of the story. The father calls attention to his own imperfect fictional construct. His ethos is defined by his relationship to his son, and, as such, it is malleable; his character is constantly revised and reshaped by the son who is in the process of coming to terms with his father.

Julian thus cannot "read" his father out of a "text" that is of his own making. He can see his father only in relation to himself. Our narrator, however, at least initially, desires to know his father in a way he never can. So in many ways he attempts the impossible. To know his father in any context that would preclude him, in other words, to know his father as not his father, defines and obfuscates his goal for the interview. For to understand his father in any way but as his father is to do what he desires least: to separate them. In trying to make sense of his father's character, the narrator of "What Happens Next?" really is attempting to understand himself, his identity within a larger ethical and emotional context, that of his father and his father's past. And in ironizing his motives so self-consciously, he shows through this transparent though entertaining attempt at self-protection how desperately he wants the answers, how desperately he wants to be validated by his father's life. This is why the implied and explicit associations made by the father in his intentionally offhand postscript in a return letter to his son finally offers the narrator the kind of "information" he so doggedly seeks. The narrator's anxiety about his father's character and ethical choices cannot be separated finally from his anxiety about himself.

Although Julian's father does, indeed, answer his questions in the same itemized form in which they were delivered, it is in the postscript to his letter from Fort-de-France, Martinique, received after his father's return home, that the father finally provides Julian with a piece of information that almost imperceptibly cuts to the heart of the interview.

> P.P.S. Did I ever tell you that my father, whom you never met, wrote, too? I don't know what, but I think it was poetry. Otherwise, you are dissimilar. You were hovered over during the first part of your life, and have all the stigmata of the artist: essentially self-centered, forbidding, a nonconformist. You were not a friendly child, and smiled rarely, but when you did it lit up your face so. My father was a very decent, gentle, literate human being who was ground down by economic pressures. He was slightly built and never considered strong, but I remember him carrying me in his arms when I fell in the wagon shop on Cherry Street. (126)

This narrative aside, the father's authorial digression, as it were, conveyed ironically as a virtual afterthought, tells the son more than any answer to questions of "great themes" ever could. In this postscript, the father provides his son with the longed-for connectedness to a past, to others before him. Just as the father gives his son that connection, affirms his resemblance to a grandfather he never knew, the father takes it back: "Otherwise, you are dissimilar." But his remarks are, after all, an expression of love and a recognition of his son's needs. Our narrator wants to be connected to the past, but he wants to be "dissimilar" as well; he wants to be his own person, a desire for the possibility of continuity and change.

And the father's "memory" here of his relationship with his own father reinforces the continuity of generations that the narrator has been leading to all the while. Julian virtually pushes his father into a response that his father has been playfully ironizing and avoiding thus far. In his postscript, however, he finally agrees to play his son's "game"; he provides Julian with a response that defines his own identity. In this passage, Julian's father establishes a link, a generation of fathers and sons. The memory of his father "carrying me in his arms when I fell" calls attention to the kind of intimacy that the narrator, too, has with his own father. The brief descriptive passages in the narrative define this relationship. In the midst of the interview, for example, the narrator describes their postures: "I am leaning against my father's shoulder, and he has his arm about me" (123). In this recognition of intimacy, however, both author and character pay ironic tribute to our insecurities in attempting to find solace in a familial past.

In fact, what our narrator really wants to hear about is his own past. As his father reminds him in the postscript above, he is "essentially self-centered." It is his own "limited" history that interests him most. The author ironically reminds us here, once again, of the futility of making identity out of a stable past. Identity is not static; it is not a garment one puts on. Rather, identity is always *in the making*. At the conclusion of the story, Julian, "sitting in the dark at my father's feet," asks the final question of his interview, a question that returns Julian to his own past: " 'Dad,' I am saying, 'remember when you used to push me in my stroller along the river and sing to me about the crocodile? How did it go?' " (127). The response, at first not forthcoming but then finally called forth, is: "My father sings faintly. . . . 'Croc, croc, croc crocodile, / Swimming in the shining Nile' " (127). His is a past he need not fictionalize in the way he must in reinventing his father's elusive past. Ironically, he can no more identify with his own history than he can with a country and a grandfather he never knew. And so with resignation Julian asks this final question, a silent acknowledgment that he can know finally no more than himself, the specifics of his own personal history.

"There is no way around it: you enter history through my history and me" (370), pronounces Philip Roth's character Nathan Zuckerman in *The Counterlife*. When we try to do otherwise we get into trouble. When we subordinate our own lives to a perception of the importance of a historical symbol or event, when, in other words, history becomes an emblem, an icon by which to measure our value, we lose our individual identities in the very struggle to form them. More often than not, we find characters who deny their histories in the attempt to define them. Rogin, throughout "What Happens Next?" ironizes his character-narrator, who attempts to fashion his identity by investing in a history that belongs to someone else. In such a pantomime is the loss of self. This is what Roth's rather blasphemous character Nathan Zuckerman imposes on his brother, Henry, who flees the "cultural isolation" of gentile America to "make history" in Israel. Nathan confronts Henry, now re-made Hanoch:

> "In Hebron Abraham pitched his tent. In the cave of Machpelah he and Sarah were buried, and after them Isaac, Jacob, and their wives. It's here that King David reigned before he entered Jerusalem. What's any of it got to do with you?" (122)

As Nathan exhaustively tries to explain to the brother he considers deluded, it is not one's identification with the "burning bush" or the "golden calf" that provides one with a sense of identity or a measure of integrity but rather an identification with the making and acceptance of personal histories, establishing personal identities in a limited, since individual, context. According to Nathan Zuckerman, it is people making history in ordinary ways that counts. Henry in Israel, attempting to identify with, indeed, to represent Jewish history, fails to create his own. Perhaps. But, more often than not, in the literature that reflects this haunting preoccupation with Jewish history, it is not so easy to separate oneself from the past. And whether it is one's uneasy identification with the immigrant's expectations for America, or with a vague sense of the values and lives of the Eastern European Jews, or with Israel's promise of a Jewish homeland, such identification preoccupies these characters in very disconcerting ways.

Aside from Henry Zuckerman's radical flight to Israel, most of these characters are drawn to a Jewish past virtually despite themselves. We find in the literature characters who are secular Jews at best, or more often characters who do not define themselves as Jews but who nonetheless are drawn to or caught up in a particular history defined by Judaism. Even as I write this, I want to ask, What is a peculiarly Jewish history? Surely the sense of history to which these characters, for the most part, feel a connection is not Moses leading his people in the wilderness. Instead, it seems to be an ill-defined feeling of consanguinity with a collective ethos, an ethos of struggle, of marginality, and of tension. These characters are intuitively reminded of something they are not but something they might have been, of circumstances they inevitably would have encountered but, born too late, did not.

Such characters are haunted by a past that excluded them, not only by birth order, but because the events that happened give them a particular identity in history, whether they opt for it or not. Grace Paley's recurring character Faith Darwin, for example, typifies this:

> Faith's head is under the pillow nearly any weekday midnight, asweat with dreams, and she is seasick with ocean sounds, the squealing wind stuck in its rearing tail by high tide. That is because her grandfather, scoring the salty sea, skated for miles along the Baltic's icy beaches, with a frozen herring in his pocket. And she, all ears, was born in Coney Island.[13]

As Faith's intuitive, however unconscious, alliance with her grandfather would suggest, the "stories" from history can control one's emotional and psychological condition. They form, more often than not, a past from which an individual has been excluded but with which he or she cannot avoid confrontation.

Art Spiegelman's narrator in *MAUS: A Survivor's Tale,* the uniquely contrived cartoon depicting the Holocaust, appears as Art Spiegelman himself, a writer-cartoonist-interviewer who "draws" a story based on his father's memories of life in Poland from 1935 to 1944. His tale begins with his courtship of Art's mother, Anja Zylberberg, and takes us through the years just prior to and during the Nazi invasion of Poland, terminating with his parents' imprisonment in Auschwitz in 1944. Vladek's story, prompted by questions from his son, crosses back and forth (a literal and symbolic crossing of lives) between Poland during the war to Rego Park, New York, where Vladek Spiegelman now lives in antipathy with his second wife, Mala, also a survivor, whom he married after his first wife's suicide, an act committed long after the liquidation of the camps, their relocation in suburban New York, and Art's birth. Art, who intersperses his own sparse but nonetheless revealing judgments throughout his father's narration, is thrice disguised. He is the intellectual, the writer turned interviewer[14] armed with briefcase, notebook, and tape recorder who justifies his literary undertaking in the face of his father's admonitions that "it would take *many* books, my life, and no one wants anyway to hear such stories. Better you should spend your time to make drawings what will bring you some money." Our narrator asserts his own personal desire to know: "*I* want to hear it. Start with mom. . . . Tell me how you met" (1:12). Further, despite all expectations, the figures Art draws are depicted as animals: Jews are mice, Germans are cats, Poles are pigs, and Americans are dogs.[15] Such masking strikingly dramatizes the predatory nature of the Nazis' war on the Jews and accentuates the loss of humanity in the midst of the all-too-human responses of the "characters."[16] The use of masks, however, no more distances or protects the narrator from his father's story or from his need to hear it than it did Gilbert Rogin's narrator, whose authorial guise is transparent. In fact, Art's mask (for he draws himself as a mouse, too), like all the other "animals" in the story, is all but unnoticeable beyond the initial disjunction of subject and form. It must be so, since the fragmentation of identity, of personhood, is the inevitable outcome of Vladek's story and Art's quest.

Whereas Rogin's narrator in "What Happens Next?" concludes his story with a warm and humorously graceful acceptance of his relationship with his father and with a growing interest in the making of his own character, Spiegelman's autobiographical narrator never achieves such reconciliation. Throughout his story, he remains incapable of squaring up the kind of man his father is with the experiences of his father's past. And so the animosities between father and son, far from being resolved through the telling of stories, are heightened, are brought to the surface as—we are meant to infer—never before. Far from embracing his father's ethical choices and conduct, Art's interview culminates in his rage and fury: "God damn you! You—you murderer!" (1:159). Even with the promise of more chapters to come, such reconciliation is difficult to imagine, in part because Art's father has become, through the telling, both antagonist and symbol in our narrator's portrayal of him: antagonist because, by burning his wife's diaries, he has obstructed his son's ability to know his mother, whose premature death by her own hand excludes him all the more from understanding the past; symbol because, as a survivor of the Holocaust, Vladek Spiegelman has been robbed of an individual identity. Therefore Art's attempt to know his father in his "parental guise," to borrow Rogin's term, is thwarted by his place in a particular historical epoch. Vladek represents an era of madness and destruction. "My Father Bleeds History," writes Spiegelman's narrator as an entry into his book. In this way, Vladek is larger than life, and so our narrator is up against what the other narrators analyzed thus far are not: he is not free to accept or reject his father's values, choices, and character because they are all formed irrevocably by horrors that, even in the telling, are beyond Art's comprehension.

Vladek Spiegelman, urged on by his son, reinvents the story of his life "in Czestochowa, a small city not far from the border of Germany"

(1:12); his marriage to Anna Zylberberg; the birth of their first son, Richieu; and the beginning of the war, "synagogues burned, Jews beaten with no reason, whole towns pushing out all Jews—each story worse than the other" (1:33). Vladek describes his family's denial and then recognition of the horrors of the Nazi invasion as the atrocities begin to affect Vladek personally: the loss of his business; conscription in the "Polish Reserves Army" (1:38); capture by the Germans ("they marched me to where it was more like me. War prisoners" [1:49]). Vladek records, in an exactness made all the more vivid by Art's detailed drawings, the struggle to keep his family alive in hiding, the death of his son, and finally their capture and incarceration in Auschwitz, where "we knew that from here we will not come out anymore . . . we knew the stories— that they will gas us and throw us in the ovens. This was 1944 . . . we knew everything. And here we were" (1:157).

Although this is indeed Vladek Spiegelman's story, it is told through the filter not only of Vladek's memory, but of his son's distinctive arrangement and cartoon portrayal of it. Although Art expresses his intention "to portray my father *accurately*" (1:132), such a task is futile. No matter how distanced the writer or narrator is from the story he relates, his voice, by which I mean the implicit judgments and values conveyed through the choice and arrangement of material, can never be ignored.[17] Even though Art allows his father to tell his own story, the portrayal of Vladek's story cannot be free from Art's assessment of his father. Spiegelman calls attention to this by dramatizing himself throughout the narrative. Art, too, appears as a character in his own book (again a technique very much in the tradition of the secular Yiddish writers). In fact, father and son compete on occasion for final narrative authority, when, for example, Valdek takes over the drawing of the bunker in which they had hidden: "Show to me your pencil and I can explain you. . . . Such things it's good to know exactly how was it—just in case" (1:110). Our narrator recognizes his father's moral authority; after all, Vladek experienced what his son can only hope to grasp. Despite Artie's feeling of presumptuousness in writing the biography, the feeling that he has, in fact, misappropriated that which is not rightly his, Vladek's initial response to his son's book is positive: "I know already my story by *heart,* and even *I* am interested!" (1:133). Paradoxically, Vladek is both insider and outsider to his own experience; in this, too, his position is parallel to his son's. Although only Vladek has, finally, the "right credentials" to tell his story, Art as narrator is imbued with the moral authority that comes with the responsibility to tell.[18] As teller and writer converge, our narrator takes over the chronology of the storytelling; he orchestrates and directs the narration. Art attempts to control what should "come next." His sense of *how* a story should be told reestablishes his authority all along.

For although born after the war, Art sees himself as a product of his father's past. In urging his father to "tell *your* story, the way it really happened" (1:23), Art hopes to find the clues to his sense of fragmentation and unease in his own life. It is clear, as the layers of stories intersect—Vladek's and Anja's lives in Poland, Art's and Vladek's tense interaction in New York during the interview, Art's relationship with his wife, Françoise—that in giving shape to Vladek's character, Art hopes to clarify his own identity and to make choices for himself not in accordance with or opposition to his father, but in a way that will validate his own values. However, Art cannot separate himself from his father's choices, nor from what he imagines are his father's experiences. And despite the fact, or perhaps because of the fact, that he does not like much of what he perceives in his father, he feels enormous guilt and fragmentation.

In the narrative juxtaposition of the New York suburbs with Poland at war, we learn ever-increasing pieces of information about Art's relationship with and response to his father. Art reflects all the characteristic guilt attendant to the children of Holocaust victims and survivors. Having received a frantic summons from his father, whose feigned heart attack ensures his son's ministrations, Art and Françoise interrupt their vacation with friends to go to his aid. En route, Art tries to explain to his wife, and to himself, we suspect, his endless preoccupation with his father's past.

> When I was a kid I used to think about which of my parents I'd let the Nazis take to the ovens if I could only save one of them. . . . Usually I saved my mother. Do you think that's normal? . . . I used to have nightmares about S.S. men coming to my classroom and dragging all of us Jewish kids away. . . . Don't get me wrong, I wasn't *obsessed* with this stuff. . . . It's just that sometimes I'd fantasize zyklon B coming out of our shower instead of water. I know this is insane, but I somehow wish I had been in Auschwitz *with* my parents so I could really know what they lived through! . . . I guess it's some kind of guilt about having had an easier life than they did. (2:14–16)

Although able to ironize his discomfort, Art's guilt is exacerbated by his unavoidable difference from and antipathy toward his father. In "drawing" his father, Art cannot help but censure him. Vladek, as drawn by his son, appears intrusive, controlling, hypochondriacal, and obsessed with money, with wasted potential. But Art's admonishment of his father is constantly challenged by the guilt such disapprobation induces in him. After all, as his father reminds him, "It's for you I watch out my money!" (1:67). But even his father's chastisement cannot stand up to the root cause of Art's guilt: that everything must be measured against, must be viewed in the darkness of, Auschwitz. When Mala, for example, validates Art's assessment of his father's character—"He drives me crazy! He won't even let me throw out the plastic pitcher he took from his hospital room last year! He's more attached to things than to people!" (1:93)—we, like Art, are unable to accept this indictment without tacit amendment. It is, after all, with good reason that Vladek seems "more attached to things than to people," his young son, wife, and family having been destroyed by the Nazis. For even after surviving the loss of her child, ghettoization, and the camps, Anja Spiegelman commits suicide, so tormented was she still. Thus, Art, although not a survivor in any specific sense of the term as we know it, also is denied, by the very historical *fact* of Auschwitz, cathartic emotional responses. Art cannot even censure his father without conscious restraint, all unbridled emotion— grief, hatred, love—lost to history.

Since the Holocaust, one's view of the world is necessarily skewed. Like others before him, Alvin Rosenfeld, in *A Double Dying: Reflections on Holocaust Literature,* warns us: "The human imagination after Auschwitz is simply not the same as it was before. Put another way, the addition to our vocabulary of the very word Auschwitz means that today we know things that before could not even be imagined."[19] Yet, I think that the very problem for the narrator in *MAUS* is that although he "knows" about Auschwitz, indeed, while he imaginatively "draws" pictures of his parents hunted down in the bureaucratic Nazi "mousetrap," he cannot imagine it, like Chaim Potok's Reuven Malter, who "just couldn't grasp it. My mind couldn't hold on to it, to the death of six million people."[20] In fact, once Artie has heard his father's story, once they arrive, in Vladek's memory, at the gates of Auschwitz, he does not know how to respond. "My God" (1:158) is all Art can finally say, since words betray experience, and experience defies words. For this, too, he feels guilt and remorse. Thus his self-destructive desire to have been in the camps with his parents calls attention to his need to know experientially what they went through, indeed to *be* of them, to complete his identity as their son. Attempting to invent their experiences is insufficient. In recognizing his presumption in even attempting such a feat, Art reveals the following misgivings about his project:

Just thinking about my book . . . it's so *presumptuous* of me. I mean, I can't even make any sense out of my relationship with my father. How am I supposed to make any sense out of *Auschwitz? . . . of the Holocaust?* . . . I feel so inadequate trying to reconstruct a reality that was worse than my darkest dreams. And trying to do it as a *comic strip!* I guess I bit off more than I can chew. Maybe I ought to forget the whole thing. There's so much I'll never be able to understand or visualize. I mean, reality is too *complex* for comics. . . . So much has to be left out or distorted. (2:14–16)

Spiegelman's ironic stance here merges the voices of author and narrator in this recognition of inadequacy and violation of that which, under normal conditions, would be considered most private.

Yet, as Spiegelman makes clear, the Holocaust, even in our memory of it, denies a private life; it stands for the systematic denial of one's agency in fashioning an individual history. For example, when Art wants to include Vladek's early love affair in his book, his father protests:

"But this what I just told you—about Lucia and so—I don't want you should write this in your book. . . . It has nothing to do with Hitler, with the Holocaust! . . . this isn't so *proper,* so respectful. . . . I can tell you *other* stories, but such *private* things, I don't *want you* should mention." (1:23)

This passage strikes me as particularly intriguing because of the ironic complexities that it raises. Vladek gives voice to the obvious dilemma of Spiegelman's book: the place of one's private life in a history of the Holocaust. How can one speak of, no less write about, intimate human actions and emotions in a context that desecrated the private, that robbed individuals of their humanity?

Vladek's personal affairs at once have nothing and everything "to do with Hitler [and the] Holocaust." Ironically—tragically—Vladek wrests from his son a promise he will not keep, to omit his "private stories" from the book. This is, however, an impossible request, since how is his son to determine what is and is not "private" in this context? Paradoxically, the most obscene of events is expressed, in Vladek's terms, as more "proper" to discuss than his private affairs. In fact, Vladek himself views his experiences under Nazi rule as a public event. Comically, at one point in the narrative, long after Vladek has revealed such intimate tragedies as the death of his child, he yet again makes this seemingly arbitrary distinction. When Art suggests that Vladek and Mala see a marriage counselor in order to work out their difficulties, Vladek responds: *"Ach!* I don't want that a stranger should mix into our private stories" (1:135). This should strike us as peculiar, because the Holocaust would seem to reflect the most private of events, the eradication of individual choice, freedom, life. But the Holocaust can never be a private recollection, since in denying personal identities, human beings, human responses, are lost to the collective. Private sorrow is diminished by the enormity of the event. Whatever name we give to it, "Holocaust," "Nazi genocide," "the war against the Jews," "crimes against humanity," the fact remains that we are talking about the eradication of the sanctity and integrity of the individual, whose individuality remains forevermore subordinated to the event.

We are reminded here, I think, of Saul Bellow's Mr. Sammler, who escaped death, inexplicably hidden in a tomb by the anti-Semite Cieslakiewicz, and made uneasy by the symbolic status imposed on him.

> Symbols everywhere. . . . It was the Sammlers who kept on vainly trying to perform some kind of symbolic task. The main result of which was unrest, exposure to trouble. Mr. Sammler had a symbolic character. He, personally, was a symbol. His friends and family had made him a judge and a priest. And of what was he a symbol? He didn't even know. Was it because he had survived? He hadn't even done that, since so much of the earlier person had disappeared. It wasn't surviving, it was only lasting. He had lasted. For a time yet he might last.[21]

The problem for Spiegelman, then, in trying to bring together the specifics of his father's personal life and the history of the Holocaust, is in his attempts to reconcile the two: how to come to terms with his father as a person and also categorically as "victim," "survivor," Jew.

To do so, therefore, is, not surprisingly, to come to terms with Judaism. His father's past is inextricably bound with Judaism. His history is defined by his status as a Jew in Poland during the Nazi invasion and regime. There is, for Art Spiegelman, no getting around the fact that his father cannot be "taken out of history," cannot, in other words, be perceived as distinct from his fate as a Jew. And for Art, however, American-born, seemingly free to fashion his own history, Judaism is a past he cannot really accept, but also a past from which he cannot free himself. Vladek Spiegelman represents, for his son, a Jew trapped in history; he is at once the product of history and, unintentionally—in fact, involuntarily—a creator of it. Vladek is enslaved by history, particularly by Jewish history, not only because of his place in the Holocaust, but also because he embodies, in his son's perspective, all the worst possible Jewish stereotypes, those very characteristics from which Art, in every conceivable way, has alienated himself.

We understand, as the narrative opens, that Art has not seen his father in a long time. His self-imposed separation, caused in part by his mother's suicide and his own ambivalence toward his father, has been a separation from Judaism as well. Exasperated by his father's compulsive behavior during one of his visits, Art complains to Mala, Vladek's second wife: "In some ways he's just like the racist caricature of the miserly old Jew" (1:131). In his censuring of his father, however, Art is not free from misgivings about his own responses, because he recognizes that he is the writer-cartoonist who has created his father as such. Art's perceived identity as a Jew is very much on the surface, since many of his choices seem to have been made, one way or another, in response to Judaism. One instance is particularly telling in this regard. In rationalizing a previous relationship, Art explains to his current wife, "I just dated her to get over my prejudice against middle-class, New York, Jewish women. They remind me too much of my relatives to be erotic" (2:12). Art's reaction against Jewish women, however, is only partly mitigated by his marriage to a non-Jew, since Françoise converts to Judaism "to make Vladek happy" (2:12).

Art's unease about his own choices in relation to Judaism are comically portrayed in the following dialogue, in which Art and Françoise discuss her tenuous place in his narrative. Art's quandary in deciding whether to draw Françoise as a mouse is caused by the fact that, despite her conversion to Judaism, she is French, and, when it comes right down to it, he has trouble separating her from the position the French in general have taken toward the Jews:

> Let's not forget the centuries of anti-semitism. . . . I mean, how about the Dreyfus Affair? The Nazi collaborators! . . . I've got it! . . . Panel one: my father is on his exercycle. . . . I tell him I just married a frog. . . . Panel two: he falls off his cycle in shock. So, you and I go to a mouse rabbi. He says a few magic words and *zap!* . . . By the end of the page the frog has turned into a beautiful *mouse!* (2:11–12)

In this passage, Art criticizes his own position toward Judaism, because the comic version of his wife's conversion lacks any real sense of commitment. But conversion it is, nonetheless. Art's life has been formed by Judaism, since even in his denial of or reaction against Judaism there is a recognition and virtual affirmation of it.

Finally, I think, the meaning of Art's epigraph, "My father bleeds history," is clarified. To "bleed history" is at once to *reflect* it and to *make* it. Perhaps the definition of identity that these characters have been trying to get at all along finally is the invention of personal identity from the options presented by history. Vladek Spiegelman can no more be separated from the time and place that formed him than can his son. Art can make sense of his father and of himself only in terms of their place in history. Thus, telling "stories" of that time and place serves as a starting point for self-knowledge, not only the telling of what happened with accuracy—when, where, and who—but the emotional responses, the ways in which those events were assimilated and incorporated into the constitutive forming of the self in the perceptions of others. Telling bears witness to history and to the individual trapped in the events of the past. In this way, telling stories forms and gives meaning to the self. This is why Art feels so bereft at the end of part 1 of *MAUS*. When his father reveals to him that he has destroyed his mother's notebooks, diaries that Anja had kept with the express wish that some day, "when he [her son] grows up, he will be interested by this" (1:159), Artie accuses him of murder; Vladek, for obviously understandable reasons (though reasons perhaps justifiable only to himself),[22] has destroyed knowledge that Art believes would have freed him to fulfill his responsibilities. For Art Spiegelman is moved by the compulsion not only to know, but also to tell, to "draw," publish, and thus bear witness to his parents' lives inasmuch as they, too, stand as witnesses to what is undoubtedly the worst in human history.

This notion of bearing witness, so fundamental to Jewish history and literature, is given new meaning in the fiction of contemporary Jewish American writers. The necessity to bear witness, to make claims for the permanence and integrity of both the individual and the community, a process of telling long ingrained in the Jew's struggle for survival, has taken on a different shape and scope to fit this particular time and place. Far removed from the Eastern European shtetls, from the arduous process of immigration and relocation, from, in many instances, the religious frame and dictates of Orthodox Judaism, and half a century since the Holocaust, American-born Jews are portrayed in search of stories from the past, stories that form identity through memory. Haunted by a history they never knew and, in some instances, a past they consciously deny and reject, such characters are actively drawn to the stories and memories of those before them, those who experiences, mysteriously, have shaped their choices and identities. It is this same vague sense of connection and deference that propels Henry Roth's character Aaron Stigman, in "The Surveyor," ceremoniously to place a wreath on the site of the martyrdom of those Jews who refused to renounce their faith during the Inquisition. Although not a practicing Jew, having "left the faith of [his] ancestors many years ago" (150),[23] Stigman is drawn to the site of the burning of heretics, troubled by the excess of icons commemorating Christianity: "Too many martyrs of their faith. None for mine—or what used to be mine" (140). This commemoration of a past connects him to the faith of his ancestors and includes him in a communal identity and historical continuum.

Unlike Aaron Stigman, however, a single act of remembrance is insufficient for the contemporary generation of American-born Jews analyzed herein, mainly because they feel themselves to have been insidiously excluded from the events of the past. I am reminded in this context of Tillie Olsen's novella *Tell Me a Riddle,* in which her protagonist, a Jewish immigrant who raised her children in America, is reluctant to discuss her life in the Old Country with her grown sons and daughters. She distrusts the rabbi sent to her hospital bedside and refuses to participate in religious rituals, even at the behest of her daughter, whose attempts to reestablish tradition she scorns. And only when the end of her life is imminent does she explain to her granddaughter, "It is more than oceans between Olshana and you."[24] The ethos, the attitudes, and values of post–World War II America in a fundamental sense defy the very language of experience. And many of these characters are no less plagued by a sense of exclusion from their perception of a formative history and tradition, even when such an exclusion is self-imposed. So they remain outsiders, marginalized by their own place in history. And this exclusion is problematic for them, because they feel without an anchor to an ethical system within which they might shape their own identities. They return, time and again, to the stories of their parents in the hope of securing the kind of knowledge that will allow them either to reject or to accept their parents' values and choices and, in either case, to make sense of their own lives within a larger historical context.

Knowing stories of the past gives these characters the confidence with which to forge change, change that is not a denial but a reinvention of the past, of Judaism, of a tradition that can withstand change and thus affirm individual choice. From a tradition of remembering, of telling stories, these characters reinvent themselves, but selves anchored to history, to personal histories. Thus they bear witness not only to the past but to a future. Always in the process of rewriting the self, these characters in a sense revise history in the transmission of stories from the past. Such revision is a necessary prerequisite for establishing identity, since in it is the invention of the self, the construction of a "history" that is really a normalizing of the present. Not surprisingly, then, such characters, narrators and thus inventors in their own right, often appear in the guise of writers, since they are involved in making fictions by which they can live. Their relentless determination to hear stories from the past includes them in a history that is not of their own making, perhaps, but that, given "fresh authority," to borrow Harold Bloom's term,[25] can accept change and survive. And so these characters and, I suspect, these writers themselves remain riveted, as Grace Paley tells us, with "their ears to the ground, listening for signals from long ago."[26]

Notes

1. For a comprehensive account of the development of Yiddish fiction, see Dan Miron, *A Traveler Disguised.*

2. Sholom Aleichem, "It Doesn't Pay to Do Favors," 188.

3. Sholom Aleichem, "Hodl," 69.

4. Cynthia Ozick, "Envy; or, Yiddish in America," 92.

5. Grace Paley, "The Immigrant Story," 171. Subsequent quotations are from the edition in Works Cited.

6. Philip Roth, *The Counterlife,* 124. Roth self-ironically cites this line in the epigraph to *The Facts.* Subsequent quotations are from the editions in Works Cited.

7. Herbert Gold's linguistic masterpiece, "The Heart of the Artichoke" (in *Jewish-American Stories,* ed. Irving Howe [New York: New American Library, 1977], 270–300), is a skillful example of a story that makes sense only in terms of the multilayered narrative interplay between author and the older and younger voices of the narrator.

8. Such structures create a characteristic feature of Jewish fiction: literal veracity. Characters, since Sholom Aleichem's fictional narrators, affirm that their stories are "true," told to them by "reliable" sources, or they are witnessed or experienced personally. The possibilities for irony here are clear.

9. Grace Paley, "A Conversation with My Father," 162. Subsequent quotations are from the edition in Works Cited.

10. Gilbert Rogin, "What Happens Next?" 122–28. Subsequent quotations are from the edition in Works Cited.

11. Art Spiegelman, *MAUS: A Survivor's Tale,* parts 1 and 2. Subsequent quotations are from the editions in Works Cited, identified as 1 and 2 respectively in the text.

12. Two other characteristic texts come to mind in this regard: Jerome Weidman's very moving story "My Father Sits in the Dark," 367–71, and Delmore Schwartz's famous story "In Dreams Begin Responsibilities," 1–9. Weidman's narrator, in characteristic first-person narration, tells the story of his father's peculiar

habit of sitting in the dark in the evening after everyone else has gone to bed. Although this is the ostensible plot of the story, as the increasingly tense narrative unfolds we discover that the dramatic tension has little to do with the father's unnerving habit and everything to do with the narrator's sense of fear, denial, and loss. Delmore Schwartz constructs the conceit of a dream in which his protagonist views a movie version of his parents' lives before his birth, a dream filled with anxieties and tensions regarding his relationship with his father. For an analysis of this story, see my "Ethical Fiction of Delmore Schwartz."

13. Grace Paley, "Faith in the Afternoon," 31–32.

14. The figure of the writer/bookseller has historical significance in Yiddish literature. Mendele Mocher Sforim (Mendele the book peddler), Shalom Abramowitsch's pseudonym and character, represents mobility. He is a figure who brings news from the outside world into the shtetls. Sholom Aleichem, too, characteristically appears in his fiction as a writer, a compelling figure to whom the character-narrators appeal for guidance and often vindication.

15. Such masking is made all the more complex when Vladek and Anja, drawn as mice, put on pigs' masks (to conceal themselves as Poles) in an attempt to move about freely (1:140–41).

16. For an interesting discussion of the function of humor in the use of animal caricatures in *MAUS,* see Terrence Des Pres's "Holocaust *Laughter?"* 216–33.

17. For varied and extensive discussions of the relations among authors, readers, and characters, see Wayne Booth, *The Rhetoric of Fiction, A Rhetoric of Irony,* and *The Company We Keep.*

18. I am reminded here of Grace Paley's character in the short story "Listening," who makes explicit the responsibility that friends have to tell each other's stories. Paley's character, Cassie, steps into the story to chastise her friend, the writer.

> Listen, Faith, why don't you tell my story? You've told everybody's story but mine. I don't even mean my whole story, that's my job. You probably can't. But I mean you've just omitted me from the other stories and I was there. . . . Where is *my* life? (210)

The responsibility to record stories is a recurrent theme in Paley's fiction.

19. Alvin Rosenfeld, *A Double Dying,* 13.

20. Chaim Potok, *The Chosen,* 180.

21. Saul Bellow, *Mr. Sammler's Planet,* 91.

22. He is moved to do so by grief and despair:

> These notebooks, and other really nice things of mother. . . . One time I had a very bad day . . . and all of these things I *destroyed.* . . . These papers had too many memories. So I *burned* them . . . after the tragedy with mother, I was so *depressed* then, I didn't know if I'm coming or I'm going! (1:158–59)

In this episode, too, Art's guilt resurfaces; he draws Vladek's response in a way that foregrounds his own complicity: "For *years* they were laying there and nobody even looked in" (1:159). Despite the narrator's intentions, he is too late. Yet in blaming his father he can protect himself a while longer.

23. Henry Roth, "The Surveyor," 134–53. This story first appeared in *The New Yorker* on 6 August 1966.

24. Tillie Olsen, *Tell Me a Riddle,* 113.
25. See Harold Bloom, "A Speculation upon American Jewish Culture," 270.
26. Grace Paley, "Faith in the Afternoon," 32.

Works Cited

Aarons, Victoria. "The Ethical Fiction of Delmore Schwartz: Identity, Generation and Culture." *The Jewish Quarterly Review* 77 (1987): 255–82.

Bellow, Saul. *Mr. Sammler's Planet.* New York: Penguin Books, 1984.

Bloom, Harold. "A Speculation upon American Jewish Culture." *Judaism* 31 (1982).

Booth, Wayne C. *The Company We Keep: An Ethics of Fiction.* Berkeley: University of California Press, 1988.

———. *The Rhetoric of Fiction.* 2d ed. Chicago: University of Chicago Press, 1983.

———. *A Rhetoric of Irony.* Chicago: University of Chicago Press, 1974.

Des Pres, Terrence. "Holocaust *Laughter?*" In *Writing and the Holocaust,* edited by Berel Lang. New York: Holmes & Meier, 1988.

Miron, Dan. *A Traveler Disguised: A Study in the Rise of Modern Yiddish Fiction in the Nineteenth Century.* New York: Schocken Books, 1973.

Olsen, Tillie. *Tell Me a Riddle.* New York: Dell-Laurel, 1981.

Ozick, Cynthia. "Envy; or, Yiddish in America." In *The Pagan Rabbi and Other Stories.* New York: E. P. Dutton, 1983.

Paley, Grace. "A Conversation with My Father," "Debts," "Faith in the Afternoon," and "The Immigrant Story." In *Enormous Changes at the Last Minute.* New York: Farrar, Straus, & Giroux, 1983.

———. "Listening." In *Later the Same Day.* New York: Penguin Books, 1986.

Potok, Chaim. *The Chosen.* New York: Fawcett Crest-Ballantine, 1967.

Rogin, Gilbert. "What Happens Next?: An Uncompleted Investigation." In *Jewish-American Stories,* edited by Irving Howe. New York: New American Library, 1977.

Rosenfeld, Alvin. *A Double Dying: Reflections on Holocaust Literature.* Bloomington: Indiana University Press, 1980.

Roth, Henry. "The Surveyor." In *Shifting Landscape: A Composite, 1925–1987,* edited by Mario Materassi. Philadelphia: Jewish Publication Society, 1987.

Roth, Philip. *The Counterlife.* New York: Penguin Books, 1986.

———. *The Facts.* New York: Farrar, Straus, Giroux, 1988.

Schwartz, Delmore. "In Dreams Begin Responsibilities." In *In Dreams Begin Responsibilities and Other Stories,* edited by James Atlas. New York: New Directions, 1978.

Sholom Aleichem. "Hodl." In *Tevye the Dairyman and the Railroad Stories,* translated by Hillel Halkin. New York: Schocken Books, 1987.

———. "It Doesn't Pay to Do Favors." In *Old Country Tales,* translated by Curt Leviant. New York: Paragon Books, 1966.

Spiegelman, Art. *MAUS: A Survivor's Tale.* Parts 1 and 2. New York: Pantheon, 1986 and 1991.

Weidman, Jerome. "My Father Sits in the Dark." In *My Father Sits in the Dark and Other Selected Stories.* New York: Random House, 1961.

Nostalgia and Ambiguity

in Martha Lamont's

"Crow and Her Seagull Slaves"

TOBY C. S. LANGEN

The operation of individual intent in the performance of traditional but nonliturgical tales in Native American oral literature has been a subject as interesting when ignored as when acknowledged. At one extreme, early commentators like John Wesley Powell thought of Native American literature as the product of cultures so primitively collective that individual voices could not be heard: "The folktales collected by Mr. Cushing," Powell wrote in his introduction to *Zuni Folk Tales,* "constitute a charming exhibit of the wisdom of the Zunis as they believe, though it may be but a charming exhibit of the follies of the Zunis as we believe" (viii). Here, Powell not only dehumanizes the Zuni people, but in claiming Cushing as a scientist (as distinct from a believer in "follies") is forced to belittle his fellow white man's achievement in translating, if not Zuni "text," at least some intimations of Zuni literary skill. Did Powell ever wonder what sort of person the storyteller could be who passed along "follies"? If that person called something to mind in order to tell it to an audience, then what was called to mind cannot have been "folly"; we can remember something only if we conceptualize it in such a way that it has enough internal order to be reassemblable. Not only is information remembered via the sense it makes, but people remember things in order to make sense (Ausubel; Gagne and White; and Mink). To think about the role that memory must have played in the development, transmission, and reception of traditional verbal art enables literate outsiders to rescue their concepts of that art from the impersonal nonsense of Powell's characterization of it.

"Crow and Her Seagull Slaves" was told in 1953 by Martha Lamont, a Snohomish elder living at the Tulalip Reservation, to the tape recorder of Leon Metcalf, who as a young man had learned a few words and phrases of the Lushootseed language that Martha Lamont spoke. Some thirty years after making the tape recording, Metcalf agreed to be interviewed about his memories of Martha Lamont and some of the other storytellers he had worked with. On many subjects his memory was hazy, but even though he had not been able to follow most of what they were saying, he was in no doubt about the fact that what he had observed was the recitation of memorized narratives (Metcalf).

Sally Snyder's 1964 dissertation on Skagit folklore, the only book-length study of Lushootseed art narrative, gives a confusing picture of the role of individual creativity in the literature, and it reflects, I think, the state of mind of many scholars in the field at that time. Like Metcalf, Snyder did not speak Lushootseed, and the stories she discusses were given to her in English or via on-the-spot translation by a relative of the storyteller present at what Snyder calls the recital. If there had been a memorized Lushootseed version in the mind of a storyteller, then Snyder would not have had access to it: in relation to Lushootseed traditional models, hers is a collection of paraphrases or summaries.

> Mrs. M.X., an excellent narrator, but with an exceedingly limited English vocabulary . . . complained sometimes that she was unable to express adequately in English certain portions of stories. However[,] we discussed passages difficult for her and I usually managed, then, to elicit what she meant. (13)

Nonetheless, Snyder posits a strictly memorial tradition of Lushootseed-language narrative, repeating what elders told her about the necessity to pass down stories unchanged and attributing to failures of memory the variation that she knew had taken place, because she herself had recorded many examples of it.

Of the effects of the language shift from Lushootseed to English and the possibility of the development of an English-language style or tradition, memorial or not, Snyder has nothing to say. She does note that one of the storytellers who worked with her had memorized "carefully selected phrases" (14), which certainly suggests his having had occasions to tell the stories in English often enough to warrant preparing them. Although these phrases stand out as memorized, presumably in contrast to the rest of the utterance, and although she thought his versions of stories "drastically" (15) innovative, Snyder uses the word *recitation* to refer to his performance. In her description of performance, then, Snyder gives conflicting signals about the sovereignty of storytellers. It is interesting to note that in her larger discussion of the development of Skagit narratives over time from "yarns" into "myths," Snyder presumes a great deal of creativity on the part of "raconteurs." But once the yarn is mythified, evidently creativity stops and performance becomes mere repetition.

A decade after Leon Metcalf collected the Crow story from Mrs. Lamont, and a couple of years after the appearance of Snyder's dissertation, Thom Hess, a linguist, recorded the same story by Mrs. Lamont. Unlike Metcalf and Snyder, Hess was a student of Lushootseed, and he transcribed the story in consultation with Mrs. Lamont and her husband, Levi. Hess's manuscript is headed " 'Crow and Her Seagull Slaves,' recited by Martha Lamont." As he now recollects, he never asked her whether she told her stories from memory, but he does not think that by "recited" he meant to imply "memorized." Perhaps his choice of words is best interpreted as a reflection of the fact that in that era scholarly interest was not focused on the process of composition (Hess, forthcoming, xiii). It needs to be reiterated, too, that Indian elders, then as now, expressed the conviction that stories were passed on unchanged and that the most promising young storytellers were children who could remember things word for word.

The lucky circumstance of our having two tellings of "Crow and Her Seagull Slaves" by the same storyteller gives us a rare opportunity to test these assumptions about the role of memory in the ongoing life of Lushootseed oral tradition.

The story about Crow and her seagull slaves is an easy one to hold in the mind and so is a natural candidate for memorization. Crow sets out in her canoe to look for a husband. Oddly enough, she knows the name of the one she wants but not where he lives or what he looks like. She travels along singing of her intention, and various suitors come down to the shore in the hope of being her chosen one. Every time, though, the seagulls cry out in their characteristic seagull intonation, "He's not the one," and Crow goes on her way. Finally she comes to the right place, the village where Valuable Shell lives. Shells were used as money in the old days, so this man is a very good catch. They marry, and that's the end of the story. With its repetitive structure, to tell it is to learn it.

As Martha Lamont told it to Leon Metcalf in 1953, there seems to have been little more to the story than the outline above, filled in with dramatizations of the encounters with the various suitors. The outline is more interesting than it seems, however, because there is a joke in it. What makes people smile is the fact that Crow goes out and looks for her own husband. In the old days, the marriages of young people of good family were arranged by their relatives, and unmarried girls never made trips to other villages without an escort of family members. In fact, to go on a trip such as Crow undertakes in this story would have been enough to destroy any chance of her making the kind of marriage that she does make. So the story is one long joke.

Near the end, however, Mrs. Lamont makes an interesting remark (though it must be remembered that there is nothing in the 1953 version to indicate whether the remark is her own or part of the story as she received it from someone else).

> As soon as Crow arrived there where Shell's house was, her slaves left her, because she was married now. She was brought into the longhouse of this si?ab, and her poor little seagull slaves flew away.
> It was the whiteness of the seagulls that was the reason for Crow's attitude, the reason she made them slaves. Their being white and therefore not good for much was the reason they did all right as just slaves. It was their whiteness.
> And her being black it was that made her an aristocrat in her own mind. That was her idea.
> So that's how the wedding of poor little Crow turned out.

The word used for "white" in this passage (x̌ʷiqʷəq̓ʷ) means the color white, not "white" as in "white man" (pastəd). Whiteness, as in clean mountain-goat wool or things painted, dotted, or outlined with white, can indicate in ceremonial objects a connection with spirit power, not an attribute one associates with slavery. Black also has spiritual valency; but in Lushootseed English it can refer to skin color in an unflattering way. Is Mrs. Lamont continuing her joke, indicating that Crow is as confused about white and black as she is about propriety? If so, there is something interesting to think about here, for the iridescent sheen on Crow's own feathers is also emblematic of spiritual power, so that the "slave" and the "aristocratic" colors have in fact the same kind of reference, unforegrounded as it may be in the words of the story, and unrecognized as it may be by Crow. We also note that in this passage Crow is described as "poor little" (?ušəbabdxʷ), just like her slaves, so that on two counts the validity of her perception of a difference between her status and that of the slaves is undercut. And we have to admit, too, that although Crow does everything wrong, everything turns out right. If there is a political tone to this passage, then, it is played down in service of the continuing joke.

By the time Mrs. Lamont told the Crow story ten years later to Thom Hess, however, the political element was present throughout, not in terms of jokes that might or might not be about skin color, but in terms of a longing for a time when not only could a low-class bird be a high-class person, but the unhindered Lushootseed way of life provided access to treasures both spiritual and material for everyone.

A comparison of the beginnings of the two versions shows the change in focus very plainly. This is how the Metcalf version of 1953 opens:

[A]   This is how it was with Crow: Crow had never been married.

[B]   And Crow's slaves were seagulls.

[C]   And this young lady had it in mind that she would go husband-hunting in the direction of a certain young man, the son of xʷčiłqs.
            siʔab, he was very siʔab.

[core]   A lot of money was the kind of money he had, the son of this xʷčiłqs.
            xʷəyaliwəʔ was the name of him, the son of this xʷčiłqs, xʷəy aliwəʔ.

[C']   So now Crow says, "I'd better get going.

[core']   No one has ever been courted by this man, and no one has ever caught him, either.

[C'']   So now Crow goes and thinks that she might be the one to get that siʔab,
            Crow herself.

[B']   Right away her seagull slaves go and get ready, and they take her by canoe on her way.
            The world was very still.
            This canoe of Crow's was the only thing moving.[1]

This is a traditional concentrically organized opening, humorous and affectionate in its focus on the personal dilemma of Crow. (The concentric structure is organized according to subject: B [slaves], C [Crow's intention], core [information about xʷəyaliwəʔ, linked to C by verbal echo], C' [Crow's intention; this member of the structure itself split into a circular structure C', core, C''], B' [slaves].) By the end of this passage the joke about the young "lady" going after her own fiancé is firmly in place.

Here is the opening of the version told to Thom Hess in 1966:

People are living.
            Many of them.
They are living.
            Lots of them
in this world of ours a long time ago.

Crow and these—,
>   these seagulls are there.
>   The seagulls are Crow's slaves.
>   Her slaves are seagulls.

Crow was rather si?ab
>   when she was a person,—that's how she is then—
in the first time of ours
> in the world,
when a different world was yet laid out, at first.

It is the first time now,
>   when the world was created.

>   ][
So then Crow travels on the water.
>   The day is very bright.
>   It is calm.
>   The day is intensely bright.
Thus she travels.

>   ][
The slaves are talking, the seagulls.
Lots of them.
>   Her slaves are the seagulls
>   Just like seagulls always talking,
>   "qʷəni?, qʷəni?, qʷəni?, qʷəni?,
qʷəni?";
Thus just like that they "talked."

>   ][
And then those seagulls prepared.
> Thus they prepare their "ɋil'bid"—
>   their canoes.
And then they laid a mat, a sort of long long rug,
>   they made a woven path
>   a place for Crow to walk
>   in order to get into the canoe.
>   It is spread out all the way to the canoe.
>   There must be a covering where she walks, that Crow.
Thus she is si?ab.
>   Crow is very si?ab
>   when she was a person.
Thus
>   her slaves put her on board.[2]

It is evident that this opening is more expansive than the earlier one and that the tone has changed. (Some of the tonal difference is a reflection of differing translation practices; for a fuller discussion of this issue, see note 2; Langen and Barthold; Bierwert.) But even after translators' differences have been allowed for, it is clear to the reader that the narrator of the Hess version is no longer speaking in pure storytelling mode: we hear the cadences of longhouse ceremonial speech in the parts of the story devoted to setting, parts unique to the Hess version. The affectionate humor of the Metcalf version is still present, but it is devoted to the seagulls, not to Crow.[3] Crow is not a figure of fun, at least not yet. She is "rather si?ab"; and in case we doubt that, knowing Crow from other stories as we do, Mrs. Lamont counters with the statement that that is how she was "long ago when a different world was first laid out," and we have to accept her construction of that difference.

si?ab is untranslatable. In the old days it denoted distinguished lineage and prosperity and their attendant virtues. The root ?i?ab means "wealth," but people can be si?ab and not well off, especially in modern times. The word connotes wisdom, good manners, the habit of carefully considering one's words and being slow to anger, as well as the possession of traditional knowledge. It sums up all the finest qualities of the traditional Indian person. The provision of a valuable rug for Crow to walk on reflects a practice of long ago, when on certain occasions aristocratic feet were not allowed to touch the ground. Crow's high status, then, is validated by the community right at the beginning of the story, and we are not allowed to consider it a delusion of grandeur, as the Metcalf version allows us to. The word *si?ab* is never applied to Crow in the Metcalf version, only to her prospective bridegroom.

In the Metcalf version, the opening section ends with the statement that the weather is calm and Crow's canoe is the only thing moving. It is a convention of Lushootseed storytelling that journeys undertaken in good weather are successful. On one level, then, Mrs. Lamont is making use of literary convention to talk about this unconventional trip of Crow's—the joke continues. But there are two ways to read daẏaẏəxʷ ("alone"), the word I have translated as "the only thing": it can also mean "all by itself" (that is, without needing to be paddled). In the old days, some si?ab people could make their canoes travel by the power of thought or song, without physical effort. It is probable that Mrs. Lamont is playing with the ambiguity of daẏaẏəxʷ here in service of the story's joke. In the Hess version, the subject of Crow's way of traveling is handled very differently. The passage beginning "So then Crow travels" and ending "Thus she travels" is figured concentrically with a strict verbal parallelism not entirely reproducible in English, and Mrs. Lamont chants the lines as storytellers do when referring to spiritual matters. Though there is no verbal allusion to a canoe, the metanarration makes it clear that there is no need to paddle. At this point in the Hess version, we may still take straight Mrs. Lamont's portrayal of Crow as siʔab.

It is only at the close of Crow's encounter with the first suitor that we are reminded that she is siʔab only ambiguously. When Raccoon comes down to the water, Crow insults him by making fun of his appearance, just as she does in the Metcalf version, where she has been established as siʔab only by mocked convention. In both versions, she goes on through a succession of suitors delivering insults, a form of misbehavior that is punished by death in other stories involving other young women. But in the Hess version, Mrs. Lamont closes the Raccoon episode with a duplicated version of the rhetorical figure concerning Crow's canoe, reiterating the calmness of the day through which she is still traveling. The word six^w, which Bierwert has translated as "still," might also be taken to mean "as she usually does." Mrs. Lamont chants the lines of the reduplicated figure like the earlier ones ("So then Crow travels . . ."), and six^w might refer to the fact that Crow usually travels without needing her slaves to paddle. Thus, we have Crow offending both Raccoon and decorum, which is, after all, how the story goes. But at the end of the episode we also have the storyteller assuring us that this character in the old days was siʔab in her very Crowness.

In the Metcalf version, Crow has twelve suitors: Raccoon, Deer, Bear, Wolf, Cougar, Beaver, and various water birds, including Bufflehead and Mallard. Of these, only four are described in any detail (Raccoon, who wears face paint; Mallard and another duck, who have iridescent feathers; and Loon, who has a white necklace). The pattern episodes describing their encounters with Crow are short and focus on her insults, which are quoted in seven of the twelve encounters. In the Hess version, the list of suitors has been shortened to five: Raccoon with his face paint (in an episode of 40 lines as opposed to 11, the longest, in the Metcalf version); Bufflehead with iridescent feathers (24 lines here, 4 in Metcalf); Deer with polished antlers (8 lines here, 5 in Metcalf); Bear, whose fur shines (14 here, 7 in Metcalf); and Mallard (10 here, 7 in Metcalf).[4] The Hess episodes are longer partly because of narrative ornamentation (two are split apart so that they frame other parts of the story), but mainly because the descriptions of the suitors have been amplified. The suitors selected have qualities—iridescence, facial decoration, whiteness, shininess—that associate them with the kinds of ceremonial dressing that people do when they participate in the winter ceremonies. (Bierwert [1991] discusses these correspondences in detail.) Though there is no overt reference to winter dance equipment such as hair hats or deer-hoof rattles, the significance of each description gathers itself as the suitors are perceived as a group; our reception of their collective portrait requires us to revise as we go along. The Hess version adds no new element to the pattern found in the Metcalf version. All of the suitors and their attributes are available in the earlier version: it is by selection, juxtaposition, and expansion of material present in her first telling that Mrs. Lamont invites us to receive a different message this time.

For example, here is Bufflehead in Metcalf:

> Just then another duck came down toward the water.
> Pretty Bufflehead is the one coming down.
> It's nifty what he's wearing, this Bufflehead.

In the Hess version, Mrs. Lamont spends some time trying to pin down exactly what color Bufflehead's hair is:

> It is every color:
> > blue,
> > > sort of red inside,
> > > > sort of pink.
> That's how it is.
> > > sort of what? what would you say?
> > > sort of yellowish-green.
> . . . His headgear, whatever it is, kept changing.

The word Bierwert translates as "headgear" is the Lushootseed word for "hat," šiqʷ. Bierwert notes that when speaking in English of the ceremonial headdress used in the longhouse, Lushootseed people say "hat," and she suggests that Mrs. Lamont's šiqʷ here is probably a "back-translation" of this specialized use of "hat" and would be intelligible to her audience as such.

If the suitors are would-be winter dancers, then what is Crow? In the old days, people became winter dancers after they acquired the help of a guardian spirit. In order to do this, they had to look for one, a process that sometimes involved searching out a remote spot beside the water. We have information (for example, Haeberlin and Gunther, 73) that spirit powers used to travel around by canoe with their servants and look for young people who were seeking help. When such a spirit power encountered such a young person, he would send his servants over to take a closer look and report back (cf. Collins, 152). If the young person was acceptable, then the spirit power would become his helper, a relationship that is often likened to marriage in Lushootseed ways of speaking. In the Hess version, the story of Crow's wedding journey is being told as if it is on some level analogous to the behavior of these spirit powers.

We began this essay with some questions about the role of memory in the life of a traditional story, specifically with a question about memorization. We can see that in the case of the Crow story, very few things occur verbatim in both versions: the seagull's speech, "He's not the one"; Crow's traveling song; and, for the most part, her slot-variable formula insult to the suitors. (I do not include here such things as the commands "put in" or "shove off," since they could well occur verbatim, not on account of having been memorized, but because one usually says them that way.) Also, very few things are verbally unique to either version: the most important are the Metcalf speech about whiteness and the Hess verbalization of setting. The main differences are the Hess version's expansions of things already verbalized in Metcalf, such as the way the canoe goes through the water, or the spelling out of things latent in Metcalf, such as stating that Crow is siʔab instead of describing her thus without using the word. In the notion of "expansion" must be included the "contraction" of the list of suitors, a diminution at the surface level that opens the way for the elaboration of the pattern episodes and permits the association of the hopeful suitors with the winter dance, an association nowhere verbalized.

Would the Hess version, whose implied changes are so much more telling than its verbalized ones, impress a traditional audience as the "same" as the Metcalf version? Jack Goody, in his 1987 study of LoDagaa ceremonial literature, makes the point that without a written text, it is almost impossible to know whether two versions are the same: no one's memory is that good, he writes, and the two versions are never available at the same time (88). He does not allow, however, that it is quite possible to note individual differences in tellings one hears when they are told without too great a time lapse between them. Goody suggests that "the concept of sameness may be looser [in oral culture]; it may refer not to verbal identity but to some kind of unspecified structural similarity," such as narrative or plot, which "can provide a continuing framework which is sometimes the core of the recitation, sometimes no more than a peg on which to hang a different sort of discourse" (88–89).

Indeed, Mrs. Lamont's concept of the Crow story might well be described as a continuing framework that serves as a peg on which to hang different sorts of discourse. We have already noticed that the framework has properties (repeated structures) that enable it to continue in memory easily. What is it, then, that the storyteller recalls when she sets about retelling "Crow and Her Seagull Slaves"? Goody suggests that the framework of recall lies in "event structures," which allow "reconstruction within a schema" (173–78). This suggestion, too, seems valid for Mrs. Lamont's practice, though we may wish to look more closely at the relation between "elaboration" and "schema" (in verbal terms) or "realized" and "latent" (in conceptual terms) in these two versions of the Crow story.

The most striking difference between the openings of the two versions is the provision of a setting in the Hess version. The Metcalf version starts right in: Crow has a problem. Even the customary ʔal tudiʔ tu-haʔkʷ, "a long time ago," is present only by unverbalized convention. The opening words of the Hess version, on the other hand, constitute the most common way of beginning a story set in the myth time: ʔəsɬaɬil tiʔəʔ ʔaciɬtalbixʷ, "people were living there"; but when Mrs. Lamont follows this with "lots of them in this very world which belongs to us" ("this world of ours" in Bierwert's translation), she is adding something to the convention: that this world "belongs to us" is a political statement that the old stories did not need to make.

References to this past world recur throughout the story like a refrain, and they have a cadence more often heard in the longhouse than in storytelling. Mrs. Lamont spoke in public regularly, in particular as assistant minister of the Indian Shaker Church at Tulalip, where she opened the service by greeting the people in their ancestral language. During much of her life, there were legal and social obstacles to the practice of the winter dance, and it was in the Shaker Church that the spiritual heritage of the people could legally be honored. In some versions of Shaker belief there was a disavowal of traditional stories and of native languages, but this does not seem to have been the case at Tulalip, where some of the people most interested in the preservation of oral tradition, such as Mrs. Lamont, were Shakers.

On 5 September 1963, eleven days before she told the Crow story to Thom Hess, Mrs. Lamont tape-recorded a speech for him on the ways Snohomish children were brought up in the old days. In the following excerpts of this speech, we may hear echoes of Mrs. Lamont's Shaker public speaking style:

> This is how the teaching of the people used to be at the time when the earth was first made. This is what the people did, our people, when we began. They

gave advice long ago, at the beginning. [Mrs. Lamont summarizes the advice, which has to do with the search for spirit helpers, mentioning one by name, hiidə?, saying, "Things (things to eat) come ashore when one sings hiidə?'s song"; and "one would sing and so one's relatives would eat."] This is what they did long ago, when we were first made, we of the Indian people, on this very land where we now have our existence, this created land. . . .

They traveled over the water with ease; they ate every kind of food—salmon, duck, whatever. . . .

It was a very good way of doing things they had at the beginning, the people who came after those long ago forebears.

. . . If there is a good person, someone's fine young son, he will be betrothed to someone equally good, also a fine young person. . . . They marry according to the custom of the people. It is announced at a gathering: "It is good that our daughter is being married to him, because his are good people. They come from good people." . . . And those good families have had each other picked out for a long time.[5]

These excerpts from a seven-page transcript testify to the way the verbalization of setting in the Hess version of the story echoes statements in the speech, an echoing that is more striking in the Lushootseed than in the translations. The allusion to traveling over the water with ease also finds an echo in the story, as does the mention of the guardian spirit hiidə?: he is one of those whose servants would go out and look over young people who had come to seek help. It is against the backdrop provided by Mrs. Lamont's discussion of betrothal customs that Crow's behavior in the story would have been seen by an audience in the old days. Noteworthy also is the way Mrs. Lamont goes from the subject of spirit quest to the subject of marriage without verbalized transition. Spirit quest and marriage are associated in the speech under the rubric of raising children, but in the story they have become metaphors for each other.

It looks as though Mrs. Lamont revised the ending of the Hess version to dramatize the connection between power song and food that she makes in the speech. People at Valuable Shell's house dance and sing, and the narration of their feasting is ornamented concentrically (two small circular structures juxtaposed inside a large one; I have slightly changed Bierwert's formatting in order to foreground these structures here).

Thus, the people are pleased, according to custom.
And then they are pleased.
Crow has brought a loaded canoe.
There is lots.   what—
smelt and everything, herring and everything.

They always just went.
And they always helped themselves from the canoe.
    And they always just took that.
And they will help themselves from the piles, from
her feasting canoes.
Thus, that is the reason everyone is pleased, according to custom.

Crow is now a provider of food, specifically bringing it to Valuable Shell's people in a manner that acts out a metaphor traditionally used to describe the way spirit powers such as hiidə? can make salmon and other waterborne foods throw themselves onto the shore. In Metcalf all this is latent: "And now there will be a reason for people to get together, a reason for them to feast" is all that is said.

There seems ample reason to think that Mrs. Lamont's memory of the speech she gave on September 5 informed her telling of the Crow story on September 16. (It is also probable that at other times in her public speaking she made such a speech; she may even have selected this topic for Thom Hess's tape recorder because it was one at which she was practiced.) And there may be another remembered text informing both the Crow story and the September 5 speech. On August 28, at her first meeting with Hess, Mrs. Lamont had told a trilogy of stories about the Changer (text 1 in Bierwert, ed.). That "first world" in which the Crow story is set was lost to humankind when the Changer came along, diminishing its powers and possibilities and reducing things to the way they are today. Mrs. Lamont's Changer story includes what might be taken as a meditation on the injustice of the Change, a story in which Mink stands up to the Changer and makes a fool of him before being reduced to minkhood. The second part of the Changer story also deals with a theme integral to the story of Crow and her seagull slaves; an examination of the emotional power of the concept of class, it tells about a recent widow (another Crow) who is comforting herself with an erroneous estimation of her late husband's high rank.

The Change, that loss of a world, is often associated in Lushootseed thought with the other loss that came about with the arrival of white people, who may also be referred to as "changers" in Lushootseed. The myth time, when things were as they were planned to be and should be, is associated in some versions of Lushootseed thought with the spirit world, where Indian power still resides and therefore is still accessible through traditional lifeways (Amoss). Thus, stories taking place in the myth time have the potential to speak quite immediately to questions of personal power, equity, and political life.

Memory of the myth time leads to a realm situated not in the past but in truth and justice, the only realm in which identity flourishes. Since there is no justice on a mythical scale realized in the modern world, justice is always imaginary, and identity is never able to be acted out (except perhaps in the winter dance); it remains imagined. The Hess version of the Crow story begins ʔəsłałil tiʔəʔ ʔaciłtalbixʷ, "People were living there." ʔaciłtalbixʷ can mean simply "people" or more specifically "Indian people." In the context of a traditional story, ʔaciłtalbixʷ as "Indian people," which it seems to mean in the Hess version, implies a self-consciousness that goes along with an awareness of the difference between modern times and ancestral times: the audience is being asked not to forget itself in the story but to remember itself. Crow was siʔab when she was an Indian. Through a narrative emblem of spirit power in the old days, Mrs. Lamont is seeking to remind her audience of some possibilities that she believes are still inherent in the Lushootseed way of life.

Scholars writing about memory as it operates in oral cultures have drawn certain contrasts with memory as it operates in literacy. They describe oral memory as homeostatic, capable of keeping track of only so much data, so that obsolete information is constantly being forgotten and replaced with more recent memories. People in oral cultures are not aware of this process and continue to think of their information as having been passed down intact from ancient times (Goody and Watt, 30–33; Clanchy, 233). The notion of homeostasis generates further conclusions about how remembering feels to and works for the members of an oral culture: "The individual has little perception of the past except in terms of the present whereas the annals of a literate society cannot but enforce a more objective recognition of the distinction between what was and what is" (Goody and Watt, 33–34); there is no perceived conflict between "ancient precedents and present practice," and "no ancient custom can be proved to be older than the memory of the oldest living [person]" (Clanchy, 233); there can be no reference to 'dictionary definitions,' nor can words "accumulate the successive layers of historically validated meanings which they acquire in literate culture" (Goody and Watt, 29). Bearing in mind that Mrs. Lamont's culture is an oral one islanded in the midst of and under pressure from a vast and noisy literacy, I would like to work back through this list of conclusions and see how they describe or fail to describe the working of memory as we know it at Tulalip through the Crow story. The chief problem will be that the scholarly conclusions about memory do not incorporate an account of the values of the oral cultures they discuss, whereas the words of the

Crow story and the speech of Mrs. Lamont as a Shaker traditionalist mean what they mean only because they spring from a concern for such values. In addition, when scholars speak of memory, they seem to be thinking of it not as someone's memory but as the operation of a faculty that is the same for all people in whatever culture they are referring to.

Although oral cultures in their pristine state have no printed books, they do have dictionaries. The way people remember Mrs. Lamont is such an oral dictionary. Elders trying to define a word (an activity that goes on not just in the field sessions of anthropological linguistics, but also in conversation, reminiscence, and the instruction of young people) will refer to the way someone else used it on a specific occasion. x̌ax̌', "difficult," for example, is defined in one family by recalling Mrs. Lamont's use of it during a Shaker ceremony, when she described the inner resources necessary to do work that was so "difficult" (Moses). The present-day defining of the word goes beyond the memory of this occasion to consider whether Mrs. Lamont's use of it then comprehends all possible meanings now. By the time this "looking up of" (remembering about) x̌ax̌' is finished, one knows more about it than is ever written down in a dictionary entry, including how to use the word in varying contexts. The idea of consulting authority, including authorities who are not still living, is not confined to literacy; and historically validated depth is available in an oral lexicon, as the previous discussions in this essay of words like "hat" and "person" show.

The availability of an oral lexicon that records layers of meaning to an audience that is conscious of those layers is one piece of evidence that makes suspect the claim that people in oral cultures perceive the past only in terms of the present and are not aware of discrepancies. I know, for example, that at Tulalip determinations of status or social class may be made in part by reference to discrepancies between past and present in family histories. Here, the present is viewed in terms of the past: present events and conditions are always being checked against what is known of the past, and people are acutely aware of the distinction between what was and what is. Oppression, not literacy, enforces such awareness. It seems to me that this very awareness is one of the motivations for retellings of stories like "Crow and Her Seagull Slaves" and that one might well describe the Hess version as memory's response to colonialism. In celebrating what she remembers of the past (and what she remembers may be the story and how it was given to her, not the primordial past itself), Mrs. Lamont redefines the present, reminding people of possibilities in Lushootseed life that she sees going all too often unrealized. We speak of "what Mrs. Lamont remembers": she is not and never was the "oldest living person" on the reservation or in her cultural group, but what she remembered (as distinct from what was recorded) is still in part remembered by others—not only as part of their personal experience, but also as what may have been passed down by people long dead who were born a long time before Mrs. Lamont. There is no arbitrary cutoff point in the survival of what one person carries in memory.

In speaking of Mrs. Lamont's Crow story as politicized, do we attribute to her a sort of nationalist thought? Does Benedict Anderson's definition of nation as "an imagined political community, imagined as both inherently limited and sovereign" (1983, 15), describe the matrix of identity that we see Mrs. Lamont proposing through her construction of a world in which past and present are interpenetrable?

According to Anderson, the concept of " 'homogenous, empty time' [terminology he borrows from Walter Benjamin], in which simultaneity is . . . marked not by prefiguration and fulfilment [as is messianic or biblical time] but by temporal coincidence" (30), underpins the imagined community of nations, which has replaced with its structures of meaning the older world order of the community imagined religiously. Citizens of the community imagined religiously lived in time that had meaning because of their awareness of the fact that all events now happening were present already in the end of time, that is to say, in divine intention; simultaneity was purposeful along an axis perceived by people as vertical, extending from past through present to future. Citizens of nations are aware of no such purpose to simultaneity but think "horizontally" about discrete segments of coincidence for which a relationship must be provided by mental activity, imagining. This imagining is a product of literacy, for it is dependent for its subject matter on the rapid dissemination of information from areas distant from each other.

Mrs. Lamont's concept of time is described satisfactorily by neither of these models. Time for her may be described as religious, but the messianic model of religion carries a linear organization that is not present in all religious ideas about time. What Mrs. Lamont presents are worlds without trend parallel in consciousness and presumably therefore also in time and interpenetrable by means of religious activity. Concepts based on linearity, either horizontal or vertical, cannot describe the partnership of these worlds. Time is not "empty" for Mrs. Lamont, either, though it has no trend. Though she does seem to be proposing a political community inherently limited and sovereign, it is a community not so much imagined as remembered, and simultaneity for her is not contemporaneousness. Perhaps "empty time" and "nation" are not so inseparable as Anderson has proposed; certainly a loosening of the bond between them would leave room for conceptualizing the emergence of a nationalism from within an oral culture.

We have heard elders reiterate their belief that stories never change, even while seeing with our own eyes the record of the fact that elders themselves do "change" stories. Instead of accepting the elders' statements as descriptions of their experience as audience (and therefore rejecting those statements as definitive of any aspect of story that exists outside of performance), we might well investigate them as testimonies to a belief in the unchanging importance of traditional narrative. By asking what the statement that stories do not change means to the people who make that claim, we give ourselves a chance to get acquainted with a community that identifies itself by remembering.

Notes

I would like to thank Thom Hess for giving me access to his notebooks and tape recordings and for his comments on a previous draft of this essay. I thank Marya Moses for help in transcribing the tape recording of the Metcalf version of "Crow and Her Seagull Slaves" and Crisca Bierwert for permission to quote from her translation of "The Marriage of Crow." Mrs. Moses and I had available an earlier transcription of the Metcalf version by Vi Hilbert (1985), which we consulted and for which we are grateful. I thank the Thomas Burke Memorial Washington State Museum for permission to copy Reel 38 from the Metcalf Collection, and Laurel Sercombe, ethnomusicology archivist at the University of Washington, for providing a sound-enhanced copy of the tape recording.

1. The Lushootseed text and my English translation of this version of the story will appear in a special issue of *Oral Tradition*, edited by Larry Evers and Barre Toelken. For a discussion of rhetorical structures in Lushootseed storytelling, see Langen.

2. Quotations from the Hess version are from the translation by Crisca Bierwert (Lamont 1991). One purpose of Bierwert's lineation is to direct attention to structures of verbal repetition, whereas the principal goal of my formatting is to foreground the circular organization of the passages I quote. Bierwert's use of tense reflects the fact that in Lushootseed verbs are not marked for tense; her diction is closer to a literal translation of Mrs. Lamont's words than mine, whereas the diction of my translation tries to capture Mrs. Lamont's jovial and idiomatic style. No one translation can do everything that needs to be done to represent Mrs. Lamont's language fully.

3. Can it be a coincidence that qʷəniʔ is the word for "seagull" in the language

of the Lummi, a people who live to the north of Tulalip and with whom the Snohomish have had differences of opinion in the past? It is tempting to believe that Mrs. Lamont decided not only to reclaim the world for the Snohomish, but also to "enslave" the Lummi while she was at it. It would not have been unusual a hundred years ago for a Snohomish person residing at Tulalip to know some words of Lummi, for people from different tribes around Puget Sound and the Straits visited, spent time together at fish camps, and married each other frequently. But it needs to be said that today at Tulalip people do not recognize qwəni?, nor can we be sure that Mrs. Lamont did; qʷəni? may be something that she received along with the rest of the story, and thus somebody else's joke.

4. In his comments on a previous draft of this essay, Thom Hess pointed out that it is Mallard whose feathers preeminently change colors and that his description has been given to Bufflehead, so that there is nothing left to say about Mallard when he appears. I suspect that Mrs. Lamont chose Bufflehead (who, after all, does have some iridescent head feathers) because of his white nape and its metonymic relation to the duck down that floats in the air at some winter gatherings.

5. In preparing the translations of these excerpts from the tape recording, I consulted a transcription by Thom Hess and Harriette Shelton Dover, as well as a transcription and translation by Vi Hilbert.

Works Cited

Amoss, Pamela T. *Coast Salish Spirit Dancing: The Survival of an Ancestral Religion.* Seattle: University of Washington Press, 1978.

Anderson, Benedict. *Imagined Communities: Reflections on the Origin and Spread of Nationalism.* London: Verso, 1983.

Ausubel, David P. *The Psychology of Meaningful Verbal Learning.* New York: Grune and Stratton, 1963.

Bierwert, Crisca. "The Figure of Speech Is Amatory." *Studies in American Indian Literatures,* 2d ser., vol. 3, no. 1 (1991): 40–47, 66–79.

———, ed. *Lushootseed Texts.* Vol 1. Lincoln: University of Nebraska Press, forthcoming.

Clanchy, M. T. *From Memory to Written Record: England, 1066–1307.* London: Edward Arnold, 1979.

Collins, June McCormick. *Valley of the Spirits: The Upper Skagit Indians of Western Washington.* Seattle: University of Washington Press, 1974.

Cushing, Frank Hamilton. *Zuni Folk Tales.* 1901. Reprint, Tucson: University of Arizona Press, 1986.

Gagne, Robert M., and Richard T. White. "Memory Structures and Learning Outcomes." *Review of Educational Research* 48, no. 2 (1978): 187–222.

Goody, Jack. *The Interface between the Written and the Oral.* Cambridge: Cambridge University Press, 1987.

———, and Ian Watt. "The Consequences of Literacy." In *Literacy in Traditional*

Societies, edited by Jack Goody, 27–68. Cambridge: Cambridge University Press, 1968.

Haeberlin, Hermann, and Erna Gunther. *The Indians of Puget Sound.* University of Washington Publications in Anthropology 4, no. 1. Seattle: University of Washington Press, 1930.

Hess, Thomas M. "Recollections of the Storytellers." In *Lushootseed Texts,* vol. 1, edited by Crisca Bierwert. Lincoln: University of Nebraska Press, forthcoming.

———, and Harriette Shelton Dover. Transcription of a tape recording of Martha Lamont made by Thom Hess on 5 September 1963. Ms. in Hess's collection.

Hilbert, Vi. Transcription of Crow story from Metcalf Reel 38, 1985. Ms. in collection of Lushootseed Research, Inc., Seattle.

———. Transcription of a tape recording of Martha Lamont made by Thom Hess on 5 September 1963. Ms. in collection of Lushootseed Research, Inc., Seattle.

Lamont, Martha. "Crow and Her Seagull Slaves." In a special issue of *Oral Tradition.* Edited by Larry Evers and Barre Toelken. Forthcoming.

———. " 'The Marriage of Crow' Told by Martha Lamont." Translated by Crisca Bierwert. *Studies in American Indian Literatures,* 2d ser., vol. 3, no. 1 (1991): 49–65.

Langen, Toby C. S. "The Organization of Thought in Lushootseed (Puget Salish) Literature: Martha Lamont's 'Mink and Changer.' " *MELUS* 16, no. 1 (1989–1990): 77–94.

———, and Bonnie Barthold. "The Texts Are Compelling." *Studies in American Indian Literatures,* 2d ser., vol. 3, no. 1 (1991): 1–7.

———, and Marya Moses. "x̌ənimuličəʔ at Home: Reading Mrs. Lamont's Crow Stories at Tulalip Today." In a special issue of *Oral Tradition.* Edited by Larry Evers and Barre Toelken. Forthcoming.

Metcalf, Leon. Interview with T. Langen, Phoenix, Arizona, 1986. Tape recording in collection of interviewer.

Mink, Louis O. "History and Fiction as Modes of Comprehension." In Louis O. Mink, *Historical Understanding,* edited by Brian Fay, Eugene O. Golub, and Richard T. Vann, 42–60. Ithaca: Cornell University Press, 1987.

Moses, Marya. Personal communications. Tulalip, 1990–1991.

Powell, John Wesley. Introduction to *Zuni Folk Tales,* by Frank Hamilton Cushing. 1901. Reprint, Tucson: University of Arizona Press, 1986.

Snyder, Sally. "Skagit Society and Its Existential Basis: An Ethnofolkloristic Reconstruction." Ph.D. diss., University of Washington, 1964.

Oppression and Repression:

Personal and Collective Memory

in Paule Marshall's *Praisesong for the Widow*

and Leslie Marmon Silko's *Ceremony*

G . T H O M A S   C O U S E R

On the surface, the circumstances of the protagonists at the outset of Paul Marshall's *Praisesong for the Widow* (1983) and Leslie Marmon Silko's *Ceremony* (1977) could not be more different: Marshall's Avey Johnson is midway through a Caribbean cruise on a posh liner, whereas Silko's Tayo has returned to the Laguna Pueblo reservation from World War II by way of a V.A. hospital where he was treated, unsuccessfully, for combat fatigue. One is on a pleasure cruise, the other still reeling from the death trip of the war. But there are close and extensive parallels between the novels—parallels that reflect the crucial role of memory in (re)constructing minority experience in each novel.

Alienated in different ways from their respective ethnic groups, both protagonists are plagued by apparent hallucinations that prove to be unacknowledged memories linking them to a communal past. Both are brought into contact with an elder who embodies ethnic lore in a site characterized as mythologically significant (Lebert Johnson's rum shop, Betonie's hogan). Both Tayo and Avey are gradually induced into initiation processes that involve purging, pilgrimage, and ritual; these ordeals put them in contact with traditional ways and lead to their reaffirmation of their ethnic identities. That is, the two protagonists become recommitted to their respective tribes through a mutual process of recollection: as they gradually recall the communal past, they are in turn re-membered by their communities.[1]

The essence of genre is typically a formula with a powerful implicit message. In the case of these return-to-roots narratives, the significance

106

and continuing appeal of the underlying plot have to do with the perilous history of certain minorities. Histories of oppression, such as those of Native Americans and African Americans, are especially vulnerable to suppression and repression. With regard to such groups, written history is often amnesiac or self-justifying; it tends to marginalize or exclude the "ethnic," or other. At the same time, rather than dwell on (and in) a painful past, minority groups may sanitize memory in order to preserve positive self-images. Reviving such memories is necessary, however, precisely because, at least for groups whose traditional culture is primarily oral, the only history *is* memory. Not to remember is to accede to the erasure or distortion of collective experience; to repress memory is to reenact and perpetuate oppression. Arnold Krupat has suggested that the "theme" of tribal literature tends to be "kinship relations"; tribal stories are "tribal allegories" (222–23), whose concern is not with the individual but with the tribe, "the people." This helps to explain the persistence and power of the return-to-roots narrative even in "ethnic," as opposed to more circumscribed "tribal," narratives: it reasserts ethnic kinship by recovering what official history may "forget," omit, or obliterate.

Reflecting on recent ethnic autobiography and autobiographical fiction, Michael Fischer concludes:

> The newer works bring home forcefully . . . the paradoxical sense that ethnicity . . . is not something that is simply passed on from generation to generation, taught and learned; it is something dynamic, often unsuccessfully repressed or avoided. . . . Insofar as ethnicity is a deeply rooted emotional component of identity, it is often transmitted less through cognitive language or learning . . . than through processes analogous to the dreaming and transference of psychoanalytic encounters. (195–96)

This account of the contemporary rendering of ethnicity illuminates the two novels in question here, for both protagonists come to terms with their legacies at first through the operation of involuntary memory, when their cocoonlike consciousness is repeatedly pierced by hallucinatory and disorienting shards of their past; unable to repress these elements any longer, they learn to retrieve and reorder them in a purposeful way. The two novels do not so much reproduce ethnic customs as they model ethnicity as a cultural production dependent on the creative labor of each generation for its perpetuation.

Of the two novels under consideration here, Marshall's is perhaps more rooted in the past, insofar as her protagonist's ultimate role is revealed to be that of a medium, or conveyor, of an archetypal African American myth. Avey Johnson is named Avatara after a great-aunt's grandmother, the source of the story of the Ibos' landing. (It is a story of simple, emphatic rejection of oppression: foreseeing their fate in America upon landing in South Carolina, these chained slaves are said to have turned and *walked* back to Africa.) The plot of the novel has to do with Avey's being teased back into awareness of this heritage and finally identifying herself formally with her ancestor, whose avatar—(re)incarnation—she thus becomes. The narrative that enacts her reintegration of collective with personal memory combines an elaborate and complex achronological sequence of flashbacks with a straightforward description of her participation in a ceremony that encodes centuries of accumulated and preserved lore.

The intricate mosaic of fragmentary memories is made necessary by Avey's thorough assimilation into a middle-class lifestyle in the suburb of North White Plains (whose name is triply allegorical). Ironically, it is her cruise aboard the *Bianca Pride* ("huge, sleek, imperial, a glacial presence in the warm waters of the Caribbean" [16])—the sort of luxurious vacation for which she and her husband sacrificed so much—that recalls her ethnic heritage, including vivid memories of her pre-middle-class life. The initial reactivator of Avey's ethnic consciousness is, significantly, an *aural* memory. The patois spoken by natives on Martinique faintly echoes the Gullah spoken by the older blacks in Tatem, South Carolina, where she had summered as a youth (and been told the story of Ibo Landing):

> But reaching her clearly now was the flood of unintelligible words and the peculiar cadence and lilt of the Patois she had heard for the first time in Martinique three days ago. She had heard it that first time and it had fleetingly called to mind the way people spoke in Tatem long ago. There had been the same vivid, slightly atonal music underscoring the words. She had heard it, and that night from out of nowhere her great-aunt had stood waiting in her sleep. (67)

The aural memory thus reawakens her condensed cultural memory, which was transmitted orally (and reinforced visually and kinesthetically through walking trips to the landing).

It is only with the awakening of personal memory, then, as encoded at first in dreams, that the repressed collective history returns to consciousness. What Avey has repressed is the painful history of interracial experience in America. She has rarely dreamed (or at least remembered dreams) since the mid-sixties: "Before then, she had found herself taking all the nightmare images from the evening news into her sleep with her"—images of civil rights protests, sit-ins, the bombing of the Sunday school in Birmingham in 1963 (31). Now, her first new dream arouses Avey's memory of the emblematic event of the Ibos' landing. Expelled from the Ring Shout for dancing, Cuney had taken up as her religion the worship of her Ibo ancestors, whose story was told to her by *her* "gran": "Her body she always usta say might be in Tatem but her mind, her mind was long gone with the Ibos" (39). In Avey's dream, Cuney beckons to the mature Avey like a mother coaxing her one-year-old to walk on her own or a preacher imploring backsliders to be saved (41–42). The struggle degenerates into a tug-of-war, then an unseemly fistfight, but the process is that of persuading a lapsed believer to become not a mere disciple but an apostle. In effect, Avey is the vehicle, the unconscious medium, of an oral gospel, a purported eyewitness account of "an unrecorded, uncanonized miracle" (136).

Avey's "hallucinations"—for example, a shuffleboard game on deck seems to turn into a brawl—prove to be encoded, condensed, or symbolic memories. Although she does not immediately understand what she sees, she has begun to take on the visionary power ascribed to the Ibos. When an innocent game of quoits begins to sound like a beating, it triggers a flashback of police brutality: "Her memory seemed to be playing the same frightening tricks as her eyes" (57). In a later hallucination, at her hotel on Grenada, after she abandons her cruise, she is reproached by the ghost of her husband, Jay, for throwing away what they had worked so hard to earn. But book 2, "Sleeper's Wake," questions the worth of their sacrifices by recalling what they had lost in the process; memories of the transition from Brooklyn to North White Plains, and the concomitant change in her husband from the blues- and jazz-loving Jay to the disciplined, successful (and racist) accountant Jerome, suggest the unforeseen and perhaps unnecessary cost of upward mobility.

> Something in those small rites, an ethos they held in common, had reached back beyond her life and beyond Jay's to join them to the vast unknown lineage that had made their being possible. And this link, these connections, heard in the music and in the praisesongs of a Sunday . . . had both protected them and put them in possession of a kind of power. . . . All this had passed from their lives without their hardly noticing. (137)

Avey begins to wonder whether they could have made money, lived more comfortably, and still maintained respect for their "cullud" selves—that is, escaped oppression without abandoning their distinctive cultural heritage.[2]

Avey not only needs to remember what she has forgotten, but also needs to forget much of what she remembers; in order to regain her "soul" she must lose the "world," at least temporarily. Hence the images of a volcanic eruption burying her suburban home (196). Hence, too, the unmistakable images of regression and rebirth in the second half of the novel. Thus, when she wakes in her hotel on Grenada, "Her mind . . . had been emptied of the contents of the past thirty years during the night, so that she had awakened with it like a slate that had been wiped clean, a *tabula rasa* upon which a whole new history could be written" (151). Similarly, with her ritualistic bathing by Rosalie Parvay on Carriacou, she is somatically recalled to her infancy, when she was bathed by her great-aunt in Tatem; she is thus bodily reminded of her nurturing by her female ancestors and symbolically reborn into her tribe.

In the second half of *Praisesong for the Widow,* Avey moves toward a state of reconciliation with her ethnicity by means of a crucial journey overseen by Lebert Johnson, a trickster figure based on the ubiquitous Afro-Caribbean deity Legba; her transformation is thus induced and supervised by a character who is himself an avatar of an African survival. The journey is the annual pilgrimage of its natives to the small island of Carriacou, where they pay homage to the Old Parents, the Long-Time People, and reaffirm their connection to Africa by participating in tribal dances. Avey's journey there is conspicuously ritualized: after she is purged by seasickness en route and then ceremonially cleansed, Lebert leads her from a crossroads through a liminal gate to the site of the dances, where the very music of the Big Drum is encoded memory:

> The theme of separation and loss the note embodied, the unacknowledged longing it conveyed summed up feelings that were beyond words, feelings and a host of subliminal memories that over the years had proven more durable and trustworthy than the history with its trauma and pain out of which they had come. After centuries of forgetfulness and even denial, they refused to go away. The note was a lamentation that could hardly have come from the rum keg of a drum. Its source had to be the heart, the bruised still-bleeding innermost chamber of the collective heart. (244–45)

After watching the "nation dances"—for those who still identify with particular tribes—Avey joins in a "creole dance"—for those who have lost sight of their "nations." (Just as the local patois recalls the Gullah spoken in Tatem, this dance recalls the Ring Shout she had danced as a child. Both represent the survival of African folkways; aural memory is reinforced by kinesthetic memory.) She dances as if walking on water: "She moved cautiously at first, each foot edging forward as if the ground under her was really water—muddy river water—and she was testing it to see if it would hold her weight" (248). When, at a climactic moment, she identifies herself as "Avey, short for Avatara" (251), she situates herself in terms of both her personal history and her lineage: she is told afterward that, judging from the way she danced, she is very likely descended from the Arada people. Thus, her involuntarily initiated quest has led her metaphorically back to Africa, back to her roots in tribal life.[3] In traveling there "on water," she has reenacted, remembered, and memorialized the miraculous mythic flight of the Ibos.

Her experience also recapitulates crucial elements of African American history. Her journey by boat to Carriacou evokes the horrendous Middle Passage: "She was alone in the deckhouse. . . . Yet she had the impression as her mind flickered on briefly of other bodies lying crowded in with her in the hot, airless dark. . . . Their suffering—the depth of it, the weight of it in the cramped space—made hers of no consequence" (209). And her flight from the cruise reenacts, however genteelly, the flight of the fugitive slave.[4] Thus, the title of book 1, "Runagate," has a double meaning: at the outset she is a renegade by virtue of her repression of her ethnic past, but during the course of the book, she "runs away" to Africa. Indeed, at the end of the book, she returns to America with the intent of proselytizing—keeping her heritage alive by moving south, fixing up the old house in Tatem, and passing on her newly remembered story to any who will listen. The story of the Ibos' resistance to oppression, once readmitted to consciousness, is seen as a kind of antidote to contemporary amnesia and alienation in the African American community.

Like Cuney's gran's, Avey's mind will be in Africa while her body remains in America. Far from being an image of paralyzing self-division, this state of being is characterized as a healthy condition: she is *in* America but not entirely *of* it, engaged in American life but mindful of a valuable African legacy. Insofar as to remember is to have one's body in one place and one's mind in another, the novel's narrative line, which is determined by Avey's newly activated, volcanic memory, dramatizes the complex dynamics of African American consciousness.[5] A certain kind of memory—voluntary, active, and creative—is central to Marshall's novel because it embodies her vision of a vital African American culture.

In Silko's *Ceremony*, the protagonist is also an alienated minority American who slowly and painfully comes to terms with the traditional ways of his people. A mixed-blood abandoned by his Indian mother and raised by his aunt, and a traumatized veteran of World War II, Tayo is struggling to reintegrate himself into the reservation community. He is, however, bedeviled by a past that must be exorcised, and like Avey, he finally finds redemption only in long-forgotten cultural rituals. If anything, the relation of past to present, hallucination to memory, is even more complex in *Ceremony* than in *Praisesong for the Widow*. Much of the first half of the novel is devoted to rendering Tayo's postwar confusion—emotional, moral, intellectual, and spiritual—by plunging the reader into a narrative that switches back and forth abruptly between apparently unrelated scenes and alternates between narrative prose and traditional stories presented as verse. At times, there are flashbacks within flashbacks; not until nearly midway through the novel does the plot "advance" significantly.

The narrative begins with Tayo's muddled dreams, full of mingled voices, which are memories fused chaotically together. For Tayo, each of these is a thread:

> He could feel it inside his skull—the tension of little threads tied together, and as he tried to pull them apart and rewind them into their places, they snagged and tangled even more. . . . He had to sweat to think of something that wasn't unraveled or tied in knots to the past—something that existed by itself, standing alone like a deer. (7)

Part of Tayo's psychic work—sometimes unconscious, sometimes conscious—during the novel is to disentangle some of these threads and to weave them back together in meaningful patterns, for no experience of value can, or should, be completely severed from others. (The ultimate creative force in the novel, after all, is Thought-Woman, the spider; indeed, she is invoked as the ultimate source *of* the novel [1]. Tayo's reweaving of his memory threads is in harmony with, and a function of, divine principles.)[6] By the end of the narrative, his "dreams" no longer haunt him because they have been understood—as *memories*—within the proper cultural context of traditional myths, stories, and rituals.

Like Avey, Tayo has lost a secure sense of his relation to his past, in part as a result of his enlistment in the army and his role in combat in World War II. And like hers, his hallucinations prove to have truth value. His mistaking Japanese soldiers for Indians, a basic failure to distinguish friend from foe, at first seems a symptom of combat fatigue. Later, it can be seen as a function of guilt for having left the reservation to go to war. (His uncle Josiah, whom he had promised to help raise the Mexican cattle, dies during his absence, and Tayo feels guilty for abandoning him.) Later still, Betonie interprets this troubling memory/hallucination as an expression of a deeply buried sense of racial brotherhood with his Asian "enemies" (124). Still later, it is seen as a manifestation of a sense of the universal brotherhood of mankind in the face of the new threat of nuclear annihilation: "From that time on, human beings were one clan again, united by the fate the destroyers planned for all of them, for all living things" (246). Eventually, then, his "hallucinations" are revealed to be manifestations not of insanity but rather of misunderstood insight. This is why, despite their professed concern (and professional credentials), the V.A. psychiatrists cannot cure him: "Their medicine drained memory out of his thin arms and replaced it with a twilight cloud behind his eyes" (15). Betonie, the eccentric medicine man, can succeed where the psychiatrists fail because he elicits, rather than suppresses, Tayo's memories, and because he is equipped to appreciate their various dimensions, from the tribal to the universal.

The early pages of the novel are dominated by painful, personal memories: of being abandoned by his mother when he was four; of her death; of being told of her sexual escapades; of the death of his "brother" Rocky, whom he had vowed to take care of during the war; of stabbing his fellow veteran Emo in a bar; and so on. Susan Scarberry aptly characterizes Tayo's involuntary and harrowing experience of these memories: "His memories occur randomly. Oftentimes, an object or a sense impression triggers a host of fearful memories which Tayo is powerless to avoid" (Scarberry, 20). But perhaps she overstates the case when she asserts, "Virtually all [of Tayo's] memories are bad at this point" (20). Early in the novel Tayo's consciousness does contain some positive memories, which have to do with traditional ways and the ethic implicit in them— for example, of intimacy with the land (19), of the acquisition of the Mexican cattle (73–81), and of praying at the spring and having an incipient sense of his power as a rainmaker (11, 45–46, 93–96). At the beginning of the novel these memories are recessive, difficult for Tayo to recall clearly or fully. Thus, his memory of the spring emerges in its full personal and spiritual resonance only gradually and intermittently (over the sequence of pages cited earlier). But one of the important effects of the narrative is to undermine any simple distinction between "bad" and "good" memories. Tayo's problem is not that he has "bad" memories— that is, that he remembers unpleasant experiences—but that he has lost the ability to understand those experiences in their proper cultural context.[7]

In any case, it is not enough to "remember the story," as Josiah exhorts him to do in the case of the greenbottle flies. (Reprimanding Tayo for casually killing flies, Josiah had told him how the greenbottle fly had once obtained forgiveness from the mother of all people [101–102].) In a sense, Tayo still does this. More than that, he must begin to *recognize* (in the root sense of the word) and respect the story, to view it not as a relic of a dead or dying culture, but as an element in the ongoing "ceremony" that is (his) life. This he comes to do by virtue of his instructive contact with two medicine men, Ku'oosh and the mixed-blood Old Betonie, and with the mysterious mountain-spirit, Ts'eh. What they collectively convey to him is the traditional place of the individual in the community and the relation of that community to the land. Significantly, they do this not only by what they say but by how they say it. For example, Ku'oosh is described as speaking "softly, using the old dialect full of sentences that were involuted with explanations of their own origins, as if nothing the old man said were his own but all had been said before and he was only there to repeat it" (34). Ku'oosh, then, speaks as if *remembering* what he is saying rather than articulating something new.

The fact that memory is to be seen not as passive recall but as active re-creation is especially evident when Ts'eh takes Tayo to view a deteriorating pictograph of a pregnant she-elk. Though the pictograph is being slowly bleached away, Ts'eh insists that "as long as you remember what you have seen, then nothing is gone. As long as you remember, it is part of this story we have together" (231). The deterioration of the physical icon is negated by the active mental cultivation of the image and its cultural significance. At a climactic moment, after having acted out various ceremonies under the tutelage of Betonie and Ts'eh, Tayo approaches the mine shaft from which the ore had been taken to arm the first nuclear bomb. There he has restored to him a traditional vision of the world, which makes sense of his tortured dreams of modern warfare. His vision, at this most ominous of sites for the contemporary world, assumes the shape of a traditional tribal art form.

> He had arrived at the point of convergence where the fate of all living things, and even the earth, had been laid. From the jungles of his dreaming he recognized why the Japanese voices had merged with Laguna voices, with Josiah's voice and Rocky's voice; the lines of cultures and worlds were drawn in flat dark lines on fine light sand, converging in the middle of witchery's final ceremonial sand painting. (246)

This confirmation of what he had considered his private hallucinations is cathartic.

> He cried the relief he felt at finally seeing the pattern, the way all the stories fit together—the old stories, the war stories, their stories—to become the

story that was still being told. He was not crazy; he had never been crazy. He had only seen and heard the world as it always was; no boundaries, only transitions through all distances and time. (246)

What he had thought was sick confusion was really a matter of healthy, though misunderstood, visions of fusion. Memory is not merely a static preservative but a regenerative force, faithful to its immemorial origins but at the same time responsive to the present circumstances in which it functions.

By means of ceremony, such as the Scalp Ceremony (meant to cleanse him of the effects of the mechanized anonymous killings of World War II), quest (the recovery of the spotted cattle, which involves trespassing on white-owned land), and a pilgrimage to a holy mountain,[8] Tayo is prepared for reentry into his tribe, at which time he tells the story of his cure to the elders in the kiva. The implication of this entire process is, as Kenneth Lincoln has observed of the scene in which Tayo first meets Betonie, that

> healing involves the right triggering of memory . . . [a]nd, similarly, to name things rightly is to make medicine through memory, to heal and give strength. . . . So, to remember and breathe, according to traditional memory, places one naturally in a naming ceremony, aligned with the things that are and always have been. (241–42)

Throughout the novel, at crucial moments, Tayo is advised to exercise his memory—by Josiah (102), by Night Swan (100), and climactically by Ts'eh: "As long as you remember what you have seen, nothing is gone" (231); "Remember . . . remember everything" (235). Memory functions in this novel, as in Laguna culture, not as the thread that connects individual experiences, like beads, but as the medium that links people harmoniously with one another and to the earth. Josiah reminds Tayo that the "old people used to say that droughts happen when people forget, when people misbehave" (46). If to forget *is* to misbehave, then to remember, as Tayo learns to, is to restore the balance. Like Avey, Tayo needs to remember (how) to remember.

Although both novels incorporate cultural memory in manner as well as matter, a distinction might be made between them in their use of traditional materials, their attitudes toward those materials, and the degree to which cultural memory defines or affects their form as opposed to their content (although form and content are ultimately inseparable). In this respect, the gestures of Marshall are more limited; that is, despite her incorporation of various survivals of African culture, such as the

Legba figure and the tribal dances, her literary form is more Westernized, in that the narrative voice only occasionally partakes of the orality of traditional culture. Still, Marshall has created what we might call a Creole novel, which, like the patois spoken on Carriacou, communicates by integrating features of both minority and mainstream culture. Avey moves toward contact with her African roots aboard a vessel called *Emanuel C,* and the elder women aboard that vessel remind Avey of the church mothers of the Mount Olivet Baptist Church she had attended as a girl. Similarly, the interrogation of the young Avey by her great-aunt Cuney about the Ibos' landing, with emphasis on the plausibility of their walking on water (39–40), suggests that Marshall is proposing an equivalence, or at least an analogy, between African and Christian mythology. Thus, the novel consciously and conspicuously syncretizes African myth, ritual, and religion with New World Christian equivalents to make sense of African American experience; it stresses continuity between African tribal cultures and Christianized African American culture.[9]

Ceremony makes more extensive use of traditional forms, beginning as it does with a traditional-looking poem that asserts, in effect, that the narrator-author is "writing down" a story generated by "Thought-Woman"; that is, the novel begins by abjuring the notion of individual authorship that is tied up with the modern Western concept of originality, and the concepts of copyright and intellectual property that issue from, and reify, it. Although it does not ascribe the story to tribal memory, this gesture presents the story not as novel but as traditional—in harmony with, because issuing ultimately from, a transpersonal tribal source. Indeed, it suggests that the novel itself *presents* or *enacts* a sort of healing performance; Silko's novel, then, has a ritualistic function or dimension that is absent from Marshall's. Other manifestations of this impulse are clear in Silko's incorporation of traditional myths, stories, and poems in her text—set off from the prose paragraphs not in the left-justified lines of Western poetry but centered on the page.

Despite its more traditional or tribal form, Silko's novel is freer of nostalgia for a pure racial or ethnic past.[10] Marshall's novel does indulge in nostalgia for an implied African past, and it indicts its heroine's assimilation into middle-class suburban life in a way that risks identifying ethnic authenticity with low social status (and thus implying a "proper place" for African Americans). In contrast, Silko clearly affirms the need to adapt tradition to contemporary circumstances and to seek healthy accommodation between indigenous and Western cultures—in her choice of a mixed-blood protagonist, in the symbolism of the mixed-breed cattle, and through Betonie's unorthodox curing of Tayo. In various ways, she implies that the community cannot seek refuge in traditional customs and values.

From the close parallels between the two novels, one can induce a formula for a contemporary return-to-roots novel: take an alienated member of a minority or ethnic group; subject him or her to an unnerving experience that recalls past traumas, personal and communal; introduce a "tribal" elder, who will lead the alienated character back into contact and communion with the minority community through traditional ceremony; and so on. My intent here is not to disparage either novel as formulaic, nor to characterize the later text as derivative of the earlier. Rather, the point is to acknowledge the central importance of an underlying pattern to both novels and perhaps, by doing so, to promote an appreciation of both novels: only when a theme is familiar can one relish its variation.[11]

Having emphasized the underlying plot in these return-to-roots narratives, I want to acknowledge that Marshall's and Silko's novels are far from "generic" narratives. Because of the richness and complexity of their cultural inflections, neither novel feels formulaic. Moreover, both writers employ fractured chronology to give their novels particularity and resonance; the return of the repressed tribal consciousness is represented by means of techniques characteristic of high modernism. Both protagonists come to terms with the repressed past (and the past of oppression) via complicated reconstructions and reintegrations of memory, collective as well as individual. By means of various mechanisms of recall—associative, aural, oral, somatic, and kinesthetic—forgotten experience is belatedly remembered; as a result, the protagonists are reintegrated into their respective minority communities. What raises these novels, then, above "generic" status is, in part, the inventiveness of their narrative forms, which synthesize elements of oral and print cultures, the minority and the mainstream. Significantly, the necessity for readers to piece together a coherent story out of an achronological narrative enlists them, regardless of their own ethnicity, in the reconstruction of the lost history of the minority group.[12]

According to Abdul R. JanMohamed and David Lloyd,

> One aspect of the struggle between hegemonic culture and minorities is the recovery and mediation of cultural practices that continue to be subject to

"institutional forgetting," which, as a form of control of one's memory and history, is one of the gravest forms of damage done to minority cultures. (6)

These two novels employ, valorize, and revitalize the particular modes of memory available and essential to the minority groups most alienated from hegemonic culture in America, African Americans and Native Americans. Both expose the problematic relation between history and myth as forms of collective memory because both involve events that have traditionally been unwritten and that thus rely exclusively on memory and oral transmission to perpetuate them from generation to generation. Insofar as they recover particulars of a repressed past and move toward a recognition of oral and traditional forms of narrative, both novels challenge universalist assumptions that underwrote, until recently, the idea of "the canon." They subvert the paradigm of a single, monolithic literary tradition by reenacting the conflictual history that produced the canon and that the canon has sometimes obscured. And they suggest ways of opening and enriching the canon by illustrating the vital relevance of traditional oral cultures to contemporary American life.

Notes

1. It is more than mere coincidence that both novels are dedicated to the authors' grandmothers; both texts assert in the beginning the sort of homage to ancestors they demand of their protagonists in the end.

2. The process of Avey's assimilation is, as Abena Busia has noted, a reenactment of the diaspora:

> Marshall articulates the scattering of the African peoples as a trauma . . . that is constantly repeated anew in the lives of her lost children. The life of the modern world and the conditions under which Afro-Americans have to live, the sacrifices they must make to succeed on the terms of American society, invariably mean a severing from their cultural roots, and, as Avey learns to her cost, this is tantamount to a repetition, in her private life, of that original historical separation. (197)

3. Abena Busia has noted that as one of the easternmost of the Caribbean islands, Carriacou is literally as well as metaphorically one of the closest to Africa (201).

4. The novel's symbolic geography reworks, rather than merely reproduces, archetypal African American experiences. Thus, Avey's "middle passage" reverses the poles of the diaspora—her destination is "Africa" (Busia, 207)—and her flight to freedom takes her south, away from North White Plains (Christian, 75).

5. Christian has noted the close relation between the motif of the mind re-moved from the body and the basic technique of the novel (75–76).

6. The imagery of weaving is also important in *Praisesong,* where it symbol-izes the sense of cultural connectedness that is restored to Avey in the course of the novel (see, for example, 90–91, 190–91, 249), but it is not explicitly a meta-phor for the creative process.

7. Scarberry's diction here misrepresents, however, the thrust of her very per-ceptive essay "Memory as Medicine," which is about the healing power of mem-ory when it functions properly.

8. The novel's use of geography is in itself a rich topic. Edith Swann has treated Silko's use of Laguna "symbolic geography" extensively, and Robert Nel-son has written on the relation between geography and vision in *Ceremony.*

9. Silko's novel is, unlike Marshall's—and for reasons grounded in Native American history—implicitly hostile to the influence of Christianity, which it portrays as inconsistent with tribal customs and values.

10. In a panel discussion of *Ceremony,* LaVonne Ruoff makes the point that tribal culture in America was never absolutely pure; there was always intertribal influence (Sands, 68). The same no doubt is true of African tribal culture.

11. The formula, in any case, is not confined to African American and Native American writing; nor is it a relatively recent development. To establish the per-vasiveness and relative longevity of this formula, one need only point to its pres-ence in Philip Roth's "Eli, the Fanatic" (1959). Roth's protagonist is uneasily or incompletely assimilated to the suburban world of Woodenton, and as a result of contact with traditional, observant Jews who have survived the Holocaust, he undergoes a kind of conversion experience. Putting on the clothes of one of the survivors, he seems to take on his identity as well, becoming nearly unrecogniz-able to his neighbors, friends, and family, who view him, through a psychoana-lytical lens, as having a nervous breakdown.

12. In a panel discussion of *Ceremony,* Susan Scarberry points out that its form requires that the reader's memory function like Tayo's (Sands, 64); the same is true of *Praisesong.*

Works Cited

Busia, Abena P. A. "What Is Your Nation?: Reconnecting Africa and Her Diaspora through Paule Marshall's *Praisesong for the Widow.*" In *Changing Our Own Words: Essays on Criticism, Theory, and Writing by Black Women,* edited by Cheryl A. Wall, 198–211. New Brunswick: Rutgers University Press, 1989.

Christian, Barbara. "Ritual, Process, and Structure." *Callaloo* 6, no. 2 (1983): 74–84.

Fischer, Michael M. J. "Ethnicity and the Post-Modern Arts of Memory." In *Writing Culture: The Poetics and Politics of Ethnography,* edited by James Clifford and George E. Marcus, 194–223. Berkeley: University of California Press, 1986.

JanMohamed, Abdul R., and David Lloyd. "Introduction: Toward a Theory of

Minority Discourse: What Is to Be Done?" In *The Nature and Context of Minority Discourse,* edited by JanMohamed and Lloyd, 1–16. New York: Oxford University Press, 1990.

Krupat, Arnold. *The Voice in the Margin: Native American Literature and the Canon.* Berkeley: University of California Press, 1989.

Lincoln, Kenneth. *Native American Renaissance.* Berkeley: University of California Press, 1983.

Nelson, Robert M. "Place and Vision: The Function of Landscape in *Ceremony.*" *Journal of the Southwest* 30, no. 3 (1988): 281–316.

Roth, Philip. "Eli, the Fanatic." In *Goodbye, Columbus and Five Short Stories.* Boston: Houghton Mifflin, 1959.

Sands, Kathleen, and LaVonne Ruoff, eds. "A Discussion of *Ceremony.*" *American Indian Quarterly* 5, no. 1 (February 1979): 63–70.

Scarberry, Susan. "Memory as Medicine: The Power of Recollection in *Ceremony.*" *American Indian Quarterly* 5, no. 1 (February 1979): 19–26.

Swann, Edith. "Laguna Symbolic Geography and Silko's *Ceremony.*" *American Indian Quarterly* 12, no. 3 (1988): 229–49.

Tilling the Soil to Find Ourselves:

Labor, Memory, and Identity

in Ernest J. Gaines's

Of Love and Dust

HERMAN BEAVERS

In those empty spaces, times intersect and our relation
with things is reversed: rather than remembering the past,
we feel the past remembers us. Unexpected rewards: the
past becomes present, an impalpable yet real presence.
—Octavio Paz, "The Tree of Life"

Say it for nightmare, say it loud
panebreaking heartmadness;
nightmare beings responsibility.
—Michael S. Harper, "Nightmare Begins Responsibility"

Numerous African American authors have employed the communal idea as the repository of memory, a space where collective experience is stored and utilized in the shaping of the next generation. In this respect, communal acts of remembering can be both liberating and constitutive: by reconstructing the past, they are likewise vehicles of identity.[1] One could think here of Toni Morrison's *Song of Solomon;* an instance in which the hero, Milkman, engages in what begins as a materialistic quest for gold and ends as a journey of genealogical importance, one that brings him face to face with the knowledge that his ancestral legacy includes the power of self-generated flight. Surely, Morrison's novel fits into a corpus of novels where we find a protagonist who, individually, fails to manifest the personal resources necessary to formulate

121

a resilient identity. It is in the community (or figures in the community who represent the collective memory of the group) that the individual can find the historical and cultural impetus to undertake recovery and rebirth.

I would like to propose, however, that an equally important critical project is to be found in the examination of fictions where the individual must reach a new state of awareness or self-recovery by resisting collective memory.[2] The necessity to follow this second impulse allows for an examination of fictional black communities in a context of greater complexity. For the act of breaking out of a repressive paradigm in order to construct a new relationship to the past is just as important as using the past to manifest communal ties. To suggest that the individual will always find him- or herself within the space of the collective is likewise to suggest that personal forms of struggle become meaningful only as collective acts. Such a state of affairs is antithetical to the manner in which African American culture constitutes a performance culture. Indeed, what expressive culture—in the form, say, of the blues—often articulates is that the value of community lies not in the loss of individuality, but in the furtherance of processes that valorize acts of individualism, even when those actions endanger communal interests in the short run.[3]

These issues come to the fore in Ernest J. Gaines's novel *Of Love and Dust*. In this, his second novel, Gaines returns to his interest in depicting the conflict between old and new ways of life, the clash between old and new paradigms of identity formation.[4] Within that project, memory serves as a powerful influence in his characters' lives: their lives are mediated by the social blueprint of Jim Crow, where violence is privileged in the collective memory because it is used to reinforce the segregation and racial codes that separate black from white. In this respect, it is the memory of violence rather than actual force that enforces passivity and thus upholds the status quo.

This helps us to understand Gaines's decision to begin the novel *in medias res*, its narrative machinery already in motion. The effect of this strategy is to make the reader rely on an act of memory to fully ascertain the present. This can be accomplished only by retrieving the details from the past that will make the encounter at the novel's outset meaningful. Thus, when Jim Kelly looks down the quarters and sees the rapidly approaching dust, he lacks the intuitive equipment to discern the dust's ominous potential. But as Gaines himself has pointed out, dust functions as a metaphor for death, and so the novel's first image raises the question of survival and the kinds of resources that are needed to survive.[5]

As the title intimates, Gaines posits love as the antithesis of death. Though love is regenerative and capable of producing a new social condition, the characters lack the ability to institute it along with a resistant posture. Dust obscures and negates this possibility, stirring acts of memory that prevent the quarters from seeing beyond it to gaze forward in spite of the presence of evil and death. The fact that Gaines renders love and dust as simultaneous events proposes that life on the Herbert plantation is characterized by stasis. He introduces two characters into this scenario of social death: Marcus Payne and Jim Kelly. The moment Marcus emerges out of the dust looking for Kelly represents the moment when the latter's past, present, and future become intertwined with the former's. It could be argued that *Of Love and Dust* depicts Marcus's exploits; Marcus represents a figure of resistance, whereas Jim serves as a mere witness to the events surrounding Marcus's arrival. However, a more precise reading would lead us to conclude that the novel is a symbiosis between Marcus and Jim. Marcus needs Jim to tell his story, and Jim tells his story because of Marcus's impact on his life. Moreover, there are problems with Marcus narrating his own story, namely because the reader would become trapped in the point of view of an outsider who lacks insight into the workings of the plantation and the quarters. Thus, Marcus cannot tell his own story because his actions always indicate his distance from the community. Gaines explains:

> When you get to Marcus, you get a one-sided thing. It's like trying to get Gatsby to tell a story of *The Great Gatsby*. You can't do that. I needed a guy who could communicate with different people. I needed a guy who could communicate with Bonbon, the white overseer, with Aunt Margaret, with Marcus.[6]

Gaines's narrative strategy is realized through Jim Kelly; as the novel's overarching voice he serves the function of mediating between the plantation's various spheres. And like Nick Carraway, Jim's credibility as mediator is unobtrusive enough to lead the other characters to fill in the gaps in his narrative without displacing his narrative authority.

The mediation Jim undertakes is performed on the ritual ground of language. We find a clear example of this in his relationship with Sidney Bonbon, the Cajun overseer. Because Jim is well versed in the language of mechanization, the farm machinery provides the circumstances that lead to his relationship with Bonbon. He recounts:

It was me when I showed Bonbon I was good with any machine he had there. Maybe if I hadn't showed him how good I was he wouldn't have put so much trust in me. He wouldn't have treated me different from the way he treated all the others. He wouldn't have told me things about himself, things about his family—things he never told nobody else. No I had to show him how good I could handle tractors. And every time I did, he told me a little bit more. And since I knew all about trucks and tractors, I was the person he chose.[7]

Jim's mechanical ability leads Bonbon to cross the boundary of racial difference into the space of sanctioned remembrance. Trucks and tractors provide the means for Bonbon to ignore Jim's inequity of social status, to add flesh, blood, and bone to his authoritarian presence as overseer. What this also suggests, however, is that Gaines links labor and narration; Jim's status as "good worker" sets him apart from the other blacks on the plantation. This leads, as Keith Byerman has argued, to his medial status on the plantation; his fluency in the mechanical sphere makes him a receptacle of memory.

This is further exemplified by Jim's relationships with the other blacks in the quarters. Although he could easily be the object of resentment due to his status, Jim avoids this because the other language he speaks is that of the blues. As a guitar-playing blues performer, he gives voice to the rage, hurt, and frustration that characterize black life on the plantation. And because the blues is the cohabitation of pain and experience, Jim is a necessary presence for the community's well-being.[8] Moreover, the musical expression of these feelings is acceptable to the whites on the plantation, who lack the ability to decode the songs' utility as social commentary. In addition, the intimacy that Jim occasions in the quarters through his music positions him as both teller and character in the narrative structure of the novel. This allows him to recount Marcus's actions even as he gives voice to his (and thus, the quarters') anxieties about him. As bluesman, he can interpret the behavior issuing from Southern racial conventions, even as he can be openly critical of himself for failing to challenge them, for choosing ease over resistance.

But this points at the other aspect of Jim's character: his disillusionment. Jim's spiritual malaise translates into an inability to engage his environment. This is evidenced at its most basic level when he looks at the toilet in his backyard, "ready to tumble at the first light breeze." Though he promises to fix it "one of these Saturdays," he knows this will never happen. At a more substantial level, there is Jim's indifference to the plantation store with its two rooms, one for whites, the other for

blacks. This physical manifestation of Jim Crow represents a site maintained, at least in part, by consensus; though the blacks on the plantation may not like being segregated, the store's importance to their sustenance neutralizes their desire to challenge its racial policy. Jim observes
when he enters the store:

> If you were colored you had to go to the little side room—"the nigger room."
> I kept telling myself, "One of these days I'm going to stop this. I'm going to
> stop this; I'm a man like any other man and one of these days I'm going to
> stop this." But I never did. Either I was too tired to do it, or after I had been
> working in the field all day I was too tired and just didn't care. (43)

What makes this passage important to my critical purpose is that Gaines
uses repetition to demonstrate Jim's frustration and anger. But more important, the fact that he repeats "I'm going to stop this" illustrates Jim's
memory at work: he remembers all the times he has promised to resist
degradation, projecting his resistance into the future. But this assertion
is framed by two sentences in the past tense, indicating the way the future is overwhelmed by the past.

Moreover, the toilet and side room serve as effective representations
of Jim's disempowerment: the latter as a place where he is victimized
and feels powerless to resist, the former as a site of privacy gone awry.
Jim responds to both places with an apathy he cannot breach; he knows
that action is called for, but he cannot muster the resolve to act. Despite
his relatively comfortable status in the plantation hierarchy, Jim pays a
price both publicly and privately.

Jim's disillusionment, we discover, emanates from a deeper wellspring
of hurt. This becomes clear during the novel's opening chapters when
Jim remembers his former lover, Billie Jean. Drawn by the fast pace and
material trappings found in the city, Billie Jean abandons the plantation
and Jim. We find out that Jim comes to the Hebert plantation not because he wants to break from the past, but rather because he wants to
sustain it. Hence, when he wakes before work, Jim sits on the bed and
remembers:

> Thinking about her and remembering four, five, six years back. Remember-
> ing the nights coming in from the field and the big tub of hot water waiting
> for me; and Billie washing my back, and then us in that old Ford, heading
> for town. And dancing and dancing until late, and then hurrying back to
> that bed and loving, loving, loving until morning. Then hitting that field
> again, half dead, and then back and the tub of hot water and the dancing
> and the loving. (22)

"Maybe that's why [Daddy] hangs around here," he reflects. "It reminds him a little of the old place and he figures that one day you might pass by and decide to stop" (23). In an interesting turn, Jim refers to himself in the third person, as if to suggest a former persona, now lost. In this fragmented state, he is able to see the source of his pain but incapable of bringing the resources to bear in order to transcend it. Instead of playing the blues to achieve some emotional distance from the past, Jim hopes that Billie Jean will return to loose him from his self-imposed exile. Hence, Jim's present hinges on this faulty paradigm of memory, where all therapeutic means are located outside his purview; he cannot exert himself in any gesture oriented toward the future because he is trapped in the past.

This becomes clearer when, after a day of driving the tractor, Jim sits down with his guitar and starts to play.

> I sat on the steps and started playing the guitar. I thought about Billie Jean and played softly at first, then I tried to forget her and played something fast and hard. But I thought about her again and went back to the soft thing, then I tried to forget her and went back to the hard. (47)

Here, Jim's inability to sustain a tempo for the duration of a song suggests that he can neither reflect, which would call for a critical attitude toward the past, nor forget, which would lead him to improvise a new, concrete (for example, "hard") pattern for his life. For all his facility with tools and repair, Jim cannot engage in an act of self-repair, largely because he cannot conceptualize narrative as a form of labor. Though he plays the blues, in the passage above he demonstrates his inability to use it as a tool to put Billie Jean in a functional perspective. Sherley Anne Williams observes: "The blues deal with a world where the inability to solve a problem does not necessarily mean that one can, or ought to, transcend it. The internal strategy of the blues is action, rather than contemplation, for the song itself is the creation of reflection."[9] In short, Jim is not yet a blues performer because he fails to yoke performance to the task of reflection. Though he plays in the quarters, he subordinates the importance of interrogating his own experience to using the blues as a way of consuming his leisure time. And because of the status that accrues from his work for Bonbon and Marshall Hebert, he sees no need to project labor into the personal sphere.

However, it is important to recognize that memory frames Jim's workday, an inversion of his life with Billie Jean where work is subordinate to physical pleasure. Indeed, the act of remembering is as much an act of labor for Jim as working on the tractor. Because of his propensity for positioning relief outside himself, his crisis of agency can be relieved only by the illusion of an aggregated self provided by work. Further, as a member of a community whose sole purpose on the plantation is labor, Jim has no recourse to power, save that which is offered by religion. His religious faith takes the form of conceptualizing God as an indifferent figure, insensitive to a fault. Though Jim makes the sign of the cross before he eats, he rarely prays, due to his feeling that He "d[oesn't] hear a word," having "quit listening to man a million years ago." In Jim's mind all God does is "play chess by Himself, or sit around playing solitary with old cards." The view of God as a figure of total neutrality, coupled with his apathy, indicates the level of Jim's self-imposed marginality. If he is a medial figure, he is likewise a marginal one; although he is far from indifferent about the plight of others, he lacks the self-interest necessary to question his own plight seriously. As such, he represents the communal voice in its most expedient form, where the needs of the individual are subordinated to the needs of the group. But Gaines's attention to Jim's specific form of hurt suggests that his narrative masks a deeper imperative.

Marcus's arrival in the quarters offers Jim an opportunity to discover a new kind of responsibility. Because the reader discerns the novel's events through Jim's consciousness, *Of Love and Dust* is a significant work of fiction because it refuses to allow the reader to identify with heroic action of an individual sort. Jim's narrative describes Marcus's actions, but these come to us through the filter of his communal bias. Since Gaines does not present Marcus in a romantic contour, we cannot step outside the quarters' point of view to see his actions in terms other than those Jim privileges in his narration. As a result, Marcus is the classic badman from African American folklore. Paradigmatically, Gaines's characterizations of Jim and Marcus evoke convergence and anomaly: the voices of the plantation "converge" in Jim's act of narration, and Marcus's actions are anomalous; they resist conventional practice. Indeed, he appears to be incapable of getting along or fitting in anywhere on the plantation.[10]

As I noted earlier, Jim's status on the plantation grows out of his "bilinguality," his ability to bridge discursive domains. However, this ability to mediate the boundaries between discursive systems works to cement, rather than challenge, the status quo. By contrast, Marcus is a figure of complete resistance, largely because he remains so self-interested. Soon after his arrival at the Hebert plantation, Marcus states, "I ain't cut out for this kind of life." Jim's narrative authority is such that we interpret this in the simplest terms possible: Marcus is unwilling to take responsibility for the man he killed, and thus life on a plantation is unacceptable. Further, because Jim recounts Marcus's uncooperative posture in a number of settings, Marcus appears, through Jim's credible narration, as a threat to communal well-being.

But we need to address the manner in which the reader is prevented from formulating an alternative reading. Though Jim's life is characterized by its conformity and apathy, what shapes his relationship with Marcus is his adherence to the past, to the workings of memory. Marcus, as self-centered antihero, focuses his attention on the present and, later, on the future. He may realize the danger of such an attitude, however much he values self-determination over group acceptance. In contrast, Jim's notion of self always functions within a system that produces either interdependence or approval. Thus, he tells Marcus, "You can't make it like that. . . . They got the world fixed where you have to work with other people" (235). But this statement articulates convergence, Jim's desire to participate in an established paradigm. Hence, he believes that community should be preserved at all cost, even if it means that the individual must relinquish a claim to the right to rebel.

Ironically, Marcus is victimized, at least partly, by the constraints of oral culture. According to Berndt Ostendorf, oral cultures

> never expand beyond the horizon of the present collective. They are finite and sedentary and, one should add, conservative and nationalistic. Their chauvinism is due to a strong adherence to a policy of withholding choice and stabilizing that balance of controls which has guaranteed survival until now. By way of compensation they will create a sense, however unfree, of togetherness and the means of ritual catharsis. But this will turn into a trap whenever any one member wants to assert his individuality and advance beyond the horizon of the group.[11]

As badman, Marcus is described as "the convict," with a reputation for making trouble for the group. As such, he threatens the quarters' sense of well-being. Jim's narrative, though sympathetic to Marcus's plight, remains fixed on Marcus's rebelliousness. These acts of resistance, large and small, challenge the rituals that shape and define relationships both within and without the quarters. For example, Marcus declines to wear khakis out to the field, choosing a silk shirt and dress shoes because he refuses to accept his lot on the plantation. In one of the novel's most humorous moments, he starts a brawl with Murphy Bacheron (another badman), a man "nobody [is] crazy enough to hit." As the brawl demonstrates, Marcus's rambunctious attitude is infectious to the point where the entire house erupts into violence. After attempting to woo Pauline, Bonbon's black mistress, and failing, he succeeds in seducing his wife, Louise. As the fence around Bonbon's house symbolizes, Louise is both prisoner and prize. In a setting that has such prohibitive racial and sexual taboos, this is a transgression of the highest order, one that will most certainly have an impact on the collective.

Marcus seizes upon this opportunity, despite the fact that it endangers both himself and the quarters. The reason for this, Ostendorf alludes, is that the quarters are expected to exercise control. As the brawl suggests, antisocial behavior is not problematic until it threatens white control of the plantation. The quarters, as represented by Jim, are responsible for holding Marcus's behavior in check. Because of this imperative, the egocentricity that informs his actions is interpreted as recklessness instead of resistance. This is so despite the fact that Marcus is clearly empowered by his liaison with Louise. Jim notices that when "Bonbon came out there in the evening he made [Marcus] sweat again. But he didn't seem to mind" (119). And though Jim threatens him, Marcus continues his attempt to get closer to the overseer's wife. Jim concludes, "Sure as hell, that sonofabitch is going to start trouble before all this is over with" (123).

Jim's prediction is correct. Marcus's relationship with Louise becomes a communal threat and as such inhibits communal activity. This indicates both the excessive nature of Marcus's power and the manner in which that power is simultaneously attractive and repellent. Marshall Hebert, the plantation owner, becomes intrigued with using the prospect of a physical confrontation between Marcus and Bonbon for his own ends. But it is here that we can begin to see the past's impact on the quarters' sense of possibility. Bishop, who serves as Hebert's butler, refers to Bonbon's brothers and observes, "That boy touch Bonbon, them brothers go'n ride" (122). He knows that the lynching ritual used to enforce the sexual taboo between black men and white women is strictly, and often blindly, administered.[12] The community's need to hold Marcus in check is indicative of the necessity to sacrifice the future to preserve the ritualized present. After they learn that Hebert has recruited Marcus to kill Bonbon, the quarters fear the kind of retribution Marcus's actions will precipitate. This is evidenced in Jim's description of the quarters:

Soon as I crossed the railroad tracks, I could see how dark and quiet the quarters was. There wasn't a light on in any house. There wasn't a child playing anywhere. Nobody sat out on the gallery waiting for supper to be done. Not even a speck of smoke came from any of the kitchen chimneys. The whole place was dark and quiet, it looked like everybody had moved away. But they hadn't moved away, they had locked themselves inside the houses. All of them had heard what Marcus was supposed to do and all of them was afraid. (270)

In the face of a paradigm that consists of resourcefulness and resistance, the people in the quarters hold fast to the old ways.

Most certainly Marcus is an individual to be feared by both the folk and the white plantation owner, for he possesses the potential, were it to become collectivized, to topple the plantation system. Because his self-interest takes on such hyperbolic forms, the overt and covert forms of rebellion he enacts break the cycle of small skirmishes that hold the status quo in place. Before Marcus arrives, the quarters are satisfied with small victories gained at the system's expense or with status that, like Jim's, is calibrated inward in order to create the illusion of upward mobility. However, the plantation can accommodate this type of resistance because it leaves the larger system of Jim Crow intact. But Marcus's single-mindedness argues that defying convention through open resistance is a viable route toward an integrated self. His lack of humility, in light of the ways in which Jim Crow promotes passivity and self-immolation, is at once therapeutic and disruptive. Thus, he tells Jim, "Stop being old fashioned. . . . Where would people be if they didn't take a chance? You know where? Right here. Right here in this quarter for the rest of they life" (248–49). The problem is that the quarters, because they exercise a collective memory, equate this form of individual risk-taking with death. Because Jim narrates through the collective vehicle, he renders Marcus's act of signifying completely inert. Jim's idolatrous relation to the past makes him incapable of switching the valence of Marcus's assertion from negative to positive.

This prevents him from seeing that, as a figure of resistance, Marcus is sufficiently empowered to confront history. This is best exemplified when he puts his foot in the door to the Hebert house to keep Bishop from closing it in his face. The plantation's historical continuity with slavery is ruptured, and thus, Bishop tells Jim, "He just pushed his foot in there. . . . The house his great-grandparents built. The house slavery built. He pushed his foot in that door" (215). Bishop, comfortable as a house servant via the status quo, knows that Marcus threatens not only his status but the viability of the system that creates it. Marcus's transgressive act ruptures the plantation's illusion of pastoral tranquillity. But more than this, it reveals the spurious relationship between racial inferiority and history. Though Marcus's actions could empower the inhabitants of the quarters, their lack of interpretive equipment leads them to feel only fear and ambivalence: fear because they know that violence is a likely result and ambivalence because Marcus's actions unveil the plantation's illusion of order as unstable. Lacking a paradigm to implement in place of Jim Crow, they cannot conceptualize a way to emulate Marcus's behavior while turning it toward socially productive ends.

The other aspect of Marcus's resistant posture is his willingness to utilize Marshall Hebert as a resource to achieve his own ends. He knows that Hebert hates Bonbon and wants him to kill the overseer. Because blacks in the quarters are lower in the social hierarchy than either the plantation owners or the Cajuns, Hebert wants to manipulate Marcus by promising him that he will go free. This points at an important thread in Gaines's fiction. Despite the fact that self-defense led Marcus to kill Hotwater, African Americans' lack of standing in the Louisiana legal system nullifies this aspect of the narrative. Since the system does not place a high value on blacks' lives, acts of intraracial violence are seen as a drag on the system of due process reserved for whites. The result is that quasi-legal measures have been put in place to contend with intraracial violence: one can be sent to the state penitentiary or bonded out to a plantation and work off the time. Lacking access to the self-defense plea after he kills Hotwater, Marcus must exploit the class conflict existing between the plantation owners and the Cajuns.[13] Although I stop short of arguing for Marcus as a character possessed with capabilities of revolutionary scope, it is important to note his ability to exploit the rift between Bonbon and Hebert to his own advantage.

Part of Jim's role as narrator of Marcus's tale is to recontextualize intraracial violence, to give it a new meaning. In this sense, Jim represents the kind of perspectival shift necessary to see the macrosignificance of events taking place on the Hebert plantation. Thus, at the end of the novel Jim observes:

And what had Marcus done that was so wrong? Yes, he had killed—yes, yes— but didn't they give him the right to kill? I had been thinking about this in the field all evening and I had said to myself, "Yes, yes; it's not Marcus, it's them. Marcus was just the tool. Like Hotwater was the tool—put there to kill Marcus." (269)

This marks Jim's realization that the "plantation system" is not a source of steady labor, but an intricately designed drama whose aim is to keep blacks in their place by pitting them against one another. By constructing Marcus, Hotwater, Bonbon, Pauline, and Louise as "tools," Jim redefines the nature of work and recognizes his own complicity in the plantation scheme. The Hebert plantation offers the illusion that black labor resides outside a historical context, but it requires the individual to disconnect memory and narrative. Its numerous episodes of brutality and violence have sufficient repressive force to make physical labor a hindrance to acts of memory. Hence through labor Jim can indulge his escapist impulse and thus provide a surrogate for a life with Billie Jean, a way of confining his marginality to a personal axis without considering the social axis. He must realize that he, too, is a tool: in assisting, in even a removed way, to break Marcus he is maintaining both his own illusory status and the plantation's racial hierarchy.

Throughout his stay on the Hebert plantation, Marcus's propensity to satisfy his immediate desires clashes with Jim's more deliberate, community-minded routine. Jim's status as narrator effectively prevents the reader from making a positive judgment of Marcus's behavior. However, this is due to the fact that the latter's rebelliousness and self-centeredness are seen through the lens of family and community. Within such contexts, these characteristics are injurious, if not potentially destructive.[14] But Marcus's act of manipulating the legal system (and Marshall Hebert) in order to be with Louise requires, as Jim comes to realize, radical vision and courage to pull it off. Further, seeing Marcus within the framework of the plantation hierarchy, as a cog in a larger machine, forces Jim to shift his point of view from the quarters as microcosm to the South as macrocosm. This gesture marks Jim's shift in political consciousness and argues that Marcus is the anomaly that prefigures the paradigmatic shift of the civil rights activity of the next decade.

We must also remember Jim's original relationship to machines: the source of his medial status. However, this status is an illusion. Though it ushers him into a kind of quasi-intimacy with Bonbon, inevitably his narrative status is compromised because he is forced to remain neutral in plantation matters that would threaten his status as driver. In short, if Jim is to reach a narrative space where his voice can articulate the need to break out of the stasis that entraps him, he needs Marcus's defiance. What this means is that *Of Love and Dust* is, in Patricia Waugh's words, a "self-begetting novel."[15] Hence, we are forced to consider the tone of Jim's narration after reading the novel because of its abrupt shift. For this shift seemingly coincides with Marcus's transition from badman to hero and likewise marks Jim's transformation from mediator to bluesman. I would argue, though, that this shift is an illusory one. The novel has been a story about Jim all along. Thus, we can account for his change in attitude toward Marcus:

> No, I didn't blame Marcus anymore. I admired Marcus. I admired his great courage. And that's why I wanted to hurry up and get to the front. That's why my heart had jumped when the tractor went dead on me—I was afraid I wouldn't be able to tell him how much I admired what he was doing. I wanted to tell him how brave I thought he was. He was the bravest man I knew, the bravest man I had ever met. (270)

Jim sees Marcus's attitude of resistance as the correct response to a confined state of being. Though the plantation almost breaks Marcus (and Gaines does suggest that Marcus undergoes a transformation of his own), Jim realizes that Marcus's refusal to let go of his plan to run away is not a sign of irresponsibility. Rather, it is Marcus's refusal to allow a corrupt system to define what he should value and how he should live.

Though it is clear that Jim's transformation is substantive because it exposes the gap between de jure and de facto legal practice that the Civil Rights movement would later exploit, I want to suggest that neither Marcus's small (and failed) rebellion nor Jim's narration for that matter brings about large-scale, concrete changes on the plantation, for Jim's observation regarding Marshall Hebert is correct: "He was police, he was judge, he was jury" (198). But Jim's story does serve another, albeit abstract, purpose: his voice stands against written representation of the event. By disclosing what we know from Aunt Margaret will become a secret discourse, Jim's voice bursts from the constraints of coded discourse to establish the political element undergirding blues performance.

Further, we can see Jim's narrative as one that abandons disillusionment for faith. Though Marcus is killed before he can escape, what Jim embraces when he decides to see him off is the hidden potential of rebellion, the possibility of its success. Jim's workday is disrupted by Marcus's escape, which points to a more symbolic breakthrough; the memory of Billie Jean (the source of his ruined potential) is preempted as the iconographic force in his life and remade into a cipher, which means that Jim can assign her any kind of meaning he wishes, including that of a figure rendered inert by the past.

*   *   *   *   *

Although Gaines gives no indication of a restoration of Jim's religious faith, it is certain that he has recovered his integrity. This is best evidenced when he goes to see Marshall Hebert after Marcus's death. When Hebert offers Jim a letter of recommendation, it is at once a warning for Jim to leave the plantation and a commodity whose price is Jim's silence about what happened. However, in a revision of Bledsoe's letters of introduction in *Invisible Man*, Jim opens the letter, reads it, and tells Hebert, "No, sir, I'll get by. . . . Thanks very much" (278). Jim eschews the blind innocence that seals the fate of Ellison's hero, choosing instead to read beneath the surface of the text. This kind of active literacy occasions self-determination and thus allows Jim to break out of the cycle of corruption underpinning the plantation's hierarchy.

The necessity of Jim's departure is understood by all the folk in the quarters. Indeed, in his final exchange with Aunt Margaret (a source of Jim's narrative reach) we see how the community's memory is selective, if not repressive. "Yes, you got to leave. . . . You see you won't forget," Aunt Margaret observes. When Jim asks, "You done forgot already, Aunt Margaret?" she responds in the affirmative (279).

In a community so committed to oral history and storytelling, one would be hard pressed to believe Aunt Margaret's claim. It does, however, imply several issues. First, she asserts that on matters of interracial contact, memory and silence are an inseparable compound; to break silence and enjoin memory in such an instance is to invite punishment, if not death. Second, she knows that Jim's transformation is such that he will create a new amalgamation: he will remember Marcus, what happened to him and why, and (perhaps most important) why he was a hero. Because of this, there is no way he can live within the constraints of the Hebert plantation.

The weight of Jim's act is further underscored by the novel's last scene. As Jim departs, Aunt Margaret accompanies him to the road. But after only a short distance he observes, "When I looked over my shoulder, I saw her going back home" (281). The old woman's return to the plantation signals the solitary nature of Jim's choice: his liberation is singular. Moreover, the growing distance between him and Aunt Margaret, when contrasted with the novel's opening scene (where Marcus emerged out of the dust) suggests Jim's break with the past. In this sense, she is a double for Billie Jean, who turned her back on Jim to go elsewhere. Here, however, Jim abandons mnemonic fixation in favor of self-interest.

Jim is perhaps best characterized in terms of what Wayne Booth refers to as the privileged narrator.[16] He has access to all the people who can give his narrative its fullest shape; when his physical presence at events is not possible, he fills in these gaps through members of the community who tell him what happens. But at no point does he make the claim that the story he relates is his own. He is a narrator, whose act of telling is unsupported or corrected by the "implied author" of the text. It is left to the reader to infer that Jim's departure from the Hebert plantation and the narrative that leads up to it are interconnected. Indeed, it is necessary for the reader to perform an act of "revision" on Aunt Margaret's receding form at the novel's end.[17] Though Jim's gaze captures the moment as the end of his life on the Hebert plantation and thus the end of his life in a familiar (and loving) community, the reader must read against this impulse and equate the moment with narrative possibility. The reader gets no help from Jim in reaching this conclusion. Kelly's telling of the tale is linear (with the exception of the flashbacks he weaves into the tale to correct narrative gaps): it begins with Marcus's arrival and ends with his own departure. Further, the events of the tale and its telling take place in the same calendar year. We know this because of Jim's observation, early in the novel, that Marcus's grandmother Julie Rand has calendars on her wall that date "from the late thirties up to *this year—forty-eight*" (10, my emphasis).

Hence, one cannot assert that *Of Love and Dust* is a framed tale, unless one points out that the reader is responsible for constructing the frame around the tale. Although Jim's narrative contains questions and answers to questions from the person Jim is addressing throughout the novel, at no time does he comment on his departure. If anything, he remains in the performance mode; his act of disclosure relies on his ability to sustain his narrative's illusion as Marcus's story. Thus, Jim's narrative is one of diminishing unreliability and increasing ambivalence. It represents the former because the tale is increasingly about how Marcus's resistance liberated him, and the latter because he is in a liminal state, the character of which he refuses to acknowledge to the reader. He can offer commentary on the circumstances surrounding Marcus's death because they represent the race rituals that force his separation from the plantation's illusion of comfort.

The liminal space that Jim occupies eschews connection to a community and thus allows him to give voice to thoughts that race ritual would either privatize or silence altogether. And because the plantation insists that racial memory function in the service of self-restraint, Jim's use of memory as a catalyst for talking about racial matters signals a profound shift. His act of narrative disclosure allows him to address himself to "the color-line." Despite the fact that he has spent a long time working on a plantation, trapped in lockstep with the past, Jim articulates a profoundly twentieth-century tale.

The novel leaves space, then, not only for Jim's transformation, but for the reader's as well. Because the reader is seduced into an interpretation of Marcus as badman, Jim's change in attitude has the potential to catch the reader completely off-guard, to produce a feeling of ambivalence. This is so largely because Jim's medial status allows him to fulfill the reader's desire to see and hear events that he himself has not witnessed. Thus, Jim can indulge the reader's voyeuristic impulse, especially as it pertains to Marcus and Louise. When Jim's narrative discloses Marcus's death and thus enables the shifts to a metahistorical reading, it indicts the impulse to truncate historical utterance (in contrast to "written" history) because it identifies Marcus as a "tool" whose utility depends on the imagination of the teller.

We must understand Jim's movement from innocence to insight (in light of the fact that he does not approve of Marcus's tactics for the larger portion of the novel) as a transition from rote learning to imagination. The duration of Marcus's time is devoted to figuring out ways to beat the system, which Jim sees as self-serving and defeatist. But this is due to his propensity to see events through the lens of community. What this indicates is Gaines's reworking of the conversion narrative: Jim moves from the sin of idolatry (where the past is an idol he refuses to relinquish) to the salvation of narrative (where he eschews an idol for a process). It is a secular salvation, to be sure. However, only by weighing Jim's act of self-disclosure within the novel's unannounced circularity does this become clear. Though he is free from the collective stasis of the quarters, we have no way of knowing what awaits him beyond the plantation. Gaines's unwillingness to "lift the veil" and thus allow us to see Jim's present location speaks to the way in which breaks from the past are disorienting. Perhaps the key here is that Jim's "invisibility" corresponds to his newly found (or recovered) ability to enjoin the imagination. For it takes an act of imagination to see Marcus Payne as a courageous figure, to see his individualism as a way of projecting a resilient self. In this sense, *Of Love and Dust* fits in with other African American narratives in which protagonists must break out of a static community to establish viable identities. One thinks here of W. E. B. DuBois's John in "Of the Coming of John," Paule Marshall's Selina in *Brown Girl, Brownstones,* and Toni Morrison's Pecola Breedlove in *The Bluest Eye.* In each of these texts, we find protagonists who, for a variety of reasons, find community repressive.[18] Though not all are successful in this quest, each text argues that the effort is worthwhile. Ernest Gaines has written a novel that proffers a doubled form of closure: the ending—much like the blues—is at once tragic and triumphant. What this suggests is that memory and the acts of voice that accompany it are vehicles of identity that require imagination to make the destination a reality.

Notes

1. Some of the fictions that fall into this category are Ann Petry's *The Street,* Ralph Ellison's *Invisible Man,* David Bradley's *The Cheyneysville Incident,* Alice Walker's *The Color Purple,* Paule Marshall's *Praisesong for the Widow,* and various short stories by James Alan McPherson.

2. This chapter builds on Craig Werner's essay entitled "Tell Old Pharoah: The Afro-American Response to Faulkner," found in *The Southern Review* (Autumn 1983). It seems to me that Gaines's hero pursues a pattern that Faulkner's protagonists (one thinks here of Quentin Compson and Ike McCaslin), through gestures that privilege the past in their lives, elect not to follow.

3. We find that several African American scholars have addressed themselves to the importance of African American performance as a kind of "both/and" modality. For example, Michael S. Harper coins the term the "collective-I" in his liner notes for the album *John Coltrane.* As he configures it in the blues, the "collective-I" marks an instance in which the audience hears their individual experiences articulated within the performer's song. In short, the audience hears "we" as the performer sings "I." Consider this alongside Ralph Ellison's observation that "the jazz moment" is an instance in which the performer's expression occurs both "in and against the group," which means, again, that community (or traditional) issues of performance must not overshadow individual ones. Ellison's remarks can be found in his essay "The Charlie Christian Story," in *Shadow and Act* (New York: Vintage Books, 1964; reprint, 1972). Again we see how both speak to the idea that the notion of individuality must be carefully balanced against the idea of the group.

4. Sherley Anne Williams, *Give Birth to Brightness* (New York: Dial Press, 1972), 169.

5. John O'Brien, *Interviews with Black Writers* (New York: Liveright, 1973).

6. Ibid.

7. Ernest J. Gaines, *Of Love and Dust* (New York: Dial Press, 1967; reprint, 1979). All further references are to this edition.

8. Ralph Ellison, "Richard Wright's Blues," in *Shadow and Act* (New York: Vintage Books, 1964; reprint, 1972), 78.

9. Sherley Anne Williams, "The Blues Roots of Contemporary Afro-American Poetry," in *Chant of Saints* (Urbana: University of Illinois Press, 1979), 125.

10. The language I use here is consciously drawn from Thomas Kuhn's ground-breaking study of scientific research and process, *The Structure of Scientific Revolutions* (Chicago: University of Chicago Press, 1962; reprint, 1970).

11. Berndt Ostendorf, *Black Literature in White America* (Totowa, N.J.: Barnes and Noble Books, 1982). Although Ostendorf's analysis clarifies the nature of Marcus's plight, it is also important to note how closely Marcus resembles the "badman" examined in chapter 5 of John Roberts's fine study of the folk hero in African American expressive culture, *From Trickster to Badman* (Philadelphia: University of Pennsylvania Press, 1989). In the instance of Marcus, I would argue that the novel's plot revolves around the way that Marcus moves, at least in Jim's estimation, from "bad nigger" to "badman." Marcus's actions are perceived as being self-serving at the community's expense, but in fact his actions (set in the 1940s) are the paradigm for the kinds of resistance that will later characterize the Civil Rights (and later, black nationalist) movement of the 1960s. In this regard, we can consider characters like Marcus and Morrison's Sula as figures who articulate a new design for African American identity. Their problem is that there is no place for them because the social conditions necessary to absorb their uniqueness do not yet exist.

12. As Keith Byerman observes, open resistance in Gaines's fiction is often punished by death. *Fingering the Jagged Grain* (Athens: University of Georgia Press, 1986), 67.

13. This is a theme that Gaines first explored in his collection of stories entitled *Bloodline.* In the story "Three Men," Gaines creates a character named Proctor Lewis, who chooses to remain in jail rather than being bonded out after killing a man. Gaines noted in an interview with John O'Brien: "I should point out that Proctor Lewis and Marcus Payne are the same character; I wanted to show what would have happened to Proctor Lewis had he gotten out of prison, the chances he would have taken to attain his freedom" (81). What this suggests is that Gaines is interested in the forces acting on black manhood as well as the forms black resistance assumes "when young blacks stand up against the establishment."

14. In this regard, Marcus is literary kin to Morrison's Sula, whom Morrison describes as having an "experimental life" and who, "lacking an art form," becomes dangerous to the Bottom because there is nothing to engage her rebellious individualism. Like Sula, Marcus represents a revolutionary figure whose premature arrival makes him useful as a martyr but not as a leader. Lacking Jim's communal-mindedness, Marcus's behavior is self-oriented, and so he is incapable of assuming the leadership necessary to topple the plantation system as a whole.

15. Patricia Waugh, *Metafiction* (London: Methuen, 1984). Waugh defines the self-begetting novel as "an account, usually first-person, of the development of a character to a point at which he is able to take up and compose the novel we have just finished reading." From this perspective, Jim is "invisible," and his narrative is a sign of his burgeoning self-awareness.

16. Wayne Booth, *The Rhetoric of Fiction* (Chicago: University of Chicago Press, 1982), 159–60.

17. Credit for the term *revision,* as I use it here, goes to Adrienne Rich.

18. What these protagonists share is a position that is, like Jim's, characterized

by liminality. John returns to the South and finds that he is no longer comfortable in the folk community, even as he realizes the difficulties of enduring the degradation of Jim Crow. His dilemma is resolved by his death. Selina, at the end of Marshall's novel, departs to return to her native Barbados, leaving what is described as "the wreckage" of urban living behind. Finally, Morrison's Pecola moves into the space of insanity, forever apart from the family that have proved themselves incapable of loving her and the community that can find no way to affirm her.

Works Cited

Booth, Wayne. *The Rhetoric of Fiction*. Chicago: University of Chicago Press, 1982.

Byerman, Keith. *Fingering the Jagged Grain*. Athens: University of Georgia Press, 1986.

Ellison, Ralph. "The Charlie Christian Story." In *Shadow and Act*. New York: Vintage Books, 1964: Reprint, 1972.

———. "Richard Wright's Blues." In *Shadow and Act*. New York: Vintage Books, 1964: Reprint, 1972.

Gaines, Ernest J. *Bloodline*. New York: Norton, 1976.

———. *Of Love and Dust*. New York: Dial Press, 1967: Reprint, 1979.

Kuhn, Thomas. *The Structure of Scientific Revolutions*. Chicago: University of Chicago Press, 1962: Reprint, 1970.

O'Brien, John. *Interviews with Black Writers*. New York: Liveright, 1973.

Ostendorf, Berndt. *Black Literature in White America*. Totowa, N.J.: Barnes and Noble Books, 1982.

Roberts, John. *From Trickster to Badman*. Philadelphia: University of Pennsylvania Press, 1989.

Waugh, Patricia. *Metafiction*. London: Methuen, 1984.

Werner, Craig. "Tell Old Pharoah: The Afro-American Response to Faulkner." *Southern Review* 19 (Autumn 1985): 711–35.

Williams, Sherley Anne. "The Blues Roots of Contemporary Afro-American Poetry." In *Chant of Saints: A Gathering of Afro-American Literature,* edited by Michael S. Harper and Robert B. Stepto. Urbana: University of Illinois Press, 1979.

———. *Give Birth to Brightness*. New York: Dial Press, 1972.

Memory and the Matrix of History:

The Poetics of Loss and Recovery

in Joy Kogawa's *Obasan*

and Toni Morrison's *Beloved*

GURLEEN GREWAL

Is it inevitable? . . . Are there moments in history which
cannot be escaped or transcended, but which act like time
warps permanently trapping all those who are touched by
them? . . . No one simply passes through. History keeps
unfolding and demanding a response. . . . Everything is
waiting for the emptiness to be filled up, for the filling-up
that can never replace, that can only take over. Like time
itself. Or history.
—Irena Klepfisz, "Bashert"

A matrix is a womb, a network, a rock bearing embedded
fossils, a rocky trace of a gemstone's removal.
—Houston Baker, Jr., *Blues, Ideology, and Afro-American Literature:
A Vernacular Theory*

Shuttles in the rocking loom of history,
the dark ships move, the dark ships move

. . . .
Voyage through death,
            voyage whose chartings are unlove.
Voyage through death
            to life upon these shores.
—Robert Hayden, "Middle Passage"

Our wholeness comes from joining and from sharing our
brokenness. . . . Rather than abandoning the way of brokenness, I believe we need to remember the paradoxical
power in mutual vulnerability. . . . Beyond our doubt and
confusion lies our capacity to recognize what suffering is

and where health lies and to identify with both. I believe
that it is the identification of and with suffering at every
level, in every condition and in every person that magnetizes the compass of justice and points us to home.
—Joy Kogawa, "Is There a Just Cause?"

Western historiography struggles against fiction," writes
Michel de Certeau. Fiction "narrates one thing in order to tell something
else. . . . It is a witch whom knowledge must labor to hold and to identify
through its exorcising. . . . It is only a drifting meaning. It is the siren
from whom the historian must defend himself, like Ulysses tied to the
mast."[1] Joy Kogawa's *Obasan* (1981) and Toni Morrison's *Beloved* (1987)
perform a different kind of exorcising. Personalizing their collective histories, breathing into the past the desires and disappointments of those
who *lived* those histories, these novels are the witchery of fiction challenging Certeau's historian/scholar to hear that which is unspeakable.
Beloved and *Obasan* are a remarkable pair of novels reconstituting the
historical experience of their respective marginalized people from the
vantage point of familial relationships, the mother-daughter relationship in particular. Familial ties wrenched in the past, through slavery (in
Beloved) and through the internment/relocations of Japanese Canadians
during World War II (in *Obasan*), become the novels' pervading concern;
articulating the pain and the far-reaching consequences of that sever-
ance is the central effort of both novels. If *Obasan* reflects the anguish of
a daughter, Naomi Nakane, separated from her mother during World
War II, *Beloved* explores the consciousness of an ex-slave mother, Sethe,
as she attempts to come to terms with the fact that she killed her own
daughter in order to save her from slavery. Together they take us through
what Barbara Christian calls "the chaotic space of mother-love / mother-
pain, daughter-love / daughter-pain."[2]

Morrison and Kogawa are writing against the figure of the historian as
deaf Ulysses, making us aware of the limitations of conventional historiography. When the latter is the dominant group's version of an oppressed group's experience, it becomes imperative that the elisions, the
repressions, and the silences be explored. In both novels, however, this
silencing also takes place within the oppressed community itself. Kogawa comments on the rationale for this deliberate amnesia: "The horror

would surely die sooner, they felt, if they refused to speak."[3] *Obasan,* a historical novel dedicated to the author's parents and to "those amazing people, the Issei [the first-generation immigrants from Japan]—the few who are still with us and those who have gone," is an elegy to the painful past. Likewise, Toni Morrison's *Beloved,* dedicated to the "Sixty Million and more" who made "the voyage through death," excavates the pain of that repressed knowledge, the "veil behind the veil" that has been "disremembered and unaccounted for," "deliberately forgot."[4] In both instances, the painful reliving of the past is liberating, marking as it does a contemporary reckoning of the group's own buried identity and history.

Obasan and *Beloved* are epitaphs, elegies, testimonies. Ceremonial performances of memory, these narratives enact the process of loss and recovery. Exhorting words from the speechless landscape of grief, the novels excavate, mourn, then ceremoniously bury the past. Memory's journey into the individual and collective past becomes the means of self-knowledge, catharsis, forgiveness, and release. For both writers, insofar as the individual embodies the collective, gaining access to the collective past means getting in touch with the individual experience of abandonment. Both novels mourn the breakup of the mother-daughter dyad, pried and swept asunder by the nightmare swirl of history (the Middle Passage and slavery in *Beloved,* the relocation camps and the atomic bombing of Nagasaki in *Obasan*) on to the shores of the living. The resulting wreckage, what Kogawa calls "the way of brokenness," what Morrison calls "the unspeakable," is the terrain of both novels.

Both writers succeed in making available the experience of trauma from multiple perspectives. They have undertaken similar challenges: how to name that which is both unnamed and unnameable, how to mediate between silence and speech, and how to transform this wreckage into a body of grace. For Toni Morrison it means exorcising the horror of the past, of getting in touch with it and then letting it go. Kogawa leads us finally to a perspective of suffering that is transpersonal, to a self whose limited boundaries have dissolved in love and compassion amidst the brokenness. In *Obasan,* the abandoned daughter is able to transcend her personal pain only when she enters the grief of the absent mother. Both writers' "identification of and with suffering at every level" magnetizes our "compass of justice and points us to home."

In an article addressed to the Canadian Caucus of Human Rights in 1983, Joy Kogawa writes of her own identity as a second-generation Japanese Canadian (Nisei):

My experience of the Japanese Canadians . . . is of a vastly and profoundly disparate and broken people. . . . Many Nisei, like myself, who suffered the drawn out trauma of racial prejudice during our formative and young adult years have a deep timidity burned into our psyches with the injunction that we must never again risk the visibility of community. Perhaps as a result, no Japan town exists anywhere in Canada today.[5]

Reflecting on the succession of traumatic events affecting Canadians of Japanese origin during World War II,[6] Naomi Nakane, the third-generation narrator of *Obasan,* commemorates the experience of all three generations—ranging from the Issei (such as her grandma Nakane), who were "too old then to understand political expedience, race riots, the yellow peril" (17), to the Sansei (such as herself), who were too little to do so. Between the incomprehension of the very old and the very young lies the burdensome story of the Nisei, the narrator's absent parents and her stoic foster parents, Uncle and Obasan. Imprisoned in Canadian camps, Naomi's father dies young of tuberculosis. The unexplained disappearance of her mother, who along with her grandma happened to be visiting relatives in Nagasaki, the site of the other holocaust of World War II, creates a void in the narrator's childhood that grows well into her adult life. The breaking of the long-held protective silence regarding her mother's terrible fate is what finally enables Naomi to come to terms with the past.

Naomi Nakane, the first-person narrator, informs us early in the novel of her family's coherence before the war and its fragmentation after it. "Like two needles," the narrator's parents had "knit [their] families carefully into one blanket" (20): on her mother's side the Katos, educated and well-to-do, and on her father's side the Nakanes, boat builders whose dedication to their craft had led to prosperity. However, we see that this extended family blanket has "become badly moth-eaten with time"; it is now "no more than a few tangled skeins: the remains of what might once have been a fisherman's net" (21). Naomi's family recover neither their fishing boats the Canadian government seized and gave to white Canadians nor their home in Vancouver, British Columbia, after they were evicted from it and sent to camps. But what is worse for "the original togetherness people" (20), the entire family is scattered: of the Nakanes, the very old grandparents are relocated away from their sons, one of whom—Naomi's father—is in the camps, while the other son, Uncle, and his childless wife (Obasan) are left with the grandchildren, Naomi and Stephen. Mother and Grandmother Kato, visiting family in Japan, are suspended there. The two sides, once lovingly knit by Naomi's parents, are decisively sundered: when Grandpa Kato and Aunt Emily petition for the family's relocation to Toronto, Uncle and Obasan, being Japanese nationals, are not permitted to accompany them. Remaining with Uncle and Obasan, Naomi and her brother are moved to Slocan, a ghost mining town in the interior of British Columbia. Here, with hard work, they manage to eke out a living; however, just as they are beginning to be comfortable, they are ordered to move to Alberta, where, in great hardship, they begin at zero again.

There are resonances here between the Japanese Canadian, Native American, and Jewish experiences of dispersal. Uncle, the fisherman who is displaced into the prairie interior of Alberta, is compared to Chief Sitting Bull, and Naomi refers to her brother, Stephen, as "one of the Israelite children moving unharmed through the fiery furnace" (205). The narrator observes that the government's persecution of her people had an effect that went beyond the loss of property: "The message to disappear worked its way deep into the Nisei heart and into the bone marrow" (184). Stephen's response to the heavy grief and humiliation is to escape from his Japanese identity. A successful musician, he assimilates into the Canadian mainstream. This response to loss—passing from a stigmatized identity into an acceptable one—is not atypical. But as Irena Klepfisz, a Jewish writer whose family experienced the Holocaust, points out, "No one simply passes through."[7] Stephen is not "unharmed": History claims him as it does his sister, Naomi. In his recurrent nightmare "about a metallic insect the size of a tractor, webbing a grid of iron bars over him," he finds himself "escap[ing] the web by turning the bars into a xylophone" (220). Music is his route of escape and solace, but it does not bring any kind of reconciliation with the past or resolution within the family. Escape such as his has its own torment. It is left to his sister to bridge the past and the present. Naomi, not Stephen, is Momotaro, the fabled Japanese hero who returns to his old foster parents after recovering the treasures that the ogres stole from their village. Momotaro's role of redressing the wrongs is shared by her brave aunt Emily, who refuses to heed the message of disappearance by insisting that "Momotaro is a Canadian story" (57).

The novel begins with a prologue that is like an incantation; the task of the poet-historian is great, for

> There is a silence that cannot speak.
> There is a silence that will not speak.
> Beneath the grass the speaking dreams and beneath the dreams is a sensate sea. The speech that frees comes forth from that amniotic deep. To

attend its voice, I can hear it say, is to embrace its absence. But I fail the task. The word is stone.

I admit it.

I hate the stillness. I hate the stone. I hate the sealed vault with its cold icon. I hate the staring into the night. . . .

Unless the stone bursts with telling, unless the seed flowers with speech, there is in my life no living word. The sound I hear is only sound. White sound. Words, when they fall, are pock marks on the earth. They are hailstones seeking an underground stream.

If I could follow the stream down and down to the hidden voice, would I come at last to the freeing word? I ask the night sky but the silence is steadfast. There is no reply.

The novel then opens, in August 1972, on the anniversary of the bombing of Nagasaki, with a memorable staging of two human figures under an "unimaginably vast" prairie sky, in a landscape of "infinite night" and stretches of uncut prairie grass of Southern Alberta, Canada (3). We learn that they, a gentle, "too much old man" called "Uncle" and his niece, the narrator, have come here every year since 1954 and that there is something he knows that he will not tell her. The narrator descends into the coulee bottom to pick a flower—also an annual ritual—growing by the riverbank; we see her "inch her way down the steep path" where "the slope oozes wet from the surface seepage of the underground stream," and she "can hear the gurgling of the slowly moving water" (4). In this metaphorical language, stone and moving water signify the damming and release of emotion; memory that is not accessed is likened to a "sealed vault with its cold icon": the past that is not retrieved is just a gravestone, cold, still, and lifeless. To reach memory, the narrator must descend to a subterranean realm: beneath the grass the speaking dreams (the subconscious) and beneath the dreams a sensate sea, the source of fluid, freeing speech. The vast and deep sense of unmitigated solitude evoked by the "infinite night" of "the prairie sky" builds in the first few pages, and we find at the heart of the narrative the speechlessness of grief, a realm where language breaks down into monosyllables of muteness. The narrative present of 1972 continues with Uncle's death in September, survived by his widow, Obasan, whose old body moves silently in a "different dimension of time" (44). Mediating between the living and the dead, between silence and speech is the solitary figure of the thirty-six-year-old narrator, Naomi Nakane. It is in the wake of Uncle's death that the past begins to unfold.

Through her own patchwork of memories and dreams, the narrator is patching the frayed family quilt, piecing together their story. In this effort, she is actively assisted by her aunt Emily, who is finally the only surviving member of the Katos. When separated from her niece, she communicated over the years via letters. Neither she, at fifty-six, nor Naomi, at thirty-six, is married or has children; they are both self-supporting single women who seem to have, the narrator remarks wryly, a "crone-prone syndrome" (8). The past has prior claims on both women. As the narrator notes, "Our attics and living-rooms [spatial metaphors for the past and the present] encroach on each other, deep into their invisible places" (25). Having lost both her mother and her sister in the atomic bombing of Nagasaki, Aunt Emily's entire life is consumed by her engagement with history. The latter means documenting the known truth of what her relatives and friends lost at the hands of the racist government in Canada: their dignity, their homes, their health, their families. Gathering information, documenting facts, revealing the injustices of the past, becomes her life's work. In her vocation as her community's historian, she finds and raises her voice. It is through reading the documents and letters in Aunt Emily's package, given to her after Uncle's death, that Naomi begins to assimilate the past. Only at the end of her recollections do she and the reader learn of Grandma Kato and Mother's destruction in the catastrophe of Nagasaki—the horror of which has been kept secret all this time.

In *Obasan,* the narrative of the past is constructed and told through several narrative mediums. Kogawa employs the power of both documentary prose and poetic images accenting in elliptical haiku fashion the silent syllables of grief. The most overt telling is through Emily's newspaper clippings, letters, and diaries. The most covert telling is through Uncle's and Obasan's eloquent silences. Mediating between these two forms are Naomi's personal memories.

The diary entries Aunt Emily addresses to her elder sister, Naomi's mother in Japan, become the means by which the novel generates a powerful documentary narrative. Beginning on 25 December 1941 and ending on 21 May 1942, the diary entries document a sinister progression of events, the initial hopeful tone, evincing faith in Canadian democracy, changing to bewilderment, pain, and outrage.

> You should see the faces here—all pinched, grey, uncertain. Signs have been posted on all highways—"Japs keep out." . . . One letter in the paper says that in order to preserve the "British way of life," they should send us all away. We're a "lower order of people." In one breath we are damned for being "inassimilable" and the next there's fear that we'll assimilate. (86–87)

Then come the seizing of fishing boats and other property, evacuation from homes, imprisonment in camps, enforced labor, and relocation—

old people, children, men, and women,"shuttles in the rocking loom of history," moved from place to place: "We just disperse. It's as if we never existed. We're hit so many ways at one time that if I wasn't past feeling I think I would crumble" (88). And then the cataloguing of horrors: "Mothers are prostrate in nervous exhaustion—the babies crying endlessly—the fathers torn from them without farewell—everyone crammed into two buildings like so many pigs—children taken out of school with no provision for future education" (91). One also gets a sense of the energy, resilience, and determination of Aunt Emily and the others' "worrying, figuring, going bats with indecision" (106) to keep the family together in the face of the impersonal, relentless, and chameleon-like commission orders. And then the admission of defeat: "I asked too much of God" (106): the Nakanes (being Japanese nationals) are not permitted to relocate to Toronto with the Katos, and the family is further fragmented.

The narrative oscillates between Aunt Emily's forthright and cleansing vociferousness, her "billions of letters and articles and speeches, her tears and her rage," and Naomi's quiet and haunting meditations on the past, informed by Uncle and Obasan's stoic language of silence. That is, the narrative moves from the documentary realm of public facts to the undocumented world of emotions, the shadowy world of memories, of the lived and livid history that eludes documentation. Registering the necessity of both facts and the subjective truths of memory—the novel alternates between these two modes of understanding the past—Kogawa clearly values and enacts the "drifting meaning" that evades speech. Returned from a conference in California called the Asian Experience in North America, Aunt Emily educates her niece with a pamphlet entitled *Racial Discrimination by Orders-in-Council;* the narrator responds:

> There it was in black and white—our short harsh history. Beside each date were the ugly facts of the treatment given to Japanese Canadians. "Seizure and government sale of fishing boats. Suspension of fishing licences. Relocation. Liquidation of property. Letter to General MacArthur. Bill 15. Deportation. Revocation of nationality."
> Wherever the words "Japanese race" appeared, Aunt Emily has crossed them out and written "Canadian citizen." (33)

As her aunt goes on vehemently about the various injustices, the narrator admits: "I felt she should have electrocuted me. But I was curiously numb beside her" (34). In other words, she seems to say, here are all the facts we need to know, but they are dry and disembodied. Fiction yields a different kind of truth, the truth of the emotions; in Toni Morrison's words, "Facts can exist without human intelligence, but truth cannot" ("Site of Memory," 113). And it is the embodied truth, the living word Kogawa is after. Musing on her two aunts, the narrator wonders: "How different my two aunts are. One lives in sound, the other in stone. Obasan's language remains deeply underground but Aunt Emily, BA, MA, is a word warrior. She's a crusader, a little old grey-haired Mighty Mouse, a Bachelor of Advanced Activists and General Practitioner of Just Causes" (32). Observing Obasan, the old woman who had reared her in her mother's absence, the narrator notes: "The language of her grief is silence. She has learned it well, its idioms, its nuances. Over the years, silence within her small body has grown large and powerful" (14). Here is the other drifting meaning of history. And it is powerful with its own truth.

Aspects of both aunts blend in this narrative. In the vocal energy of Aunt Emily, the narrator implies the value of setting the record straight, of asserting one's rights. Bulldozing Aunt Emily's "marathon talking" is the medium by which the government's sham of democracy is laid bare:

> "... Why in a time of war with Germany and Japan would our government seize the property and homes of Canadian-born Canadians but not the homes of German-born Germans?" she asked angrily.
> "Racism," she answered herself. (38)

Naomi is caught between the silent modality of grief and nonverbal communion, as represented by Uncle and Obasan, and vocal modality of protest and verbal articulation, as represented by Aunt Emily. As a character whose identity since childhood has been ravaged by the injustices of the past, Naomi finds Aunt Emily's words curiously remote and empty, hot air. They do not touch the stillness of her grief. They do not reach the water of her buried emotions. The deepest part of her is aloof, cut off. Naomi comments on crusading Aunt Emily with her paper tanks and paper "missiles" aimed at the injustices of her world: "Like Cupid, she aimed for the heart. But the heart was not there" (40). Slogans and pamphlets do not reach Naomi's heart. (We recall the prologue: "The sound I hear is only sound.") What does not reach the heart does not transform or heal it. Aunt Emily's confrontational mode leaves Naomi speechless: "From both Obasan and Uncle I have learnt that speech often hides like an animal in a storm" (3).

However, the perspectives of both speech and silence are strategic to the novel's account of the past. It is Aunt Emily's parcel, containing her life's mission, and her quest for justice that stir Naomi into active recollection: "I untie the loose twine from around the middle of the envelope and a note falls loose and drops to the floor": "Write the vision and make it plain. Habbakuk 2:2" (31). Naomi confesses that unlike Aunt Emily "beaming her flashlight" upon "a dark field," she is among those who "crouch and hide, our eyes downcast as we seek the safety of invisibility"; that while the vision is "plain" to Aunt Emily, the "truth for me is more murky, shadowy, and grey. But on my lap, her papers are wind and fuel nudging my early morning thoughts to flame" (31–32). In their different but complementing ways, then, these spinsters, aunt and niece, produce together the family and group history.

But we realize that archival documentation is one thing, and bodily remembering is another. In the resistance that Naomi offers Aunt Emily one also detects the reluctance of the traumatized to activate their memory, to confront their deep wounds. In 1972, Naomi finds herself reluctant to go through Aunt Emily's package of documents. She acknowledges the value of the papers "piled as neatly as the thin white wafers": they are "symbols of communion, the materials of communication, white paper bread for the mind's meal" (182). But Naomi counts herself among the "unwilling communicants receiving and consuming a less than holy nourishment, our eyes, cups filling with the bitter wine of a loveless communion" (182). She is bone-weary. "Do I really want to read these? . . . I want to get away from all this. From the past and all these papers, from the present, from the memories, from the deaths, from Aunt Emily and her heap of words. . . . What does it all matter in the end?" Her deep fatigue, despair, and sense of futility are countered by Emily's voice: "It matters to get the facts straight. . . . Reconciliation can't begin without mutual recognition of facts. . . . What's right is right. What's wrong is wrong. Health starts somewhere" (183). That decisive affirmation by Aunt Emily eventually produces in Naomi the desire to confront the bitter past. Recalling her aunt's emphasis on getting the facts right, Naomi cries out:

> The fact is that, in 1945, the gardens of Slocan were spectacular. In the spring . . . the plants were ripening for harvest when the orders came. The fact is that families already fractured and separated were permanently destroyed. The choice to go east of the Rockies or to Japan was presented without time for consultation with separated parents and children. (183)

Health starts somewhere. And Emily, "the general practitioner of just causes," helps her niece along the process of remembering. While describing her house in Vancouver, the one that had contained the fondest memories of her mother and father, the narrator falters, overcome by emotion: "It is more splendid than any house I have lived in since. It does not bear remembering. None of this bears remembering" (49). It is at this juncture that she recalls her aunt's advice.

> "You have to remember," Aunt Emily said. "You are your history. If you cut any of it off you're an amputee. Don't deny the past. Remember everything. If you're bitter, be bitter. Cry it out! Scream! Denial is gangrene. . . ."
> All right, Aunt Emily, all right! The house then—the house, if I must remember it today, was large and beautiful. (50)

Naomi is provoked into expressing painful memories about the hardships of exile in Alberta when she finds in Emily's package a single newspaper clipping and an index card with the words "Facts about evacuees in Alberta." But here the facts are not facts. "The newspaper clipping has a photograph of one family, all smiles, standing around a pile of beets. The caption reads: "Grinning and Happy" (193). The matter-of-fact report about "Japanese evacuees develop[ing] into most efficient beet workers," quietly incenses Naomi.

> Facts about evacuees in Alberta? The fact is I never got used to it and I cannot, I cannot bear the memory. There are some nightmares from which there is no waking, only deeper and deeper sleep. . . . Aunt Emily, are you a surgeon cutting at my scalp with your folders and your filing cards and your insistence on knowing all? The memory drains down the side of my face, but it isn't enough, is it? It's your hands in my abdomen, pulling the growth from the lining of my walls, but bring back the anaesthetist turn on the ether clamp down the gas mask bring on the chloroform when will this operation be over Aunt Em? (194)

And with the older woman serving as a midwife to her niece who carries the unshared burden of the past, the narrator proceeds to deliver the painful account of "how it was" in Granton, Alberta: the extremes of heat and cold, the unrelenting physical labor and fatigue, the daily humiliating privations. Above all, she gives expression to the sense of being deeply hurt by an indifferent universe. The open horizon of blue sky with clear clouds offers no consolation: "The clouds are the shape of our new prison walls—untouchable, impersonal, random" (196). No matter how expansive the physical universe, Naomi is a prisoner of her own consciousness that is locked in the past, "unable to shout or sing or dance, unable to scream or swear, unable to laugh, unable to breathe out loud" (183).

> But we're trapped, Obasan and I, by our memories of the dead—all our dead—those who refused to bury themselves. Like threads of old spider webs,

still sticky and hovering, the past waits for us to submit, or depart. When I least expect it, a memory comes skittering out of the dark, spinning and netting the air, ready to snap me up and ensnare me in old and complex puzzles. Just a glimpse of a worn-out patchwork quilt and the old question comes thudding out of the night like a giant moth. Why did my mother not return? (26)

Paradoxically, freedom from the tyranny of the past can be had only by submitting to it. The painful operation of memory is not over until Naomi's psyche has confronted the core of the pain in her body—"the body [that] will not tell" (196)—and in her own self-image, where the pain of a collective trauma finds its specific idiosyncratic expression. For Naomi the unexplained permanent disappearance of her mother is guilt-ily connected with the secret incident of the childhood sexual abuse she suffered at the hands of a neighbor, Old Man Gower. This self-inflicted guilt is strengthened by the absence of knowledge about her mother. For Naomi history is "murky," full of what she does not know: "The memo-ries were drowned [by the elders] in a whirlpool of protective silence. . . . Kodomo no tame. For the sake of the children" (21). But there is no protection from history. To not confront the past is to be "consumed" by it and "devoured alive"; it is to be suspended in time and space. Naomi notes: "I am sometimes not certain whether it is a cluttered attic in which I sit, a waiting room, a tunnel, a train. There is no beginning and no end to the forest . . . no edge from which to know where the clearing begins. Here, in this familiar density, beneath this cloak, within this carapace, is the longing within the darkness" (111). Having lived a childhood of painful exile and led an existence of loss, powerlessness, and not knowing, at thirty-six Naomi realizes she is "unwilling to live with randomness" (5). Thirsting for meaning, for understanding and de-liverance, her memory leads her to Old Man Gower and the secret abuse that marked for the four-year-old Naomi the first and permanent separa-tion from her mother.

> "Don't tell your mother," he whispers into my ear. This is what he always says. Where in the darkness has my mother gone?
> I am clinging to my mother's leg, a flesh shaft that grows from the ground, a tree trunk of which I am an offshoot—a young branch attached by right of flesh and blood. . . . But here in Mr. Gower's hands I become other. . . . My arms are vines that strangle the limb to which I cling. . . . If I tell my mother about Mr. Gower, the alarm will send a tremor through our bodies and I will be torn from her. But the secret has already separated us. The secret is this: I go to seek Old Man Gower in his hideaway. I clamber unbidden onto his lap. His hands are frightening and pleasurable. In the center of my body is a rift.

... My mother is on one side of the rift. I am on the other. We cannot reach each other. My legs are being sawn in half. (65)

Naomi suffers from the victim's guilt at her "participation" in her own sexual abuse. The child is unable to make sense of the contradictory but typical responses to such abuse: "I do not wish him to lift me up" (61); "If I am still, I will be safe" (62); "I do not resist. One does not resist adults" (63); "His hands are frightening and pleasurable"; "I am ashamed" (64). Her self-loathing at her own seeming complicity condemns her to secrecy and silence. This story of the daughter's separation from her mother recalls one of the oldest of patriarchal myths: the Greek myth of Persephone's separation from earth mother Demeter by Pluto's abduction of the daughter into the underworld. However, in Naomi's case, it is not the daughter who disappears but the mother, whose absence is mourned by a daughter whose grief is inconsolable because it is compounded by guilt:

> It is around this time [of Gower's sexual abuse of Naomi] that mother disappears. *I hardly dare to think, let alone ask, why she has to leave.* Questions are meaningless. What matters to my five-year-old mind is not the reason she is required to leave, but the stillness of waiting for her to return. After a while, the stillness is so much with me that it takes the form of a shadow which grows and surrounds me like air. Time solidifies, ossifies the waiting into molecules of stone, dark microscopic planets that swirl through the universe of my body waiting for light and the morning. (66, italics mine)

The simultaneous loss of her self-esteem and her mother and the endless waiting and unknowing subject Naomi to a life of profound sadness and silence. "A double wound. The child is forever unable to speak. The child forever fears to tell" (243). Freud defines sadness as "the most archaic expression of a non-symbolizable unnameable narcissistic wound."[8] In *Obasan* its realm is silence and stone, that is, deep emotional withholding. The narrator knows the cure and follows her own sure instinct for health: "Unless the stone bursts with telling, unless the seed flowers with speech, there is in my life no living word." It is only when the silence surrounding her mother's absence begins to "speak" that she finds release from her negative self-identification.

Aunt Emily's package containing Grandma Kato's letters from Japan releases the painful past of Nagasaki into which Naomi's mother has disappeared forever. Grandma Kato's graphic description of the disfigured women and children of Nagasaki is read by a priest at the family gathering. When we finally discover the long-absent mother, it is in the most silencing of conditions. Naomi translates:

> One evening when she [Grandma Kato] had given up the search for the day, she sat down beside a naked woman she'd seen earlier who was aimlessly chopping wood to make a pyre on which to cremate a dead baby. The woman was utterly disfigured. Her nose and one cheek were almost gone. Great wounds and pustules covered her entire face and body. She was completely bald. She sat in a cloud of flies and maggots wriggled among her wounds. . . . It was my mother. (239)

In the hushed spell that follows, Sensei (the priest) adds: "That there is brokenness" (240). The daughter sees now how her own grief and hurt at being abandoned are surpassed by her mother's suffering and that of the other victims of the atomic explosion.

> Silent Mother, you do not speak or write. You do not reach through the night to enter morning, but remain in the voicelessness. . . . You wish to protect us with lies, but the camouflage does not hide your cries. Beneath the hiding I am there with you. Silent Mother, lost in the abandoning, you do not share the horror. . . . Young Mother at Nagasaki, am I not also there? . . . Gentle Mother, we were lost together in our silences. Our wordlessness was our mutual destruction. (241–43)

The daughter is able to transcend her own woundedness only by entering the woundedness of the young mother at Nagasaki. The priest's prayer finds its flowering in the daughter: "Teach us to see Love's presence in our abandonment. Teach us to forgive" (243). Finally, the daughter is able to address her mother from a place of maturity: "I am thinking for a child there is no presence without flesh. But perhaps it is because I am no longer a child I can know your presence though you are not here. The letters tonight are skeletons. Bones only. But the earth still stirs with dormant blooms. Love flows through the roots of the trees by our graves" (243). In relation to her mother, the daughter realizes that she is no longer the Grand Inquisitor; the daughter's mostly silent but relentless and accusing inquisition of her mother is over. The fact that Naomi is ready to attend to her mother's voicelessness is evident from her Grand Inquisitor dream in which her mother appears dancing in a flower ceremony holding in her mouth a rose, "red as a heart," with a "knotted string stem, like the twine and string of Obasan's ball which she keeps in the pantry" (227). Naomi recalls, in relation to the dream, the "two ideographs for the word 'love.' The first contained the root words 'heart' and 'hand' and 'action'—love as hands and heart in action together. The other ideograph, for 'passionate love,' was formed of 'heart,' 'to tell,' and 'a long thread' " (228). The entire novel is summed up in this series of images. The whole narrative is like the "dance ceremony of the dead" attempting to realize the vocal presence of the silent absent mother, whose love is received by the abandoned daughter only after she has shed her accusing role of Grand Inquisitor. The narrative, a "dance cere-mony of the dead," is "a slow courtly telling, the heart declaring a long thread knotted to Obasan's twine, knotted to Aunt Emily's package" (228). The daughter's story of the mother—the "tale is a rose with a tan-gled stem" (229)—is mediated by the two aunts, each represented by an ideograph of love. Silent Obasan's hands are "resourceful hands" that "serve" and are "busy with survival tasks" (160): *love as hands and heart in action together.* Communicative Aunt Emily is represented by the ideo-graph for "passionate love," "formed of 'heart,' 'to tell,' and 'a long thread.' " Aunt Emily's package of communications tied with string is the lifelong labor of her love. The title *Obasan* (meaning "aunt" in Japa-nese) embraces both aunts' contributions. However, if the title specifi-cally honors the silent suffering, love, and endurance of Obasan, the novel's concluding pages (an "Excerpt from the Memorandum sent by The Cooperative Committee on Japanese Canadians to the House and the Senate of Canada, April 1946") honor the impact of the paper mis-siles aimed at the government. The countless letters and untiring acts of conscience of the Emilys of the world do make a difference.

The titular Obasan, referring to womanhood, is also a tribute to the long-suffering Issei, the first-generation immigrants who suffered di-rectly the consequences of racism, bureaucratic trickery, and neglect. Ko-gawa's novel is a tribute to the Issei, to whom she refers in her essay not just as "the ones most abused" and "forgotten," but as "the pioneers who with their lives and limbs cleared Canadian forests and created farms, established mines . . . built churches, community halls and in-fused this land with their gentle dignity and their endurance."[9] Naomi shows her gratitude and pays respect to Obasan when she says: "Every-where the old woman stands as the true and rightful owner of the earth" (16). The historian as deaf Ulysses needs to heed the meaning of her life, for the silent old woman is "the bearer of keys to unknown doorways" (16).

While the figure of the Grand Inquisitor, whose "demand to know was both a judgement and a refusal to hear," resembles Ulysses, the patri-arch/historian who is deaf to the sirens, he also represents our own limi-tations: What the Inquisitor "has never learned is that the avenues of speech are the avenues of silence. To hear my mother, to attend her speech, to attend the sound of stone, he must first become silent. Only when he enters her abandonment will he be released from his own" (228). A lesson on receptivity.

Having entered this abandonment, Naomi is freed from the past. She now sees that grief has its place and its time. Dark night of the soul, it is the "stillness" of the "pre-dawn hour . . . filled with emptiness. How thick the darkness behind which hides the animal cry. . . . Grief's weeping. Deeper emptiness. Grief wails like a scarecrow in the wild night, beckoning the wind to clothe his gaunt shell" (245). The "cluttered attic" must be left behind. A "waiting room," a "tunnel," grief is a station at which the "train" stops but from which it must move on. The narrator takes her leave of grief: "This body of grief is not fit for human habitation. Let there be flesh. The song of mourning is not a lifelong song. . . . My loved ones, rest in your world of stone. Around you flows the underground stream. How bright in the darkness the brooding light. How gentle the colors of rain" (246).

The novel began with a prologue, a desperate need: "If I could follow the stream down and down to the hidden voice, would I come at last to the freeing word?" In coming to terms with her loss she accesses the flowing stream of life. At the end, the narrator returns to the familiar landscape of the prairie sky, which is now "a faint teal blue" (246). The novel began with infinite night, the vastness of grief, and the stone vault of silence, and it ends with the dawning of light: "I can see the faint shaft of light . . . straight as a knife cutting light from shadow, the living from the dead" (246). There is a new dispensation here in the image of the moon/stone immersed in water: "Above the trees, the moon is a pure white stone. The reflection is rippling in the river—water and stone dancing. It's a quiet ballet, soundless as breath" (247). If water and stone were separate before, the final immersion indicates a psychological restoration, the harmony of emotions in a balanced dance of life.

Houston Baker, Jr., notes, "A matrix is a womb, a network, a fossil-bearing rock, *a rocky trace of a gemstone's removal . . .*" (italics mine).[10] It is the absence, separation, or forceful removal of a daughter from her mother, of a mother from her daughter, that constitutes the core of Toni Morrison's *Beloved.* Baby Suggs and her daughter-in-law Sethe are both rocks bearing embedded fossils, carrying the traces of loss. Whereas Baby Suggs has given up counting her lost children, for Sethe, her daughter is the forcibly removed gemstone whose absence is always present. Beloved is the ghostly figure who haunts her mother's matrix, the matrix of black history. Sethe's house becomes a metaphor for the women's interiority; situated on Blue Stone Road, the house, and by extension *Beloved* (the house of fiction), has a blues tone—governed by "a blues muse," aptly described by Wilson Harris as "an ancient mother of scarred freedom/ unfreedom."[11]

In her piece "Mourning," Alice Koller answers the question "What is it to mourn?" as follows: "It is to be hurled into pain so vast that . . . it usurps all other thinking, all other feeling, *a pain that occupies you as you occupy the house you live in*" (italics mine).[12] The house at 124 Blue Stone Road is, indeed, occupied territory; Beloved, who occupies the house and Sethe's consciousness, is the very embodiment of pain, which is also an unexpressed rage. Koller tracks *mourning* etymologically through various languages, noting that "these derivations from language to language carry living seed":

> "Mourn" from Greek for "care," in turn relating to "memory," "remembering." "Pain" from Greek for "payment," "penalty"; "to pay," "to punish"; "price." "Grief" from Latin and from Greek for "heavy." "Grieve," from Middle English, Old French, Latin for "to burden," from Latin for "heavy," "grave," like Gothic, Greek, Sanskrit for "heavy." "Sorrow" from Middle English *sorow,* from Old English *sorg.* Like Old High German *sorga* "sorrow," and Old Slavic *sraga* "sickness." "Anguish" from Latin for "straits," for "narrow," like Old English for "narrow."[13]

Toni Morrison remarked in an interview that in her treatment of slavery she wanted to do something "narrow" and deep, instead of attempting the breadth of historical accounts.[14] This narrowing translates into a sustained and mournful commemoration of the past.

Based on a documented incident, *Beloved* (1987) is a historical novel revealing the silences in the generic, first-person slave narratives and crossing the boundaries between fiction and history. In giving each of her characters a distinct interior life, and in exploring the characters' memories (something the slave is not supposed to have by virtue of being less than human), something that is absent from "objective" historical accounts and repressed in subjective (autobiographical) ones, Toni Morrison is, in William Andrews's phrase, "telling a free story."

Sethe, the central protagonist of *Beloved,* incurs the rancor and resentment of the women in the community because of her extreme refusal to define herself as a breeder of slaves. The conflict at the heart of the social drama in *Beloved* gets to the heart of slavery: Sethe is the slave mother who dares to claim her children as her own property instead of the slaveholder's; if the master can subject the slave in bondage to a slow "social death,"[15] the mother can release them through instant death. Infanticide, Sethe's raw act of defiance, runs counter to the slave community's response of resistance, namely, their determined effort to keep alive family ties despite the master's attempt to sunder them. In the course of the novel, Morrison redirects the moral outrage Sethe incurs to the institution of slavery.

The seeds of the novel were planted in the 1970s when Toni Morrison undertook the editing of *The Black Book,* a collection of "original raw material documenting our [black] life"; in the process she discovered many painful incidents of black history, including the infamous story of Margaret Garner. She cites an article, titled "A Visit to the Slave Mother Who Killed Her Child," published in the *American Baptist* in 1856.

> She [Margaret Garner] said that when the officers and slave-holders came to the house in which they were concealed, she caught a shovel and struck two of her children on the head, and she took a knife and cut the throat of the third, and tried to kill the other—that if they had given her time, she would have killed them all—that with regard to herself, she cared but little; but she was unwilling to have her children suffer as she had done.
>
> I inquired if she was not excited almost to madness when she committed the act. No, she replied, I was as cool as I now am; and would much rather kill them at once, and thus end their sufferings, than have them taken back to slavery, and be murdered by piecemeal.[16]

Morrison was moved to reconstruct imaginatively the life of Margaret Garner, on which she reflects: "I wondered if they [young blacks] knew the complicated psychic power one had to exercise to resist devastation."[17]

Morrison sums up the limitations imposed on the nineteenth-century writer of the slave narrative: "It was extremely important" that "the writers of those narratives appear as objective as possible—not to offend the reader by being too angry, or by showing too much outrage"; they had to be careful not to be "inflammatory."[18]

> Over and over, the writers pull the narrative up short with a phrase such as, "But let us drop a veil over these proceedings too terrible to relate." In shaping the experience to make it palatable to those who were in a position to alleviate it, they were silent about many things, and they "forgot" many things. There was a careful selection of the instances that they would record and a careful rendering of those that they chose to describe. . . .
>
> But, most importantly—at least for me—there was no mention of their interior life. . . .
>
> . . . My job becomes how to rip that veil drawn over "proceedings too terrible to relate." The exercise is also critical for any person who is black, or who belongs to any marginalized category, for, historically, we were seldom invited to participate in the discourse even when we were its topic.[19]

In *Beloved,* Morrison is explicit about the white master, "school teacher," and his nephews' brutality and obscenity. Morrison is explicit about the rape of the maternal body: "school teacher" and his nephews steal Sethe's milk, and after putting her pregnant stomach in a hole in the ground (so as to save the unborn slave), lash her back.[20] Focusing on every phase of a slave woman's life, from infancy to childhood, from girlhood to motherhood, and on to old age, Morrison is able to demonstrate the truth of Harriet Jacobs's statement: "Slavery is terrible for men; but it is far more terrible for women"; superadded to the burden common to all, "*they* have wrongs, and sufferings, and mortifications peculiarly their own." Morrison's novel makes brutally clear that aside from the "equality of oppression" that black men and women suffered, black women were also oppressed as *women.*[21] They were routinely subjected to rape, enforced childbirth, and natal alienation from their children. As Morrison's novel shows, although physical abuse is humiliating, the added emotional pain of a mother is devastating. The pathos of Baby Suggs, the grandmother, whose resilient spirit is eventually broken, is captured by the image of her retiring to ponder pieces of color. Margaret Garner's story enables Morrison to explore the passion of the slave mother and the anguish of the mother-child relationship.

Beloved highlights black women's persistent resistance to slavery. Morrison portrays the mother's deed as an act of resistance, one among many that constituted the quotidian experience of slaves. Sethe's act of killing her child is not the only anomaly: Ella, the good woman of the town who assists Stamp Paid on the Underground Railroad, "had delivered, but would not nurse, a hairy white thing, fathered by 'the lowest yet,' " a white father and son who had held her in captivity and raped her; the child dies after five days of neglect. We are told that Sethe's mother abandoned the children white men forced upon her, keeping only Sethe, who is born of an African father; Sethe's mother "threw them all away but [her]. The one from the crew she threw away on the island. The others from more whites she also threw away" (62). By making resistance central to the experience of slave women, not just the Nat Turners of history books, Morrison wipes out the stereotype of the mammy figure.

In *Beloved* Morrison is interested in investigating the cost of such "heroic" resistance, in exploring what the killing of the child did to the psyche of a mother like Margaret Garner. What is the psychological, emotional state of these individuals? What does it feel like inside? Let us recall that of the seven long years Harriet Jacobs spends hiding from her master in a garret, in a place so cramped she does not have room to stand, hearing her children but unable to reach out to them, we are told remarkably little. What must she have endured? It is *Beloved,* with its confinement of the reader to 124 and its inmates' interiority, that gives us some sense of that experience in all its claustrophobic intensity. From the first lines of the novel ("124 was spiteful. Full of a baby's venom."), the reader is plunged *in medias res* into the haunted house and the troubled memories of Morrison's characters. Now, a century later, it is possible for the black artist to remember, to grieve, to undertake the labyrinthine journey into unacknowledged regions of pain and anger and loss. As a race, it was expedient to keep going, to forget. Observing that "nothing came down orally to my generation of that experience on the slave ship," Morrison attributes this collective effacement of the past to "some survivalist intention to forget."[22] It takes Toni Morrison's *Beloved* a hundred years to emerge; in the novel, it takes Sethe eighteen years to stop lingering over the crevices in the self, and when she does, they engulf her. Remembering makes Sethe lose her job, lose herself in the past. Historically, a beleaguered people could not afford to look back but had to keep going to meet the demands of the present.

Set in 1873–1874, ten years after Emancipation, the free characters are slowly beginning to take stock of the past. In most slave narratives, the slave past, its typicality and inhumanity having been sketched, is something to leave behind. *Beloved,* charting the journey back from the free present to the slave past, reverses the progressive movement of slave narratives. Further, while the slave narratives privileged the individual's account of coming to selfhood, where the single, heroic self is fixed in the "I" of the subject and the tale ends with the victory of freedom, Morrison's narrative decenters the individual, giving way to a multiplicity of voices. The novel invokes the "polyphonic ideal" of Mikhail Bakhtin, the Russian scholar who in articulating the sociological poetics of the novel envisions "the ideal of the coexistence, interaction, and interdependence of several different, relatively autonomous consciousnesses that express simultaneously the various contents of the world within the unity of a single text."[23] In *Beloved* the memories are as complex as the people who tell, repeat, and improvise them; narrative becomes a collective, interactive enterprise. The effect of several individuals dealing with their past has the effect of a collective remembrance and purging.

The entire novel is conceived psychologically: how to reclaim the freed self, body and soul, for "freeing yourself was one thing; claiming ownership of that freed self was another" (95). The plot is structured by the principle of "the return of the repressed"; the spirit of the past comes to possess the principal characters. It is a ghost story that is healing because the characters move from being possessed by the past to possessing the past and themselves. The plot of the novel has to do with the possession of 124 and its inmates, Sethe and her daughter Denver, by a ghost, whose eventual exorcism brings peace. As the dedication indicates, the writing of the novel is an act of reparation, central to which is the affirmation of the discredited beliefs and traditions of black culture. In the nineteenth-century African American ethos that Morrison creates, the presence of the ghost is taken very seriously. The reader is required, from the first line of the novel, to suspend disbelief in spirits and to enter the house on 124 Blue Stone Road understanding that it is haunted. The cupboard shakes, a doleful red aura surrounds the door, and small anomalous incidents accumulate over time to establish the identity of the ghost: the spirit of Denver's sister, the "crawling already" baby girl who is buried beneath the pink stone inscribed with the word *Beloved*. The possession is not a singular occurrence, for Baby Suggs says that houses of black folk all over the land were peopled by ghosts: "Not a house in the country ain't packed to its rafters with some dead Negro's grief" (5). According to West African belief, the dead are not "finished" with the living, because the past (the dead) and present (the living) and future (the unborn) are coexistent; the ancestors can communicate with their descendants, and they do, especially if certain rites for the dead have not been performed. The character Beloved is what the Yoruba would call Abiku, a "wanderer child," "the same child who dies and returns again and again to plague the mother."[24] Such a world view posits a fluidity and continuity between the past and the present, and fidelity to this milieu gives Morrison the latitude to move freely between the literal and the metaphorical, between various dimensions of reality.

In *Beloved*, a West African religious worldview blends with Christianity to produce an African American ethos. The biblical cadences and echoes in the language are appropriate, since the slave culture did appropriate the Bible for solace and survival. As Lerone Bennett, Jr., points out, "The slaves reinterpreted white patterns, weaving a whole new universe around biblical images and giving a new dimension and new meaning to Christianity." Their God was not the one who demanded of servants obedience to their masters, but the one who "delivered the Israelites."

> In a total and passionate quest for *this* God, the slaves . . . turned American Christianity inside out, like a glove, infusing it with African-oriented melodies and rhythms and adding new patterns, such as the ring shout, ecstatic

seizure and communal, call-and-response patterns. . . . The emblem of this creation was the invisible black church of slavery, which centered in the portable "hush-harbors."[25]

Grandmother "Baby Suggs, holy" has her own "hush-harbor" in the Clearing, where communal praying, singing, crying, and dancing merge together in a collective ceremonial act of healing love. In the novel, various verses from the Bible are given another meaning: the transmutation from the word *Beloved* inscribed on the tombstone of Sethe's daughter to the living Beloved reinterprets the Gospel According to St. John: "And the Word was made flesh, and dwelt among us" (1:14). "I am my beloved's, and my beloved is mine" (in Song of Songs, 6:3) becomes "I am Beloved and she is mine" (210). Sethe trying to appease the "hungry" Beloved enacts the truth of the biblical statement "Many waters cannot quench love"—or the absence of love—"neither can the floods drown it: if a man would give all the substance of his house for love, it would utterly be contemned" (Song of Songs, 8:7). Sethe does give all her substance to Beloved, who feeds on her and is still unsatisfied. The novel is an evocation of "The Witness of the Spirit" in the First Letter of John: "This is he that came by water and blood, *even* Jesus Christ, not by water only but by water and blood. And it is the Spirit that beareth witness, because the Spirit is truth" (5:6); "And there are three that bear witness in earth, the spirit, and the water, and the blood: and these three agree in one" (5:8). Indeed, at the center of the novel, Beloved, Sethe, and Denver agree: they have found their truth in each other. The novel subverts the male trinity with a female one. (*Beloved:* In the *name* of the mother, the daughter, and the sad ghost.) Speaking of Beloved, Ella tells Stamp Paid, "You know as well as I do that people who die bad don't stay in the ground." Stamp "couldn't deny it. Jesus Christ Himself didn't" (188). Beloved is the tormented spirit who has not yet experienced the forgiveness that allows for the resurrection or liberation of the spirit.

In the novel, storytelling, remembering, and retelling the past become ways of feeding the hungry and neglected dead. According to West African belief, the dead live as long as they are remembered. Beloved, the ghost demanding attention, is both thirsty and hungry. Hers is a sensual hunger for Sethe: looking, hearing, and touching are food to her starved senses. Above all, storytelling is the food Beloved craves: she makes both Denver and Sethe tell her stories. The appeasement of physical hunger by the oral intake of food is interchanged with the aural intake of story and song, oral forms of communication indigenous to African culture.

By the end of the novel, the well-fed ghost leaves with a "big belly," thanks to both Paul D and Sethe; here, as in the rest of the novel, the literal meaning blends cryptically with the metaphoric.

Indeed, the complexity of the novel stems from the fact that it constantly merges the physical and the psychical, the literal and the metaphoric. The arrivals and departures of Beloved easily lend themselves to a metaphorical reading. The novel begins in 1873 with Sethe's house, which has been haunted ever since Sethe killed her baby daughter rather than let her be taken, in accordance with the Fugitive Slave Act, back to slavery. Both Sethe and her daughter Denver are used to the presence of the ghost, whom they accept as being not evil but "sad." They live their lives in resigned solitude under a pervasive gloom. It is only when Paul D meets Sethe after eighteen years that Sethe's past and present are stirred into life. Each recalls for the other buried images and tumultuous emotions connected with their slave days. Each also brings the other hope for the future. After Paul D touches her back, which is etched with scars resembling a branching tree and numb to any sensation, Sethe wonders if she should "feel the hurt her back ought to"; she feels she can "trust things and remember things because the last of the Sweet Home men was there to catch her if she sank" (18). But as she thinks these thoughts, we are told, "The house itself was pitching" and Paul D was physically fighting an invisible adversary; he "did not stop . . . until everything was rock quiet," until "[it] was gone" (18). Here a connection is made between the opening of Sethe's scarred back and the rocking of the house, a site of interiority: "Merely kissing the wrought iron on her back had shook the house, had made it necessary for him to beat it to pieces" (20). Paul D is really *activating* or letting loose the past; the ghost leaves the house in spirit but returns, in the figure of Beloved, assuming real-life proportions, a concrete shape to contend with. Sethe realizes there had been "no room for any other thing or body until Paul D arrived and broke up the place, making room, shifting it" (39). It is Paul D who ushers in Beloved by asking Sethe, who is unsure about making room for him in her life, "What about inside?" "I don't go inside," replies Sethe. Paul D reassures her: "Go as far inside as you need to, I'll hold your ankles. Make sure you get back out" (46). Going inside is like embarking on a voyage through the underworld, remembering, going past Lethe, river of forgetfulness, back to life. Part 3 begins with the statement "124 was quiet" (239); only after Sethe has dealt with the catastrophe of infanticide can peace and Paul D come to stay in her life.

However, it is not a one-way influence; if Paul D makes the tree of death on Sethe's back stir with life, Sethe also invigorates him. As Paul D knows, "This was not a normal woman in a normal house. As soon as he had stepped through the red light he knew that, compared to 124, the rest of the world was bald" (41). After his soul-breaking experience in the underground slave camp of Alfred, Georgia, "He had shut down a generous portion of his head, operating on the part that helped him walk, eat, sleep, sing" (41). With the pleasure of seeing Sethe, however, "The closed portion of his head opened like a greased lock" (41). Since Sethe, too, makes him grapple with his own past, the flesh-and-blood Beloved is the spirit of the past that touches them both. For Paul D is literally and figuratively "moved" by the past/Beloved. The slave pasts of Sweet Home, Kentucky, and Alfred, Georgia, are traumatic enough to keep him moving, make him a restless wandering man unable to be still in one place. Then, in 124, Beloved starts him "moving" again, this time involuntarily, because he genuinely wishes to settle down with Sethe, to make a life together. Paul D experiences Beloved as a mysterious force exerted upon him; the past will not let him rest, the unresolved, unacknowledged pain will not allow him to form a stable relationship with Sethe, even though he would like to.

Paul D is peeved and bothered by the timing of Beloved's appearance: "She had appeared and been taken in on the very day Sethe and he had patched up their quarrel, gone out in public and had a right good time—like a family" (66). However, before Sethe and Paul D can create an emotional space for each other, they must deal with the past. The haste with which Paul D and Sethe move toward lovemaking—"It was over before they could get their clothes off"—is necessarily followed by a slow period of self-recovery. This is particularly critical for Sethe, who has undergone a terrible trauma. So, Beloved is the unresolved past that comes between them; for both Sethe and Paul D, she is the return of the repressed. The distracted state of their minds is made clear when they first make love; both are caught up in their own memories, and though these do converge sensuously in the image of the corn flowing with juice, though they have much to share, judging by their mutual disappointment they are not yet ready for each other. If Sethe is numb to physical touch—the white master's infliction of brutal pain has made her block her capacity to feel—Paul D's own red heart has been covered by a tobacco tin of memories shut tight with a rusty lid. He has to recover his heart. We are told, "By the time he got to 124 nothing in this world could pry it [the tobacco tin] open" (113). Sethe succeeds in loosening the lid of the rusty tin, a Pandora's box of memories. Beloved's is the voice of the past confronting Paul D in the cold house: "You have to touch me. On the inside part. And you have to call me my name" (117). Metaphorically, in touching Beloved, Paul D is touching the past inside him and is in the process of being healed: the lid of his rusty tobacco tin has been dislodged, and as the tightly guarded contents of the past are spilling out, he begins to find his "red heart."

Beloved is reminiscent of Jung's archetype of the maiden, who is "often described as not altogether human in the usual sense; she is either of unknown or peculiar origin, or she looks strange or undergoes strange experiences, from which one is forced to infer the maiden's extraordinary, myth-like character."[26] Archetypes are "living psychic forces that demand to be taken seriously"; having an "unconscious core of meaning," "an archetypal content expresses itself, first and foremost, in metaphors."[27] If, metaphorically speaking, Beloved is desire, a black Aphrodite, rising from the waters of the unconscious, on the realistic plane, Beloved is also a plausible character with a specific past, "a *fully dressed* woman [who] walked out of the water" (50, italics mine), enabling Morrison to introduce the Middle Passage.

In this nonfigurative reading, Beloved is a child who is captured with her mother in Africa and packed with other slaves on a ship making the voyage through the Atlantic. When her mother apparently jumps ship—it was not uncommon for slaves to commit suicide—the child is left deeply disturbed by her disappearance. We can only imagine what happens to her afterward from her monologue and from Sethe's surmise, which corroborates Stamp Paid's hearsay about a white man imprisoning a pup. Sethe "believed Beloved had been locked up by some whiteman for his own purposes, and never let out the door. Then she must have escaped to a bridge or someplace and rinsed the rest out of her mind" (119). Stamp Paid recalls a tale about "a girl locked up in the house with a whiteman over by Deer Creek. Found him dead last summer and the girl gone. Maybe that's her. Folks say he had her in there since she was a pup" (235). We are led to assume that she escapes, comes to a bridge from which she peers into the water, where she sees images of her mother's disappearing face. Her development has been arrested at an early stage; her self-image is deeply fragmented. She has no face of her own, because the mother in whose eyes the child would become whole has left her. She jumps in after her and emerges from the stream near 124 Blue Stone, where she fixes upon Sethe's face. Here she is taken in by

Sethe as a stranger in need of food and rest. Denver, in her profound loneliness, clings to her as the drowning would to a boat.

Like Paul D and Sethe, Beloved is a character who is haunted by a traumatic past, compelled to relive different moments of it. Earlier, on being asked by Denver about her name, she replies, "In the dark my name is Beloved" (75). Her driving Paul D out of Sethe's house to the cold house and cornering him there to touch her and call her by her name may be variously interpreted. Morrison may be revising the Oedipus complex here; it is not the father but the mother whom the daughter seeks. Although Beloved does seek out Paul D, she tells him that it is "her face" she wants: "I don't love nobody but her" (116). Her trips to the cold house seem to be governed by the desire to drive a wedge between him and Sethe; by seducing him, she intends to shame him and weaken his claim on Sethe. It is a cunning motivated by desperation. When she is with Denver in the cold house, a damp, cold place, Beloved is reliving the trauma of the slave ship; "I'm like this," she demonstrates, and "bends over, curls up and rocks." All she says is "Over there. Her face." Beloved is a disturbed personality, a nubile girl whose mind is unable to absorb the layers of shock her body has been subjected to since a child.

It is not until later, after Paul D confronts Sethe with the newspaper clipping of eighteen years earlier and leaves, that Beloved's identity as a ghost is confirmed by a Sethe driven in upon herself; under the emotional strain, she begins to see Beloved as her own baby girl returned to her. We are told, "When the click came Sethe didn't know what it was" (175). But the click, "the settling of pieces into places," comes after Paul D confronts Sethe with the notorious paper clipping from eighteen years ago and accuses her of behaving like an animal, of having four feet, not two. It is then that she welcomes Beloved as her own daughter come back from the dead. The narrator remarks, "Things were where they ought to be or poised and ready to glide in" (176). Now, after the desolation of Paul D's departure, Sethe has something to look forward to: she is "eager to lie down and unravel the proof for the conclusion she had already leapt to" (181). The desire to believe precedes the "proof." Events of the past are recast in the light of this desire, so that "the hand-holding shadows she had seen on the road were not Paul D, Denver and herself, but 'us three' " (182). After convincing her that "there was a world out there," Paul D leaves her to shrink the world to her room. Echoing the novel's epigraph, Sethe calls her Beloved who is not *her* Beloved. Sethe wants to believe Beloved is her daughter come back to her from the dead, because it gives her a chance to explain her actions and demonstrate her love. It means that forgiveness, her redemption, is at hand.

The fact that Beloved, Denver, and Sethe should emotionally spiral into each other is inevitable. Each serves to fulfill the deepest, most dire need of the other. For Denver, who is desolate since her two brothers ran away in terror, whose ears voluntarily shut out sound for two years to compensate for hearing the terrible story of her sister's death at the hands of her own mother, and who is even more lonely since Grandma Baby Suggs's death, Beloved is a savior. Simply put, she is delicious company Denver cannot afford to lose. What binds Sethe and Beloved to each other is the heart of this heart-wrenching story.

Marianne Hirsch rightly points out that "the psychoanalytic plot has . . . silenced the mother's response to separation" and that what we have is "an untold maternal experience."

> Even as feminist theorizing, based in psychoanalysis, urges feminists to shift their political allegiance back from father to mother, even as it urges us to sympathize with our mothers' position in patriarchy, it is still . . . written from the child's primary process perspective: permeated with desires for the mother's approval, with fear of her power, and with anger and resentment at her powerlessness.[28]

Morrison presents the untold story of the mother and the daughter in a rewriting of the Demeter-Persephone myth. (Pluto in Greek mythology is black, envisioned as the dark god of the underworld.) In Beloved, it is the slave catcher who is Pluto in both instances of Beloved/Persephone's and Sethe/Demeter's trauma: whether it is the daughter of the African mother gathering flowers "in a round basket" (210) who is taken captive on the slave ship, or the "crawling already?" daughter Sethe saves from slavery by killing, it is white men who come to tear the daughter and her mother apart. The same is true of Sethe and her mother. The mother's language and the love that flows with her milk are both denied the daughter, who in turn grows up to be a mother whose daughter's milk is stolen from her. C. G. Jung's comment is of interest here: "The psyche pre-existent to consciousness (e.g., in the child) participates in the maternal psyche on the one hand, while on the other it reaches across to the daughter psyche. We could therefore say that every mother contains her daughter in herself and every daughter her mother, and that every woman extends backwards into her mother and forward into her daughter."[29]

This lack binding mother and daughter is as painful as Paul D's non-verbal communication with other slave men through the chain, "the best hand-forged chain in Georgia." However, Paul D is left out of the vortex of mother-daughter guilt and pain; he cannot decipher their "code." In a way, 124 must be evacuated by the men—no Howard, no Buglar, and no Paul D must be around—so that the suffering women endure by virtue of being women can take center stage. One must note here that *Beloved* also portrays the black man's pain with great sensitivity. The painful memories of Paul D (the collar, the bit, the lynching, the sodomy) create a composite picture of the male slave, showing the breaking of his spirit, so that a lame rooster, a cock called Mr., has more going for him than a black man. The account of the strong and responsible son and husband Halle finally breaking down at the sight of his wife being raped is very painful; as Paul D insists, "A man ain't a goddamn ax. Chopping, hacking, busting every goddamn minute of the day. Things get to him. Things he can't chop down because they're inside" (69). However, in her narrative, Morrison clears a separate space for the women so that we may better understand Harriet Jacobs's following statement: "*They* [black women] have wrongs, and sufferings, and mortifications peculiarly their own." So, we are told that once "Sethe locked the door, the women inside were free at last to be what they liked, see whatever they saw and say whatever was on their minds" (199). As Jung remarks, the Demeter-Kore (Persephone) myth "exists on the plane of mother-daughter experience, which is alien to man and shuts him off."[30]

When Julia Kristeva wrote that "a mother is a continuous separation, a division of the very flesh. And consequently a division of language,"[31] she did not have the slave mother in mind. She was referring to the mother under the category of "woman." Slavery, however, puts into high relief every psychoanalytic feminist utterance describing "woman" and the family in patriarchy. The number of Sethe's house, 124, suggests the slave woman's reproduction of labor under slavery: $1 + 1 = 2$; $2 + 2 = 4$; it recalls Paul D's cruel reminder to Sethe about her having two feet (being a human), not four (being an animal); the truth is that under slavery black women were listed under the latter category as breeders and valued as such. The extreme and unspeakable nature of the slave woman's oppression enables it, when spoken, to convulse the symbolic order of patriarchy. However, in doing so, *Beloved* also lets us recognize the need for a historically specific differentiation of women's bodies, psyches, and oppressions. Kristeva's suggestive positing of a maternal semiotic, a pre-Oedipal language prior to the child-subject's formal acquisition of language, is complicated in *Beloved*. Sethe remembers hearing as a child an African language, speaking as a child her mother tongue, traces of which now elude her memory. Here, we are speaking not (as Kristeva does) of a universally repressed, preverbal maternal semiotic, but of a specific violence done to a verbal mother tongue. In *Beloved*, not only is the mother tongue obliterated from consciousness, the very tongue of the speaking subject is harnessed or clamped by an iron bit. Morrison's use of poetic language is an attempt to articulate the pain of this violence.

The language attempts to articulate the very matrix of the slave woman's pain as mother, as daughter. When Stamp Paid passes by 124, he hears "voices": "The speech wasn't nonsensical, exactly, nor was it tongues . . . he couldn't describe or cipher it to save his life" (172):

> You are my face; I am you. Why did you leave me who am you?
> I will never leave you again
> Don't ever leave me again
> You will never leave me again
> You went in the water
> I drank your blood
> I brought your milk
> You forgot to smile
> I loved you
> You hurt me
> You came back to me
>
> You left me
>
> I waited for you. (216–17)

Here are the sirens that the historian as deaf Ulysses does not hear, that even sensitive and caring Paul D cannot comprehend. It is a specific and gendered language of abandonment.

However, the individual ego is defenseless against the unbuffered assault of the repressed. After the joy of discovering each other, Beloved's recriminations begin and Sethe cannot apologize enough. There is no filling the void, the irreparable damage done to Beloved, or the deep guilt that plagues Sethe. She relinquishes control, her job, her sanity, "broke down, finally, from trying to take care of and make up for" (243). Denver has been locked out of the gaze of mother-daughter, who are "locked in a love" that is draining them, driving them to "the edge of violence, then over." Their roles changed; Sethe "was like a chastised child while Beloved ate up her life" (250). The past is in danger of engulfing the present.

The plot, built on the principle of the return of the repressed, reenacts the fatal configuration of events that took place eighteen years earlier. As in a Greek tragedy, events move toward an inexorable end as the tragic characters' flaws close in upon themselves. With the desperate realization that her mother's life is in danger, Denver is galvanized into taking charge and leaving her mother's house to seek help. When news of the ghost's revenge on Sethe reaches the community, they intervene. Led by Ella, thirty women gather outside the house to pray. Although times have changed and the situation that brings a white man driving a carriage to 124 is benevolent—Mr. Bodwin, the abolitionist who had appealed on behalf of Sethe, is coming to take Denver to her first day of work at his house—Sethe is locked in the past. The memory of past danger makes Sethe fly on reflex to attack the approaching man. Fortunately, the community of women and Denver save her from herself. Beloved, who has been standing naked on the porch holding Sethe's hand, is also prey to the past; in Sethe's sudden departure from her, and in the crowd of black people, she is reminded of the hold of the slave ship; in the white face of Mr. Bodwin she sees "the man without skin, looking . . . at her" (262). She runs from the scene that is unfolding the double horror of her past.

We do not know what becomes of Beloved, whether she lives or dies. Beloved goes as she comes; the unaccountability of her whereabouts, her physical absence, constitutes the experience of loss at the heart of slavery. On the metaphorical level, Beloved is gone because the past she represents has been confronted. Events have come full circle, and Sethe has been saved. In facing the past, Sethe emerges, released from it into the present. Beloved disappears, having served her function of "rememory"; the sound and the fury is over, and "spiteful," "loud" 124 is finally "quiet." Now Sethe may realize, as Paul D does, that she is her "own best thing." Now Paul D may lay his story beside Sethe's.

In a way it is important that Beloved remain a little inaccessible and mysterious so as to be a suggestive symbol of the unconscious, of desire, of the past, of memory, for none of these is fully graspable by the conscious mind. Like the footprints that fit everyone's feet, Beloved is the past of those "ordinary unheralded lives" silenced in history.[32] Like Denver, the author "construct[s] out of the strings she had heard all her life a net to hold Beloved" (76). But "the past is infinite,"[33] and Beloved slips out again. A mermaid, with hair like fish, she is associated with that liminal zone between land and water, the bridge. Jean-Pierre Vernant's formulation of an alternative history aptly describes *Beloved* as a historical novel: "History as celebrated by Mnemosoune is a deciphering of the invisible, a geography of the supernatural. . . . It throws a bridge between the world of the living and that beyond to which everything that leaves the light of day must return."[34]

Remembering and mourning become signs of the subject's agency and recovery in *Obasan* and *Beloved,* both of which end on a quiet elegiac note. J. Hillis Miller notes that "the process of mourning has a kind of intrinsic rhythm."[35] Joy Kogawa closes her memories of the past with a statement about the need to live in the present: "The song of mourning is not a lifelong song." Morrison, too, covers the exposed wound of the past with the repeated statement, "It was not a story to pass on" (275). Morrison implies at the end of her novel what Kogawa says at the beginning of hers: "There is a silence that cannot speak." When all is said and done, there is a reservoir of all that which remains unspoken, untouched. The gaps and the silences become quietly recriminating, refuting the possibility of any posthumous recompense that claims to be adequate to the past. All cannot be accounted for.

In both novels the return to nature also signals a quiet acceptance following a cathartic release of the past. The narrator in *Obasan* returns to the natural landscape she and the late Uncle frequented: "Between the river and Uncle's spot are the wild roses and the tiny wildflowers that grow along the trickling stream. The perfume in the air is sweet and faint. If I hold my head a certain way, I can smell them from where I am" (246). Melancholy gives way to an awareness of the sweetness of life. Kogawa concludes the narrative with a description of the predawn prairie landscape in which light and dark, water and stone are balanced in "a quiet ballet, soundless as breath" (247).

A similar harmony is restored in Beloved. When Paul D finally tells Sethe that she is her "best thing," and Sethe repeats incredulously, "Me? Me?" (273), we know a psychological resolution has occurred. Healing is at hand. At the end of *Beloved* we are left with an image of natural closure: a lock, "a latch latched" and covered with the "apple-green bloom" of lichen. Authorial control gives way to the agency of natural elements: "The rest is weather. Not the breath of the disremembered and unaccounted for, but wind in the eaves, or spring ice thawing too quickly. Just weather. Certainly no clamor for a kiss" (275). The ghost—with its clamor for a kiss—has left her. With emotions no longer out of balance, life breathes again with its natural rhythms restored.

The sirens of Mnemosoune have emerged from the "sensate sea," "that amniotic deep," and have sung their song from the very matrix of history. We have heard their drifting meaning. In both novels the reader partakes in the triumph of what Kogawa calls in her prologue the "living word": in their fiction, "the stone bursts with telling" and "the seed flowers with speech"—the speech that frees.

Notes

1. Michel de Certeau, *Heterologies: Discourse on the Other*, tr. Brian Massumi (Minneapolis: University of Minnesota Press, 1986), 200, 202.

2. Barbara Christian, " 'Somebody Forgot to Tell Somebody Something': African-American Women's Historical Novels," *Wild Women in the Whirlwind: Afra-American Culture and the Contemporary Literary Renaissance*, eds. Joanne M. Braxton and Andree Nicolas McLaughlin (New Brunswick, N.J.: Rutgers University Press, 1990), 339.

3. Joy Kogawa, *Obasan* (Boston: Godine, 1981), 236. All subsequent references are included in the text.

4. Toni Morrison, *Beloved* (New York: Knopf, 1987), 274. All subsequent references are included in the text.

5. Joy Kogawa, "Is There a Just Cause?" *Canadian Forum* (March 1984): 21.

6. For a historical account of Japanese Canadians during World War II, see Ken Adachi, *The Enemy that Never Was: A History of the Japanese Canadians* (Toronto: McClelland and Stewart, 1976); Patricia E. Roy et al., eds., *Mutual Hostages: Canadians and Japanese During the Second World War* (Toronto: University of Toronto Press, 1990); Muriel Kitagawa, *This Is My Own: Letters to Wes and Other Writings on Japanese Canadians, 1941–1948*, ed. Roy Miki (Vancouver: Talonbooks, 1985). The plight of Japanese immigrants in America following the bombing of Pearl Harbor in 1942 was not dissimilar to that of their Canadian counterparts. In *Race, Gender, and Work: A Multicultural Economic History of Women in the United States* (Boston: South End Press, 1991), historians Teresa L. Amott and Julie A. Matthaei record the "anti-Japanese hysteria" that spread in the United States, although

> not one incident of sabotage or espionage was reported throughout the duration of the war. Nevertheless, on February 19, 1942, President Roosevelt signed an executive order authorizing the evacuation of 110,000 Issei and Nisei—virtually all the ethnic Japanese in the United States—from the so-called Western Defense Command, the coastal areas of Washington, Oregon, and California. . . . Japanese American families . . . were given one week to dispose of their possessions. . . . Many farmers who had invested years of painstaking effort to raise orchards from seedlings were forced to liquidate them at low prices. . . . Japanese Americans were tagged like luggage and transported to 10 'permanent relocation camps' in Utah, Arizona, Colorado, California, Wyoming, Idaho, and Arkansas. Each camp held an average of 10,000 people. The camps, located in desert or swamp areas where temperatures fluctuated between freezing and broiling, were surrounded by barbed wire. (228)

7. Irena Klepfisz, "Bashert," *A Few Words in the Mother Tongue: Poems Selected and New (1971–1990)* (Portland, Oreg.: Eighth Mountain Press, 1990), 183–200.

8. Sigmund Freud, "Mourning and Melancholia," in *On Metapsychology: The Pelican Freud Library,* vol. 6 (Harmondsworth: Penguin, 1964), 251–68.

9. Kogawa, "Is There a Just Cause?" 21.

10. Houston A. Baker, Jr., *Blues, Ideology, and Afro-American Literature: A Vernacular Theory* (Chicago: University of Chicago Press, 1984), 3.

11. Wilson Harris, *Womb of Space: The Cross-Cultural Imagination* (Westport, Conn.: Greenwood Press, 1983), 28.

12. Alice Koller, "Mourning," in *The Stations of Solitude* (New York: William Morrow, 1990), 307.

13. Ibid., 308.

14. *Toni Morrison,* an RM Arts production, produced and directed by Alan Benson, ed. Melvyn Bragg (Chicago: Home Vision, 1987).

15. The concept of social death is developed in Orlando Patterson's *Slavery and Social Death* (Cambridge, Mass.: Harvard University Press, 1982). I am indebted to Abdul JanMohamed for pointing out the theme of social death in *Beloved.*

16. Toni Morrison, "Rediscovering Black History," *New York Times Magazine,* 11 August 1974, 16, 18.

17. Ibid., 18.

18. Toni Morrison, "The Site of Memory," in *Inventing the Truth: The Art and Craft of Memoir,* ed. William Zinsser (Boston: Houghton Mifflin, 1987), 106.

19. Ibid., 109–111.

20. Anne E. Goldman suggestively connects the theft of Sethe's milk with the appropriation of Sethe's ink by "school teacher": "Both the body and the word become commodified," "texts upon which the white man makes his mark." See Goldman, "I Made the Ink: (Literary) Production and Reproduction in *Dessa Rose* and *Beloved,*" *Feminist Studies* 16, no. 2 (Summer 1990): 314.

21. For an insightful analysis of the nature of the slave woman's oppression, see Angela Davis's essay "The Legacy of Slavery: Standards for A New Womanhood," in *Women, Race, and Class* (New York: Vintage, 1983), 3–29.

22. *Toni Morrison,* TV interview with Alan Benson.

23. Robert Anchor, "Bakhtin's Truths of Laughter," *Clio* 14, no. 3 (1985): 253.

24. Wole Soyinka, "Abiku," in *Idanre and Other Poems* (New York: Hill and Wang, 1987), 28–30.

25. Lerone Bennett, Jr., *Before the Mayflower: A History of Black America* (New York: Penguin Books, 1984), 99, 102.

26. Carl Gustav Jung, "The Psychological Aspects of the Kore," *The Archetypes and the Collective Unconscious* (Princeton, N.J.: Princeton University Press, 1969), 186.

27. Ibid., 156, 157.

28. Marianne Hirsch, "Clytemnestra's Children," in *Alice Walker,* ed. Harold Bloom (New York: Chelsea House Publishers, 1989), 200.

29. Jung, "The Psychological Aspects of the Kore," 188.

30. Ibid., 203.

31. Julia Kristeva, "Stabat Mater," in *The Kristeva Reader,* ed. Toril Moi (New York: Columbia University Press, 1986), 178.

32. Ibid.
33. Ibid.
34. Quoted in Michael M. J. Fischer, "Ethnicity and the Post-Modern Arts of Memory," in *Writing Culture: The Poetics and Politics of Ethnography,* ed. James Clifford and George E. Marcus (Berkeley: University of California Press, 1986), 194–233.
35. J. Hillis Miller, "Symposium," in *Rhetoric and Form: Deconstruction at Yale,* ed. Robert Con Davis and Ronald Schleifer (Norman: University of Oklahoma Press, 1985), 97.

Works Cited

Adachi, Ken. *The Enemy that Never Was: A History of the Japanese Canadians.* Toronto: McClelland and Stewart, 1976.

Amott, Teresa L., and Julie A. Matthaei. *Race, Gender, and Work: A Multicultural Economic History of Women in the United States.* Boston: South End Press, 1991.

Anchor, Robert. "Bakhtin's Truths of Laughter." *Clio* 14, no. 3 (1985): 237–57.

Baker, Houston A., Jr. *Blues, Ideology, and Afro-American Literature: A Vernacular Theory.* Chicago: University of Chicago Press, 1984.

Bennett, Lerone, Jr. *Before the Mayflower: A History of Black America.* New York: Penguin Books, 1984.

Christian, Barbara. " 'Somebody Forgot to Tell Somebody Something': African-American Women's Historical Novels." In *Wild Women in the Whirlwind: Afra-American Culture and the Contemporary Literary Renaissance,* edited by Joanne M. Braxton and Andree Nicholas McLaughlin. New Brunswick, N.J.: Rutgers University Press, 1990.

Davis, Angela Y. "The Legacy of Slavery: Standards for a New Womanhood." In *Women, Race, and Class.* New York: Vintage, 1983.

de Certeau, Michel. *Heterologies: Discourse on the Other.* Translated by Brian Massumi: Minneapolis: University of Minnesota Press, 1986.

Fischer, Michael M. J. "Ethnicity and the Post-Modern Arts of Memory." In *Writing Culture: The Poetics and Politics of Ethnography,* edited by James Clifford and George E. Marcus. Berkeley: University of California Press, 1986.

Freud, Sigmund. "Mourning and Melancholia." In *On Metapsychology: The Pelican Freud Library* Vol. 6, Harmondsworth: Penguin, 1964.

Goldman, Anne E. "I Made the Ink: (Literary) Production and Reproduction in *Dessa Rose* and *Beloved.*" *Feminist Studies* 16, 2 (Summer 1990): 313–30.

Harris, Wilson. *Womb of Space: The Cross-Cultural Imagination.* Westport, Conn.: Greenwood Press, 1983.

Hirsch, Marianne. "Clytemnestra's Children." In *Alice Walker,* edited by Harold Bloom. New York: Chelsea House Publishers, 1989.

Johnson, Barbara, Louis Mackey, and J. Hillis Miller. "Marxism and Deconstruction: Symposium at the Conference on Contemporary Genre Theory and the Yale School." In *Rhetoric and Form: Deconstruction at Yale,* edited by

Robert Con Davis and Ronald Scheifer. Norman: University of Oklahoma Press, 1985.

Jung, Carl Gustav. "The Psychological Aspects of the Kore." In *The Archetypes and the Collective Unconscious*. Princeton, N.J.: Princeton University Press, 1969.

Kitagawa, Muriel. *This Is My Own: Letters to Wes and Other Writings on Japanese Canadians, 1941–1948*. Edited by Roy Miki. Vancouver: Talonbooks, 1985.

Klepfisz, Irena. *A Few Words in the Mother Tongue: Poems Selected and New (1971–1990)*. Portland, Oreg.: Eighth Mountain Press, 1990.

Kogawa, Joy. "Is There a Just Cause?" *Canadian Forum*, (March 1984): 20–24.

———. *Obasan*. Boston: Godine, 1981.

Koller, Alice. *The Stations of Solitude*. New York: William Morrow, 1990.

Kristeva, Julia. "Stabat Mater." In *The Kristeva Reader*, edited by Toril Moi. New York: Columbia University Press, 1986.

Morrison, Toni. *Beloved*. New York: Knopf, 1987.

———. "Rediscovering Black History." *New York Times Magazine*, August 11, 1974, 14–24.

———. "The Site of Memory." In *Inventing the Truth: The Art and Craft of Memoir*, edited by William Zinsser. Boston: Houghton Mifflin, 1987.

Patterson, Orlando. *Slavery and Social Death*. Cambridge, Mass.: Harvard University Press, 1982.

Roy, Patricia E., et al., eds. *Mutual Hostages: Canadians and Japanese During the Second World War*. Toronto: University of Toronto Press, 1990.

Soyinka, Wole. "Anbiku." In *Idanre and Other Poems*. New York: Hill and Wang, 1987.

Toni Morrison. TV interview with Alan Benson. An RM Arts production, produced and directed by Alan Benson, edited by Melvyn Bragg. Chicago: Home Vision, 1987.

The Role of Memory

in August Wilson's

Four-Hundred-Year Autobiography

SANDRA G. SHANNON

Sometime during 1980 a relatively unknown playwright named August Wilson submitted a play about a group of black cab drivers to the Playwrights Center in Minneapolis. Already much accustomed to rejection notices as an aspiring poet-turned-playwright, Wilson was elated when the Playwrights Center not only accepted *Jitney* but also awarded him $2,500. He recalls thinking, "Wow, I must be a playwright" (Savran, 291). With this newfound confidence in himself, along with a growing network of support from seasoned directors and accomplished playwrights, Wilson churned out a succession of plays about the black experience. But Wilson's most rewarding discovery in the early stages of his career as a playwright was that his plays—*Joe Turner's Come and Gone, Ma Rainey's Black Bottom, Fullerton Street, Jitney,* and so on—were fortuitously set in separate decades (1911, 1927, 1941, and 1971, respectively). Once he had observed a pattern in his work, Wilson went on to adopt an impressive ten-play mission and an equally impressive artistic agenda:

> To focus upon what I felt were the most important issues confronting Black Americans for that decade, so ultimately they [the plays] could stand as a record of Black experience over the past hundred years presented in the form of dramatic literature. What you end up with is a kind of review, or re-examination, of history. Collectively they can read certainly not as a total history, but as some historical moments. (Powers, 52)

Guided by what seems to be a spiritual calling to purge the demons of his past from his memory, this dynamic playwright from the streets of Pittsburgh's Hill District has, since then, constructed a veritable museum of plays featuring recognizable moments from the African American past.

Wilson's grand-scale revision of African American history through drama is inspired by resources as diverse as blues lyrics; the paintings of Romare Bearden; the poetry, plays, and political ideology of Amiri Baraka; and the short fiction of Argentine-born Jorge Borges. However, the richest resource for his plays is his own memory. By varying degrees each of the plays that make up Wilson's ten-play chronicle is a product of the playwright's own remembered past—a past that combines his personal experiences of growing up poor and fatherless in a Pittsburgh slum area, his quest for his own ties with Africa, and his sustained belief that African Americans of the present generation urgently need to ground themselves in Africa's cultural past. When asked during a 1987 interview what fuels his ongoing dramatic agenda, Wilson responded:

> For the most part I make them [stories] up. Sometimes they are things I heard 20 years ago. These stories are repeated over and over. As soon as you hear them, you go and tell somebody. These are things that the community has decided you need to know to survive. I'm trying to remember stories that I heard, and understand why I heard them and what people are trying to pass along. ("He Gives a Voice to the Nameless Masses," 47)

In the process of remembering these stories, Wilson becomes a medium for passing along the cultural language embodied in them. His plays are manifestations of a conscious mind teeming with people, conversations, and images from both his experienced and his imagined past. Consequently, these thoughts, shaped largely by his memory, become gateways to the larger African American past.

August Wilson's dependence on his memory as the master text for a dramatic revision of African American history raises some important theoretical issues. For example, how does Wilson's memory fit into his scheme of rewriting certain historical moments of African American history? And in what ways does Wilson's memory influence the action, dialogue, and structural framework of the completed plays? Now that he has succeeded in completing more than half of his promised project, critical attention must accordingly begin to assess the impact of this soon-to-be-completed history package as a collective body of work with an articulated agenda of its own. This essay seeks to provide a basis for such future scholarship by demonstrating how memory informs each of the plays that he has, so far, completed in his cycle.

Wilson's ten-play chronicle challenges the authority of history. Preferring dramatic conflicts that evolve fundamentally from his own memory, he consciously avoids historical research and turns instead to the blues as inspiration for mood, place, time, subject, and dialogue for each play. The blues evoke an atmosphere conducive to remembering the past. Codified in the lyrics and musical notes of Wilson's favorite blues pieces are voices from the past—what he calls "an emotional reference" (Moyers, 168). These songs and musical pieces move him to summon the experiences of the people to whom he gives voice in his work.[1] Thus, his memory, combined with an active artistic imagination inspired by the blues, overshadows any need for historical accuracy and forms the basis for dramatic texts that treat history as merely a way of knowing the present world and of predicting and shaping the future. Wilson's mission is not so much to challenge the wrongs of the past as to bring them once again into focus to exemplify how African Americans addressed these wrongs and emerged from them.

By relying on his memory, Wilson maintains a measure of personal control over history during this process. In the playwright's hands sacrosanct records of the African American past are molded into useful examples of thought and behavior for present and future generations. At a lecture at Manhattan's Poetry Center, he noted, "What I hope to do is to 'place' the tradition of black American culture, to demonstrate its ability to sustain us. We have a ground that is specific, that is peculiarly ours, that we can stand on, which gives us a world view, to look at the world and comment on it" ("How to Write a Play Like August Wilson," H5). With this mission in mind, Wilson makes possible a continuous dialogue with the past, especially targeted at African Americans who have denounced or ignored their African heritage. This opportunity to engage the past invites redefinition, introspection, and ultimately a reassessment of current attitudes and modes of behavior.

Ma Rainey's Black Bottom (1981), the play most responsible for launching Wilson's career, is a still shot of an imaginary day in the life of the controversial blues legend Ma Rainey. With the help of his imagination plus a good deal of intuition, Wilson reexamines an era in African American history tainted by the plundering of his people's cultural heritage. By assembling a group of fictitious musicians around his interpretation of the actual blues legend and by placing them in a 1927 Chicago setting, Wilson effectively peels back the covers on the blues-recording industry of this period to expose the rampant greed and opportunism among white promoters as well as the frustrations of professionally stunted African American artists.

At the center of the conflict in *Ma Rainey* is the gross plundering of profits from blues performers. Whites enjoyed financial prowess over all aspects of the recording industry in 1920s Chicago. Using this control to their advantage, they plundered the profits of blues singers and musicians unable to market their own talents because of unchecked racism and meager funds. The musicians in the play react in various ways to their virtual shutout from this profitable scheme by soothing their pain with the "psychic balm" (Freedman) of the blues. Their music, their conversations, and the vivid stories of their past are seasoned by the blues.

That part of Wilson's life which most influences his art as well as his attitude is the blues. In *Ma Rainey* it functions in three ways: as the subject of the dramatic conflict, as the subliminal force that conveys the oppression of the characters, and as the impetus behind the playwright's creative imagination. This pervasiveness of the blues is best explained by Ma Rainey's own admission: "You don't sing to feel better. You sing 'cause that's a way of understanding life. . . . The blues help you get out of bed in the morning. You get up knowing you ain't alone. There's something else in the world" (*MR*, 82–83).[2]

August Wilson creates the tense scenario of *Ma Rainey's Black Bottom* out of emotions inspired by the blues. The creative process at work in the play includes a mixture of imagination and memory; he selectively borrows various features from each medium to suit his design. For example, because Ma Rainey's reputation precedes her, she is immediately recognizable on stage. However, Wilson is not obliged to be faithful to the details of her life. As one critic notes,

> Because Wilson's intention was to depict an imaginary incident in the career of Ma Rainey, not to write a biography, he avoided the extensive study of her life that might have had a "straitjacket" effect on his portrait. His interest was in what lay behind the blues, music that he believes represents the total experience of blacks in the earlier South. ("Wilson, August, " 53).

Without research and without the advantage of actually having met or known Ma Rainey, Wilson turned to her music as the best way to acquaint himself with her ethos. He told one *Theater Week* writer, "For *Ma Rainey*, I read the liner notes on the back of her albums and then I thought the best way to know her was to listen to her sing" (Barbour, 11). Implicit in this admission is that Ma Rainey's persona emerges from the playwright's mystical reunion with the blues singer, whom he reincarnates by listening to her music.

Despite Wilson's claims to eschew the "straitjacket" of research, *Ma Rainey's Black Bottom* does bear evidence of more than a very active imagination or extraordinary sensitivity to her music. For example, Sandra Lieb's study of her, *Mother of the Blues* (1981), reveals intimate details of her life that are knowable only as a result of in-depth research. The fact that Ma Rainey's jug band music was threatened by more avant-garde, more danceable tunes, that she was bisexual, or that she had a sister are all details that appear in the play and, despite Wilson's claims, required some degree of investigation or prior knowledge.[3] Moreover, the play's very credible depictions of race relations during the late 1920s and its moving portrayals of blues performers of this decade require some intimate knowledge of the time period.

Unlike Ma Rainey, the diverse group of musicians show more of the influence of the playwright's personal manipulations. In fact, Ma Rainey is the only historically "real" character in the play. Toledo, Cutler, Levee, and Slow Drag are reflections of Wilson's past acquaintances—most likely from his days in Pittsburgh—filtered through the prism of his imagination. As agents of Wilson's memory, they function as props set in place mainly to advance the tragic story line. He admits:

> As for the characters, they are all invented. At the same time they are all made up out of myself. So they're all me, different aspects of my personality I guess. But I don't say, "Oh, I know this guy like this. I'm going to write Joe." . . . So I write different parts of myself and I try to invent or discover some other parts. ("How to Write a Play," 5)

The vivid stories these characters tell of their own troubled experiences or their lighthearted anecdotes enrich the play's emotional context and allow the audience to view them as three-dimensional individuals. For example, Levee's recollections of his mother being raped by white men suggests the motive for his loathsome attitude toward his fellow band members. He tells the group, "There was my mama with a gang of white mens. She tried to fight them off, but I could see where it wasn't gonna do her any good, I didn't know what they were doing to her . . . but I figured whatever it was they may as well do to me too" (*MR*, 69). The musicians also add touches of humor to their recollections. Cutler interrupts an intensifying round of dozens with a tale of how Slow Drag got his name:

> They had a contest one time in this little town called Bolingbroke about a hundred miles outside of Macon. We was playing for this dance and they was giving twenty dollars to the best slow draggers. Slow Drag looked over the competition, got down off the bandstand, grabbed hold of one of them gals, and stuck to her like a fly to jelly. (*MR*, 55)

Like each of Wilson's dramatic chronicles, *Ma Rainey's Black Bottom* is a chapter in what he calls "a 400 year old autobiography, which is the black experience" ("He Gives Voice to the Nameless Masses," 47). In re-creating this record of the past, Wilson, as autobiographer, is at once author and subject; his life experiences assume allegorical dimensions as he relates the story of his people through the prism of his memory. *New York Times* critic Samuel Freedman observes, "If Wilson's mission is memory, his method is more artistic than archival. . . . He is a storyteller, and his story is the African diaspora—not because it suits a political agenda but because everything in his life conspired to make it so."

The 1987 Broadway play *Fences* (1986) best demonstrates the incorpo-ration of Wilson's private past into the larger scheme of rewriting African American history. The conflict of this 1950s play set in "the slag slippery hills of a middle American urban industrial city that one might mistake for Pittsburgh, Pennsylvania" (*F*, vii), closely resembles Wilson's own troubled relationship with his misunderstood stepfather, David Bedford. The parallels between the fictional Troy and Cory Maxson and between Bedford and young Wilson are obvious:

> In 1969, when Wilson was 24, his stepfather, David Bedford, died. The two had not been close for almost a decade, since Wilson quit his high school football team against Bedford's wishes, and the late 1960s was a time when young black men like Wilson often disparaged their fathers as a generation of compromisers. Then Wilson heard a story about Bedford that changed his life.
>
> Bedford, it turned out, had been a high school football star in the 1930s, and had hoped a sports scholarship would lead to a career in medicine. But no Pittsburgh college would give a black player a grant and Bedford was too poor to pay his own way. To get the money, he decided to rob a store, and during the theft he killed a man. For the 23 years before he met Wilson's mother, Bedford had been in prison. By the time he was free, only a job in the city Sewer Department beckoned. (Freedman, 40)

Before David Bedford came into the life of Wilson's African American mother, Daisy, Wilson had had an even more unstable relationship with his German biological father, who had little to do with Wilson's mother, his sisters, or him. The young boy grew to dislike his white father and eventually identified with his mother's African heritage. Consequently, the pattern of paternal detachment in Wilson's life inspired *Fences*. Based on the playwright's own quest for a father figure, *Fences* demonstrates the bittersweet relations between a misunderstood African American fa-ther and his headstrong adolescent son. Certain identifiable aspects of Wilson's past have been altered, but for the most part the gist of his recollections remains intact: the seemingly tyrannical father who once served time in prison for murder, who aspired to become a sports legend, who found unfulfilling work as a garbage collector, and who attempted to dictate his son's future. Thematically, however, the most important parallels between Wilson's memory and the conflict in *Fences* are the eventual epiphanies that both young Wilson and Cory experience about their fathers' integrity. Both young men mature to some extent when they learn the entire context of their fathers' actions.

The angelic, long-suffering Rose Maxson is the result of equal borrowing from the playwright's imagination and from his memory. As an extremely tolerant, self-sacrificing African American mother, Rose is the stage equivalent of the late Daisy Wilson, whom her son, August, admires for having instilled in him "the forces that have shaped me, the nurturing, the learning" (Moyers, 174). Supporting characters, such as Bono, Gabriel, Alberta, and Lyons, are essentially imaginary backdrops who complement the portrait of father Troy's controversial world. Wilson told journalist Bill Moyers, "I crawl up inside the material, and I get so immersed in it that as I'm inventing this world, I'm also becoming a part of it" (178).

While Wilson's memory of his adolescence does provide a good deal of the framework for *Fences,* certain characters' remembrances of days gone by provide another perspective on his preoccupation with the past. Wilson allows memory in *Fences* to extend beyond his recognized moments from the past to include the recollections of the characters he creates. While this play, set in 1957, edges toward revolutionary change on the eve of the Civil Rights movement, Troy Maxson, its fifty-three-year-old main character, can still recall his experiences as a sharecropper's son. Indeed, the play is strategically set in a time that invites nostalgia or regret over the past and, at the same time, promises positive change.

David Bedford's alter ego, Troy Maxson, is eloquent as he reminisces about past events, such as his glorious days in the Negro League or his conviction for homicide and time spent in jail. He recalls the callous ways of his sharecropper father, who regularly placed farming above his family: "The only thing my daddy cared about was getting them bales of cotton in to Mr. Lubin. That's the only thing that mattered to him" (*F,* 51). During other moments of reflection, Troy recalls how he courted and won Rose, how he acquired "three rooms [of furniture] for two ninety eight" (*F,* 15), and how he wrestled with death for three days and three nights during a bout with pneumonia.

Troy spends a great deal of rhetoric remembering the past, but he is just as focused on the future, albeit largely through his son. Although he is not happy to recall his father's limited thinking, he has boundless hopes for Cory.

> You go on and get your book-learning so you can work yourself up in that A&P or learn how to fix cars or build houses or something, get you a trade. That way you have something can't nobody take away from you. You go on and learn how to put your hands to some good use. Besides hauling people's garbage. (*F*, 35)

Rose Maxson's character noticeably grows once she resorts to remembering her past. The most revealing aspects of her character do not surface during lighter moments with her husband, Troy, as he ribs her in front of his friend Bono or during her many intercessions on behalf of Gabriel, Lyons, or Cory. But Rose immediately becomes a fuller, more complex character once she reaches back into her memory to explain the degree to which she has neglected herself for Troy. She tells him, "I gave eighteen years of my life to stand in the same spot with you. Don't you think I ever wanted other things? Don't you think I had dreams and hopes? What about my life? What about me?" (*F*, 70). Dredging up the past becomes a desperate measure for Rose as she roars out her disapproval of Troy's infidelity. However, at the close of *Fences*, memory becomes a healing measure as Rose mends the broken fences between Cory and his father.

Troy's place in Wilson's temporal scheme is important to the playwright's focus on generational differences between father and son. His memory is valuable in demonstrating causal relationships between past difficulties with his father and the present confrontation with his own son. Patricia Schroeder observes in *The Presence of the Past in Modern American Drama*, "It takes only a modest creative leap to imagine a drama in which those carefully chosen past incidents are both more and less than facts, a drama in which the memories of the characters, reliable or not, are permitted to determine the spectator's understanding of what has happened in the past" (20). Although Troy tries desperately to reclaim some of his life's fleeting gusto by sequestering his brother's veteran benefits, by arguing for a promotion at his job, by imposing his trademark iron will on Cory, and by having a lusty affair with Alberta, he is a veritable dinosaur who has, through no fault of his own, missed his life's calling. The various temporal perspectives influencing Troy Maxson's behavior show the complexities of the African Americans of this decade. Wilson explains:

> White America looks at black America in this glancing manner. They pass right by the Troy Maxsons of the world and never stop to look at them. They

talk about niggers as lazy and shiftless. Well, here's a man with responsibilities as prime to his life. I wanted to examine Troy's life layer by layer and find out why he made the choices he made. (Watlington, 110)

Among the chronicles Wilson has already added to his ambitious ten-play mission to retell African American history, *Joe Turner's Come and Gone* (1988) and *The Piano Lesson* (1990) feature the most poignant emotional links to slavery and its ramifications. By Wilson's design, these emotional links to slavery become spaces for dialogue between contemporary African American audiences and their slave past. The dramatic forums that he creates in *Joe Turner* and *Piano Lesson* invite these audiences to perceive that through acknowledging their history, they uncover an untapped source of emotional support needed to withstand today's problems.

Joe Turner's Come and Gone, like all of Wilson's plays to date, is grounded in recognizable moments in African American history yet acquires its form and substance from the playwright's imagined reality of certain time periods. The time period featured in this play is charged with the emotions associated with displacement, alienation, and isolation. The historical context out of which *Joe Turner* evolves includes a backdrop of frustrated sharecroppers; hundreds of unemployed, unskilled laborers; countless broken families; and a pervasive rumor of a better life up north. W. E. B. Du Bois, like Wilson, saw drama in the very existence of African Americans who endured such oppression. In his exhaustive sociological study *Black Reconstruction in America*, he notes, "Easily the most dramatic episode in American history was the sudden move to free four million black slaves in an effort to stop a great civil war, to end forty years of bitter controversy, and to appease the moral sense of civilization" (3). In epic fashion Richard Wright's *Twelve Million Black Voices* documents the lean years following the Emancipation Proclamation when freedmen and their families could not escape the engulfing system of sharecropping. After leaving dilapidated shacks encircled by rows of cotton stalks, they headed north to cities like Chicago, Washington, D.C., Philadelphia, and Pittsburgh.

As he does in *Ma Rainey's Black Bottom*, August Wilson avoids the so-called straitjacket effect of researching the respective decades for his dramatic history series, taking cues instead from his own intuitive perceptions of what African Americans must have experienced and how they must have reacted and felt during each play's separate conflicts. The seeds for *Joe Turner* germinated as Wilson listened to a W. C. Handy album, *W. C. Handy Sings His Immortal Hits*. He explains:

There's a cut on the album where Handy says, "The story of the blues cannot be told without Joe Turner." Joe Turner was the brother of Pete Turner, governor of Tennessee, who oppressed Negroes into peonage. He had a chain with forty links to it. And the men would be late coming home from their work in the fields. And someone would say, "Haven't you heard? Joe Turner's come and gone." (Barbour, 10)

Set precariously within the disorientation of the Reconstruction and post-Reconstruction, the play focuses on cultural fragmentation, that is, the emotional and physical effects associated with the displacement of freedmen. Wilson consciously suppresses his persona in *Joe Turner's Come and Gone*, merging his identity with the collective consciousness of all of his ancestors. He admittedly strives to create another world so that "you're looking at the familiar in a new way" (Powers, 54). In the process, he stretches the concept of memory to encompass four hundred years of African American presence in America and to create a link between past and present descendants of Africa.

Herald Loomis is both a native son and a prodigal son of this instability. Although just becoming accustomed to the bittersweet joys of freedom made possible by the Emancipation Proclamation, Loomis is once again enslaved—but this time by the legendary white Tennesseean Joe Turner, who forces him to labor on his plantation for seven years. Once released, Loomis returns, scattered and disillusioned by the long separation from his wife and daughter. The outlawed Tennesseean Joe Turner, therefore, is both Loomis's captor and the personification of all the antagonistic forces facing freedmen in this post-Reconstruction era. But when Loomis seeks shelter at a boardinghouse during one of many stopovers in search of his wife, he learns that she has become saved and no longer wishes to have anything to do with him. Left with the custody of his daughter, Loomis now feels especially incomplete. Deeply frustrated, he slashes his chest in a ritualistic act of exorcism, declaring, "I don't need nobody to bleed for me! I can bleed for myself" (*JT*, 93).

Joe Turner's Come and Gone reintroduces modern African American audiences to certain atavistic images and emotions prevalent during the post–Civil War era in the United States. Out of his vivid imagined reality, Wilson conjures up scenes of how it must have been for the masses of newly emancipated bondsmen. In a prefatory note to the play, he writes:

From the deep and the near South the sons and daughters of newly freed American slaves wander into the city [Pittsburgh]. Isolated, cut off from memory, having forgotten the names of the gods and only guessing at their faces, they arrive dazed and stunned, their hearts kicking in their chest with a song worth singing. ("The Play," *JT*)

Joe Turner provides audiences with a dramatic forum for grappling with the emotional wasteland confronting African Americans in the post-Reconstruction era. Accordingly, its most valuable assets are those which suggest to its audiences that Africa is an extended yet still very powerful backdrop. Such ties with Africa are manifest in the play's emphasis on the archetypal search for home, the patterns of storytelling, and elements of magic and the supernatural.

Although Herald Loomis's long and desperate search for his wife, Martha Pentecost, is the basis of the play's conflict, his quest is also a mirror image of the subconscious self whose stability is predicated upon knowing its source. Thus Loomis's quest for home assumes archetypal dimensions that make possible nonverbal dialogue with the past. He tells Martha, "Joe Turner let me loose and I felt all turned around inside. I just wanted to see your face to know that the world was still there. Make sure everything still in its place so I could reconnect myself together" (*JT*, 89). Because of the play's archetypal framework, the audience can fathom not only one African American man's struggle to regain footing, but also his or her own urgent need to get in touch with a private past.

Herald Loomis's archetypal quest for home also suggests nonverbal parallels with a larger quest for Mother Africa. Unlike the emigrationist Marcus Garvey, August Wilson, in the late 1980s, is aware of the impracticalities of advocating that all African Americans return to Africa. Instead, he adapts the dramaturgy of his play to call for a spiritual journey back to their ancestral past. He asserts, "We're not in Africa anymore, and we're not going back to Africa. You have to understand your parents and understand your grandparents. I like to say I'm standing in my grandfather's shoes" (Watlington, 106).

Just as the archetypal familiarities of *Joe Turner* open channels for dialogue with Mother Africa, so too do the pressing stories of select members of the cast of post–Civil War characters. The storytelling tradition, which Wilson has woven into all of his plays to date, is distinctly African. His director/mentor Lloyd Richards observes that "the oral tradition brought from Africa was not only useful but essential to pass on history, custom, and the names, nature and practices of ancient gods" (64). Closely linked to the oral history preserved by the African griot, the stories of Herald Loomis, his wife, and several tenants of the Pittsburgh boardinghouse convey the verbal history spanning years of private struggle.

The prodigal son Herald Loomis seems particularly anxious to tell his story. After years of following his wife's trail, Loomis tells the resident conjure man details of a haunting vision of bones rising up and walking on top of the water. In an interview, the playwright interpreted the significance of these reactivated bones as "Loomis's connection with the ancestors, the Africans who were lost during the Middle Passage and were thrown overboard. They are walking around here and now and they look like you because you are these very same people. This is who you are" (Powers, 54). Loomis has apparently become an unwitting medium for transmitting the pain and suffering of his ancestors—indeed the entire African American race. Their songs haunt him for exposure while he seeks to find his own.

African rituals and elements of the supernatural also converge in *Joe Turner* to bridge present and past. A conjure man, or African healer (Bynum Walker), practices puzzling bloodletting rituals involving pigeons dangerously close to his landlord's garden; a restless spirit (Miss Mabel) returns from the grave to haunt a mischievous young boy for failing to release some pigeons; and a recently released farmhand (Herald Loomis) slashes his chest in another bloodletting ritual that apparently denounces Christianity and mimics an African sacrificial rite. Although these images of Africa in *Joe Turner* are prevalent, they often become part of the play's subtext; that is, Wilson does not spend much time creating complete pictures of these African touches. Indeed, the very gaps that he creates or the questions he leaves unanswered serve as invitations to think, to come to grips with one's personal ancestral ties with Africa. He explained in an interview:

> Blacks have taken Christianity and bent it to serve their African-ness. In Africa there's ancestor worship, among other kinds of religious practices. That's given blacks, particularly southern blacks, the idea of ghosts, magic and superstition. . . . Relating to the spirit worlds is very much a part of African and Afro-American culture. (Savran, 302)

In *The Piano Lesson* Wilson establishes a line of communication between Africa and the modern African American audience by galvanizing the symbolic resonance of a nearly two-hundred-year-old piano. This powerful icon of African Americans' slave past, though static in itself, moves a brother and sister to find solutions to the question "What should we do with our past?"

Whereas a W. C. Handy blues album inspired *Joe Turner*, a painting by Romare Bearden moved Wilson to write *The Piano Lesson*. The image of a young girl at a piano being coached by an authoritative female yielded the idea that a piano could be used to teach a history lesson. Wilson explained to a *New York Times* feature writer:

> So I got the idea from the painting that there would be a character who was trying to acquire a sense of self-worth by denying her past. And I felt that she couldn't do that. She had to confront the past, in the person of her brother, who was going to sweep through the house like a tornado coming from the South, bringing the past with him. (Rothstein)

Central to *The Piano Lesson*'s conflict is an old piano, which functions as an emblem of African folk tradition and American capitalism. The pictorial history carved into its surface by the great-grandfather of Berneice Charles Crawley and Boy Willie Charles has increased both its monetary and its sentimental values. Berneice reveres the piano to the point of paranoia and refuses to let her brother turn it into a down payment for land. However, Boy Willie is not dissuaded by her obsession for what is, to him, a sensible investment in his future; he maintains that he can reap more practical good from an otherwise useless object by using it to promote his career and thereby taking advantage of an opportunity that was denied his sharecropper father. With impeccable logic, he rationalizes against his sister's less forcibly argued need to preserve the family heirloom.

Boy Willie is not alone in his designs on the piano. Also apparently bent on retrieving the controversial object is the pesky ghost of the piano's former white owner, Robert Sutter. This spirit is the direct descendant of the slave-owning Sutter family, who acquired the piano from a poor white farmer in a barter for Berneice and Boy Willie's paternal great-grandparents. This spirit, who still lays claim to the piano, tinkles its keys from time to time and terrorizes both Berneice and her daughter with several intrusions into their home. Exasperated by the ghost's claim to the piano, Boy Willie finally exorcises it in a symbolic wrestling match, which is followed immediately by Berneice's decision finally to play the piano.

The carvings etched onto the piano's wooden surface transform the musical instrument and furniture piece into a memento of the Charles family's slave past. Because the piano was offered in exchange for Boy Willie and Berneice's great-grandparents, it is imbued with their ancestors' very essence. Indeed, to Berneice, the piano is the embodiment of each member of her family who was forced to endure slavery.

Yet the symbolism of this piano runs deeper than as an object responsible for a feud between siblings. More than a controversy over a piano, their strife becomes a public debate recognizable to any African American family at a similar crossroads. Still more important, the piano forces them to remember their ancestors and call on them to intervene in their heated discussions so that their debating can yield understanding, appreciation, and wise decisions. Ancestors in the Charles family as distant as great-grandparents and as immediate as their recently deceased father, in effect, assume form through Berneice and Boy Willie's verbal battle over the piano. For each, the past, as represented by his or her ancestors, offers equally convincing support for quite different positions. For example, Boy Willie's recollections of his late father's life as a sharecropper inspire him to avoid a similar mistake. Pressing images of his father's unfulfilled life prompt him to explain his designs on the piano. He tells his uncle, "If my daddy had seen where he could have traded that piano in for some land of his own, it wouldn't be sitting up here now. He spent his whole life farming on somebody else's land. I ain't gonna do that" (*PL*, 46).

Although Boy Willie's opportunism is understandable, albeit risky, Berneice's reverence for the piano also deserves a measure of respect. She tells her brother, "Money can't buy what that piano cost. You can't sell your soul for money. It won't go with the buyer. It'll shrivel and shrink to know that you ain't taken on to it. But it won't go with the buyer" (50) and "You ain't taking that piano out of my house! Look at this piano. . . . Mama Ola polished this piano with her tears for seventeen years. She rubbed on it till her hands bled. Then she rubbed the blood in . . . mixed up with the rest of the blood on it" (52).

The resolution of Boy Willie and Berneice's conflict is not immediately clear at the close of *The Piano Lesson*. Its open-ended final scene leads one to surmise that Wilson invites his audience to weigh the evidence and arrive at their own conclusions. What will happen to the piano? Does Boy Willie persuade his sister to release it to him, or does Berneice continue worshiping it from afar? Whatever its fate, it is certain that its value increases as it is transformed from an object of conflict to one that inspires the Charles family to engage in conversations with their past.

August Wilson's most recent play, *Two Trains Running* (1990), is weighed down by the omnipresence of memory. Set in 1969, the play is a static, two-act succession of stories about the past trials of a motley group of restaurant regulars. As they gather daily at a Pittsburgh restaurant scheduled for demolition, they press on each other their life experiences in search of both causes and cures for their troubles. When they cannot get at the source of their blues, they turn to Aunt Ester, a reportedly 322-year-old sage whose extraordinary longevity and unorthodox manner of collecting her fees from a river baffle but do not deter her customers.

The regulars of this soon-to-be-demolished restaurant, positioned across the street from West's funeral parlor, include a mentally retarded man who is obsessed with getting a ham that was promised to him for a paint job he completed some nine and a half years ago; a newly released inmate from the penitentiary where he served time for robbing a bank; a wealthy mortician who once doubled as a numbers runner and bootlegger but who now owns a posh funeral parlor, where he displays the body of an extremely influential religious leader whose death has attracted throngs of mourners and curious onlookers; a pretty young waitress who has mutilated her legs with razor cuts to deflect unwelcome attention from men; and the restaurant's owner, who is rightfully nervous about the compensation the city of Pittsburgh plans to offer him for his establishment.

Because the substance of *Two Trains* is conveyed largely through conversations about the past, very little action transpires. Indeed, during the course of this rhetorical display, only two major developments occur: Hambone's landlady finds his scarred body sprawled across his bed, and the restaurateur Memphis discovers that the city's payment to buy out his business far exceeds the $10,000 he expected. A love affair between Sterling, the ex-inmate, and the waitress stirs up the action a bit, but aside from a steamy kiss and suggestions of marriage, any future plans the two entertain seem hopelessly stalled.

In addition, death permeates the setting, further retarding any movement in the play. Malcolm X's murder looms in the background; the mortician West has gained both popularity and wealth by inheriting the bodies of numerous Pittsburgh citizens; Prophet Samuel's body draws hundreds of viewers as it lies in state in West's funeral parlor; and Hambone's body is discovered mysteriously sprawled across his bed and riddled with stab wounds. These patterns of stagnation and death are reinforced by Wilson's recurring emphasis on memory. Like Eugene O'Neill's group of has-beens in *The Iceman Cometh*, these self-made philosophers rarely move beyond their present circumstances and get their greatest thrills by remembering experiences.

The digressive tendencies of several characters who narrate their experiences in Memphis's cafe also contribute to the play's lack of momentum. Although the memories of men such as Memphis and West do provide some useful perspectives, several speakers use the opportunity to speak in order to cram in as much of their life's experiences as they can. Their recollections begin as thoughtful responses to some issue at hand but eventually branch off into a medley of remotely related snatches of memory. Memphis, for example, is quick to counter West's belief that it is futile to challenge white city officials once they make him an offer for his land. Memphis professes to "know how to deal with white folks" (*TT*, 60) and proceeds to tell a story that begins with his being run off his Jackson, Mississippi, farm. In the middle of relating the tale, he proceeds to relate the story of the murder of a mule he loved by white outlaws eager to grab his land, now rejuvenated by his discovery of a subterranean water supply. Memphis laments, "But I loved that old mule. Me and him had been through a lot together. He was a good old mule. Remind me of myself" (*TT*, 60). Sterling also rambles through a series of experiences whenever he gains an audience: "We had one boy down at the Toner Institute . . . name of Eddie Langston. I never will forget that. We was about thirteen. I tried to wake him up in the morning and the whole bed was filled with blood. He cut his wrist and bled to death" (54–55); "I got in a fight one time. This woman kept looking at me and the man she was with come over and got mad at me. I told him he ought to be talking to her. He punched me in my mouth" (55); and "This woman told me one time, 'Sterling, I wanna have your baby.' I told her if we have a baby he might live to be 75 years old. Just think how much hell he gonna catch. I wouldn't do that to nobody" (56). To these characters, the stories dredged up from their memories provide definition for their present lives. They take advantage of each opportunity they get to connect with their past and capitalize on the attention of any ready-made audience.

As in *Fences*, the time in which *Two Trains* is set energizes the play with a sense of restlessness about imminent change. The politically and racially detonated time period, which Wilson designates as "one month after Martin Luther King Jr.'s assassination, against a backdrop of Malcolm X rallies and riot police" (Courtmanche), is appropriate. Images of past, present, and future intersect in free-fall lunchroom debates punctuated by long, winding narratives dramatizing moving experiences. For example, Memphis is very cynical about all of the hoopla around him concerning an impending birthday rally for Malcolm X. His cynicism is tinged with bad memories of what becomes of such hype:

> They had that boy, Begaboo. The police walked up and shot him in the head and them same niggers went down there to see the mayor. Raised all kind of

hell. Trying to get the cop charged with murder. They raised hell for three weeks. After that it was business as usual. (63)

Memphis's memories demonstrate lessons he has learned from his past—wisdom that leads him to dismiss the birthday rally as a phony agitation propaganda tactic. But Sterling, fresh out of his prison fatigues and not as informed of the town's history as Memphis is, sees value in this cause. The day after he and Risa attend the rally, he tells the group, "I woke up this morning trying to look around and see what I can do to help the people and that's when I thought about getting me a soapbox" (70). Memphis, like the self-righteous Troy Maxson, is one of that breed of African American men who have grown tired of the impetuosity of youth and the futility of constant rebellion. Ironically, however, *Two Trains* conveys the belief that the future of African American interests in America rests with the likes of Sterling—a noticeably naive ex-con whose no-work ethic and get-rich-quick schemes are ominous signs for the generation soon to take Memphis's place.

Aunt Ester, the 322-year-old offstage counselor, is a questionable addition to the cast of *Two Trains*. She exemplifies all of African American memory—what Wilson refers to as "a testament to the long line of connection that stretches across 346 years to the first African who set foot on the continent of North America" (42). Existing on the fringes of the play's reality, she demonstrates mystical powers by "laying on the hands" and by doling out sound advice. Holloway, one of her staunchest supporters, sings her praises: "I go up to see her every once in a while. Get my soul washed. She don't do nothing but lay her hands on your head. But it's a feeling like you ain't never had before. Then everything in life get real calm and peaceful" (48). Aunt Ester fills a spiritual void in the lives of Memphis's group of incomplete souls. Instead of resorting to Christianity (which they claim to be the white man's religion) for spiritual sustenance when overcome by the blues of their lives, they find their way to the red door on 1839 Wylie Street, behind which Aunt Ester works her soothing brand of faith healing and psychiatry.

Aunt Ester is an obvious attempt to personify an expansive memory of experience; her age is equivalent to the number of years African Americans have been in America. William Gale of the *Providence Journal Bulletin* observed at the play's Yale Repertory Theater opening, "Wilson makes her presence talked about and felt, representing the strength and depth of blacks . . . in all those years, we have a tradition to remember and fall back on, he [Wilson] says" (D2).

Each of the five plays examined in this essay demonstrates Wilson's commitment to reestablishing ties with the African American past. As he notes in the preface to his first published collection of plays, "Each of these plays was a journey. At the end of each, out of necessity, emerged an artifact that is representative, the way a travel photo is representative, of the journey itself. It is the only record" (*Three Plays*, vii). The four-hundred-year-old biography of African American experience that Wilson has been diligently recording for more than a decade documents a journey of the playwright's own mind across the broad expanse of his memory.

For Wilson, the process of reestablishing a link with Africa involves tapping the resources of his memory—both private and collective. He becomes a willing medium for synthesizing elements of his past and the imagined past of thousands of African descendants in order to produce inspirational new adaptations of recorded history. Wilson's revisionist scheme makes room in the history books for renewed dialogue between past and present. Aided by the melancholy strains of blues lyrics, a poet's sensitivity, and superior intuitive abilities, he makes repeated mental voyages to the past.

Notes

1. Wilson explains how he became an early convert to the blues aesthetic in the April 1989 issue of *Vanity Fair* (Watlington). After buying a $3 record player that played only seventy-eights, he discovered a record store that proved to be a veritable gold mine of seventy-eights that were no longer in circulation. There he found a copy of Bessie Smith's "Nobody in Town Can Bake a Sweet Jelly Roll Like Mine" and was so moved by its lyrics that he played it repeatedly. He later recalled, "I'd never heard of Bessie Smith. I listened to it twenty-two times, and I became aware that this stuff was my own. Patti Page, Frank Sinatra—they weren't me. This was me. The music became the wellspring of my work. I took the stuff and ran with it."

2. To help identify and distinguish Wilson's works discussed in this essay, I have assigned the following abbreviations:

F	*Fences*
JT	*Joe Turner's Come and Gone*
MR	*Ma Rainey's Black Bottom*
PL	*The Piano Lesson*
TT	*Two Trains Running*

3. Wilson told *Theater Week*'s David Barbour that he did not know that Ma Rainey had a sister. "I wrote her a sister in the play. And I was glad to find out that she had one," he stated.

192

Works Cited

Barbour, David. "August Wilson's Here to Stay." *Theater Week* (18–25 April 1988): 8–14.

Courtmanche, Elleanor. "August Wilson Trains His Sights on the 60s." *After Hours* (6 April 1990): 3.

Du Bois, W. E. B. *Black Reconstruction in America.* New York: Atheneum, 1971.

Freedman, Samuel. "A Voice from the Street." *New York Times Magazine,* 15 March 1987, 40.

Gale, William. "August Wilson's Vision of Light at the End of the Tunnel." *Providence Journal Bulletin,* 6 April 1990, D1–D2.

"He Gives Voice to Nameless Masses: The New York *Newsday* Interview with August Wilson." *Newsday,* 20 April 1987, 47.

Lieb, Sandra R. *Mother of the Blues: A Study of Ma Rainey.* Amherst: University of Massachusetts Press, 1981.

Moyers, Bill. *A World of Ideas.* New York: Doubleday, 1989.

Powers, Kim. "Theater in New Haven: An Interview with August Wilson." *Theater* 6 (Fall–Winter 1984): 50–55.

Reed, Ishmael. "In Search of August Wilson." *Connoisseur* 217 (1987): 92–97.

Richards, Lloyd. "Preface to *Joe Turner's Come and Gone.*" *Theater* 7 (Summer–Fall 1986): 62–88.

Rothstein, Mervyn. "Round Five for the Theatrical Heavyweight." *New York Times,* 15 April 1990, 2:8.

Savran, David. *In Their Own Words: Contemporary American Playwrights.* New York: Communications Group, 1988.

Schroeder, Patricia. *The Presence of the Past in Modern American Drama.* Rutherford, N.J.: Fairleigh Dickinson University Press, 1989.

Shannon, Sandra. "From Lorraine Hansberry to August Wilson: An Interview with Lloyd Richards." *Callaloo* 14 (Winter 1991): 133.

Watlington, Dennis. "Hurdling Fences." *Vanity Fair* (April 1989): 102–13.

"Wilson, August." *Current Biography* 48 (August 1987): 53.

Wilson, August. *August Wilson: Three Plays.* Pittsburgh: University of Pittsburgh Press, 1991.

———. "How to Write a Play Like August Wilson." *New York Times,* 10 March 1991, H5, H17.

———. *Joe Turner's Come and Gone.* New York: New American Library, 1988.

———. *Ma Rainey's Black Bottom.* New York: New American Library, 1981.

———. *The Piano Lesson.* New York: Plume, 1990.

———. "Two Trains Running." *Theater* 22 (Fall–Winter 1990–1991): 41–72.

Beyond Mimicry:

The Poetics of Memory and Authenticity

in Derek Walcott's *Another Life*

SANDRA POUCHET PAQUET

Between 1970 and 1974 Derek Walcott published several essays on Caribbean literary culture: "What the Twilight Says: An Overture" (1970), "Meanings" (1970), "The Caribbean: Culture or Mimicry" (1974), and "The Muse of History" (1974). These essays articulate an overarching set of philosophical and methodological considerations that are central to any discussion of a modern Caribbean aesthetic and sensibility, and are central to an understanding of the aesthetic personality Walcott creates in *Another Life* (1973), a poetic autobiography published in the same period. In *Another Life,* one of the great archetypal poems of the polyglot Caribbean, Walcott creates a prototype of the Caribbean poet as possessor and transmitter of knowledge about his culture.[1] The poem and essays together constitute an integrated poetic vision, a kind of cultural manifesto, in which Walcott determines his own legitimacy as Caribbean poet and, by extension, affirms the authenticity of Caribbean literary culture.

The overarching themes in all these works are the New World themes of a new civilization and a new poetic tradition that bind the disparate elements of an evolving society into a moral and artistic whole. The Caribbean poet is not just a creature of language, but the creator of a language that illuminates the regional quest for identity.[2] To name the New World of the Caribbean is to share in the drama of its creation. These themes are central to Walcott's art; they are perhaps central to the self-definition of all New World peoples who seek to transcend the authority of European cultural traditions. These themes are not new, but Walcott writes with the energy and vigor of a modern Caribbean poet in whom the distinctive poetics of Walt Whitman, Pablo Neruda, Aimé Césaire, and St. John Perse are reconceived with a freshness and clarity that illuminate core values of a distinctly Caribbean sensibility ("Muse," 2–7).

Walcott's vision of the Caribbean is essentially Adamic ("Muse," 2–3; "Caribbean," 13). He defines Caribbean man, regardless of ancestry, in elemental terms of transformation and rebirth.[3] In Walcott's New World mythology, the soldering of Africa and Europe in the American archipelago led to a new beginning that is symbolized for Walcott in the Creole languages that proliferated in the Caribbean and in the indigenous folk cultures that sprang up around them.[4] "It was the experience of a whole race renaming something that had been named by someone else and giving that object its own metaphoric power" (Hirsch, 287). The genesis of Creole languages was a primal act of self-identification, an original scripting of cultural values that forms the basis of modern Caribbean culture.[5] It was an elemental process of dismantling and reconstitution, the genesis of a second Eden without any pretense of innocence or naivete: "The apples of its second Eden have the tartness of experience. . . . [T]here is a bitter memory and it is the bitterness that dries last on the tongue. It is the acidulous that supplies its energy" ("Muse," 5). Reconstruction of self and society was not only a social necessity, but also the foundation of a new cultural tradition that required "the re-creation of the entire order, from religion to the simplest rituals" ("Muse," 5).

Walcott's celebration of his Caribbean roots, of his beginnings "on a small island, a colonial backwater" ("Twilight," 14), is the foundation of a distinctly Caribbean sensibility that links him functionally to Césaire and Guillen on one hand and to continental poets like Whitman and Neruda on another. His celebration of the Caribbean landscape as a site of creativity and renewal is an affirmation of the uniqueness of the culture that produced him. But in the 1970s this had the added significance of ferreting out and legitimizing the pervasive African influence on the culture in contradistinction to the European. Walcott tells Edward Hirsch: "Our music, our speech—all the things that are organic in the way we live—are African" (285).[6] Cultural and poetic synthesis in the modern Caribbean is not a sign of cultural degeneracy spawned by colonialism, but a creative enterprise initiated by Africans in an oppressive and hostile environment. Walcott aspires to nothing less than the spirit and tone of the "new naming of things" ("Muse," 13) that gave the region its peculiar cultural momentum and uniqueness.[7]

In "What the Twilight Says: An Overture," Walcott describes the process by which African slaves laid claim to the New World and, in so doing, devises an inspirational model that shapes his own poetics:

> What would deliver him [the New World Negro] from servitude was the forging of a language that went beyond mimicry, a dialect which had the force of revelation as it invented names for things, one which finally settled on its own mode of inflection, and which began to create an oral culture of chants, jokes, folk-songs and fables; this, not merely the debt of history, was his proper claim to the New World. For him metaphor was not symbol but conversation, and because every poet begins with such ignorance, in the anguish that every noun will be freshly resonantly named, because a new melodic inflection meant a new mode, there was no better beginning. ("Twilight," 17)

In the framework of the Antillean quest for identity and cultural authenticity, the rebirth of tradition in this new naming of things is not mimicry but metamorphosis. To fashion one's own mask, the mask through which one may speak to and for the gods, is to move beyond mimicry, to speak with god's tongue, and in turn to find one's own voice.[8]

The metaphor of the mask is appropriate to both the search for voice and the achievement of voice in the Caribbean. In Trinidad's carnival, the masquerade is an image of mimicry on one level and, on another, an original reconstitution of European and African cultural traditions.[9] Since its inception in 1783 Trinidad's carnival has functioned as one of the few reliable keys to the evolution of Trinidad's moral and artistic identity. It is a cultural phenomenon that fuses disparate cultural elements of island life into an artistic whole peculiar to itself. The fusion is myriad and the ensuing "chaos" ritualized and repeated in self-conscious celebration of the spiritual forces shaping the culture.[10] In its various manifestations—the steel drum, calypso, and carnival costume—carnival becomes for Walcott the embodiment of art forms "originating from the mass, which are original and temporarily as inimitable as what they first attempted to copy" ("Caribbean," 9).

In "The Caribbean: Culture or Mimicry?" Walcott observes that "like America, what energizes our society is the spiritual force of a culture shaping itself, and it can do this without the formula of politics" (4). The recognition of an authoritative cultural voice in indigenous cultural traditions provides Walcott with an effective counterbalance to the colonizing influence of European culture: "What I have tried to do . . . is combine my own individual poetic sensibility with the strength of the root, the mass racial sensibility of expression" (Walcott interview, 287–88). Voracious about art and culture in their myriad forms,[11] Walcott has something more in mind than reproducing the Creole languages of the Caribbean, something more than mimicking folk cultural forms:

> It did not matter how rhetorical, how dramatically heightened the language was if its tone were true, whether its subject was the rise and fall of a Haitian king or a small-island fisherman, and the only way to re-create this language was to share in the torture of its articulation. This did not mean the jettisoning of "culture" but, by the writer's making creative use of his schizophrenia, an electric fusion of the old and new. (17)

These values engage Walcott directly in the critical debate surrounding ancestry, colonial history, cultural diversity, and assimilation in Caribbean literature. Walcott takes a position that is diametrically opposed to the terms of V. S. Naipaul's rejection of the Caribbean in *The Middle Passage*, for its multiracial, multiethnic character and for its alleged lack of history: "Racial equality and assimilation are attractive, but only underline the loss, since to accept assimilation is in a way to accept permanent inferiority" (181). Naipaul's rejection of cultural assimilation as a creative process is reinforced by his equation of history with creativity: "History is built around achievement and creation, and nothing was created in the West Indies" (29). Though much bandied about in Caribbean discourse since it was first published in 1969, *The Middle Passage* raised questions about Caribbean culture as a conceptual need to which Walcott responds by creating the counterdiscourse of a new and authentic Caribbean cultural identity engendered by the place and the people: "You build according to the topography of where you live. You are what you eat, and so on; you mystify what you see, you create what you need spiritually, a god for each need" ("Caribbean," 12).[12]

If there is a failure of creativity in the region, it is the failure of colonialism: "Nothing was created *by the British* in the West Indies" (213), Walcott tells Hirsch. He argues that "for the colonial artist the enemy was not the people, or the people's crude aesthetic which he refined and orchestrated" ("Twilight," 35), but "shame and awe of history" ("Muse," 2). He rejects "the idea of history as time for its orignal concept as myth, the partial recall of the race" ("Muse," 2). Caribbean man is "a being inhabited by presences," rather than "a creature chained to his past" ("Muse," 2). This shift in focus from past to present is seen not as an acceptance of defeat, but as a deliverance from servitude to colonial history, a strategy for survival that is the beginning of a new poetic tradition.

> The slave converted himself, he changed weapons, and as he adapted his master's religion, he also adapted his language, and it is here, that what we can look at as our poetic tradition begins. Now began the new naming of things.

197

> Epic was compressed in the folk legend. The act of imagination was the creative effort of the tribe. Later such legends may be written by individual poets, but their beginnings are oral, familial, the poetry of firelight which illuminates the faces of a tight, primal hierarchy. ("Muse," 13)

Walcott argues that cultural assimilation was not surrender to bondage but a victory of epic proportions for the New World African. The interpenetration of conflicting and apparently irreconcilable cultures shaped a new moral and artistic imperative in the Caribbean.[13]

This is Walcott's lifeline as a Caribbean poet whose sensibility bridges Africa, Asia, and Europe in a Caribbean setting. Walcott accommodates a plurality of cultures in a poetic tradition that evolves out of the epic experience of African slaves in the Antilles and locates that tradition in the larger context of a New World experience: "It is this awe of the numinous, this elemental privilege of naming the new world which annihilates history in our great poets, an elation common to all of them, whether they are aligned by heritage to Crusoe and Prospero or to Friday and Caliban" ("Muse," 5). Walcott rejects colonialism, an act of empire, as the beginning of the modern Caribbean in favor of "the new naming of things": "The shipwrecks of Crusoe and of the crew in *The Tempest* are the end of an Old World" ("Muse," 6). The reconstitution of community in the Caribbean begins with the reconstitution of language in that place, a new language that is the beginning of a new way of life for an entire community. The poet's task, as it emerges in this period of Walcott's development, is to continue this process of creation, to remain faithful to the moral and cultural imperative initiated as a collective enterprise by our African ancestors in the New World. The colonizing imperative meets its end here; selective assimilation signals metamorphosis as cultural process rather than historical event.

In his essays and in numerous interviews given during this period, Walcott engenders a conception of Caribbean culture that legitimizes the range and depth of his own literariness and, in the process, validates the authenticity of Caribbean literary culture. In the terms dictated by his essays, Walcott is most Caribbean when he lays claim to the artistic traditions of the world as his legitimate sphere of influence. Rei Terada calls the creative process Walcott's Creole poetics.

> We find creole and classical, native and foreign, individual and communal, singular and multiple, doubled one within the other; as a result, we have to see all of Walcott's poetry as creole poetry, for it incorporates myriad idiolects, glimpses of private language, and glimpses of universal language alike into a creole of creoles. (118)

Yet, in Walcott's concept of Caribbean culture, the authorizing, validating presence is autochthonous, telluric, and oral in its outward manifestations. Walcott's ideal of the good man is "a man who is dependent on the elements, who inhabits them, and takes his life from them. Even further, the ideal man does not need literature, religion, art, or even another, for there is ideally only himself and God" ("Caribbean," 12); his wisdom owes no necessary debt to the ideal of reading and writing that is the poet's medium. Walcott's poet is possessor and transmitter of this ideal knowledge as he traverses the world. The ambiguity is ultimately without crisis because he remains rooted in the "oral, familial, the poetry of the firelight" ("Muse," 13).[14]

The relationship between Walcott's essays and *Another Life* exemplifies the way that very personal, even private, details in Walcott's works are linked to a more encompassing poetics. The ordeal of memory has its correlative in the exile's ordeal of distance and return to a truer vision (Gonzales Echevarria, 10). The poet's life as written becomes a repository of cultural signification. If culture originates in nature, it is embedded in collective memory and in the idiosyncrasies of the individual poet's life and language. In *Another Life*, the ideal poet is the creation of the collective community:

> People entered his understanding
> like a wayside church,
> they had built themselves.
> It was they who had smoothed the wall
> of his clay-colored forehead,
> who made of his rotundity an earthy
> useful object
> holding the clear water of their simple troubles,
> he who returned their tribal names
> to the adze, mattock, midden and cookingpot.
> (20.iv)

Walcott implants himself as authoritative cultural source, as the one who both validates and is validated by the collective culture. The autobiographical mode Walcott employs identifies him as an insider and allows him to define the relationship of self to culture in ideal terms. If culture is embedded in memory and memory is rooted in language, the process of literary self-constitution in *Another Life* locates the poet at the creative center of community and authorizes him to speak of and for the collective.[15] The poet and his art merge in a cluster of tropes around self and collective culture that privileges the poet as authentic and authoritative cultural voice. In the four books of *Another Life*, memories are organized loosely into epochs and historical changes. Idiosyncratic personal experiences are fashioned as a repository of signification for the metaphorical transformation of life into art and the poet's narrative into the narrative of an entire people within his lifetime. In the process, the poet is transformed into cultural archetype and poetic autobiography gains credence as both the lived historical reality and the myth generated by that experience.

In *Another Life*, the process of becoming a Caribbean poet is narrated as the resolution of cultural conflicts engendered by European settlement of the Caribbean islands through plunder, genocide, slavery, and indenture. It is a process of simultaneous dismantling and self-constitution in the aftermath of empire. In "Meanings" Walcott describes himself as "a kind of split writer; I have one tradition inside me going one way, and another tradition going another. The mimetic, the narrative, and dance element is strong on one side, and the literary, the classical tradition is strong on the other" (48). In *Another Life*, Walcott emerges from such conflicts as the unifier, "carrying entire cultures in his head, bitter perhaps, but unencumbered" ("Muse," 3). Like the steelbandsman who listens assiduously to Beethoven as he refines Ogun's instrument in a Trinidad panyard, Walcott places himself at the meeting point of the different cultural traditions of Europe and the Third World in the Caribbean, in a passion for creation that rejects inherited antipathies for a New World identity "in which all our races are powerfully fused" ("Negritude," 22).

What *Another Life* details is that the poet's growth to this maturity of vision, his recovery of cultural values that would allow the warring parts of himself and his culture to interact creatively, was an exhilarating, though painful experience begun in his childhood.[16] Walcott records that it was a learned appreciation of the folklife and folklore of St. Lucia that provided the necessary counterbalance to European culture in his formative years. It was his passion for the people and the landscape of St. Lucia, nurtured variously by Harry, Dunstan, and Andreuille, the three figures around whom books 1, 2, and 3 of *Another Life* are organized, that initiated his recovery from a boyhood sense of cultural orphanage and prompted him to reject the history and rhetoric of empire, of conquest and defeat, to recover another way of seeing himself in the world. The urge to be legitimate heir to Marlowe and Milton ("Twilight,"

31) fuses with the momentousness of "Adam's task of giving things their name" (*Another Life*, 145; henceforth abbreviated as *AL*).

It is Simmons, his mentor, his teacher, and an authority on local folklore, who first shows the poet the way out of his childhood perceptions of himself as "a prodigy of the wrong age and color" (*AL*, 7). The poet discovers through Simmons another way of seeing himself and his landscape in the works of Jamaican poet George Campbell, who is represented as full of reverence for the Jamaican landscape and people. Walcott quotes him selectively:

> "Holy be
> the white head of the Negro,
> Sacred be
> the black flax of a black child . . ."
> And from a new book,
> bound in sea-green linen, whose lines
> matched the exhilaration which their reader,
> rowing the air round him now, conveyed,
> another life it seemed would start again.
> (*AL*, 7)

Inspired by Harry Simmons and the different sense of values that pervades George Campbell's poetry, the young poet's passion for art intensifies as a passion for describing the St. Lucian landscape and people.

Schooled in the heroes of Greek and Roman myths, in Kingsley's *Heroes* and *Tanglewood Tales* (*AL*, 17), the mature poet identifies cultural equivalents in the rhythms of life around the child. He devises another mythology, which places the St. Lucians around him at the center of his creative impulse. In chapter 3, the poet sketches some of them in a series of cameo portraits: Ajax, Berthilia, Choiseul, Darnley, Emmanuel, Farah and Rawlins, Gaga, Helen, Philomene, Ligier, Midas, Nessus, Submarine, Uncle Eric, Vaughan, Weekes, Xodus, and Zandoli.

> These dead, these derelicts,
> that alphabet of the emaciated,
> they were the stars of my mythology.
> (*AL*, 22)

The portraits are revealing in their swift characterization of aspects of folk life in St. Lucia and in what they indicate about the poet's developing sensibility. The divided child walks with Homer and Milton and Methodism among a people rooted in a culture of their own making and their own language, St. Lucian Creole. It is a mythology that in a colonial context is perceived as antithetical to the tone and spirit of Western culture because it is oral and African and because it exists outside the school syllabus and church dogma. The poetic impulse is to unite both traditions in a primal act of self-identification.

The "dry rocks" (*AL,* 23) of an English-derived Methodism invite the divided child to become a preacher and writer of great hymns on its behalf. But this child is rooted in a framework of African Caribbean belief that some call devil worship and others superstition, that the poet recognizes as the spiritual life and creative resource of his community.

> Traumatic, tribal,
> an atavism stronger than their Mass,
> stronger than chapel, whose
> tubers gripped the rooted middle-class,
> beginning where Africa began:
> in the body's memory.
> (*AL,* 24)

The poet's childhood absorption in folk beliefs and the rituals around him, and his keen sense of their creative power, their independent life in his community, provide him with a counterbalance to the classics of European culture. Chapter 4 indicates that the mature poet clings to the folk songs, tales, and rituals of St. Lucia as an essential part of his creative impulse. In this chapter he recounts a story from his childhood that he calls "The Pact." It is the story of Auguste Manoir, "pillar of business and the church" (*AL,* 25), who also practices obeah. "The Pact" is tonally true to the folktales of its type and a highly accomplished narrative poem in itself. But Walcott's debt to the folk imagination goes beyond the literary applications of folklore.

In "What the Twilight Says," Walcott writes about the shaping influence of the songs and tales he heard as a child:

> All these sank like a stain. And taught us symmetry. . . . It had sprung from the hearthside or lamplit hut-door in an age when the night outside was a force, inimical, infested with devils, wood-demons, a country for the journey of the soul, and any child who has heard its symmetry chanted would want to recall it when he was his own story-teller, with the same respect for its shape. ("Twilight," 24)

Walcott identifies himself as the inheritor of a living tradition of folk belief and custom and with it a way of seeing the world and his place in it. In "Meanings," Walcott makes it clear that for him the landscape and the people of St. Lucia are a singular inheritance.

> There is a geography which surrounds the story-teller, and this made physical by things like mist or trees or whatever—mountains, snakes, devils. Depending on how primal the geography is and how fresh in the memory, the island is going to be invested in the mind of the child with a mythology which will come out in whatever the child grows up to retell. (50)

Walcott's lifelong efforts to keep at bay the weight of history and the authority of a European classical tradition in a small British colony rest here, in the landscape and people of the Caribbean. The poet stays rooted spiritually and geographically while, Janus-like, he gazes in different directions, assimilating different cultural traditions without uprooting himself.

Another Life is expansive in its connections, patterns, metaphors, themes, and resonances. Walcott uses St. Lucian folklore as he uses multiple references to the classical traditions of Western Europe, as a way into himself; as a way of tracing the growth of his aesthetic personality across cultural boundaries that are national, racial, and class derived. It is a way of approaching himself, of defining his artistic sensibility in the elemental terms of "a being inhabited by presences, not a creature chained to his past" ("Muse," 2).

Walcott's intimate revisiting of his native landscape in book 1 of *Another Life* culminates in a moment of intense lyricism and reverence for the people and the place, a moment of dedication in which the poet surrenders to his vocation. When the poet is just fourteen, he loses himself in a trance one afternoon as he wanders alone on the hills overlooking a coastal village.

> I drowned in laboring breakers of bright cloud,
> then uncontrollable I began to weep,
> inwardly, without tears, with a serene extinction
> of all sense; I felt compelled to kneel,
> I wept for nothing and for everything,
> I wept for the earth of the hill under my knees,
> for the grass, the pebbles, for the cooking smoke
> above the laborers' houses like a cry,
> for unheard avalanches of white cloud.
> (*AL*, 41–42)

The poet's dedication to art assumes an intensely felt geographic and spiritual context: "The body feels it is melting into what it has seen. This continues in the poet. It may be repressed in some way, but I think we continue in all our lives to have that sense of melting, of the 'I' not being important" (Hirsch, 203). The achievement of voice begins for the poet in the merging of self with the social reality around him: "I have felt from my boyhood that I had one function and that was somehow to articulate, not my own experience, but what I saw around me" (Hirsch, 210). In *Another Life,* the mature poet remembers and renews his identification with the social world embodied in St. Lucia then and at the time of writing.

> For their lights still shine through the hovels like litmus,
> the smoking lamp still slowly says its prayer,
> the poor still move behind their tinted scrim,
> the taste of water is still shared everywhere,
> but in that ship of night, locked in together,
> through which, like chains, a little light might leak,
> something still fastens us forever to the poor.
> (*AL,* 42)

The poetic impulse is inextricably linked to the landscape and the people of St. Lucia.

Walcott's passionate attachment to his native landscape is given a new context in book 3 of *Another Life,* where the poet explores in his love for Andreuille, his love for St. Lucia and the nature of his own art.

> The disc of the world turned
> slowly, she was its center.
> (*AL,* 83)

Walcott describes the transforming power of an imagination nourished by "the literature of Empires, Greek, Roman, British, through their essential classics" ("Twilight," 4). The apparent betrayal lies in the nature of art, in the distinctive life of the imagination which exists independently of actual experience and yet exists simultaneously with it: "There is a memory of imagination in literature which has nothing to do with actual experience, which is, in fact, another life" ("Muse," 25). By the same token, in *Another Life,* Andreuille is transformed by the literary imagination into Anna, an aesthetic object.

> The hand she held already had betrayed her
> then by its longing for describing her.
> (*AL,* 90)

Walcott makes a Kantian distinction between the realm of the mind and the world. Anna, "already chosen / as his doomed heroine" (*AL,* 92), speaks on her own behalf in the poem.

> I became a metaphor, but
> believe me I was unsubtle as salt.
> (*AL,* 96)

Anna the material object and Anna the aesthetic object, though distinct, are linked in the poet's art. The transforming power of the imagination is linkage. The dualism that characterizes the poet's aesthetic sensibility is only superficially betrayal. It is characteristic of the spiritual forces shaping the culture of the region, from Haitian vodun to Rastafarianism, from "The Pact" to *Another Life.*

> No metaphor, no metamorphosis,
> as the charcoal-burner turns
> into his door of smoke,
> three lives dissolve in the imagination,
> three loves, art, love, and death,
> fade from a mirror clouding with this breath,
> no one is real, they cannot live or die,
> they all exist, they never have existed.
> (*AL*, 109)

In *Another Life* the search for some ancestral, tribal country ends where it started, in the Caribbean (*AL*, 41), in a dramatic shift in focus away from ethnic ancestral homelands to New World beginnings.

As Walcott describes it in *Another Life*, the process of discovering his voice as a Caribbean poet was a struggle for the fourteen-year-old youth searching for a way to resolve the cultural conflict between Europe and Africa in colonial St. Lucia. It is in this context that Walcott describes the poet's youthful fascination with British history and how it contributes to the conflict within him. The conflict is embodied in the mutually exclusive claims of two grandfathers, one white and one black; one European and one African; one prompting him to follow in the footsteps of European masters, the other rooted in the landscape of his birth.[17] The young poet grows frustrated with the pressure to choose, to accept and reject.

> But I tired of your whining, grandfather,
> in the whispers of marsh grass,
> I tired of your groans, grandfather,
> in the deep ground bass of the combers,
> I cursed what the elm remembers,
> I hoped for your sea-voices
> to hiss from my hand,
> for the sea to erase
> those names a thin,
> tortured child, kneeling, wrote
> on his slate of wet sand.
> (*AL*, 64–65)

One end to the conflict is erasure and new beginnings. Ultimately, the poet rejects servitude to the muse of history as essentially uncreative: "The truly tough aesthetic of the New World neither explains nor forgives history. It refuses to recognize it as a creative or culpable force" ("Muse," 2). He claims the freedom to shape the meaning of his inheritance anew, to create his own context for being. At the end of "The Muse of History," Walcott addresses his two grandfathers, prototypical ancestors, black and white, in a spirit of independence and gratitude.

> I accept this archipelago of the Americas. I say to the ancestor who sold me, and to the ancestor who bought me, I have no father, I want no such father, although I can understand you, black ghost, white ghost, when you both whisper "history," for if I attempt to forgive you both I am falling into your idea of history which justifies and explains and expiates, and it is not mine to forgive, . . . and I have no wish or power to pardon. (27)

The poet substitutes dialogue for servitude and veneration. He cuts himself loose from the enervating bonds of history and redefines the terms of his relationship to the past and the future.[18]

In the final book of *Another Life*, the poet as traveler arrives in Rampanalgas. It is a place of rest, Resthaven. "Rest, heaven. Rest, hell" (*AL*, 138). He remains firmly rooted in the Caribbean landscape, unworried by its lack of ruins and monuments, by its lack of history. He rejects the inherited conflict of colonial history for the child's clean slate of wet sand.

> They will absolve us, perhaps, if we begin again,
> from what we have always known, nothing.
> (*AL*, 137)

Naipaul's sardonic view of a place with no history, the scourge of a colonial sensibility, is laid to rest in a different truth. The absence of history is a new world. "If there is nothing, there is everthing to be made" ("Twilight," 4). In *Another Life*, "nothing" is "the loud world in his mind" (141). Refashioned in a language beyond mimicry, it has the force of revelation, of new names for all things. The poet emerges as keeper of the faith, with his revolutionary embrace of "no history" as a blessing, as the chance to begin anew.[19] History as the ultimate cultural mask is a carnival throwaway.[20] The ritual divestment is renewal, an act of faith.

Walcott's Caribbean poetics rests on rethinking history, time, and traditional concepts of the self. Walcott's primary point of cultural identification is the "New World Negro" who, in a language of his own creation, embarked on a new naming of things: "My real language, and tonally my basic language, is patois" (Hamner, 417). The advent of being in the modern Caribbean is the invention of a new language, the word incarnate. It follows that Walcott's archetypal "hero" is a poet. His prototypical Caribbean man is a conjurer of words who creates new contexts for being and keeps alive the original quest for identity in the New World of the Caribbean. The aesthetic personality of *Another Life* articulates a Caribbean aesthetic for life and for art, for another life than that of the region's old world forbears.

Notes

1. A classic American precedent in the forging of an aesthetic personality based on self and collective culture is Walt Whitman's *Leaves of Grass*: "This was a feeling or ambition to articulate and faithfully express in literary or poetic form, and uncompromisingly, my own physical, emotional, moral, intellectual, and aesthetic Personality, in the midst of, and tallying, the momentous spirit and facts of its immediate days, and of current America—and to exploit that Personality, identified with place and date, in a far more candid and comprehensive sense than any hitherto poem or book" (444). Even more specific to the evolution of Caribbean literary discourse is the affinity with Aimé Césaire's poet-hero in *Notebook of a Return to the Native Land*. Rei Terada observes that "Walcott considers himself the type of the American poet, and . . . that the American poet is for him the type of *the* poet" (7).

2. This is St. John Perse's national-poetic ideal: "What a prodigious destiny for a poet, creator of his language, to be at the same time the unifier of a national tongue long before the political unity that it promises. Through him, speech restored to a living community becomes the life lived by an entire people in search of unity" (Perse, 21). This unity, Walcott acknowledges, may be possible only in art: "I see no possibility of the country becoming unified and having its own strengths except in art" (Hirsch, 284).

3. The discourse in the essays and *Another Life* is characteristically male; thus *Caribbean man* seems the appropriate designation.

4. Walcott conceives of his poetic sensibility as a bridge between different ancestries, Europe and the Third World of Africa and Asia ("Muse," 20). He is not alone in this. Césaire tells Decraene: "The Amerindian, even the Indian component, the African foundation and three centuries of life in common with France, all that makes up an indivisible whole. How do you slough that off, I mean one or another of these elements, without impoverishing reality, without sterilizing it?" (64). Wilson Harris uses the term "gateway complex" to describe the metamorphosis of the poetic imagination after the shock of the Atlantic crossing and the interpenetration of different cultures that followed (12).

5. Rei Terada finds Walcott's use of the American Adam mythology duplicitous: "Each of Adam's words is indeed a beginning; but these are beginnings *over*, not primal beginnings" (151).

6. Césaire makes the same point in an interview with René Depestre: "I said to myself: it's true that superficially we are French, we bear the marks of French customs; we have been branded by Cartesian philosophy, by French rhetoric; but if we break with all that, if we plumb the depths, then what we will find is fundamentally black" (68).

7. As Wilson Harris, one of the great architects of Caribbean literary culture, explains, "Caribbean man is involved in a civilization-making process (whether he likes it or not) and until this creative authority becomes intimate to his perspectives he will continue to find himself embalmed in his deprivations—embalmed as a derivative tool-making, fence-making animal. As such his dialectic will remain a frozen round of protest" (29).

8. In *Derek Walcott's Poetry: American Mimicry*, Rei Terada explores a wide range of issues around the mimicry-originality dichotomy on an individual scale, a cultural scale, and as expressive of the relation between representation and the object world, and between culture and nature in Walcott's poetry. Note especially her introductory chapter, "American Mimicry" (1–12).

9. In "History, Fable and Myth," Wilson Harris identifies such cultural phenomena as part of an original "West Indian architecture of consciousness" (21).

10. Césaire tells Philippe Decraene: "That dualism, that ambiguity if you will, is the very basis of the West Indian soul. It is the ambiguity one has to accept and make one's own" (66–67).

11. In *Memoirs*, Pablo Neruda writes: "With feelings, beings, books, events, and battles, I am omnivorous" (264). In *Song of Myself*, Walt Whitman writes: "I know perfectly well my own egotism, / Know my omnivorous lines and must not write any less, / And would fetch you whoever you are flush with myself" (60). In a recent interview, Césaire explains: "I am a man who loves—I won't say culture—cultures, all cultures" (Césaire interview, 55). Walcott seems to prefer the more violent image: "You know that you just ravage and cannibalize everything as a young poet; you have a very voracious appetite for literature" (Walcott interview, 282).

12. Wilson Harris's emphasis on the primacy of the subjective imagination in Caribbean societies is illuminating here: "In the first place the *limbo* imagination of the West Indies possesses no formal or collective sanction as in the old Tribal World. Therefore the gateway complex between cultures implies a new catholic unpredictable threshold which places far greater emphasis on the integrity of the individual imagination" (16).

13. Césaire makes a careful distinction between assimilating French culture and being assimilated. Like Walcott, he resists the alienation of the culturally assimilated by rooting himself culturally in the Caribbean rather than in Europe (interview with Decraene, 64).

14. In effect, Walcott repeats a central tenet in George Lamming's essays on cultural politics, *The Pleasures of Exile* (1960), with respect to the centrality of the folk in Caribbean literature and culture, and revises another with respect to Lamming's emphasis on politically determined cultural formula.

15. I explore these issues of autobiography as an exemplary space for the reconstruction of self and community in Caribbean literature in my essay "West Indian Autobiography."

16. The authoritative interpretive text on *Another Life* is Edward Baugh's *Derek Walcott: Memory as Vision, Another Life*. The autobiographical and factual details underlying the poem are richly explored by Baugh in relation to the overarching themes of memory, history, art, and life.

17. In Nicolas Guillen's "Ballad of the Two Grandfathers," the poet conjures up his prototypical grandfathers, black and white, out of the shadows of his mind and brings them together (67).

18. Walcott adds a new dimension to Césaire's substitution of acceptance and love for hatred and anger in *Notebook* (73, 77).

19. In *Notebook,* Césaire's celebrated "Eia for those who have never invented anything" also ends in a celebration of the poet-hero as "a man of germination" (70–71).

20. An essential feature of Trinidad's carnival is the annual invention and discarding of costumes. Where the costumes are retained and reused, the performance is characteristically satirical, obscene, or grotesquely humorous. Walcott comments on this phenomenon at some length in "The Caribbean: Culture or Mimicry?" (9–10).

Works Cited

Baugh, Edward. *Derek Walcott: Memory as Vision, Another Life.* London: Longman, 1978.

Césaire, Aimé. "Aimé Césaire: Black Rebel." Interview with Philippe Decraene. *Callaloo* 6, no. 1 (1983): 63–70.

———. *The Collected Poetry.* Translated by Clayton Eshleman and Annette Smith. Berkeley: University of California Press, 1983.

———. "An Interview with Aimé Césaire." With René Depestre. *Discourse on Colonialism.* Translated by Joan Pinkham. New York: Monthly Review Press, 1972.

———. "It Is through Poetry that One Copes with Solitude." Interview with Charles H. Rowell. *Callaloo* 12, no. 1 (1989): 47–67.

———. *Notebook of a Return to the Native Land.* In *The Collected Poetry,* translated by Clayton Eshleman and Annette Smith. Berkeley: University of California Press, 1983.

Gonzales Echevarria, Roberto. *The Voice of the Masters: Writing and Authority in Modern Latin American Literature.* Austin: University of Texas Press, 1988.

Guillen, Nicolas. *Man-Making Words.* Translated by Robert Marquez and David Arthur McMurray. Amherst: University of Massachusetts Press, 1972.

Hamner, Robert. "Conversation with Derek Walcott." *World Literature Written in English* 16 (1977): 409–20.

Harris, Wilson. "History, Fable, and Myth in the Caribbean and Guianas." *Caribbean Quarterly* 16, no. 2 (1970): 1–32.

Lamming, George. *The Pleasures of Exile.* 1960, 1984. Reprint, Ann Arbor: University of Michigan Press, 1992.

Naipaul, V. S. *The Middle Passage.* Middlesex: Penguin, 1969.

Neruda, Pablo. *Memoirs.* Translated by Hardie St. Martin. New York: Farrar, 1977.

Paquet, Sandra Pouchet. "West Indian Autobiography." *Black American Literature Forum* 24, no. 2 (Summer 1990): 357–74.

Perse, St. John. *Two Addresses.* New York: Pantheon, 1966.

Terada, Rei. *Derek Walcott's Poetry: American Mimicry.* Boston: Northeastern University Press, 1992.

Walcott, Derek. *Another Life.* Washington, D.C.: Three Continents, 1982.

———. "The Art of Poetry." With Edward Hirsch. *Paris Review* 101 (1986): 197–230.

———. "The Caribbean: Culture or Mimicry?" *Journal of Interamerican Studies and World Affairs* 16, no. 1 (February 1974): 3–14.

———. "An Interview with Derek Walcott." With Edward Hirsch. *Contemporary Literature* 20 (1979): 280–92.

———. "Meanings." *Savacou* 2 (1970): 45–51.

———. "The Muse of History." In *Is Massa Day Dead?*, edited by Orde Coombs, 1–27. New York: Anchor, 1974.

———. "Necessity of Negritude." In *Critical Perspectives on Derek Walcott*, edited by Robert D. Hamner. Washington, D.C.: Three Continents, 1993.

———. "What the Twilight Says: An Overture." In *Dream on Monkey Mountain and Other Plays*, 3–4. New York: Farrar, 1970.

Whitman, Walt. *Complete Poetry and Selected Prose.* Edited by James E. Miller, Jr. Cambridge: Riverside Press, 1959.

The Politics of Memory:

Remembering History

in Alice Walker and Joy Kogawa

DAVID PALUMBO-LIU

Discussions of ethnic literature nearly always contain some explanation of how ethnic literature demands a particular attention to history—the histories of nations, cultures, and people. This is appropriate because, if nothing else, ethnicity is a product of material history—not a predetermined and static essence, but rather something always constructed and re-articulated with regard to a particular historical location of groups within a dominant culture.

Critics have configured in various ways the specific nature of the engagement of ethnic literature with history. The ethnic narrative presents an occasion for a subversive revision of the dominant version of history; it gives voice to a text muted by dominant historical referents; and it makes possible an imaginative invention of a self beyond the limits of the historical representations available to the ethnic subject. However, critics have paid less attention to the ways in which such acts of revision are highly problematic; to perform such acts, ethnic writers are often caught in a double dilemma. First, to make a space of articulation for themselves, to carve out an area for revision, they must first dis-place history, and yet such destabilization of the dominant history necessitates a preliminary critique of *any* history's epistemological claims. Any counterhistory, furthermore, must legitimate itself by laying claim to a firmer epistemology than that claimed by the dominant history. The question then becomes, how can one deconstruct the dominant history on the basis of its ideologically suspect nature, and *not* admit that one's revision is also overdetermined?

Second, the formal properties of literary narrative engage ethnic writers in the ideologically problematic nature of closure. The narrative's ending may be predicated upon a stabilization of history in which the ongoing dialectical relationship between minor and dominant discourses is suppressed. What starts off as a contestive counterhistory may thus be objectified and stabilized as merely a smaller instance within the greater metanarrative of history. It will become clear that the two issues I focus on in this essay—that of the truth claims of any minor history and that of the status of the personal within the politics of history—are deeply linked to the general problematic of the postmodern, which has already amassed a significant body of works on the epistemological crisis that is opened up with the "death" of the project of modernity. I cannot here rehearse the fuller implications of these links; instead I confine my remarks to the more particular questions raised in this anthology, that is, of the particular politics of ethnic memory.

In this essay on the relationship between history, memory, and ethnic narrative, I use the word *history* in a particular manner: to name the dominant discourse assigning significance and order to things. Thus, I extend the term to include both formal and informal, official and unofficial articulations that affirm and confirm what is taken to be the natural understanding of events and their significance—the "natural" is, as Raymond Williams tells us, a sign of ideology's work (55). This conceptual move is important, for it allows us to see how history is disseminated much more widely, and perhaps more convincingly, than by "official historical" texts alone; it is transmitted and reaffirmed by and in a number of representational fields, one of which is literature.[1]

However, literature may also provide a space for the revisionary act— "literature" configured as a privileged arena of the free play of the imagination, unbounded by utilitarianism, objectivity, and "ordinary truth." Literature "liberates" its author from the confines of the immediate and turns him or her toward the timeless and universal. But as I noted earlier, the insertion of counterhistory calls for an epistemological foundation that can challenge history's authority to narrate the past; that is, if one seeks to offer a counterhistory within literary narrative, then one must still subvert history via a discourse that is equally, if not more, stable.

This alternative site of epistemological grounding, central to the positioning of the ethnic self in the realm of historical significance and most particularly promised in the realm of imaginative literature, brings us to consider another term alongside, and within, ethnic literature and history: memory. All notions of ethnic writing as revision of history point to this term, for it is through memory alone, as the repository of things left out of history, that the ethnic subject can challenge history. The texts treated here share methods of inverting the history-memory relation—

both stabilize memory, imbuing it with the status of history, and destabilize history, critiquing its modes of assigning significance. In this double movement, ethnic narrative reinscribes memory as history.

The topic of ethnic memory is well studied in a number of essays, but few have really explored the problematic of the unequal and vacillating relationship between memory and history. For example, the best-known essay on the subject is Michael M. J. Fischer's "Ethnicity and the Post-Modern Arts of Memory." Although provocative, this essay reveals some of the drawbacks of uncritically transposing anthropological discourse and methodology to literary texts.[2] Intent on finding a "family resemblance" among ethnic literatures and expanding it into a metaphor for the entire postmodern condition, Fischer does not examine the ways in which ethnic memory is blocked, deflected, and problematically reconstituted according to the overdeterminants of ideology and aesthetics and their historicity, that is, those things that form the very foundation of ethnicity and its *mediated* representation in literary works.

This essay is meant to intervene in the simplification of the relation between ethnic literatures, memory, and history, which reduces the ethnic to simply a synonym for the postmodern. This reinscription ironically yet effectively wipes out ethnic literatures' historical and ideological specificities.[3] To discuss the cultural politics of ethnic literature and the work of memory on history, I have chosen two seemingly dissimilar texts: a short story by Alice Walker entitled "Elethia" and Joy Kogawa's novel *Obasan*. In both texts we find a deep desire to narrate a self predicated upon and within a particular stabilized notion of history. In their mutual attention to memory and history, both texts revolve around the possibilities of belief—both protagonists are seduced by the notion of memory as providing the basis for an authentic self that can be freed from the silence and suppression brought upon it by history. Both embark on a project to manipulate memory to the point of history, taking deeply personal memory and elevating it to the status of the historical. Yet, when transferred to the realm of social and political action, these narrative negotiations between memory and history are shown to be highly problematic.

Even with its opening sentence, "Elethia" begs to be questioned: "A certain perverse experience shaped Elethia's life, and made it possible for it to be true that she carried with her at all times a small apothecary jar of ashes" (27). The sentence opens onto question after question: the indeterminacy of "certain," the immediate seductiveness and danger behind "perverse," and the emphatic "shaping" of Elethia's life. But most conspicuously begging for an answer is the notion of the *possibility* of truth: the experience has "made it *possible* for it to be true" (that is, for Elethia *to be*) (my italics).

Elethia's name derives from the Greek *aletheia*, meaning "truth," and surely truth is the key to the story. However, I want to show how the question of the *possibility* of truth, weighed in the balance of history's mechanisms of deletion, distortion, and omission, comes to supersede "truth" as a focal point and opens up issues particular to the discourse of ethnic memory.

The cultural politics of truth/memory become clearer if we examine briefly Heidegger's particular attention to *alethia* as a historicized term. He engages the term *alethia* in ways that both show the influence of Nietzsche and later inform Foucault's writings on history (discussed later). The relationship between power and knowledge formed in this trajectory gives us a critical vantage point from which to view the problematics of ethnic memory. Heidegger discusses *alethia* most particularly in the section "The Primordial Phenomenon of Truth and the Derivative Character of the Traditional Conception of Truth."

> "Being true" ("truth") means Being-uncovering. But is not this a highly arbitrary way to define "truth"? By such drastic ways of defining this concept we may succeed in eliminating the idea of agreement from the conception of truth. Must we not pay for this dubious gain by plunging the "good" old tradition into nullity?

Heidegger locates truth in the act of concealment and unconcealment—truth is that which is made possible in the founding gestures of Western philosophy, which predicates truth upon agreement, correspondence, adequation, and, very important for our discussion, the concealment of pre-Socratic "truth." *Alethia* designates the *un*concealing of that truth, the *not forgetting* (*a-lethia*) of it, the recovery of what was sacrificed. In this, the *logos* becomes one with *alethia*.

> Thus to the *logos* belongs unhiddenness—*a-lethia*. To translate this word as "truth," and, above all, to define this expression conceptually in theoretical ways, is to cover up the meaning of what the Greeks made "self-evidently" basic for the terminological use of *alethia* as a pre-philosophical way of understanding it. (262)

To this is attached the very idea of being:

> Being-true as Being-uncovering is a way of Being for Dasein. What makes
> this very uncovering possible must necessarily be called "true" in a still more
> primordial sense. *The most primordial phenomenon of truth is first shown by the
> existential-ontological foundations of uncovering.* (263, my italics)

I want to use this notion of truth as problematized precisely by the work
of ethnic memory to un-forget that which has been covered up in the
historical accounts of ethnic peoples.[4]

In Walker's short story, we find that Elethia becomes absolutely linked
to her (and its) embodiment, that is, their *un*concealment: the figure of
the young woman and, most important, her hermeneutic uncovering of
truth-in-memory. But this uncovering also involves the covering over of
truth-as-history. Returning to the story's opening sentence, and bearing
in mind Heidegger's conception of *alethia*, we can argue that this dual
act of unconcealing and concealing is predicated upon an all-important
distinction: Elethia's experience leads directly and simply not to truth,
but to the possibility of truth: truth is thus dependent on something else
for its possibility. What is more, truth is produced, not simply given. Our
question then becomes not "What is true?" but "What *makes it possible*
for this or that to be regarded as true?" And the possibilities of truth are
intimately tied to memory, that mental activity which might produce
alternative truths and histories that have been glossed over by the dominant discourse. Just as it focuses on the idea of truth as a possibility, the
text addresses the possibilities of memory *to be truth*.

In "Elethia," a white man in the South has erected a statue of a smiling
black servant in the window of his segregated restaurant. The happy
slave is named Uncle Albert, and the restaurant is called Old Uncle Albert's. The problem is that the restaurant emphatically and ironically is
not Uncle Albert's; we must read the name Uncle Albert not as the name
of a person or his property, but as a sign of a relationship of power that
points beyond the named to a (different) namer who has named Albert
as property and not as proprietor.

Most important for our purposes, the name is a sign of power precisely
because of the elisions of memory. The narrator tells us:

> This grandson of former slaveowners held a quaint proprietary point of view
> where colored people were concerned. Not in the present—it went without
> saying—but at that time, stopped, just on the outskirts of his memory: his
> grandfather's time. (27)

The restaurant owner has no direct memory of the days of Uncle Albert; his "view" stops conveniently short of his lived experience. His "memory" is lodged instead in the safety of the unassailable past scripted by the history he enjoys as his inheritance from the days of slavery (and in this sense and others slavery lives on). Thus his memory can selectively represent the past as it wishes and construe Uncle Albert as an icon of those times (as he "remembers" it) carried over unproblematically into the present. It is this ability to cover both the past and the present with its discourse that marks the fact that (the dominant's) memory here is transformed into history: this memory is not authentic; it is derived from a history of a powerful political economy, strong enough to elide the falsity of the owner's memory. Uncle Albert is "old," but his "pastness" presents no problem in his translation into the present, for who is to refute *this* memory? It enters unquestioned into the realm of historical truth and is carried into the present, established in even the most mundane and seemingly innocuous setting, yet it carries with it profound effects.

The narrator shows how the hegemony of history is both overpowering and seductive:

> Only the very old people remembered Albert Porter, and their eyesight was no better than their memory. Still there was a comfort somehow in knowing that Albert's likeness was here before them daily and that if he smiled as a dummy in a fashion he was not known to do as a man, well, perhaps both memory and eyesight were wrong. (28)

The fact that Albert has entered the forbidden region of whites (if only to serve them) imbues him with a kind of fame, and the only ones who actually knew him take a "vicarious pleasure" in this status—it is their sole "positive" representation in history. The actual witnesses of history thus accept the representation of Albert as set forth by the "memory" of the restaurant owner and relinquish any claim to represent Albert any differently; their memory is negated, concealed, as surely as time has diminished their eyesight, superseded by the imagined memories constructed by the slaveowner's grandson which comply with and fortify the historical record.

But the young woman Elethia discovers "the truth" about Uncle Albert: "He was not a dummy; he was stuffed. Like a bird, like a moose's head, like a giant bass. He was stuffed" (28). She and her friends then decide to steal the figure and burn it, which they indeed do.

The text breaks off abruptly, then starts up again by asking, "What kind of man was Uncle Albert?" It immediately proceeds to answer its own question:

> Well, the old folks said, he wasn't nobody's uncle and wouldn't sit still for nobody to call him that, either. Why, said another old-timer, I recalls the time they hung a boy's privates on a post at the end of the street where all the black folks shopped, just to scare us all, you understand, and Albert Porter was the one took 'em down and buried them. (29)

These people remember a different Albert, an Albert who provides Elethia with a model for her act of revising history. The text thus moves us toward "making it possible" for this image of Albert to be true. But we must pause and ask ourselves, why? Why do we believe this second memory and not the first?

The memory of the slaveowner's grandson, granted the power of historical authority and institutionalization, has surpassed the memory of the minority culture, calling it into question and smoothing out any inconsistencies between memory and the history it intends to enshrine as truth. Critically, it solicits the consensus of the actual witnesses of history, the old black men, who are drawn into an identification with the hegemonic representation of history. However, if we are led to suspect this memory on the grounds of its ideological investments, then we must also transfer the same critique to Elethia: What guarantees her memory any greater possibility of truth? It may be that we cannot accept either version of Albert as necessarily true; Elethia's history is not necessarily any more certain than the restaurant owner's. Why are *her* old folk more reliable than the others? Either choice is ideologically saturated and suspect. This is most likely not the reading Walker intends, but the logic of the text opens onto such questions.

The text, thus deconstructed, now leads the reader to contextualize both history and ethnic memory's revision of history. We have to ask: What has "made it possible" for it to be true that we believe in the image of the militant Albert? Why is Elethia's voice particularly suited to give word to the dum/b/my Albert? This ultimately leads us to examine our own historical position as late-twentieth-century U.S. intellectuals "doing" ethnic literature in the American academy, inclined to grant certain histories more credibility than others. Yet if the ethnic minority subject seeks to unconceal its history by an intense and directed act of countermemory, we have to understand as well its own operations of concealing and that which it may need to conceal.[5]

This questioning of the grounds of possibility, this confrontation with our own modes of knowledge-making, recalls Foucault's description of Nietzsche's "effective history":

> The final trait of effective history is its affirmation of knowledge as perspective. Historians take unusual pains to erase the elements of their work which reveal their grounding in a particular time and place, their preferences in a controversy—the unavoidable obstacles of their passion. Nietzsche's version of historical sense is explicit in its perspective and acknowledges its system of injustice. (156)

The evocation of a "counter-memory," according to Foucault, involves a radical disruption of the usual readings of history, that is, reading backward in time to retrace a uniform evolutionary process. Instead, a counter-memory places its attention on the "heterogeneous systems which, masked by the self, inhibit the formation of any form of identity" (162).

In the case of ethnic memory we have an added complication, for the ethnic subject's will for countermemory, fed by its desire to disengage itself from the oppression of the historical voice (to unconceal itself), is confronted by two interrelated problems: first, it must acknowledge the vertigo that accompanies this turn toward discontinuity; it must find an epistemological stronghold to ground its notion of history, one that is more reliable than that which founds the now delegitimized inscription of history by the dominant. It must argue for a metanarrative even in suspecting such moves. Second, it must renounce the lure of the dominant ideology that would accommodate the objectification and thereby containment of minority memory. Even though the dominant ideology may present the ethnic subject with only a subaltern position in history, the ethnic subject can still be seduced into accepting that place within the grid of hegemonic representation (for example, the old black folks who would rather mistrust their own memory than give up the vicarious identification with the dominant). Counterposed to this stable but subordinated position in history is the problematic *minor* narrative, which risks instability in the margins for the sake of a contestive narrative of self, accepting its instability as the price for a dynamic engagement with the dominant.

Foucault concludes his essay with a discussion of the destructive aspect of Nietzsche's "history":

> The purpose of history, guided by genealogy, is not to discover the roots of our identity but to commit itself to its dissipation. It does not seek to define our unique threshold of emergence, the homeland to which metaphysicians promise a return; it seeks to make visible all of those discontinuities that cross us. (162–63)

If we extend this critique to the negotiations between ethnic memory and history, we find that contradictory ideological imperatives weigh against each other. To revise history is not to step outside its functional paradigms, and yet some moment of discontinuity must be introduced. Nevertheless, *that* discontinuity becomes counterbalanced by another kind of continuity, which lapses back into the same will to know, haunted by the same visions of "homeland" (both as a cultural "base" and as a way of knowledge). For the ethnic writer, this reinstatement of continuity is highly fraught.

The argument that the stabilization of ethnic memory may remove it from the dialectical, contestive engagement with history and refigure it as an *object* of history is confirmed by many of the critical assessments of ethnic literature that argue for precisely that kind of resolution—call it assimilation, unity, reconciliation, wholeness, or any number of other models of stability and health for the ethnic subject, each of which is purchased at the cost of recognizing heterogeneous and heretofore unnamed subjectivities.

R. Radhakrishnan's discussion of the problem of "in the name of" bears importantly on this topic: "In whose name is this new name being authorized, authenticated, empowered? This appeal to an authority that 'enables' but is extrinsic to the immediate or historical name betrays the desire for the Absolute and the irrefragable Self" (208). Yet I would argue that the appeal to the "historical" name is itself not unproblematic and cannot be relied on precisely because of the unstable ratio of concealment, unconcealment, and "truth." Medvedev and Bakhtin note the following:

> For in the ideological horizon of any epoch and any social group there is not one, but several mutually contradictory truths, not one but several diverging ideological paths. When one chooses one of these truths as indisputable, when one chooses one of these paths as self-evident, he then writes a scholarly thesis, joins some movement, registers in some party. But even within the limits of a thesis, party, or belief, one is not able to "rest on his laurels." This course of ideological generation will present him with two new paths, two truths, and so on. The ideological horizon is constantly developing—as long as one does not get bogged down in some swamp. Such is the dialectic of real life.[6]

I am not arguing for a kind of radical skepticism with regard to the historical as real that would write out the factuality of racist violence; rather, I am interested in tracing the deployment of historical discourse

and counterdiscourse around such realities, as they become foundational documents for the constitution of ethnic (and nonethnic) subjects.

Obasan is nearly universally portrayed as a model for just such reconciliation and health. For example, one review excerpted on its back cover
claims, "This quiet first novel burns in your hand. Rage mellows into
sorrow; sorrow illuminates love. It is love that you come away with, finally." Another reads, "Kogawa's novel must be heard and admired; the
art itself can claim the real last word, exposing the viciousness of the
racist horror, embodying the beauty that somehow, wonderfully, sur-
vives."[7] I do not necessarily find these interpretations outlandish or even
implausible. What is interesting to me is that both readings (from the
usual mass newspapers) are only too quick to elide rage and horror in
favor of survival and love. But the novel's ending throws those kinds of
pronouncements into question, as it emphatically resurrects the horror
of history, a horror absolutely linked to the distortion and erasure of
memory. As in "Elethia," *Obasan* is deeply engaged in a struggle to negotiate a way for memory to supersede history.

One can argue that in *Obasan* this problematic is worked out and contained, but if it is not vulnerable to the same kind of resurgent instabilities of "Elethia" that "make it possible for it to be true" that *two* versions
of history stand side by side, each equally unreliable, then in *Obasan* a
slightly different dilemma involving the same terms—memory and history—is found to be irresolvable in a different sense.

The relation of memory to history is sketched out in the text of *Obasan*
even before the narration begins. In the acknowledgments, Kogawa
thanks a number of people, and the Public Archives of Canada, for permission to use documents and letters from the files of Japanese Canadians involved in the evacuation. It is from these documents that Kogawa,
like her protagonist Naomi, constructs her narration, a narration that
juxtaposes the cold, orderly dictates of the Canadian government with
the personal correspondence of the Japanese Canadians—the history of
the dominant ideology versus the "unauthorised" minority representations of that historical moment. And they are unauthorized because
those who wrote the texts are denied status as authors of history; they
can only be subjects of it and subjected to it.

Naomi's narration is engendered in the empty space left bare by these
texts. Hers is a narration that seeks not to find facts as much as it seeks
to imbue them with significance. Hers is a deeply personal hermeneutic

project; the references to the Bible that form the epigraph of the novel confirm this connection.

> To him that overcometh
> will I give to eat
> of the hidden manna
> and will give him
> a white stone
> and in the stone
> a new name written.

In pursuing her project, Naomi finds that both the government documents and the newspaper accounts that form the "proper" materials for history and the personal letters and photographs found in Aunt Emily's packet contain ellipses, but ellipses of quite different natures. For the texts of the dominant history, these gaps are epistemological—for the dominant history, truth exists in plentitude within the boundaries of its discourse. What may seem missing to us, then, is not even a question for the dominant history—what it neglects to say simply does not exist.

In the texts of the minority discourse, the gaps are the product of many things. Readers may sense most strongly the evocation of the value of silence and its particular semiotic within Japanese culture; but we are wrong to leave it at that, for this valorization of silence cannot be taken as emanating solely from some essentialized notion of traditional Japanese culture; it must be understood within a historical context that deprived the Japanese Canadians of a voice.

In accepting the authority of the dominant culture to speak for them, Japanese Canadians would endorse history as truth. But the text sets out to argue against such a capitulation. The narrator speaks directly of the constitution of *her* history via a radical revision of the government documents that profess simply to provide facts:

> There it was in black and white—our short harsh history. Beside each date were the ugly facts of the treatment given to Japanese Canadians. "Seizure and government sale of fishing boats. Suspension of fishing licenses. Relocation camps. Liquidation of property. Letter to General McArthur. Bill 15. Deportation. Revocation of nationality." (33)

To this sort of representation, Emily scoffs, " 'Interior Housing Projects'! With language like that you can diguise any crime" (34). Again,

> The fact is that families already fractured and separated were permanently destroyed. The choice to go east of the Rockies or to Japan was presented without time for consultation with separated parents and children. Failure to choose was labelled noncooperation. (183)

Another example of history's power to assign meaning is found in a newspaper photograph of Japanese Canadians working the beet fields which carries the caption: "Grinning and happy." Naomi retorts, "That is one telling. It's not how it was" (197). The overall effect of history then is to deprive the Japanese Canadian subjects of any possibility of self-representation; rather, the "facts" presented are laden with a particular meaning by the context that dominant history provides. A headline from the *Vancouver Daily Province* noting the stoic expressions of Japanese Canadians reads, "*Indifferent* Jap Repats Start Homeward Trek" (185, my italics).[8]

Counterposed to the legalistic discourse of the "evacuation," the established protocols of displacement and disenfranchisement, we find the documents of memory: the diary of Aunt Emily, and the nonverbal icons of Naomi's childhood—the images of herself and her family—that beg to be narrated. All this despite, or because of, their curious double nature of fragility and persistence. Naomi speaks of these memories: "The memories that are left seem barely real. Grey shapes in the water. Fish swimming through the gaps in the net. Passing shadows" (21). The texts of the dominant history and the ethnic memory thus vie with each other to posit significance upon the Japanese Canadian subjects. It is crucial to note that it is Naomi, who has vested interests in maintaining the silenced gaps of both, who finally takes upon herself the task of arguing for a significance for herself. And it is not the words of the Other (here represented both by the government's history and by her family's memory) that will set her free, but the words she uses to ascribe particular significance to the words of the Other that ultimately offer her whatever freedom she may enjoy.

This tension between the historically documented and regulated past and a present that reconstitutes those moments as memory is no better attested to than when Naomi responds to a mock questionnaire: "Personality: Tense. Is that the past or the present tense? It's perpetual tense" (7). The dialectical tension between the past and the present, the historical and the continuing memories of the past in the present that contest the significance (or nonsignificance) history has assigned these memories, is stressed throughout the narrative: "All our ordinary stories are changed in time, altered as much by the present as the present is shaped by the past. Potent and pervasive as a prairie dust storm, memories and dreams seep and mingle through the cracks" (25).

The entire novel is a series of displacements and erasures that make knowledge of the ethnic subject impossible. Years after the end of the evacuation, Naomi and her family return to their former homes and attempt to find traces of that existence.

> We looked for evidence of our having been in Bayfarm, in Lemon Creek, in Popoff. . . . Where on the map or on the road was there any sign? Not a mark was left. All our huts had been removed long before and the forest had returned to take over the clearings . . . the Slocan that we knew in the forties was no longer there, *except for the small white community which had existed before we arrived* and which watched us come with a mixture of curiosity and fear. Now, down on the shore of the Slocan lake, on the most beautiful part of the sandy beach, where we used to swim, there was a large new sawmill owned by someone who lived in New York. (117–18, my italics)

Only a few bones remain: "The part of the cemetery that holds [the] bones [of the Japanese Canadians] is off by itself in the north-west corner of Forest Lawn. Perhaps some genealogist of the future will come across this patch of bones and wonder why so many fishermen died on the prairies" (225). It is precisely these "bones" that have the potential to "speak," yet we must remind ourselves that this potential is contingent upon the "*possibility* for it to be true"—some archaeologist of a vaguely distant future must find the graves, recognize the contradiction between the patrimony of the dead and their place of burial, and, furthermore, find *significance* in this alienation.

As I have noted, in *Obasan* the absence and absenting of significance finds a countermovement, one that seeks to inscribe significance where the dominant history has declared (through omission) that there is none. Part of this attempt on Naomi's part is attached to the idea that to understand history, one must seek the human being who is responsible for writing it. To inject the human dimension into the facts may bring out a corollary movement toward finding one's own humanity. Yet this attempt is consistently frustrated. Naomi finds a series of documents signed by a mysterious Mr. Good, and wonders,

> What did Mr. Good feel, I wondered, as he signed his letters . . . did he even read them? He must have had similar form letters ready to send out automatically. Did he experience a tiny twinge of pleasure at the power his signature must represent? (37)

Years later, in 1972, Naomi remarks, "I still do not see the Canadian face of the author of those words" (173).

The impossibility of reading behind the words of history complements the futility of Emily's quest for justice. As the Japanese Canadians try to read behind the facts of history to find some human voice, their own voices are silenced:

> All of Emily's words, all her papers, the telegrams and petitions, are like scratchings in the barnyard. . . . They do not touch us where we are planted here in Alberta. . . . The words are not made flesh. Trains do not carry us home. Ships do not return again. All my prayers disappear into space. (189)

One consequence of recognizing this impasse is for Naomi to seek shelter in silence—she tries to absolve the Canadian government and remove the question: "Crimes of history, I thought to myself, can stay in history. What we need is to concern ourselves with the injustices of today. Expedience still demands decisions which will one day be judged unjust" (41). Naomi's compromise thus exchanges significance in the present for justice in the future, but when the final recognition of injustice comes it brings no certain change. It is here that we find the most brutal and emphatic assertion of the power of history, and it comes at a most conspicuous point. The last page of the novel does not end with reconciliation and forgiveness, as we might expect from the back cover (which, interestingly, seems to give the dominant culture the last word). Instead, Kogawa ends her novel by citing a passage from history that attests to the utter failure to revise history.

It is an excerpt from the memorandum sent by the Cooperative Committee on Japanese Canadians to the House and the Senate of Canada, April 1946, which begins as follows: "It is urgently submitted that the Orders-in-Council [for the deportation of Canadians of Japanese racial origin] are wrong and indefensible and constitute a grave threat to the rights and liberties of Canadian citizens." But despite this eloquent plea, it is three more years before the orders are lifted. One might argue that this mode of closing the novel provides the reader with an admission from the halls of history of the injustice perpetrated on the Japanese Canadians, and it does do that. But it also has the effect of reopening certain questions that would seem to have been resolved.

The wholeness brought about by reading history with full memory, of finding the power through memory to write a deeply personal counter-history that injects the historical facts with a significance that had been hidden, distorted, or erased, redeems Naomi but does not outweigh the crimes of the past. Even the recognition of injustice, which has been Emily's battle all along, is reabsorbed by the dominant ideology that alone has the power to forgive itself. It may well be that the real "message" of the novel foregrounds the personal while problematizing the political, ending with an uneasy compromise between personal optimism and political skepticism. Naomi has her answer, but Emily has yet to find her justice.

This ambivalence around how, exactly, to negotiate the imperatives of the bourgeois novel form (toward personal enlightenment versus collective politics) points us back to the dialectical nature of memory in the ethnic narrative, its link to history, and its dual allegiance to discontinuity and continuity. In both "Elethia" and *Obasan*, the protagonists enter into certain negotiations with history. Both attempt to find a kind of personal freedom through revising the history of the dominant culture by means of a memory that can inscribe significance where none was allowed or acknowledged. What I have hoped to do here is to show how these two terms cannot be simply balanced or stabilized; both are contingent upon a strategy of reading that rejects the "homeland" proffered by history but has yet to find a stable alternative site on which to found its memory and which can move memory to the point of history. Yet this delay, this lack of closure, and this *in*determinancy, must also be seen positively for its utopian potential to name heretofore unnameable truths.

Notes

1. For ideological apparatuses, see Louis Althusser, "Idéologie et appareils idéologiques d'Etat," *La Pensée* 151 (1970), translated into English by Ben Brewster in *Lenin and Philosophy* (New York: Monthly Review Press, 1971).

2. For another critique of Fischer, see José David Saldívar, "The Limits of Cultural Studies," *American Literary History* 2, no. 2 (Summer 1990): 251–66.

3. For an extended discussion of the use of postmodern critical language in the study of Asian American literature, see my "The Ethnic as 'Post-': Reading *Reading the Literatures of Asian America*," forthcoming in *American Literary History*.

4. Cf. Homi K. Bhabha, "The World and the Home," *Social Text* 31–32 (1992): 141–54.

5. Here the issue of gender comes in most forcefully.

6. P. N. Medvedev and M. M. Bakhtin, *The Formal Method in Literary Scholarship* (Baltimore: Johns Hopkins University Press, 1978), 19–20. Cited in Radhakrishnan, 209.

7. At this point in the history of the study of ethnic literature, I think it is extremely important *not* to ignore the ideological force of such "marginal" discourses as advertising, for it is precisely in the mode of dissemination and representation of ethnic texts by the dominant culture that we find the most telling and powerful indices of the ongoing construction of history. After all, ethnic best-sellers are sold on the basis of their appeal to hegemonic values, not academic criticism. These kinds of representations can even be considered more significant than academic critical assessments that refuse to link academic discourse with cultural practice.

8. For a discussion of photo captions and Asian Americans in another context, see my "LA, Asians, and Perverse Ventriloquisms: On the Functions of Asian America in the Recent American Imaginary," *Public Culture* (Winter 1994). In it I refer to Roland Barthes's important essay "The Photographic Message," in his *Image-Music-Text* (New York: Hill and Wang, 1977).

Works Cited

Fischer, Michael M. J. "Ethnicity and the Post-Modern Arts of Memory." In *Writing Culture: The Poetics and Politics of Ethnography*, edited by James Clifford and George E. Marcus, 194–233. Berkeley: University of California Press, 1986.

Foucault, Michel. "Nietzsche, Genealogy, History." In *Language, Counter-Memory, Practice*, edited by Donald F. Bouchard, 156. Ithaca: Cornell University Press, 1977.

Heidegger, Martin. *Being and Time*. Translated by John Macquarrie and E. Robinson. New York: Harper & Row, 1962.

Kogawa, Joy. *Obasan*. Boston: Godine, 1984.

Radhakrishnan, R. "Ethnic Identity and Post-Structuralist Differance." *Cultural Critique* 6 (1987): 199–220.

Walker, Alice. "Elethia." In *You Can't Keep a Good Woman Down*. San Diego: Harcourt Brace Jovanovich, 1971.

Williams, Raymond. *Marxism and Literature*. Oxford: Oxford University Press, 1977.

Producing History and Telling Stories:

Maxine Hong Kingston's *China Men*

and Zeese Papanikolas's *Buried Unsung*

YIORGOS KALOGERAS

Buried Unsung: *Louis Tikas and the Ludlow Massacre* (1982) concludes with a photograph: Louis Tikas poses in a photo studio in Rethymno, Crete, at the turn of the century. His life has finally been traced to a concrete pre-American beginning. The narrator's research has been concluded; he has discovered Louis Tikas's native village on the island of Crete and has given back to history his real name, Ilias Anastasios Spantidakis. The picture of Tikas/Spantidakis places the long-dead labor organizer within a specific Old World historical past. The fear that Greek Americans are "a people without a history" is essentially exorcised (Papanikolas, 56). But this special moment generates discomfort of a different kind: the narrator's historical search has uncovered important and indisputable facts, such as a name, a village, and finally an old photograph, to ground them all in historical reality. And yet "all a photograph can tell you, really, is the present. Maybe it is only our overmastering hunger for something more that makes us fill that moment with our own terrible nostalgia, our myths of history or of ourselves. And yet it is just here, in this little seed of light, that we become that future the actors are posing for, that we become their posterity" (266).

This Greek American historical beginning testifies to the truth of all beginnings: it signifies a return, a repetition, and an invention; the narrator undertakes to combine "the already familiar with the fertile novelty of human work in language" (Said, xii). Tikas's village, Loutra, as well as his Greek name, Ilias, had already existed before the narrator launched on his discovery project, but they both acquire a particular meaning in the context of the author's research and writing. The Greek past of an immigrant laborer suddenly connected with American history. The elucidation of Tikas's ethnic past remains partial, inadequate, and inconsequential, and in the end very little is actually known about him. Zeese Papanikolas's project nevertheless is significant because it unearths a story that official history ignored or suppressed out of blatant discrimination or embarrassment. In the attempt to provide the labor organizer with a coherent life story, official historiography took into consideration only his American beginning. Thus, the research into Louis Tikas's ethnic identity becomes an act of resistance to assimilation. Equally important is the revelation of how history is produced. In a sincere gesture of self-understanding, the narrator confronts the reader of his book with the intentional and rhetorical character of all history writing. His story is largely constructed out of "our myths of history or of ourselves," albeit self-consciously.

This essay focuses on two texts that are problematic in terms of genre and that share a common issue: how an ethnic subject, retaining its historical integrity/difference, can be determined, defined, and placed within American official history. The writers/narrators of these books seem to have a personal as well as an ethnic stake in this project. Maxine Hong Kingston in *China Men* (1980) sketches the biographies of the men in her family, thus recording the history of discrimination against the Chinese and the history of disempowerment of Asian Americans, which still remains a fact in our "liberal" present.[1] Zeese Papanikolas, in *Buried Unsung: Louis Tikas and the Ludlow Massacre*, focuses on a virtually unknown event in American labor history: the particular story of Louis Tikas, a Cretan labor organizer for the United Mine Workers who was murdered in Ludlow, Colorado, on 20 April 1914, and the more encompassing history of Greek immigrants in the Southwest.[2] He thus makes a significant contribution to the history of an immigrant group that has been characterized as politically conservative and whose cultural/historical heritage has been stereotyped in the sounds of bouzouki music and in the rhetoric of Zorba the Greek American.

Underlying this personal motivation, however, there is an important project that the two authors undertake: they force the reader to reconsider the function of historiography as institutional practice. Focusing on ethnic history, the narrators surface the ethnic historical text and in the process emphasize its eccentric position within the official, mainstream American historiography. The eccentricity of the ethnic text in the respective books consists of its primarily folkloric orientation; it has its roots in a preindustrial, precapitalistic past. It constitutes a mystical, mysterious, and muted heritage for the protagonist and the narrator which could function as a resistance mechanism to social oppression, as well as to assimilation. Michel de Certeau claims that "history is our myth, [which] combines the 'thinkable' and the origin, in conformity with the way in which a society can understand its own working" (86). Post-Enlightenment historiography has long been associated with objective, scientific, documented, and coherent discourse that can precisely define the thinkable and logically pinpoint the origin. The emergence of an ethnic heritage proposes a countermyth or counterhistory; the oral, the circumstantial, and the folkloric determine this history, which furthermore is recoverable only in fragments. The ethnic story defies the epistemological presumptions of post-Enlightenment historiography.

The oral, fragmentary, and undocumented story depends on imagination and interpretation and raises numerous questions about historiography. More specifically, it challenges the premise that historiography is mirror writing, which relies on strict documentation. The role of imagination and interpretation is transformative, as these deconstruct the old belief in the didactic and magisterial (Certeau, 86) nature of the documentary. Moreover, imagination and interpretation reconstruct the historical text in such a way that the historian is better able to understand her or his biases.[3] It is in this capacity that ethnic history in the two books I treat here becomes the pivotal force for inscribing the Other, the silenced and oppressed, perhaps not in a position of equality but clearly in a position to generate questions.

These two books are biographies, not of well-known historical subjects, but of figures who have been relegated to the footnotes of history. The more historical of the two is *Buried Unsung*, not only because Louis Tikas was involved in a major labor strike in the Southwest, but also because the author approaches him from an overtly documentary point of view. With an arsenal of institutional conventions that range from newspaper clippings, photographs, and footnotes to investigative trips to actual locations in order to interview eyewitnesses and record their oral histories, the author seems to emphasize to the maximum the documentary dimension of historiography.

By contrast, although Maxine Hong Kingston's Chinamen are more intimate figures for the narrator, they are intentionally less clearly documented. Kingston approaches history by resorting to imagination and interpretation, even though she does not completely disregard the purely historical conventions (Sledge, 3–22). Yet the predominance of the oral and the reliance on the mythological and the folkloric in Kingston's book does not necessarily establish a clear-cut distinction between the two texts. Both the documentary and the fictional biographies are concerned with defining an eccentric ethnic historical object of study. Furthermore, they pose the question of "what is a documentary model of knowledge and how prevalent it [has] been in the self-understanding of historians" (La Capra 1985, 18). This is an urgent question for ethnic groups to ask, especially in regard to their respective representations in official history. The awareness that sources are usually treated "in narrowly documentary terms, that is, in terms of factual or referential propositions that may be derived from them to provide information about specific times and places" (La Capra 1985, 18), essentially precludes the questions that the biographies discussed in this essay raise. In fact, Papanikolas and Kingston demonstrate how the folkloric and the oral, rather than underrating the documentary, predicate that the boundaries between the latter and the fictional are not hermetically sealed; neither do these boundaries designate a no-man's-land. On the contrary, their very existence depends on a problematic and a dialogue that allow the marginal and the disenfranchised to speak.

Early in Papanikolas's book, the narrator admits that he started his research on the Ludlow strike in order to write a novel (53); however, in attempting to write a work of fiction, he inadvertently produced a biography, a history, and an autobiography.[4] The oral stories about the Ludlow strike and massacre are traced to their historical facts. Thus Louis Tikas and the Ludlow strike and massacre emerge as historical objects of study by force of a fictionalizing, novelistic impulse. In a way, this fictional impulse informs and guides the writing of the biography to the end. It is not difficult to see why, given the circumstances under which the research is conducted. After all, Louis Tikas and the Cretan strikers, the main object of the book, are shadowy figures, whereas the historical events leading to the strike, the strike itself, and the consequent massacre are fairly well documented.

Tikas, the organizer and the immigrant, is a blurred image recorded in five photographs: one shows him as a corpse in the field of the strike, another as an unidentified body in the local morgue. The other three are taken during the strike and in Tikas's official capacity as organizer, standing next to John R. Lawson or marching with Mother Jones. In other words, Tikas emerges and exists only within the historical circumstances of the strike. Without the strike his face or name might not have been recorded. There is more than a little irony to all this: Louis Tikas after all is the American name that subsumed the ethnic one. Thus the strike is both the beginning and the end of Louis Tikas. His life and death are obscure historical facts within the history of the strike. He comes from nowhere and disappears into the blurred, retouched photographs, leaving no traces behind him. Consequently his presence in the strike posits an enigma that is intensified by the tantalizing photographs and by the reports of the eyewitnesses who provide accounts that concur with official records. Personal anecdotes and firsthand accounts of the man's previous life are absent, so that the enigmatic pictures of the man and his corpse are left open to interpretation.

Hence one understands Papanikolas's decision to establish the paradoxical dialogue between the well-documented historical event and the obscure historical figure. Tikas's elusiveness essentially emphasizes the limits and limitations of conventional research; documentation is not sufficient to establish and define the object of research, nor to establish it in any other way other than that of radical alterity. Under the circumstances, the following statement by the narrator seems justified: The book "deserts the conventional ways of writing history to tell its story" (xii). Here the author admits that his project is also a self-conscious meditation on the act of "producing" history; he turns toward the rhetorical, the imaginative, and the interpretive possibilities of storytelling to frame the historical incongruity and eccentricity of Tikas's and the Greek immigrants' story (La Capra 1985, 18). He freely explores the transformative function that analogy, irony, and other rhetorical devices play in historical texts that claim a strictly representational and objective status. Furthermore, he attempts to explore the critical and political potential of such an undertaking.

The relationship between the historian, the text, and the object of study, however, is only part of the story *Buried Unsung* tells; equally significant is the relation between mainstream and ethnic historiography. The narrator exposes the blind spots of discontinuity and upstages the silences that official historiography seeks to occult. To accomplish as much he predicates and demonstrates the eccentricity of the ethnic story in terms of both narrative development and structure. In the long run, Tikas's story of immigration and of his early days in the United States lacks narrative continuity and cohesion because of the scarcity of facts. The narrator provides Tikas's record with what is missing; the long-dead labor organizer acquires a written record only by analogy, through the oral histories of men who participated in the strike. But since his interviews do not provide the narrator with adequate facts, he fills in the gaps of Tikas's story with incidents drawn from the personal odyssey of his own grandfather, George Zeese. The meagerness of facts became the challenge and starting point of research for the narrator, yet by the end of the book he has recorded primarily an analogical, oral account that may or may not fit Tikas's life. Such a practice refutes the exceptionality of a man like Tikas; the reviews that followed the publication of the book as well as the historical records suggest that within the Greek community Tikas was unique. *Buried Unsung,* however, analogically confers the same exceptionality upon a great many people of Tikas's generation; moreover, it supplies a politically radical genealogy for a community that supposedly had reached a unique level of complacency, conservatism, and conformity in the 1960s and 1970s.[5]

All things considered, however, it is the radical alterity of Louis Tikas that challenges any easy paradigms of social assimilation and/or integration. The discontinuity that the change of name signifies for Louis Tikas is reflected in the ideological reorientation of the young peasant that has puzzled the historians. Ilias Spantidakis emigrated to the industrialized, capitalist United States to become the union organizer whom we come to know under the alias Louis Tikas. How can a historian subsume this development under a social paradigm without betraying the difference and eccentricity of the ethnic object of research? On a broader level how can the historian/biographer view the relation between the striking Greek miners singing a revolutionary Cretan song and the National Guard, which responds with an imperialist ditty shortly before they confront one another on the battlefield? In the midst of labor unrest the Greeks are singing a revolutionary song that protests the Turkish occupation of Greece. On the other side, the National Guard sings of its imperialist exploits in the Philippines and its contempt for the people it encountered there. For the narrator, continuity can be recovered only by analogy and metaphor in this confrontation between Greeks and Americans: "[The Greeks] did not kill for aesthetics or for an idea, but to even up an imbalanced internal world" (81). Yet the metaphor covers only thinly the resisting blind spot of the narrative. The subject's radical alterity refuses to submit to narrative continuity or to textual coherence. Thus on a broader level, the narrator ponders the relation between class and ethnicity as this relation is appropriated by official, historical discourse. The challenging question remains: How can one account for Louis Tikas's and his fellow Cretans' political transition from a medieval consciousness to twentieth-century American industrial politics? It is easy to read such a political transformation in terms of a rebirth experience of the new American immigrants. Surely one can give credit for it to American ideology and predicate an American beginning for the immigrants. This would downplay their ethnic past. But the narrator does not allow for such easy answers; instead he focuses on this blind spot. He perceives it as a resistance against American ideology, which seeks to appropriate ethnic diversity and eccentricity as exoticism.

The tendency to exoticize, marginalize, and demote the ethnic in the struggles of these early immigrants can be seen in some of the unanimously enthusiastic reviews that followed the publication of *Buried Unsung*. It was compared to Alex Haley's *Roots* and was called "a representative man book" that pitted the "epic old world values of the immigrants and the impersonal values of a modern, industrialized America"; it recreated the life of the immigrants who lacked a "working epistemological model" that would allow them to understand corporate America and industrial struggle. It was, after all, "ethnic heterogeneity [that functioned as] a fetter to increased class-consciousness."[6] These reviews, although openly admiring Papanikolas's excellent study of Louis Tikas and the strike, fail to discern the ambiguous and problematic ways in which the author relates ethnicity to the development of class consciousness. In fact, by refusing to confront the issue, these reviewers perpetuate the same mistake that essentially leads the narrator to his almost fruitless search: they marginalize the particular ethnic history of a man and of a group in the context of a more important issue, that of the strike and the massacre. They perceive ethnicity and class as quite separate, assuming that the latter played a far more important role in the events of the strike. For these reviewers ethnicity is represented by a few picturesque and quaint tableaux such as the lyre-playing Cretans who wear their national dress and dance in the memory of various survivors.

The narrator transcends the exotic category by providing a series of analogical and often ironic parallels between the Old and New World experience of the immigrants. He surmises how these Old World primitives might perceive the strike. They can interpret the sociopolitical conditions of their new country in the ambiguous light of their Old World experience. For the narrator such an action can be called heroic, enduring, and epic, but also ironic: "Eleven hundred years of Arab pirate and Venetian overlords and Turkish conquerors had taught them this. If they fought, it would not be for some abstraction. It would be for personal vengeance" (29). If anything, such statements cut both ways: they capture the heroic, historical knowledge of the tribe, which can be transferred to the New World with rather pathetic and catastrophic results. In fact, Old World experience becomes a definite liability for the strikers, many of whom have just returned from the Balkan Wars (1912–1913): "With the battles of late October and the coming of the militia, a myth began to grow around the Greeks—a myth of them forming a little Balkan army among the strikers in the tents, armed, efficient, ruthless. . . . Much violence will be blamed on the Greeks and much trouble" (116).[7] The Greeks allow the press to exploit and perpetuate this stereotype; quite naively they believe that it enhances their personal sense of honor, thus failing to comprehend the class dimensions of the struggle. They are the primitives par excellence. A radical alterity informs the discourse on the Greeks as the narrator presents it through documents, oral histories, and personal memories. This radical alterity signifies that they have no place in America or in this particular struggle.

Then what is their place according to the official documents of the strike? There is a strong sense of exclusion. Karl Linderfelt, the man who kills Louis Tikas, refers to the Greeks as "Apaches" and compares them to the Filipinos he persecuted during the American invasion of the islands; the United Mine Workers Union seems uncomfortable with them; the Anglo witnesses think of them as strange birds who wear outlandish costumes and practice heathen customs. I believe that Papanikolas's achievement is to have captured this sense of discomfort and ambiguity, which was reflected in official reports. The latter attempt to include these foreigners and yet make them distinct; thus they depict them as culturally and politically anachronistic and inadvertently exclude them. In short, the inclusion of the immigrants, since it amounts to an exclusion, is tangential and incidental, and is attributed to their exoticism. The reason for this is that their ethnic background remains incongruous to the class struggle they are involved in. Their history of ethnicity does not connect with the history of the class struggle, and the two do not merge in a coherent, congruent story. Hence the uncomfortable gaps that the research uncovers: Louis Tikas starts, according to an unverified rumor, as a strike breaker and ends up as a labor organizer, with no credible conversion to connect the two phases of his life. There is a report of a wound he receives in Lafayette, Colorado, in 1913 during labor unrest; the same report criticizes his unwillingness to allow the union to exploit the incident: "Later on Tikas would learn the value of such a wound to union publicists. But at the time he simply 'hid it,' like a guerrilla in the Cretan hills, trusting to his own wit to console him" (52). Ultimately the challenge rests with the documents, which cannot contain this historical incongruity but are content to reduce it either to a few blurred photographs or to some transcendental ideal of exotic and exceptional life and heroic death congruent with his glorious ancestry: "Who knows what blood flowed in his veins? / Perhaps the blood of Pericles" (246).

The narrator foregrounds the role that ethnicity plays in the class struggle in Ludlow, Colorado. He includes the incongruities and the fragments, the contradictions and the rumors, and upholds the ironies and the analogies they entail in the playful activity of proliferating stories. The Greeks and the Bulgarians strike together, although a few months before they were enemies in Macedonia during the second of the Balkan Wars (1913); Tikas describes his countrymen's determination to confront the Rockefeller empire in terms of the Greek uprising of 1821; the Greeks join the strike only after they add up their individual ethnic grievances. The strike against the Rockefeller empire begins almost simultaneously with the Balkan Wars. Louis Tikas applies for his American citizenship the day Crete gains its independence from Turkey. The conflicts among the Greek strikers are reminiscent of the fights that followed the Greek War of Independence (1821–1827). The ethnic rivalry among the Greeks expedites the union's attempt to remove Tikas from his administrative position; the celebration of Greek Easter becomes a pretext for class solidarity among Greeks and *xeni* (foreigners). For Papanikolas, the imaginative potential of all these parallels, analogies, and ironies becomes the sum total of the joint function of class and ethnicity in American immigrant history. Tikas, reconstructed by Zeese Papanikolas, seems to understand this, as he finds it very important to mediate between the two; he presents himself as the *leventis* (full of spunk and pluck) among his compatriots and as a cool negotiator among the militia and the company representative in order to expedite the interests of both his ethnic group and his class. The story that the narrator ultimately tells is that of the proliferating story lines that ethnicity allows a labor organizer to explore in trying to decipher the meaning of corporate America. Tikas is the mediator for Zeese Papanikolas, whose presence and enigma weave in and out of the oral and the written, the documented fact and the unverifiable rumor. His story or stories of life and death are those of the ideological praxis involved in the construction of texts and in the production of history.

Papanikolas attempts to write a novel in order to write history but ultimately writes neither fiction nor history. Maxine Hong Kingston, however, in *China Men* fictionalizes her material and emphasizes the legendary dimension of history, biography, and autobiography. The book contains a number of short chapters that are purely mythological; the narrator invents, borrows, and adapts tales from the Chinese tradition, Western literature, newspapers, and personal diaries and then interpolates these tales in the main chapters, which supposedly recount the biographies of the men in her family.

The combination of the historically specific, such as the Chinese emigration to the United States, and the folkloric, such as the story of Tang Ao, characterizes the core chapters of the book. Although both the historical and the folkloric are often interwoven within particular sections of the book, the book also presents a number of purely historical or documentary chapters. In fact, the very center of *China Men* comprises a chapter called "The Laws," which recounts the discrimination, social coercion, and oppression of the Chinese immigrants by the U.S. government. Because of its central position in the book, this account functions to reiterate various facts that are scattered throughout. Do they signify that the book is founded on reliable research? Do they imply that it is a documentary account despite its flight into myth, fairy tale, unverifiable rumors, gossip, and family tradition? If the central chapter states as much, then it betrays the narrator's attempt to ward off the allegation that she has contaminated historical facts with fictional or semifictional embellishment. It betrays an attempt to maintain, however ironically, a certain integrity for the biographical text, allowing at the same time the inevitable slipping toward the fictional and the mythological.

In short, the mythological stories are openly fictional, allegorical, and metaphorical. The stories that focus on family members are equally problematic and their main characters equally elusive. A perfect example of this quality can be observed in the narrator's original attempt to recover in writing her father's transoceanic trip from China to the Gold Mountain/United States. Faced with her father's silence concerning his trip ("No stories. No Past. No China") (14), a silence imposed largely by the fear of deportation, the narrator relies on the commonplaces of Chinese immigration. First she presents a realistic account of her father's immigration from China to the New World. She explains how her father, a bookish scholar, is seduced by the tales of the Gold Mountain and decides to emigrate to the United States. He passes through Ellis Island, adroitly responds to the immigration authorities, who try to trick him with difficult questions, and finally gains legal entrance to the New World. Then after relating her father's experience, the author herself questions the supposedly factual basis of her account.

> I tell everyone he made a legal trip from Cuba to New York. But there were fathers who had to hide inside crates to travel to Florida or New Orleans. Or they went in barrels and boxes all the way up the coast to New York harbor. BaBa may have been in charge of addressing those crates, marking the "Fragile" in Chinese and English and Spanish. Yes, he may have helped another father who was inside a box. (48–49)

This passage offers another possible immigration story. Consequently, the narrator imagines an illegal passage to the Gold Mountain for her father, then questions the veracity of this account: "Of course, my father could not have come that way. He came a legal way, something like this" (53), and she continues by narrating his legitimate arrival to the New World. Thus, she interprets her father's silence, first, according to a legal paradigm of emigration (he is cross-examined by the authorities, answers questions correctly, and is allowed in the country), and then according to an illegal one (he is locked up in a crate, and so on). Both legal and illegal paradigms are generated according to the premises of legitimate historiography, since they are plausible versions of an immigration story. However, the narrator persists in reminding us that they are also fictional accounts that function as comic-serious substitutes for the blind spots of family/ethnic history. Moreover, they implicitly criticize the discrimination that "The Laws" describes and that results in the irrational fear of deportation haunting the entire immigrant community. However, in the process, the two paradigms expose the rhetorical nature of this particular writing of history. Hence, in order to construct the subject of her biography, the narrator appropriates the historically paradigmatic, in other words the legal and illegal versions of immigration; she constitutes and defines her father as historical subject and as immigrant by exhausting the imaginative possibilities of the topoi.[8]

Yet the historically plausible is too limited to guarantee safety from legal extradition. In "The American Father," a new set of possibilities is introduced: the grandmother gave birth to BaBa after she came to San Francisco disguised as a man; or "Chinese women once magical, she gave birth at a distance, she in China, my grandfather and father in San Francisco" (237); or the narrator's grandfather had the baby by himself. BaBa's life story is not one but many; in fact, so many that plausibility and verifiability become irrelevant. What matters is the final statement: "My father nevertheless turned up in San Francisco an American citizen" (237). BaBa and his family must escape from the legal nightmare of official deportation.

The fantasy of the storytelling is used to protect BaBa from extradition. But this irrational fear that the narrator jokingly refers to throughout the narrative underscores the precarious position of the immigrants in the New World. This fear is assuaged only in the last pages of "The Brother in Vietnam." There by implication the brother and his family are given the official reassurance that they are bona fide American citizens, in fact, super-Americans. This serves as an ironic comment on the politics of racial discrimination that "The Laws" so blatantly states. But the apparent happy ending of an immigrant family's journey into fear also introduces a set of new questions: Have these people, who essentially had no legal status in the United States, crossed another boundary? Are they now to be considered ghosts by Chinese standards? Is one kind of invisibility to be replaced by another?[9]

The narrative as a whole crosses from one fantasy into another, or from one nightmare into the next. The transformative processes of folk imagination have turned the United States and California into the Gold Mountain of the Chinese tradition in an attempt to legitimize the Chinese presence in the new country. On the level of the imagination, the United States becomes a Chinese utopia (Chua, 61–70). But the new reality proves unwieldy for their imagination and discourse. For one thing, their mythology does not fit the industrial landscape of the New World (Rabinowitz, 179–80). If the brief chapter called "The Ghostmate" is meant to elaborate on the Arcadian, utopian dimensions of the United States that inform Chinese storytelling in the Old Country, its story line has only a passing and ironic resemblance to Bak Sook Goong's actual experience as an immigrant on Hawaii. In "The Great Grandfather of the Sandalwood Mountains," Bak Sook Goong's fantastic encounter with and marriage to a Hawaiian woman offers scant relief for the atrocious conditions of exploitation he encounters on the island.

The second great-grandfather, Bak Goong, uses the trick he knows from the folk tale "Chan Moong Gut and the Gambling Wives" at the expense of the "Jesus demonesses"—the women missionaries—in a futile attempt to reaffirm the power of the oral.[10] With the Bible and their bookish Cantonese, the missionaries come among the Chinese immigrants in order to "talk story" and proselytize. They behave condescendingly and fail to understand that they remain outsiders, since they cannot comprehend the jokes or the special language the men use with one another. The Jesus demonesses might know Cantonese and how to talk story but lack knowledge of the culture and its context. In the end, Bak Goong sends them "to the outhouse to piss" (113) by offering them too much tea to drink; the missionaries do not recognize that the trick Bak Goong played on them was suggested to him by the folktale "Chan Moong Gut and the Gambling Wives." When he tells this story to his companions not only does he affirm the power of the oral, but he also creates a community of men laughing at the missionaries and at the exploitative culture they represent. But in his case too this is a temporary triumph compared with the overwhelming ban on speech the overseers impose. Ultimately, the oral fails to connect these great-grandfathers with the New World, the Gold Mountain of their fantasies. The latter remains for them a place of unfulfilled desires. After all, Bak Sook Goong fulfills his fantasy only by taking his Hawaiian wife to the Old Country; as for Bak Goong he also departs for China.

At the end of "The Great Grandfather of the Sandalwood Mountains," the Chinamen invent and perform a new ritual, which helps them fantasize that they become the founding fathers of the United States. They dig a hole and express their inmost desires and grievances by shouting into it: " 'Hello, Mother. Hello, my heart and liver.' Or 'I want home. Home. Home. Home' " (117). In the end, they can claim, in Bak Goong's words: " 'That wasn't a custom. . . . We made it up. We can make up customs because we're the founding ancestors of this place' " (118). Their act signifies their resistance to the ban on speech imposed by the overseers; it also ironically accentuates their unfulfilled desire to be included in the history of the United States. Their exclusion, which the narrator documents so meticulously in "The Laws," would not allow the newly arrived ethnic group to ratify its historical presence and legitimacy in the New World. This confers upon the group a sense of social and historical invisibility.

The sense of unreality that the New World promotes in the Chinese immigrant is emphasized even more in Ah Goong's story. But here a subtle deprivileging of mainstream American history takes place; ethnic history is favored. Ah Goong emigrates from China to work on the Central Pacific Railroad. His story takes him through the Civil War and presents him as an eyewitness to the gradual materialization of the American Dream of westward expansion. He experiences the exploitation of foreign laborers in the Northwest and participates in the labor strike that started on 25 June 1867, which ended in victory for the strikers. The Civil War is given a brief sentence in the text; however, the word "exploitation" that this sentence introduces characterizes the history of the Chinese laborers as the narrator records it. The larger part of the chapter recounts the story of the strike and the ultimate victory of the Chinese laborers. Then, as the transcontinental railroad is finished and its completion is recorded in newspapers and photographs, Ah Goong and his fellow workers literally slip out of the celebration and melt into the background of these photographs and newspaper accounts. A new phase of their immigrant history begins: it is the time of the Driving Out.

> It was dangerous to stay. . . . Ah Goong does not appear in railroad photographs. Scattering, some China Men followed the north star in the constellation Tortoise the Black Warrior to Canada, or they kept the constellation

Phoenix ahead of them to South America or the White Tiger west or the Wolf east. . . . They built railroads in every part of the country. . . . After the Civil War, China Men banded the nation North and South, East and West, with crisscrossing steel. They were the binding and building ancestors of this place. (145–46)

Ah Goong's trek through the Northwest and toward San Francisco is the antithesis of the American Dream of the West. Rather, for him and his fellow workers the journey leads to brutalization, discrimination, and expulsion. Hence his trek resembles an underground movement in which he evades the persecution and expulsion of the Chinese that this chapter enumerates. Ah Goong's story, however, lacks the neat conclusion that we see in the stories of Bak Sook Goong and Bak Goong. While he stays underground, he avoids expulsion, but as long as he leads this kind of life, the narrator cannot record his life in a linear and coherent manner. In fact, the two situations seem related, such that the first necessitates the second. Facts are missing; therefore, we cannot be given a complete story. In the end we are left with only potential conclusions. Does he eventually go back to China? Does he return to the United States? Does he die? Does he marry again? Does his family borrow money to bring him back to China? Or does he emerge from the fire that followed the San Francisco earthquake in 1906, carrying a child of his own? The text remains inconclusive and serves to dislocate rather than remove Ah Goong from existence. However, the inconclusiveness enhances the legendary aspect of Ah Goong's story, which concludes by focusing on the Chinaman's law of desire: "He had built a railroad out of sweat, why not have an American child out of longing?"

Desire places this ancestor within American history; Ah Goong is the only one in the book who fulfills his desire to become a founding father. In this sense, his story represents the emergence of the legendary into the open fields of official history, which has kept both Ah Goong and his legendary tradition underground. So the story of an ancestor passes through the official history of the Gold Mountain/United States and redirects the reader's attention away from the official records and the documentary dimension of historiography—that is, photographs, newspapers, and history books—to the legendary dimension of the story of a Chinese American grandfather. Ah Goong witnesses and participates in all of these important events but deprivileges them to turn our attention to the other history, to the eccentric events that constitute the return of the historically repressed, that is, the ethnic. Moreover, the other history and the eccentric events establish themselves firmly at the beginning of a Chinese American genealogy, that of the narrator. But in the long run, Chinese American and Chinese histories constitute the historically repressed dimension of the community's life story. The narrator's father hides his name and the story of his immigration; her relatives suppress similar stories and furthermore refuse to acknowledge a Chinese genealogy; they are also reluctant to trace their historical origin in China. But the repressed returns in articulate, albeit eccentric ways, in the course of the book.

Uncle Bun's story is a case in point. When he first appears in the text he is depicted as the eccentric uncle who talks from the point of view of an enlightened New World citizen, rather than from that of a backward peasant from the Old Country. In a long humorous scene we hear his voice expounding on the virtues of eating wheat germ, analyzing its nutritional value, and urging young and old alike to try it. But this attempt at enlightened, rational, and scientific discourse eventually carries over to Bun's discussions of Red China with BaBa. His rational analysis leads him to cast communism in the role of a utopia. It is but one step away from casting the United States in the role of a dystopia. Bun is obsessed with two main ideas, American scientific progress and Chinese revolutionary fervor. These ideas short-circuit his thinking with their paradoxes and ultimately result in his paranoia. His discourse is transformed into a critique of institutional dependence and consumer mania. But his harangues grow increasingly less rational; he attacks American consumer culture as a nightmarish garbage-producing mechanism that will eventually asphyxiate its consumers. His persecution mania, humorous and frightening at the same time, looms over the narrator's family. Bun implicates everybody in a plot to poison him; moreover, he accuses the government of initiating a plot to eliminate him as a Communist. In this way, he implicitly criticizes the historical reality of the House Un-American Activities Committee. Inevitably, the image of an enlightened American immigrant who criticizes the negative sides of the American Dream as well as the paradox of American democracy is transformed into the one of the newcomer who is driven to paranoia by nostalgia. Bun responds to his real and imaginary dangers by reverting to a dream of China before the revolution and decides to return to his village appropriately enough, disappearing into this never-never land. Thus the legendary constitutes an alternative historical vision, a metacultural point of view from which an eccentric critique of history in America can be launched.

But if American history is associated with ethnic history in a dialogical relation, it can make its comeback by intellectually and physically un-mooring the subject. The visibility of the one is predicated on the invisi-bility of the other. This is the law that determines their boundaries. Hence the repressed and marginalized ethnic past is predicated as unreal; not only does it criticize the official historiography, but it can also con-sume the subject.

Orality, circumstantiality, and fragmentation characterize the past that the narrators of the two books recover. In the end, they both con-front the fact that imagination and interpretation have guided the re-construction of the reclaimed history. The two books conclude with statements that combine satisfaction with discomfort: "All a photograph can tell you, really, is the present" (Papanikolas, 266); "It was past mid-night, or it was his accent, but I could not hear if he was saying that looking for the Gold Mountain was like looking for a needle in a hay-stack" (Kingston, 307). The researcher never loses sight of the fact that knowledge of the ethnic past is knowledge of a legend, that is to say, knowledge of a nonplace or an absence. The two narrators reclaim the mystical, mysterious, and muted heritage, but both insist that it is not only rediscovered but also invented. After all, Tikas has been appro-priated within a certain labor history/mythology; Uncle Bun and Ah Goong have been written out of existence. To reinstitute them as ethnic historical subjects is a slippery issue. One goes into the past in order to find oneself again in the present, as Papanikolas's narrator openly admits. Imagination and interpretation introduce a dialogue with offi-cial documents and extrapolate from scanty evidence to propose new ways of looking at research. These alternative ways are not extolled, however; what is emphasized and finally proposed is the need for a self-conscious approach to historiography. This approach opens the text to a critique of its ideological praxis. In the end, the disempowered speak by inscribing their difference on the discourse of the hegemonic; but inadvertently their legendary stories introduce the possibility of rearticu-lating the ethnic past or official history while avoiding narrative closure and totalization.

Notes

1. "To call a people exotic freezes us into the position of being always alien—politically a most sensitive point with us because of the long history in America

of the Chinese Exclusion Acts, the deportations, the law denying us citizenship when we have been part of America since its beginnings" (Kingston 1982, 57).

2. Earlier accounts of the strike include those by Barron B. Beshoar, and George S. McGovern and George F. Guttridge.

3. La Capra has proposed the concept of the worklike as possessing functions similar to those of the legendary proposed by de Certeau. According to La Capra, the "worklike involves dimensions of the text not reducible to the documentary, prominently including the roles of commitment, interpretation and imagination. The 'worklike' is critical and transformative for it deconstructs and reconstructs the given. . . . The documentary marks difference, the 'worklike' makes a difference" (La Capra 1983, 30).

4. It is interesting to note that although reviewers felt drawn to this kind of history writing, they expressed, nevertheless, their discomfort with the deeply personal voice that permeates the description of the research and that questions its own premises.

5. On this issue see Charles Moskos, *Greek Americans: Struggle and Success*, and Theodore Saloutos, *The Greeks in the U.S.* On the recent attempt to revise this image, see the discussion between Charles Moskos and Dan Georgakas in the pages of *The Journal of the Hellenic Diaspora* 1, no. 2 (1987) and Dan Georgakas, "Demosthenes Nicas: Labor Radical."

6. William Greever, *The Historian* (February 1984); Bill Bryans, *Journal of the West* (October 1983): 92–93; Gerald Sorin, *Labor History* 25 (1984): 603–605; Polly Stewart *Southwest Folkore* 6, no. 1:73–74.

7. The first Balkan War was fought between the Christian nations of the Balkan Peninsula and the Ottoman Empire; the second was fought among the victorious allies, and it determined the new national borders in the Balkans.

8. Neubauer claims essentially a metafictional intention on the part of the narrator, who provides the reader with a number of different immigration story versions in order to indicate the painstaking process of selection and arrangement. For me it is a more serious political act of recognition and historical revision (19).

9. Leslie W. Rabine, in a very interesting article, elaborates on the notion of crossing gender boundaries; in her view, this is associated with homelessness and permanent exile: "Most of the legends incorporated into *China Men* are about exiles who wander in search of returning home, and, in at least two of these legends, exile is symbolized by the men being transformed into women. To be a woman, whose birth is not recognized by the family, is to be a permanent exile, without any home, without a place. To be a man who loses one's home is to cross over into the feminine gender" (480).

10. Alfred S. Wang notices that, apart from the oral stories the Chinamen exchange and invent, folk medicine functions as another form of political discourse, "which alleviates the pain of Bak Goong and the other laborers" (11).

Works Cited

Beshoar, Barron B. *Out of the Depths: The Story of John R. Lawson, a Labor Leader.* Denver: Golden Bell Press, 1942.

Bryans, Bill. Review of *Buried Unsung,* by Zeese Papanikolas. *Journal of the West* (October 1983): 92–93.

Cheng, Lok Chua. "Two Versions of the American Dream: The Golden Mountain in Lin Yutang and Maxine Hong Kingston." *MELUS* 8, no. 4 (1981): 61–70.

de Certeau, Michel. *The Writing of History.* Translated by Tom Conley. New York: Columbia University Press, 1988.

Georgakas, Dan. "Demosthenes Nicas: Labor Radical." In *New Directions in Greek American Studies,* edited by Charles Moskos and Dan Georgakas, 95–109. New York: Pella Publishing, 1991.

Greever, William. Review of *Buried Unsung,* by Zeese Papanikolas. *The Historian* (1984).

Kingston, Maxine Hong. *China Men.* New York: Knopf, 1980.

———. "Cultural Mis-readings by American Reviewers." In *Asian and Western Writers in Dialogue,* edited by Guy Amithanayagan, 55–65. London: Macmillan, 1982.

La Capra, Dominick. *History and Criticism.* Ithaca: Cornell University Press, 1985.

———. *Rethinking Intellectual History: Texts, Contexts, Language.* Ithaca: Cornell University Press, 1983.

McGovern, George S., and George F. Guttridge. *The Great Coalfield War.* Boston: Houghton Mifflin, 1972.

Moskos, Charles. *Greek Americans: Struggle and Success.* Englewood Cliffs, N.J.: Prentice-Hall, 1980.

Neubauer, Carol E. "Developing Ties to the Past: Photography and Other Sources of Information in Maxine Hong Kingston's *China Men.*" *MELUS* 10, no. 4 (1983): 17–36.

Papanikolas, Zeese. *Buried Unsung: Louis Tikas and the Ludlow Massacre.* Salt Lake City: University of Utah Press, 1982.

Rabine, Leslie W. "No Lost Paradise: Social Gender and Symbolic Gender in the Writings of Maxine Hong Kingston." *Signs* 12, no. 3 (1987): 471–92.

Rabinowitz, Paula. "Eccentric Memories: A Conversation with Maxine Hong Kingston." *Michigan Quarterly Review* 26, no. 1 (1987): 179–80.

Said, Edward. *Beginnings: Intention and Method.* New York: Columbia University Press, 1975.

Saloutos, Theodore. *The Greeks in the U.S.* Cambridge, Mass.: Harvard University Press, 1964.

Sledge, Linda Ching. "Maxine Hong Kingston's *China Men*: The Family Historian as Epic Poet." *MELUS* 7, no. 4 (1980): 3–22.

Sorin, Gerald. Review of *Buried Unsung,* by Zeese Papanikolas. *Labor History* 25 (1984): 603–605.

Stewart, Polly. Review of *Buried Unsung,* by Zeese Papanikolas. *Southwest Folklore* 6, no. 1 (1983): 73–74.

Wang, Alfred S. "Lu Hsun and Maxine Hong Kingston: Medicine as a Symbol in Chinese and Chinese American Literature." *Literature and Medicine* 8 (1989): 1–21.

Yearning for the Past:

The Dynamics of Memory

in Sansei Internment Poetry

STAN YOGI

The Nisei, or second-generation Japanese Americans, almost succeeded in realizing Stephen Dedalus's desire to awaken from the nightmare of history. The particular nightmare for Nisei was the World War II internment, an episode that left many of them emotionally and psychologically scarred.[1] Between July and December 1981, the Commission on Wartime Relocation and Internment of Civilians convened public meetings throughout the United States to receive testimony on the forced removal of Japanese Americans and Aleuts from their homes after the United States entered World War II.[2] These meetings gave many Nisei a forum to acknowledge the injustice of their wartime treatment and to vocalize, often for the first time in forty years, their memories and feelings about the internment. But what of the Sansei (third-generation Japanese Americans), who were deprived of a personal and collective history by their parents' decades-long silence?

The poems of three Sansei—Lawson Inada, Janice Mirikitani, and David Mura—explore the effects of this generational silence and the poignant longing for an acknowledgment and understanding of the past. Although these three poets differ in background and poetic style, they nonetheless are drawn to examine the effects of internment on their lives. In confronting the lack of both public history (as expressed, for example, in textbooks and public discourse) and personal history (as passed on through family stories and personal narratives), these poets present a dilemma that Sansei have collectively faced: the lack of knowledge about events that dramatically marked their families.

In the wake of ethnic pride movements in the 1960s and 1970s, many Sansei sought history that reflected Japanese American experiences. This often meant confronting their parents' wartime internment. Although

245

eager to receive firsthand accounts of the camp experience, Sansei were often frustrated by the silence of their parents, who still had not psychologically and emotionally come to terms with their internment.[3]

What historian Roger Daniels calls the collective social amnesia of the Nisei had tremendous implications for the Sansei generation (Nagata, 51). The absence of personal narratives and family stories about the war years left Sansei not only without a complete sense of their parents' histories, but also with an incomplete sense of themselves. If we accept the arguments of Sharon Kaufman, who observes that themes emerge from family stories and become the means by which people "interpret and evaluate their life experiences and attempt to integrate these experiences to form a self-concept" (Kaufman, 25, as quoted in Wilson), we can understand how Nisei's silence about significant events in their lives would leave them and their Sansei children without a complete sense of self-understanding. Expanding on Kaufman's ideas, the folklorist William Wilson adds that "as we listen to [family] stories, we also are creating a meaningful, coherent sense of self, constructing our own lives in the process" (Wilson, 145). Wilson's comments apply to the Sansei generation, for the lack of family history through stories could result in incomplete Sansei self-identities.

Michael Fischer further complicates ethnic self-identity by arguing that "the search or struggle for a sense of ethnic identity is a (re-)invention and discovery of a vision, both ethical and future-oriented" (196). Fischer elaborates by commenting that ethnic identity, grounded in an understanding of the past, buttresses against cultural homogenization and contributes to a "richer, more powerfully dynamic pluralistic society" (197). Fischer's ideas raise the question: How does Nisei silence about the internment affect Sansei ethnic identity?

Many Sansei were aware that the internment was a "monumentally controversial episode . . . in the lives of their parents and grandparents but they [were] strangely out of phase with the impact that internment should have had on their forbears" (Miyoshi, 55). This mystery, in turn, left Sansei wanting "a more personal understanding and connection with their roots" that only their parents could provide (Miyoshi, 1). They hungered for an understanding of the legacies received from previous generations.[4]

In certain respects, Sansei had the luxury to ask questions about the past that would have caused tremendous psychic pain for Nisei. At the same time, though, this exploration was a necessary step in self-understanding and the development of collective identity. But how does one recall a history never experienced or locked in silence? How do Inada, Mirikitani, and Mura recover their lost family and ethnic history? In Inada's case, this is done by conveying and building on his own memories of camp life and its effects, and with Mirikitani and Mura, by creating memories for their parents and in the process establishing a sense of their own legacy.[5] By recovering or creating the past, these poets transform private memories and speculations into public statements.[6] Memory thus becomes not only a subjective internal construct of past events, but a necessary imaginative component both in the telling of a larger collective history and in the development of personal identities that defy attempts (by Nisei parents and by a nation unwilling, until recently, to acknowledge the injustice of internment) to forget and to bury the wartime past.

Lawson Fusao Inada, unlike Mirikitani and Mura, was old enough at the time of the war to have memories of internment. Born in Fresno in 1938, Inada and his family returned there after the war. A groundbreaking writer and editor of Asian American literature, Inada was one of the first Sansei to have a collection of poetry published by a major press.

His poem "From Our Album" (which appeared in his 1971 book *Before the War: Poems as They Happened*) is a series of shattering portraits of camp life. Structured in four parts, the poem moves chronologically from an opening section entitled "Before the War," which depicts prewar life, to the final section, "Song of Chicago," which captures the traumas of postwar survival. Inada constructs "From Our Album" as a series of memories, tempering a child's perspective with an adult's insights into ironies of loyalty and legacies of violence (physical and psychological) among Japanese Americans. This dual perspective allows him not only to comment on his own camp experiences, but also to envision the impact of camp on his father and thus obliquely give voice to the Nisei generation.

The poem opens with an acknowledgment of memory that marks the poem in time:

> Before the war
> means Fresno, a hedged in house,
> two dogs in the family.

These lines announce that the war was a defining moment in the lives of Japanese Americans, who organize personal histories in relation to the war. This opening succinctly idealizes life before the war with classic images of American middle-class life and suggests an almost mythical time before the trauma of internment.[7]

The opening section goes on to describe one of the family's dogs:

> Jimmy, my father's shepherd,
> wouldn't eat after the evacuation.
> He wouldn't live with another master
>
> and pined away, skin and bone.
>
> With feelings more than pride,
> we call him our one-man dog.

Through this image, Inada introduces the idea of loyalty—a central theme in the justification of internment; the general public and government officials were convinced that Japanese Americans were disloyal and consequently needed to be removed from the West Coast and locked under guard.[8] Inada cogently links the loyalty of the dog with the unacknowledged loyalty of Japanese Americans.[9]

The third section of the poem, "Desert Songs," is composed of six subsections that explore memories of violence. In the first of these, entitled "All that We Gathered," Inada uses a childhood memory to explore the intersection between physical and psychological violence:

> Because there was little else to do,
> they led us to the artillery range
> for shells all that we gathered,
> and let us dig among the dunes
> for slugs, when they were through.

The danger suggested in the image of children being led to an artillery range is undercut by the discovery that the children gather shells. The pun in the word *shells,* however, contributes to the irony and outrage of the image. Although *shells* conjures images of seashells, the reader realizes that the children are searching for artillery shells. The violence inherent in the image is revealed in the next stanza.

> Because there was little else to do,
> one of them chased a stray
> with his tail between his legs
> and shot him through the head.

The repetition of the opening line reinforces the sense of the soldiers' boredom and highlights the random brutality of the killing. The dog's death, however, is emblematic of deeper concerns. The image of the dog recalls the dog in the first section of the poem. Unlike the loyal dog of the earlier image, this dog has its tail between its legs, suggesting shame. Feelings of shame permeate Nisei recollections of the war years. Many were ashamed of their internment, as it reminded them of their second-class status in America. Inada subtly connects the dog's shame to that of Japanese Americans. The dog in this instance becomes a symbol of the psychological violence wrought against Japanese Americans. Echoing the earlier image of the loyal dog, the murdered dog not only represents the internal shame of Japanese Americans, but is also a reminder of Japanese American loyalty. Teasing out this association, Inada symbolically represents the active denial, suppression, or "killing" of the possibility of Japanese American loyalty in the minds of those who engineered the internment.

The next subsection of "Desert Songs," entitled "Shells," resonates with the association of shells in the previous section while depicting further violence that remains in the poet's memory.

> A desert tortoise—
> something mute and hard—
>
> something to decorate
> a desert Japanese garden:
>
> gnarled wood, smooth
> artillery shells for a border.
>
> When a guard
> smashes one, the shell
>
> cracks open and the muscles ooze.

The image of the tortoise presents yet another association with shells: an outer protective cover for a living creature. If read symbolically, the shell, accentuated by the words "mute" and "hard," subtly suggests the protective layer Japanese Americans developed to deal with the psychological trauma the internment created. The violence the artillery shells imply (in this section of the poem as well as the echo of the previous section) is manifest in the next image: the killing of the tortoise. Another random act of violence, the death becomes a symbol for the psychological violence done to Japanese Americans, their self-esteem smashed like the tortoise.

The fifth subsection of "Desert Songs" moves from a focus on the child to an examination of the internment's effects on the poet's father. It explores with the intensity of a haiku the father's reactions to camp and the contradictions and frustrations that Nisei endured. The title "Steers" alludes to driving and to cattle—both central images here.

> Because a dentist
> logically drives a butcher truck,
>
> I rode with my father
> to the slaughterhouse on an afternoon.
>
> Not hammers, not bullets,
> could make him close his eyes.

The sarcasm of the two opening lines evokes the randomness of camp life by pointing out the absurdity of a dentist becoming the driver of a butcher truck. The reference to driving also implies control, which the father now lacks because he is interned. The final two lines suggest the hardening of the poet's father to the violence he witnesses. The image not only represents an inuring to physical violence, but also hints at the psychological and emotional hardening necessary to endure the frustrations and humiliations of internment. The use of hammers and bullets recalls the previous deaths by shooting and bludgeoning, thus linking the deaths of the dog and tortoise with the killing the father witnesses and more significantly with his own emotional death resulting from the internment.

"Song of Chicago," the poem's final section, hauntingly conveys the troubling legacies of shame and degradation some Nisei took with them into postcamp life. The section's final stanzas are revealing:

> When the threat lessened,
> when we became tame,
> my father and friends
> took a train to Chicago
>
> for factory work,
> for packaging bolts.
> One grew a mustache
> and called himself Carlos.
>
> And they all made a home
> with those of their own—
>
> rats, bedbugs, blacks.

The section begins with animal associations, recalling previous animal imagery and making explicit the association of Japanese Americans with animals. The idea of a people's becoming "tame" disturbingly associates Japanese Americans with wild animals and suggests the spirits broken by the internment. The final line—"rats, bedbugs, blacks"—surprises as it outrages with the suggestion of humans being equated with vermin. The disturbing power of the line reveals the extent to which Japanese Americans felt dehumanized and related to a group of Americans who had for hundreds of years been at the bottom of the social hierarchy. That the poem ends on such a somber tone, capturing the shame of Nisei, is indicative of the era in which the poem was published. In the early 1970s, Nisei were not yet willing to turn a critical gaze on their wartime experiences and instead chose, for the most part, to suppress memories of internment.

Janice Mirikitani's poems "Lullabye" (from the 1978 collection *Awake in the River*) and "Breaking Silence" (from the 1987 book *Shedding Silence*) explore the effects of that suppression. Read in tandem, the poems function as a call and response. "Lullabye" explores Nisei shame and the refusal to remember history, whereas "Breaking Silence" seizes personal history as a vindication of past wrongs.[10]

"Lullabye" opens with the poet's dilemma in confronting her mother's silence.

> My mother merely shakes
> her head
> when we talk about the war,
> the camps, the bombs.
>
> She won't discuss
> the dying/her own
> as she left her self
> with the stored belongings.

The mother's metaphorical death in these opening lines recalls the hardening of spirit suggested in "From Our Album" and is linked with a resistance to acknowledging the impact of the camps. Despite the dramatic imagery of death with which the poem opens, Mirikitani does not insist that the past is forever buried. On the contrary, the image of the self stored with belongings implies that the past is waiting to be reclaimed.

Because of her mother's silence, the poet must imagine her mother recognizing the losses endured during the internment. In a remarkable shift in poetic voice, a second persona, the mother, appears.

> *Futokoro no ko*
> > Child at my breast
>
> *oya no nai*
> > parentless.

The shift is dramatic in part because the change in language suggests subversion: Japanese was the language of the enemy during the war. The shift in persona also implies the loss the Sansei generation experienced; Nisei silence has ramifications for the Sansei daughter, who is "orphaned" by the mother's refusal to speak of the past. By using the mother's voice, the daughter creates the recognition of loss that her mother cannot yet acknowledge but that nonetheless is a first step in recovering the past.

In yet another dramatic shift, a third persona appears—an official Orwellian voice.

> It is privilege
> to pack only what you can carry
>
> It is dignity
> to be interned for your own good
>
> It is peace of mind
> constituted by inalienable right.

By interjecting the official voice and actual justifications for the internment, Mirikitani points to the absurdity of internment and the forces that silenced the Nisei. It is to this voice that the poet imagines her mother is responding, "pledging allegiance / to those who would have turned / on the gas mercifully."

As if in response to the indictment implicit in the image of acquiescing to death, the mother's voice returns: "*Shikata ga nai* / It can't be helped." The term *shikataganai* conveys the Japanese concept that there are forces beyond the individual's control. Although it can be a realistic reaction, the *shikataganai* response could also represent a relinquishing of responsibility. The appearance of the concept here is interesting, for it implies justification for inaction as well as the suppression of emotion at the time of the internment.

Mirikitani goes on to create another memory, which literalizes the previous metaphorical notions of death.

> She rode on the train
> destined for omission
> with an older cousin
>
> who died next to her
> gagging when her stomach burned out.
> Who says you only die once?

Just as an internal physical illness kills the cousin, so too did the internment kill the spirit of some Nisei. The cousin's death thus becomes a powerful symbol for the emotional and psychological death suggested in earlier stanzas. The rhetorical question "Who says you only die once?" forcefully connects the notion of physical death with the tremendous psychic loss Nisei suffered. The question is one that the mother cannot answer but one that the daughter must ask.

In the final stanzas of the poem, mother and daughter reverse roles. Mirikitani once again uses the Japanese language, making a direct connection between herself and the Japanese used earlier to present her mother's voice. In this instance, the poet speaks.

> My song:
>
> *Watashi ga kadomo wa matte eru* [sic]
>   I am a child waiting
>   waiting
>
> *Watashi no hahaga umareta* [sic]
>   for the birth of my mother.

Mirikitani weaves together several ideas in these lines: the mother is incomplete, in a sense unborn, because she will not recognize the past. The daughter, in turn, is incomplete because she lacks the knowledge of the past that the mother refuses to share. But in another sense, the daughter has taken on the role of parent because she has the strength to confront the past that the mother cannot acknowledge. Through the use of Japanese, earlier associated with the mother, Mirikitani claims a history that the mother wants to escape. The poet's identity, however, is incomplete. The daughter cannot be whole until the mother is "born."

In "Breaking Silence" the birth awaited at the end of "Lullabye" occurs. Mirikitani echoes many of the literary devices she utilized in "Lullabye": the dance of voices, the conflation of mother and daughter, the themes of death and rebirth, and the creation of memory. The poem is constructed like a hymn, with refrains in the form of testimony that Mirikitani's mother presented before the Commission on Wartime Relocation and Internment of Civilians. These refrains are intercut with verses consisting of memories the poet creates about her mother's life before the war.

The opening lines shatter the silence that pervades "Lullabye."

> There are miracles that happen
> she said
> From the silences
> in the glass caves of our ears.
> from the crippled tongue,

from the mute, wet eyelash
testimonies waiting like winter.

Given the depth of silence in "Lullabye," it is not hyperbolic to claim that to break the silence is a miracle. By setting off the words "she said" in the second line, Mirikitani highlights the notion of the title; the mother speaks of events previously unacknowledged. The images that follow imply the silence from which the liberating voice emerges. Glass caves of the ear suggest the echoing of memory in minds still fragile with pain that keeps speech hostage. The "crippled tongue" and the "mute, wet eyelash" distill the inability to speak because of pain. Testimonies of the buried past thus become a liberating force, partial vindication for past wrongs left unredressed.

This celebratory initiation into the poem is dampened by an official voice, internalized by Nisei, a voice that told them

that silence was better
golden, like our skin,
    useful like
go quietly,
    easier like
don't make waves.
    expedient like
horsestalls and deserts.

These lines recall the Orwellian voice in "Lullabye" and remind the reader of the institutional pressure to acquiesce to internment orders and remain silent about that experience in the following decades.

Mirikitani explodes this official voice with her mother's quoted testimony before the Commission on Wartime Relocation and Internment of Civilians.

"Mr. Commissioner . . .
. . . the U.S. Army Signal Corps confiscated
our property . . . it was subjected to
vandalism and ravage. All improvements
we had made before our incarceration
was stolen or destroyed. . . .
I was coerced into signing documents
giving you authority to take . . ."

This speech directly contradicts the silence implicitly ordered by the preceding official voice. By quoting her mother, Mirikitani elevates her mother's testimony to the level of poetry. As with the opening lines, this is not hyperbolic, because the mother's words carry the power of poetry; packed within her words is a forty-year history of pain.

The poet comments on her mother, comparing her to a candle, "soft as tallow / words peeling from her / like slivers of yellow flame." This image establishes the recurring use of the color yellow throughout the poem, a not surprising poetic choice given the negative associations of Japanese as "yellow" people. Mirikitani turns these connotations on their head, as in the candle simile, by assigning positive meanings to the color. In this case, the yellow flames free the expression of anger and pain that has been withheld for decades.

Mirikitani next presents images of the mother's prewar past and uses cultivation as a metaphor for the nurturing and development of her life as an American. The landscape, both literal and metaphorical, is full of "reed and rock and dead brush," but the mother

> labored to sinew the ground
> to soften gardens pregnant with seed
> awaiting each silent morning
> birthing
> fields of flowers,
> mustard greens and tomatoes
> throbbing like the sea.

The literal cultivation of the land attests to the hard labor of Japanese Americans, who often transformed discarded land into fertile ground. But read metaphorically, the images also suggest the work of Nisei to make America their land, not only physically but emotionally and psychologically. The idea of fertility, suggested by the images of pregnancy and birth, indicates that both the literal and metaphorical cultivations have not yet reached maturity, but the anticipation of a great harvest is building.

This anticipation, however, is silenced by the return of the official voice:

> All was hushed for announcements:
> "Take only what you can carry. . . ."

Referring to the order that allowed internees to bring with them only what they could carry, the lines succinctly recall the evacuation orders that forced Nisei to leave all that they had built and to throw into turmoil their conception of themselves as American.

An ambiguous voice that could be the mother's or the poet's follows the official voice:

> We were made to believe our faces
> betrayed us.
> Our bodies were loud
> with yellow screaming flesh
> needing to be silenced
> behind barbed wire.

The image of loud bodies and yellow screaming flesh is intriguing. The justification for internment was based on the notion that Japanese Americans could not be trusted; they were "loud" in the sense that people believed they would reveal secrets to the enemy Japanese. The use of the words "loud" and "screaming," though, is doubly ironic because Japanese Americans never engaged in sabotage; nor were they "screaming" in protest about internment.[11] Mirikitani, however, plays with the connotations of the images. When read in light of Nisei silence about internment, both during and after the war, the reader sees that she twists the meaning of these images into something positive. The need to be loud, to scream about the injustice is a good thing.

Mirikitani returns to the metaphor of cultivation through another imagined memory of prewar life.

> She had worn her work
> like lemon leaves
> shining in her sweat
> driven by her dreams that honed
> the blade of her plow.
> The land she built
> like hope
> grew quietly
> irises, roses, sweet peas
> opening, opening.

The positive associations with the color yellow continue in this passage, with lemon leaves (and by extension, lemons) suggesting the valor of hard work and intangible hopes. The previous images of pregnancy reach maturity as represented in the blossoming of flowers. The metaphorical cultivation of hopes and dreams is intricately bound to the land, as success in the land translates into a further realization of dreams. The positive associations of growth and fruition, however, are destroyed by the return of the official voice.

> All was hushed for announcements
> " . . . to be incarcerated for your own good."

These lines dovetail with the previous appearance of the official voice: "Take only what you can carry." Indeed, the two phrases operate together, as the second instance of the official voice is a continuation of the first and completes the initial injunction: "Take only what you can carry to be incarcerated for your own good."

The merging of mother and poet hinted at previously is realized in the final instance of what is presented as the mother's testimony. In this final refrain, there no longer are quotation marks to indicate that Mirikitani quotes her mother. Rather, her voice merges with her mother's into a cascading confession of silence, anger, and redemption.

> Mr. Commissioner . . .
> So when you tell me I must limit
> testimony,
> when you tell me my time is up,
> I tell you this:
> Pride has kept my lips
> pinned by nails
> my rage coffined.
> But I exhume my past
> to claim this time.
> My youth is buried in Rohwer,
> Obachan's ghost visits Amache Gate.
> My niece haunts Tule Lake.
> Words are better than tears,
> so I spill them.
> I kill this,
> the silence . . .

The section opens with a reference to time constraints: testimony before the commission was limited. The merged voice of poet and mother, however, explodes notions of time to express the rage of lost years and lives claimed by the internment. The names of three concentration camps—Rohwer, Amache, and Tule Lake—represent the lost youth of the poet's mother and the lost lives of the poet's grandmother and cousin. The testimony becomes a healing force. The rebirth suggested by a past exhumed recalls the birth Mirikitani awaits at the end of "Lullaby." This birth occurs the moment the mother utters her first words of testimony and literally speaks the death of silence by admitting her anger over injustice.

The final section frames the poem. Mirikitani repeats the lines that open the poem—"There are miracles that happen / she said"—and continues:

We see the cracks and fissures in our soil:
We speak of suicides and intimacies,
of longings lush like wet furrows,
of oceans bearing us toward imagined riches,
of burning humiliations and crimes by the government.
Of self hate and of love that breaks
through silences.
    We are lightning and justice.
    Our souls become transparent like glass
revealing tears for war-dead sons
red ashes of Hiroshima
jagged wounds from barbed wire.

The imagery of cultivation used throughout the poem to indicate personal growth here is altered to indicate the strength to examine emotional "cracks and fissures" wrought by suicide, humiliations, and self-hatred. Speaking frees memory, even tragic memory, and transforms pain and denial into strength and power. Souls "transparent like glass" supersede the image of fragility suggested in the opening lines by the "glass caves of our ears" and suggest that transparency indicates the strength to reveal fear and recognize the pain of history.

In the poem's final lines, Mirikitani celebrates the collective growth of Japanese Americans in claiming their history and owning up to the pain, frustration, and anger that were internalized for decades:

We hear everything.
We are unafraid.

    Our language is beautiful.

In these simple declarative sentences, Mirikitani captures the power of accepting a troubled past and the necessity of sharing that past both as vindication and for the creation of a fuller and more complete sense of self.

Unlike Inada and Mirikitani, who were connected to Japanese American communities during childhood and the ethnic pride movements of the 1960s and 1970s, David Mura, growing up in the Midwest in the 1950s and 1960s, had little contact with other Japanese Americans. Consequently, his search for an understanding of the internment is perhaps charged with more mystery and need. Mura has written of the internal contradiction he felt as a Japanese American.

Much of my life I had insisted on my Americanness, had shunned most connections with Japan and felt proud I knew no Japanese; yet . . . my Japanese ancestry was there in my poems—my grandfather, the relocation camps, the *hibakusha* (victims of the atomic bomb), a picnic of *Nisei* . . . my uncle who fought in the 442nd. True, the poems were written in blank verse, rather than *haiku, tanka,* or *haibun.* But perhaps it's a bit disingenuous to say I had no longing to go to Japan; obviously my imagination had been traveling there for years, unconsciously swimming the Pacific, against the tide of my family's emigration, my parents' desire, after the internment camps, to forget the past. (*Turning Japanese,* 9)

The desire to learn about the past despite his parents' efforts to escape history is the driving force behind Mura's poem "An Argument: On 1942." Written in roughly rhyming quatrains, each stanza illuminates the contradictions inherent in the injunction to forget the internment experience.

> *Near Rose's Chop Suey and Jinosuke's grocery,*
> *the temple where incense hovered and inspired*
> *dense evening chants (prayers for Buddha's mercy,*
> *colorless and deep), that day he was fired . . .*

> —No, no, no, she tells me. Why bring it back?
> The camps are over. (Also overly dramatic.)
> Forget *shoyu*-stained *furoshiki, mochi* on a stick:
> You're like a terrier, David, gnawing on a bone, an old, old trick . . .

> Mostly we were bored. Women cooked and sewed,
> men played blackjack, dug gardens, a *benjo*
> Who noticed barbed wire, guards in the towers?
> We were children, hunting stones, birds, wild flowers.

> Yes, Mother hid tins of *utsukemono* and eel
> beneath the bed. And when the last was peeled,
> clamped tight her lips, growing thinner and thinner.
> But cancer not the camps made her throat blacker.

> . . . And she didn't die then . . . after the war, in St. Paul,
> you weren't even born. Oh I know, I know, it's all
> part of your job, your way, but why can't you glean
> how far we've come, how much I can't recall—

> David, it was so long ago—how useless it seems . . .

The opening quatrain sets a scene that insists on Asian ethnicity. The chop suey restaurant and Japanese grocery store as well as the rich sensuality of incense burning in a Buddhist temple create a distinctly Asian "foreignness" (at least for non–Japanese American readers) yet a very local familiarity (especially for Japanese American readers). This familiarity, developed from the specific names associated with the restaurant and store, directly contrasts with the insistence to forget an ethnic past argued by the poetic voice that dominates the poem. The final phrase of the quatrain—"*that day he was fired*"—also raises questions. Who, we wonder, was fired? How is it related to the scene?

The second quatrain introduces the mother's voice, which commands the rest of the poem. Going a step beyond the mother in "Lullabye" (who refuses to talk of the war), the mother in this poem actively discourages any talk of the camp and insists that the poet dismiss a connection with anything Japanese as represented by rice cakes (*mochi*) and by a *furoshiki* (cloth used for carrying) stained by soy sauce (*shoyu*). This admonition to forget is especially curious given the context of the conversation as established in the first quatrain. The final line of the stanza ("You're like a terrier, David, gnawing on a bone, an old, old trick") suggests the tenacity of inquiries into the past that must have preceded this encounter. The poet insists on an understanding of the past as forcefully as the mother insists on escaping it. Read in light of Inada's associations of dogs with loyalty and shame, the image takes on new resonances: It can also represent the loyalty of the son by *not* abandoning his history and by recovering and maintaining a past of which his parents are ashamed.

Despite her protests that there is no use in resurrecting camp memories, the mother inadvertently conveys the confinement and loss in camp life. Although she tries to downplay the notion of imprisonment, she nonetheless mentions the barbed wire and guard towers that kept Japanese Americans penned. Although she tries to minimize the effects of the war, the mother accomplishes the opposite. In the fourth quatrain she personalizes the loss wrought by the war. The poignant image of the poet's grandmother hiding Japanese pickles (*utsukemono*) and eel (a Japanese delicacy) reinforces the theme of maintaining an ethnic identity in the face of a system that denied anything positive in things Japanese. When the last of the food is eaten, the grandmother "clamped tight her lips, growing thinner and thinner." Imposed starvation becomes a metaphor for the ways in which Japanese Americans were made to feel that anything Japanese was bad and were thus starved of their own cultural heritage or denied access to it through official prohibitions.

The question the mother poses in the final quatrain—"why can't you glean / how far we've come, how much I can't recall"—succinctly summarizes the argument that the past can be escaped by focusing on contemporary success as well as the failing of memory. Both routes to escape, however, are undercut. The notion of Japanese American success is undermined in the first quatrain of the poem with the cryptic reference to a firing. That the mother's question is prefaced by the statement "I know, it's all / part of your job" is a subtle reminder of the firing. Although the firing could refer to a non–Japanese American, its appearance in the beginning of the poem within the context of an ethnic community suggests otherwise. The claim of faulty or failing memory, moreover, is tempered by the memories presented in the third and fourth quatrains.

Just as the mother's attempts to run from the past have double meanings, so does the poem's final line. When the mother tells the poet "David, it was so long ago—how useless it seems . . ." the reader can interpret the statement in two ways. The mother most likely means that the pursuit of the past is useless. She sees nothing of value in her history and wonders what her son can claim from it. The line also implies, however, the uselessness of the camps. This second reading is one that the mother, most likely, does not intend. But it is nonetheless one that, given the images of camp life and the death of the grandmother, the reader can infer. The use of ellipses to conclude the poem reinforces the ambiguity and open-endedness of the final line and the poem itself and the poet's ongoing efforts to recover the past.

In the years since these internment poems were written, Japanese Americans, spurred on by the Civil Liberties Act of 1988, which provided an apology and monetary redress for internees, have increasingly felt confident to confront their wartime past, criticize the government for its actions, and reflect self-critically on their own behavior. As these poems indicate, however, that confidence was hard-won. The Nisei poet Toyo Suyemoto Kawakami has written of revisiting the past.

> Camp Memories
> I have dredged up
> Hard fragments lost
> I thought, in years
> Of whirlwind dust.
>
> Exposed to light,
> Silently rough
> And broken shards
> Confront belief.

Kawakami reminds us of the shards of memory that can still carry powerful emotional resonances. Writing in the generation after Kawakami, these poets are haunted by the effects of internment, but they have also undertaken the work of restoring a past that the generation before them might have abandoned. Although those rough and broken shards of memory have left deep emotional wounds in the collective psyche of Japanese Americans, Inada, Mirikitani, and Mura remind us that these memories must be exposed and the injuries acknowledged for healing to take place.[12]

Notes

1. The Nisei writer Wakako Yamauchi has written eloquently of Nisei reaction to the internment and the silence that ensued.

> The sansei accuse us of not wanting to talk about the evacuation. And it's true. I speak for hundreds of Nisei like myself, or perhaps just *people* like myself, who are sometimes overwhelmed by a current of events we can neither understand nor stem, and from self-defense cope with only what directly applies to the self . . . political, social, or economic. Sure, the times affected us, moved us here or there, shaped our attitudes, our destinies, but how many of us know why or how?
>
> Or maybe we do know, intuitively, but deep inside something tells us what has happened is past history and [asks] what good does it do to bring back those events that might prove we could have, should have behaved more courageously.
>
> And when we do see those old photographs of the mass evacuation, we search the faces of our brothers and sisters, and in that backward look, in those old faces, young faces, we can see the mirror of our tragedy. Few of us can hold back the tears that most often smack of self-pity, but maybe somewhere behind those tears we know that this is the event that changed the course of our lives, and though there were those among us who had more insight, more courage, whatever path we chose, we have survived—whole. Maybe that's why so many of us remain silent about our camp experience. Maybe in our silence we ask you to honor us for that—survival. We ask that you not indulge us with pity, neither then nor now. The fact of our survival is proof of our valor. And that is enough. (lxxi)

2. For the commission's findings and recommendations, see *Personal Justice Denied*.

3. This topical silence was compounded by what sociologist Stanford Lyman identifies as a Nisei desire to manage feelings and avoid emotional entanglements and emotionally charged situations. He traces these tendencies to Japanese cultural traits as passed on through the Issei generation and argues that "Nisei will sometimes not tell about an important event, or will casually dismiss it with a denial or only a partial admission, suggesting by style and tone that it was not important at all" (55). Sociologist S. Frank Miyamoto expands on and critiques Lyman's ideas.

Amy Iwasaki Mass argues that Nisei adopted defense mechanisms such as repression, denial, rationalization, and identification with the aggressor to defend "against the devastating reality of what was being done to [them]" during the war (Mass, 160). These psychological defenses would contribute to Nisei silence regarding internment.

4. Michael Fischer notes a similar dynamic when discussing Michael Arlen's *Passage to Ararat* (1975). Fischer observes, "Michael Arlen's ethnic anxiety begins with the silence of his father about the Armenian past. By attempting to spare children knowledge of painful past experiences, parents often create an obsessive void in the child that must be explored and filled in" (204).

5. The creation of memory has also been noted among children of Holocaust survivors. Many children of survivors "have created myths about the Holocaust or their parents' Holocaust experiences based on their own fantasies, particularly in families where parents had been silent about their personal experiences" (Bergmann and Jacovy, 311).

6. As public constructions focusing on the will to remember (to the point of creating memory), these poems could be considered what the French historian Pierre Nora calls *lieux de memoire*, a loosely defined term that encompasses objects, symbols, places, and texts that embody and condense memory and provoke explorations of how the past relates to the present and the future. Nora argues that memory is sharply distinguished from history. He contends that we live in an age of hyperhistoricism (as opposed to an age in which memory is infused with daily life). "*Lieux de memoire*," Nora observes, "originate with the sense that there is no spontaneous memory, that we must deliberately create archives, maintain anniversaries, organize celebrations, pronounce eulogies, and notarize bills because such activities no longer occur naturally. The defense, by certain minorities, of a privileged memory that has retreated to jealously protected enclaves in this sense intensely illuminates the truth of *lieux de memoire*—that without commemorative vigilance, history would soon sweep them away" (12). Because of a seemingly deliberate suppression of Nisei memory and the lack (until relatively recently) of a formal Japanese American history, Nora's theories have intriguing implications for Japanese Americans. My thanks to Dominique Leblond for alerting me to the relation of Nora's work to my own.

7. This is somewhat ironic, because life before the war was not necessarily idyllic. Japanese immigrants were barred from citizenship, and in several states Japanese immigrants could not own or lease land. Racial discrimination denied college-educated Nisei jobs in the fields in which they had trained.

8. For a discussion of accusations of disloyalty, evidence of Japanese American loyalty, and government efforts to suppress evidence favorable to Japanese Americans, see respectively ten Broek, Weglyn, and Irons.

9. The connection between the dog and the Japanese American community is interesting, because the Japanese word *inu* (literally "dog") was applied pejoratively by internees to those suspected of collaborating with camp authorities and thereby being "disloyal" to the Japanese American community.

10. This shame and suppression of abuse is similar to that of Naomi Nakane, the protagonist of Joy Kogawa's novel *Obasan*. Naomi, the victim of molestation as a child, is ashamed of her abuse and does not speak of it. My thanks to Amritjit Singh for pointing out this parallel.

11. This is not to imply that Nisei offered no resistance to internment. On the contrary, many Nisei refused to be drafted into the U.S. armed services in protest over internment. Other Nisei brought court cases challenging the constitutionality of exclusion orders.

12. I thank Michael Owen Jones, Michael Omi, Michelle Nordon, Susan Gordon, Jay Mechling, and David Takeuchi for generously sharing references and material with me.

Works Cited

Bergmann, Martin, and Milton Jacovy, eds. *Generations of the Holocaust*. New York: Basic Books, 1982.

Daniels, Roger. *Concentration Camps: North America, Japanese in the United States and Canada During World War II*. Malabar, Fla.: Krieger, 1981.

Fischer, Michael M. J. "Ethnicity and the Post-Modern Arts of Memory." In *Writing Culture: The Poetics and Politics of Ethnography*, edited by James Clifford and George E. Marcus, 194–233. Berkeley: University of California Press, 1986.

Inada, Lawson Fusao. *Before the War: Poems as They Happened*. New York: Morrow, 1971.

Irons, Peter. *Justice at War: The Story of the Japanese American Internment Cases*. New York: Oxford University Press, 1983.

Kaufman, Sharon R. *The Ageless Self: Sources of Meaning in Late Life*. Madison: University of Wisconsin Press, 1986.

Kawakami, Toyo Suyemoto. "Camp Memories: Rough and Broken Shards." In *Japanese Americans: From Relocation to Redress*, edited by Roger Daniels et al., 27–30. Salt Lake City: University of Utah Press, 1986.

Lyman, Stanford. "Generation and Character: The Case of the Japanese Americans." In *Roots: An Asian American Reader*, 48–71. Los Angeles: UCLA Asian American Studies Center, 1971.

Mass, Amy Iwasaki. "Psychological Effects of the Camps on Japanese Americans." In *Japanese Americans: From Relocation to Redress*, edited by Roger Daniels et al., 159–62. Salt Lake City: University of Utah Press, 1986.

Mirikitani, Janice. *Awake in the River*. San Francisco: Isthmus, 1978.

———. *Shedding Silence*. Berkeley: Celestial Arts, 1987.

Miyamoto, S. Frank. "Problems of Interpersonal Style among the Nisei." *Amerasia Journal* 13, no. 2 (1986–87): 29–45.

Miyoshi, Nobu. "Identity Crisis of the Sansei and the American Concentration Camp." *Pacific Citizen*, 19–26 December 1980, 41 ff.

Mura, David. *After We Lost Our Way*. New York: Dutton, 1989.

———. *Turning Japanese: Memoirs of a Sansei*. New York: Atlantic Monthly Press, 1991.

Nagata, Donna. "The Japanese American Internment: Exploring the Transgenerational Consequences of Traumatic Stress." *Journal of Traumatic Stress* 3, no. 1 (1990): 47–69.

Nora, Pierre. "Between Memory and History: *Les Lieux de Memoire*." Translated by Marc Roudebush. *Representations* 26 (Spring 1989): 7–25.

Personal Justice Denied: Report of the Commission on Wartime Relocation and Internment of Civilians. Washington, D.C.: U.S. Government Printing Office, 1982.

ten Broek, Jacobus, et al. *Prejudice, War and the Constitution*. Berkeley: University of California Press, 1970.

Weglyn, Michi. *Years of Infamy: The Untold Story of America's Concentration Camps*. New York: Morrow, 1976.

Wilson, William A. "Personal Narratives: The Family Novel." *Western Folklore* 50 (April 1991): 127–49.

Yamauchi, Wakako. "The Poetry of the Issei on the Relocation Experience." In *CALAFIA: The California poetry*, lxxi–lxxviii. Berkeley: Y'Bird Books, 1979.

Arab American Literature

and the Politics of Memory

LISA SUHAIR MAJAJ

> Shadows are all a camera saves.
> Meaning's born from memory and faith
> and presence. These faces will be
> passed on, shadowed, illuminated,
> altered by what we name them
> and the current of our own quick flesh.
>
> —David Williams, *Traveling Mercies*

$\mathbf{M}$emory plays a familiar role in the assertion of identity by members of ethnic and minority groups; family stories frequently ground ethnic identification, and the popularized search for "roots" is often articulated as "remembering who you are."[1] Memory functions on both a cultural and a personal level to establish narratives of origin and belonging; myths of peoplehood, like memories of childhood, situate the subject and make agency possible. It is thus no surprise that Arab American literature turns repeatedly to memory to explore, assert, critique, and negotiate ethnic identity.[2] But the role of memory in this literature is not monolithic. The texts explored in this essay—autobiography, fiction, and poetry written by Arab immigrants in the early twentieth century, by their descendants, and by more recent Arab immigrants—turn to memory not just to substantiate ethnic assertion and invoke nostalgia, but also to facilitate assimilation, ground feminist critique, and make possible transformative relationships to ethnicity.

This diversity of uses suggests that memory, like other modes of knowledge, is mediated and constructed at historicized and politicized junctures. Although Arab American literature resists neat generational categorization, the representation of ethnicity and ethnic memory in individual texts reflects the concerns of particular historical periods. Arab

266

American immigrant autobiographies written in the first half of the century frequently reflect the ideology of assimilation, whereas texts of second- and third-generation authors are embedded in the affirmation of ethnicity popularized in the 1960s and 1970s. Throughout all these texts, however, a strategic reliance on essentialized depictions of ethnic identity emerges, suggesting their situatedness within particular discursive contexts, including that of Arab American exigencies: the difficulty of achieving panethnic group articulation, the uneasy political relationship between Arabs and Americans, and the general delegitimation of Arab culture within mainstream American contexts.

Such recourse to essentialism, articulated most clearly through biological metaphors of cultural affiliation, often endorses nostalgia for an idealized, patriarchal ethnic past. However, contemporary Arab American writers increasingly critique this static conception of culture, turning to memory to negotiate an ethnic identity that is heterogeneous and engaged across cultural borders. In particular, current writers frequently interrogate the gendered assumptions implicit in essentialist models of ethnicity, articulating an affiliative model of identification in which ethnicity, reconstrued as a transformative engagement with the past, grounds and facilitates action in both present and future.

Ethnic Strategies

Arab American identity is perhaps best understood as a panethnic identity, in which the coherence of group identity among Arab Americans from diverse geographical and religious backgrounds and contexts of migration is predicated upon "both a *common interest* ([a] . . . need for unity, often political), and a *common identity*, solidified and expressed by an overarching symbol system or 'cultural umbrella' that has the power to appeal across individual ethnic lines."[3] On a political level, Arab American "common interest" typically focuses on anti-Arab discrimination and violence, stereotypes of Arabs in popular culture, and Middle Eastern events and their repercussions in the United States. On a cultural level, "common identity" invokes the conscious remembrance of Arab culture and history as a heritage relevant to contemporary Arab Americans. Memory grounds both identity and interest: invocation of a communal past and a projected communal future provides the basis for an emotionally resonant and politically coherent "imagined community" (Anderson).

267

Projects such as Gregory Orfalea and Sharif Elmusa's anthology *Grape-leaves: A Century of Arab American Poetry* (1988), which seeks to construct and claim an Arab American literary tradition, typically invoke Arab communal legacy through touchstones of cultural memory: Arab contributions to world civilization, the Arab traditions of poetry, family and community ties, remembered ethnic foods, and Old World scenes of natural beauty. Such delineation often presumes a cultural essence latent within ethnic groups, accessible through and transmitted by personal and communal memory. For instance, Mary Zoghby, in a review of *Grapeleaves*, describes Arab American authors as being "awakened to" the influence of ethnicity within their creative works, and Lebanese Americans as having their consciousness raised to "recognize" their Arab identity. In such a context, memory serves to resurrect a forgotten or suppressed cultural essence, identify precursors, and celebrate traditions.

Such "awakenings," however, suggest that the category "Arab American" refers to an identity still constructing itself. As Mary Layoun has argued, national culture is "not 'out there' somewhere waiting to be recognized"; rather, the elements of cultural identity occupy "a critical site of conflict, a literal and metaphorical arena for national definition" (55–56).[4] Attempts to reify an Arab American cultural essence reveal internal contradictions, as any attempt to conflate the experiences of, for instance, third-generation Christian Lebanese Americans, exiled Palestinians, and Muslim Yemeni migrants quickly demonstrates. Moreover, the very insistence on categorizing Arab American literature as ethnic sometimes functions as an assertion of its *American* identity. For instance, Orfalea and Elmusa's comment that "there exist poetry anthologies for virtually every American ethnic group . . . Until now none has existed for a group whose love of poetry is native and deep: the two million Arab Americans" (xiii) implies that to have achieved the status of an ethnic group with its own poetry anthology is to have become truly "American."

Such attempts to claim a cultural heritage that also facilitates assimilation into American society recur throughout discussions of Arab American identity, suggesting both the power of cultural inscriptions and their constructed nature. Assumptions about the role of poetry in Arabic culture provide a useful example of the tensions at work here. Depictions of Arab culture typically emphasize its poetic tradition, portraying such legacies as natural, even genetic. For instance, Orfalea and Elmusa argue that Arab Americans have an intrinsic relation to poetry, stemming in part from a transhistorical memory passed down through blood and history to Arabs and Arab Americans alike. "The great Arab love of poetry [has] not been drained from New World veins," they write, in a description that lends poetry the validation of nature as well as of history (xiii). Similarly, poet Samuel Hazo, commenting on the poetry of Naomi Shihab Nye, asserts a naturalizing link between inheritance and culture.

> It [a poem by Nye] is a genuine American poem in the sense that . . . the vision is American. But the sensibility as well as the sense of tradition echo the Arabic proving even that a generation gap cannot distort or destroy what is finally a matter of the soul and the blood. (54)

Hazo's suggestion that Nye, daughter of a Palestinian father and an American mother, is heir to an Arab essence passed down across generations construes cultural memory as both biological and spiritual, situating Nye in a tradition of Arabic culture by virtue of her poetry and in a poetic tradition by virtue of her Palestinian background.

This insistence on a naturalized Arab cultural identity echoes, though to different ends, the strategies of Arab American authors before midcentury whose writing asserted their claim to American identity. In depicting their homelands, authors such as Rev. Abraham Mitrie Rihbany, Gibran Kahlil Gibran, and Salom Rizk typically invoke as core cultural elements the venerability of Arab civilization, its poetic tradition, and the scriptural legacies of Syria and Lebanon. However, their pronounced use of biblical language and analogy suggests their concern to present themselves in terms to which an American audience would be receptive. Despite invoking Arab culture as a heritage of global importance, these writers, with the notable exception of Ameen Rihani, typically distance themselves from its Islamic context, in a strategy reflecting not just their personal religious beliefs, but also their wariness of anti-Arab and anti-Muslim discrimination.[5] Moreover, their texts structure memory teleologically, so that depictions of childhood scenes, presented through biblical analogies at once familiar and "exotic" to American readers, in fact serve to substantiate the authors' progress toward Americanization. Thus, in his autobiography *A Far Journey* (1914), Rihbany depicts his religious and intellectual life as following a gradual but inevitable movement toward the "American" realms of Protestantism and enlightenment: an early encounter with a boy who "knew a great deal about America" is termed "destiny" (114), whereas his attendance at an American missionary school and subsequent conversion to Protestantism are described as an "awaken[ing]" (140).

Despite their reflection of assimilationist concerns, however, even those texts most concerned with Americanization are multilayered. The memories that Rihbany invokes to portray the limitations of his Middle Eastern past often substantiate instead the richness of that same past: descriptions of his origins as meager, primitive, and dismal are juxtaposed with enthusiastic depictions of the beauty of the Syrian seasons and the richness of Syrian wedding celebrations. Even Rihbany's dedication to Protestantism proves ambivalent, as the following passage suggests: "So did we ignorantly practice the modes of worship of our remote Oriental ancestors, who poured their gifts to Astarte into the streams of Syria ages before Christianity was born. *And who are you, child of but yesterday, to say it was all empty superstition?*" (93–94, my italics). The distance between Rihbany and his "ignorant" ancestors quickly diminishes in his implicit invocation of the ancient wisdom of these same ancestors—wisdom to which Americans, as children of "but yesterday," have no access. Such attempts to claim Americanization while simultaneously affirming Arab cultural heritage recur throughout Arab American autobiographies, illustrating the tensions implicit in the negotiation of cultures.

More recent efforts to delineate a unified Arab American ethnicity, however, often run the risk of reductionism. Gregory Orfalea's *Before the Flames: A Quest for the History of Arab Americans* (1988) provides a notable example. Orfalea writes in his introduction: "Arab Americans and their ancestors always seem to be caught standing before flames, staring into the ruins, heartbroken, more or less powerless to help those in them, at best taking their loved ones or just themselves to a new world" (x). Although concern over war and political turmoil in the Middle East is certainly a significant part of Arab American discourse, Orfalea's depiction effectively reduces all of Arab history to tragedy, depicting the past as static, pessimistic, and lacking relevance to the present. The book's cover provides a graphic representation of this summation of Arab American identity, demonstrating the limitations of reified ethnic symbols. The illustration features an empty, faceless *hatta* (Arab man's headdress), *abayyah* (man's robe), and *dishdash* (man's shirt-gown)—all clothing unlikely to be worn regularly in the United States—against a background of the American flag framed by a slightly off-color red, white, and blue arabesque design. Inside the *hatta* a flame burns. The empty headdress is eerily suggestive of a lack of internalized knowledge; the flame, suspended in thin air where a human face should be, seems to have burned away historical and cultural memory as well as future vision. What remains is the trappings of ethnicity with nothing inside except a consuming grief. Although the text does present a more complex view of Arab Americans than this market-based cover suggests, the image nonetheless brings into sharp relief the risks of cultural reductionism.

However, while such images, with their elision of Arab American complexity, reinforce the notion of Arabs as ahistorical, exotic "others," they also suggest that the work of cultural consolidation may not have progressed far enough to allow the productive interrogation of complexity. As Lisa Lowe argues with reference to Asian American ethnicity, "The very freedom, in the 1990s, to explore the hybridities concealed beneath the desire of identity is permitted by the context of a strongly articulated essentialist politics" (39). Focus on an essentialized cultural identity—like the use of biological metaphors to assert an intrinsic relation to Arab tradition—points toward an initial, crucial need for cultural consolidation while also laying the groundwork for the further articulation of cultural differences.

Memory and Nostalgia

Such consolidation is frequently arrived at in Arab American writing through an invocation of the past, in which personal and familial memories acquire representative cultural significance. Eugene Paul Nassar's prose poem *Wind of the Land* (1979), which has been described as "the closest thing we have to a narrative defining the second-generation Arab-American experience and thus rescuing it from possible oblivion,"⁶ turns to autobiography to celebrate and preserve Lebanese folk culture, invoking familiar ethnic markers: the emotional resonance of Arabic, reverence for traditional familial relationships and communal values, nostalgia for Arabic food, poetry viewed as an intrinsically Arab form of expression, and a celebration of gardens. His narrative seeks to integrate the memories constituting familial and folk discourse into a wider Lebanese heritage, one that Nassar wishes both to preserve and to make the basis for present-day Arab American identity.

This emphasis on memory takes the preservation of familial and ethnic history as constituting identity itself. Indeed, Nassar's depiction of ethnic identity as a familial inheritance posits memory not just as a vehicle of knowledge, but as a virtual bodily link, so intrinsic that the boy in *Wind* feels "he was becoming them [the men of the older generation]."

(16). "The vivid imaginations of [the boy's] parents, their values and their humor, flowed into him as the spring flows through the branch or vine . . . it seemed later, as his mind grew full of symbols, that he knew himself best by remembering it all" (13). Memory here acquires redemptive power: though life in the present is celebrated, it acquires meaning only through the traditional values of the Lebanese past—family, authority, filiality, the home. As the past assumes moral authority over the present, the simplest actions take on mythic stature: observing the kindling of a ritual fire in his father's village, the narrator imagines generations of Lebanese boys lighting that fire; the sound of Lebanese village women singing seems to him to have "been part of the earth's life for ages and ages" (67). In this poignant depiction, memory holds out the hope of escaping not just the alienation of American life, but the passage of time itself.

This opposition of an organic Lebanese sphere to a sterile American present provides a recurring trope in Arab American literature. Vance Bourjaily's "The Fractional Man" in his autobiographical novel *Confessions of a Spent Youth* (1960) turns on just this contrast. On visiting Kabb Elias, his father's Lebanese village of origin, the narrator, Quincy, longs, briefly but intensely, to reclaim the heritage he has known only indirectly from his Lebanese grandmother. Lebanon here offers the simplicity and strength, the nurturance and community, that Quincy's American life has failed to provide; it offers, moreover, the foundational memory lacking in his family, which did not "preserve as anecdote or legend" cultural or familial narratives (237). Quincy's alienation from his ethnic past, his lack of familial memory, and his desperate attempt, in chapter after chapter of *Confessions*, to define himself anew contrasts vividly with the security and timelessness of the Lebanese village that represents his grandmother's world, and hence his own past made present. But despite his longing to stay in Kabb Elias, the gap between the village and the American world to which Quincy returns is, like the distance between childhood and adulthood, finally unbridgeable. Because Quincy is unable to establish the relevance of memory to his present identity, as his approach to his Arab identity as "role-playing" suggests (Shakir, "Pretending"), memory ultimately becomes nostalgia—poignant but untranslatable into the present context.

The sense of radical loss that informs this text emerges in the poetry of H. S. Hamod as well. In his writing, Hamod, son of an immigrant Lebanese imam, turns to memory to negotiate his alienation as a Muslim in the American context. In "After the Funeral of Asam Hamady"

Hamod describes his youthful embarrassment at having to stop his car in the middle of South Dakota so that his father and grandfather could perform their prayers by the side of the highway. From the perspective of time and age, Hamod views the older men's faith as representative of a realm of value and meaning to which he has failed to earn access. All of the United States' speed, mobility, and possibility are inadequate here, since they can neither restore his relationship to his father and grandfather nor provide the spiritual peace these men possessed. As in "Dying with the Wrong Name," an exploration of the truncation of immigrant names at Ellis Island, memory offers hope of gaining access to an earlier, ethnic realm: a place before loss, where memories of people and events, the resonance of Arabic language and names, all coalesce into a Lebanese reality submerged under the Americanized version of Hamod's father's name. But this reality is "unspeakable," "sealed away / with the wrong name / except in this poem" ("Dying," 170).

As elsewhere in Arab American writing, poetry assumes great cultural importance here; like memory, it holds out the hope of reclaiming the legacy of the past, as well as offering generational connection to his father, who also "made up poems" ("Leaves," 73). But neither poetry nor memory finally alleviates Hamod's sense of the alienation of American life. In the poem "Moving," the sense of family cohesion that his father and grandfather were able to take for granted is depicted as dissipating inexorably:

> . . . my children
> move further away   like lost
> shipmates crying to me for help . . .
> . . . I sometimes think about a life . . .
> in some old country of time that I remember my father and
>   grandfather
> talking about . . .
> a certain amount of a reality
> where at least the whole tribe moved *together* . . .
> everyone   everything stuck together   things stayed
> and when they moved
> grandfathers   grandmothers   fathers
> mothers   children   grandchildren
> moved together, in the tents, the whole world
> moved in that tent.
> (175–76)

Hamod's distance from the "reality" of that earlier world echoes the breach between himself and his children—a gap marked by the difficulty of translating that reality to the "new patterns" of his children's lives. Memory is infused with loss: the poem concludes, grieving, "now / I carry no one in my tent."

_____

(En)Gendering Memory

The desire of Hamod, Nassar, and other writers to claim the ethnic past as a model for present life, and their insistence on reclaiming traditional familial structures as redemptive features of ethnicity, offers a poignant but problematic interpretation of ethnicity. The distinction that such writers draw between the "reality" of the past and the diminished present often results in a reification of the past, making transformation of oppressive elements singularly difficult. As Adrienne Rich observes, "The obsession with origins . . . seems a way of stopping time in its tracks. . . . The continuing spiritual power of an image lives in the interplay between what it reminds us of—what it *brings to mind*—and our own continuing actions in the present" (227). Celebration of and longing for the past are not, I would argue with Rich, sufficient; nostalgic longing for a return to origins privileges a static conception of identity unamenable to change. Moreover, the metonymic slippage in nostalgic texts between family, community, tradition, ethnicity, and the past implicitly affirms patriarchy as an ethnic value. This comment by John Zogby, the former director of the American-Arab Anti-Discrimination Committee (ADC), is illustrative: "We Arab-Americans need to know who we are and where we have been in order to understand where we are going. . . . [W]e must restore the authority and respect of the family, where traditionally each person has had a special role" (9, 10). Although Zogby's vision of the Arab American family as the repository of tradition and value affirms the need for historical consciousness, his validation of hierarchical authority ignores the oppressive elements of such structures.

One of the staples of nostalgia is the desire for a stable referent—in the family structure, in meaning, and in language itself. In nostalgic writing, as Janice Doane and Devon Hodges note, women fulfill the function of this stable referent: nostalgic discourse longs for a world of fixed gender roles, "a past in which women 'naturally' function in the home to provide a haven of stability that is linguistic as well as psychic" (14). The embodiment of ethnicity through traditional images of women merges memories of childhood safety, warmth, and comfort—usually symbolized through maternal figures—with longing for the similar comforts of ethnicity: ethnic food, an intimately structured community context, the familial/ethnic language, traditional social roles. Although this emphasis invests the past, ethnicity, and the women who represent these with mythic stature, such mythologization traps women in a static representational structure, within which attempts to alter traditional roles are often taken as attempts to subvert ethnicity itself—an accusation that takes on particular potency when ethnic identity is fragile or contested.

Wind of the Land provides especially clear examples of ethnicity reified in images of women. Nassar elsewhere describes the Lebanese culture of the immigrant generation as "one that humanizes nature, the universe, and God in terms of the Lebanese family, its garden, and its mountain village. The Father ideally rules the family, but only in the context of the worship of the Mother . . . all natural phenomena are seen in terms of brothers, sisters, cousins" ("Cultural Discontinuity," 33). This patriarchal vision posits Lebanese culture and the traditional family as a bulwark against the presumed instability of American life. In *Wind of the Land*, Lebanon, Lebanese women, the narrator's mother, and the Lebanese American community merge into a "natural" order where hierarchies are honored and filiality is the basis for relationships. Zahleh, the Lebanese village of the narrator's father, becomes the apotheosis of passionate lover, chaste maiden, and yearning mother, while romantic longing for Lebanon transmutes to nostalgic longing for home and mother. In contrast to the American context, where "the women have strings around the men's testicles" and "the child punishes the father" (*Wind,* 24), ethnicity offers the dream of a world defined by traditional familial relationships. A patriarch declaims at the text's conclusion:

> Our bread is in the tales of our grandmother
> and the wisdom from her lips.
> Our wine in the pomegranate cheeks and the
> gentleness of roses in our wives.
> The sanctity of our mothers of the whiteness
> of orange blossoms,
> And our sisters' strength of the hills and
> streams of Lebanon.
> (147)

In such depictions, the family becomes the measure of all things.

Such conflation of ethnic longing with nostalgia for a traditional order is hardly unusual. Micaela di Leonardo points out that "ethnic identity in the United States today is popularly assumed to imply an adherence to tradition, and tradition . . . encodes the ideal of the patriarchal family.

. . . A woman, in this ideological frame, is properly ethnic when she provides the nurturing, symbolically laden environment for which ethnic men can take credit" (221). Celebrations of Arab American ethnicity typically point with pride toward the reverence of the mother in Arab culture, a representation that appropriately refutes the pervasive stereotypes of passive, victimized Arab women.[7] But romanticization of ethnic mothers obscures the ways in which oppressive elements of fixed gender roles may be reified into ethnic expectations. D. H. Melhem's depiction in *Rest in Love* (1978) of the nurturing but constraining domestic labor of her mother and grandmother provides a useful counterpoint to male nostalgia.

> Kneading dough, shelling peas, measuring pine nuts. . . . I bear witness to a daily translation of two women's lives into pots and pans, the circumscription of kitchen walls . . . into patterns and patience, interchangeable days carried by movements worn to such precision that hand and object extend each other. How many times does the body yearn beyond clothesline and tar roof? Dough sticks to fingers; clock hands restrain. (17)

Although Melhem does invest ethnic foods and figures with symbolic weight, her intimate knowledge of what such symbolism entails for women, in terms both of labor and of foregone alternatives, prevents her from romanticizing their redemptive qualities.

Challenging discursive frameworks to subvert traditional gender roles is particularly difficult when these roles are heavily invested with ethnic or national significance. Although these tensions are perhaps most obvious in Palestinian American discourse, where the exigencies of exile and nationalist priorities result in an urgent projection of the home culture onto women,[8] they emerge throughout Arab American literature. Lebanese Canadian Abla Farhoud's play *The Girls from the Five and Ten* (1985) demonstrates the difficulties immigrant and ethnic women may face in conceptualizing alternative frameworks for identity and memory. Farhoud's play depicts the alienation of two French-speaking Lebanese immigrant sisters, Amira and Kaokab, from Canadian society, their peers, their family, their Lebanese past, and their own futures. Taken out of school by their father to work in the family store, the sisters exist in an isolation poignantly depicted through Kaokab's attempts to articulate into a tape recorder what she cannot express directly to her parents: her desperate need to leave the store, to go back to high school, and to find connection and meaning in her life. The recordings offer a counternarrative through which Kaokab seeks to reconstruct memory and possibility: "This is for us," she tells Amira, "so we'll remember when we get older.

. . . Maybe someday I'll understand why" (136). Unable to speak Arabic, since she knows only the "everyday words," Kaokab depends on her sister to translate, but Amira—"the big pitcher that swallowed everything" (153), as she sardonically terms herself late in the play—is unable to use her father's language to disrupt the paternal order: a point that becomes crucially clear when the sisters, having decided to ask for a vacation, realize that they know neither how to say *vacation* in Arabic nor even whether the word exists. Their lack of facility in Arabic distances them from their parents and from the Lebanese immigrant society; their lack of facility in English and their foreignness excludes them from Canadian culture. Kaokab miserably puts it: "We're all alone" (123).

In such isolation the power of familial discourse is all-encompassing. The story that Farhoud relates is in many ways the typical immigrant narrative, defined by the exigencies of economic struggle, the loneliness of cultural dislocation, and the chasm of linguistic barriers. It is, however, a gendered narrative. Although Kaokab desperately longs to return to high school, her brother goes on to college; although the sisters are trapped in the claustrophobic setting of the store, their brother is exempted from working. The gap between the girls and their family is figured through the attenuation of the home language, Arabic, and its failure to represent or mediate the external world of their experience. Though Kaokab struggles to find a means of articulating both past and future, she has neither the literal nor the conceptual language to communicate her despair.

This failure of communication is in part a result of incompatible memories. The father's image of Lebanon is, in the play's narration, nostalgic, patriarchal, and absolute, whereas the sisters' memories are more ambivalent. Kaokab longingly invokes Lebanon as a land of plenitude and sunshine: "In the orchards of my village / There was sun enough for all / . . . there were oranges aplenty" (121). But she knows this image is a construct of memory; they did not, as Amira points out, eat oranges all the time. Kaokab's father, however, views Lebanon uncritically through a film of nostalgia: he thinks that in Lebanon, Kaokab acidly notes, "everything's so much better. . . . The mountains are higher, the ocean is bluer, the stars brighter, the moon bigger, the fruit juicier, the vegetables fresher. . . . Heaven on earth, huh? Even the people are nicer; they have a sense of *honor*" (122). The father's vision of Lebanon differs from Kaokab's not so much in his longing for redemptive organicism as in her understanding that this romanticism coexists with a social code often oppressive to women. The sisters' fate is to be married off; Amira warns,

"None of us escape" (140). And marriage, in the stories they recount, is indeed a fate to escape; their examples include a young girl sent from Lebanon to the Yukon with a man twenty years her senior, and an immigrant aunt whose family, fearful of having an unwed daughter, arrange a marriage that leads to her early death. Clearly, to remember the utopian organicism of Lebanon is to remember only part of the story.

Memory finally ruptures the claustrophobia of the sisters' entrapment in the store, facilitating their angry claim to agency. Amira remembers filling the pitcher at the village well and watching it spill over; her recollection of the "woman who could take anything . . . poverty, misery, anything," but who picked up a butcher knife one day when her husband was about to beat her and said "not ever again" (153) erupts into her own furious determination that she too will tolerate no more. Unwilling to abandon their parents, or to sever their family ties, the sisters claim the only escape they can imagine: they decide to set the store on fire. Significantly, however, in their wild relief at the prospect of freedom, they turn to modes of expression grounded in Lebanese culture: dancing as their mother used to when they were little, ululating like Arab women at a wedding. Memory both impels them to drastic action and resituates them within the cultural and familial context that claims yet marginalizes them. Amira's cry that "when you burn, you have to burn everything" is countered by Kaokab's rush back into the burning store to save her tape recorder, a gesture that suggests her desperate desire for some connection to the grounds of her selfhood. At the play's conclusion, Kaokab's taped voice emerging from the smoke sets memory and narration against destruction and despair, poignantly delineating her foreclosed struggle to claim a future commensurate with the lyric possibilities of childhood: "When I was little, I ran barefoot on the red earth, I ran barefoot on the red earth, I ran barefoot, I ran and ran and ran" (158).

Despite the difficulties of imagining alternatives to such foreclosure of possibility, feminist reconstructions of memory and of the past offer some recourse. Elmaz Abinader's autobiographical novel *Children of the Roojme: A Family's Journey* (1991), based on her dissertation "Letters from Home: Stories of Fathers and Sons" (1989), draws on diaries, letters, and family history to narrate the Abinader family's emigration from Lebanon, exploring what romanticized depictions of the Lebanese emigrant's past often overlook: war, famine, Ottoman rule, migration and displacement, as well as the exigencies of gender and class oppression. The reconstruction of memory from a multiplicity of subject positions, as evident in Abinader's division of the text into "Stories of Fathers and Sons" and "Stories of Mothers and Daughters," suggests her concern with the ways in which gender inflects memory and narration. Although both women and men in these narratives experience fear, starvation, and alienation, the nature as well as the framing of their memories differs. Abinader's father, Jean, recalls thinking that "like the Phoenicians, their ancestors, they would leave Lebanon and return with knowledge and fame" (*Children of the* Roojme, 20); like his father, Rachid, he "wanted to come back rich and successful" (12). When his cousin and wife, Camille, leaves Lebanon as a child, however, after suffering extreme poverty, her mother, Mayme, intent upon getting her daughters out at all costs, speaks "not [of] the future, nor the past" (159). Instead of the Phoenician legacy, Mayme turns to small mementos for their journey's framework: "Here are the things we carry with us. . . . Sheets, towels, bowls, a flowered dress . . . a memory of songs, a heart full of prayers" (182). Whereas the narratives of Rachid and Jean, Abinader's grandfather and father, recount adventures on the Amazon and the dangers of life under Ottoman rule, the narratives of Mayme and Camille explore the dailiness of what it means to be left behind when men emigrate. Their relation of the grim struggle for survival bears witness as well to the exigencies of gendered experience: the requirement of silent obedience to men, the necessity of bearing sons, and the insistence on public proof of virginity.

Abinader invests the *roojme* (a pile of rocks extending out from the mountainside in Abdelli) with symbolism, depicting it as representative of the Abinader family and of her own identity: "What I stood on, this pile of rocks, was my foundation" (5). The result of the joint labor of the Abinader brothers early in the century, the *roojme* represents familial unity and prosperity, its symbolism taking on great poignancy in the ensuing narratives of familial division and impoverishment. In the novel's first chapter, "The Poetry of Men," Abinader evocatively describes the *roojme* and the Lebanese village, noting the ways in which Lebanon had stayed unchanged in the thirty-six years of her father's absence. But later chapters document the inevitable gap between memory and present reality—a gap paralleling the distance between Abinader's American life and the Lebanese experience of her father and previous generations. Memory connects Abinader to family history but also underscores her distance from both previous generations and her own future: "I am not a foreigner with adventures to tell, and I am not an American," she writes in *Letters*. "I am one of the children, with the strange name, who cannot choose a culture. I must always live in-between" (11).

The question of memory's function and sufficiency reverberates throughout Abinader's writing and through other Arab American texts. Jean recalls his own father insisting, "Remember who you are"; he tells the family stories to his own children, asking, "Is it not enough?" (*Children of the* Roojme, 27). Though narration offers a means of claiming memory, a return to the past is impossible, as even Abinader's father realizes: reclamation of familial memory does not resolve liminality. However, in charting the complexity of memory's interaction with history, Abinader not only preserves the family stories for their own sake, but also explores the relation of family history to her own agency. In the poem "The Burden of History" she writes, "And I rise, a gold ring / pressed into my hand. They gave them to me: the letters, / the diaries, the language, strange and stubborn. All the ones / who died before my birth are visible to me" (*Letters*, 16). Her assumption of this "burden of history" construes the past as both a personal and a communal legacy, one that not only invests her with the responsibility of remembrance and articulation, but also empowers her own voice. As the poem "Arabic Music" ventures, "soon it is quiet, and I start my own small song" (*Letters*, 180).

Writing Across Borders

The struggle to define a mode of agency capable of responding to the historical and political exigencies of the identity "Arab American" resonates throughout contemporary Arab American literature. In the texts of Lawrence Joseph, Joseph Geha, David Williams, Naomi Shihab Nye, and others, cultural identity is negotiated not within but across boundaries of inclusion and exclusion. Writing as an Arab American becomes defined in their work as an accountability to location and an engagement with difference; these authors interrogate the grounds of their cultural location, their relationship to intersecting contexts, and the ways in which the process of transiting boundaries yields possibilities for agency and activism. Memory occupies a crucial role in this process, for it provides the knowledge through which positionality is delineated, articulated, and transformed.

Lawrence Joseph maps the complexity of this ground of identification in his poetry. The collections *Shouting at No One, Curriculum Vitae,* and

Before Our Eyes emphasize the impact of historical, social, and political contexts on individual negotiations of identity. Joseph's writing, notable for its interrogation of cultural and racial tensions, moves beyond a culturally insular celebration of Lebanese culture to an exploration of the racial divisions riving contemporary American culture. The poem "Sand Nigger" (*Curriculum Vitae*, 27–29) offers a particularly clear example of his efforts at "critiquing . . . the racial—or ethnic or nationalist— designations or categorizations that exist throughout the American language" (Interview, 2). Situating his evocation of Arab American identity within the racially fraught Detroit context, Joseph examines the ways in which cultural and racial definitions divide and delineate American and Arab cultures. The poem begins by invoking the domestic inscription of Lebanon into immigrant households through familiar cultural markers: Lebanese foods, names, and places chanted like a litany, familial intimacies. But the terms of their articulation shift, so that ethnicity, far from evoking nostalgia, is reconstituted at the fault lines of racial and intercommunal violence: family quarrels, relatives killed in Lebanon's civil war, and the violence and poverty of Detroit. This shift signals both an insistence on exploring the meaning of the past to the present and a refusal to obscure the complexity of group identification. Mapping Arab American identity at the liminal site between black and white, Lebanese and American contexts, Joseph interrogates the cross-cutting delineations that both situate and exclude Arab Americans. The term "sand nigger," for instance, invokes both the stark racial divisions of American culture and ethnic ambiguity: it thrusts Joseph into the American context while simultaneously relegating him to its fringes. The familiar Arab proverb with which the poem concludes—"against my brother, with my brother against my cousin, with brother and cousin against the stranger"—similarly locates him at a site of shifting and overdetermined lines of inclusion and exclusion, this time within Arab culture. (29)

As Joseph's writing suggests, the process of border crossing frequently emerges in contemporary Arab American literature as an attempt to articulate an identity in relation not just to the Arab past and the ethnic American present, but to other groups as well. Joseph Geha's collection *Through and Through: Toledo Stories* (1990), which delineates the difficult passage through time and loss from Arab to Arab American, also addresses the overdetermined relationship between Jews and Arabs. The story "News from Phoenix" begins, "After three years in America, Isaac's mother was still afraid of Jews. Damascus remained fresh in her, the dark

evenings huddled with her sisters, fearful and giggling around the bra-
zier while her uncle told stories" (64). Exploring Sofia's fear of Erwin and
Charlotte Klein, the Jewish couple who befriend the immigrant family,
the story traces the transformation of old identities and the forging of
new relationships and possibilities. By the end of "News from Phoenix"
it is clear that the boundaries of family and community have been re-
drawn to include Erwin and Charlotte. This shift also redefines the possibilities available to the child Isaac, whose later memories will include
not just his mother's fear, but the generosity of Charlotte and Erwin.
Turning on the construction of memories and their implications, the
story's conclusion gestures toward what Isaac will remember of these
moments, invoking both the bitterness of loss—Erwin's implicit death—
and the necessity of change, both of which are symbolized by the bitter
yensoun (anise tea) to which Isaac realizes he must "accustom himself."
(81)

For Naomi Shihab Nye, the process of challenging boundaries is central: her poetry explores the markers of cross-cultural complexity, moving between her Palestinian and American heritages, the culture of the
Southwest where she resides, and the different countries to which she
travels. While honoring the specificity of culturally rooted lives, Nye also
emphasizes the liberating possibilities of border crossings; her poems
trace the gift of knowing "that there are travelers, that people go places /
larger than themselves" (*Yellow Glove*, 42). As the title poem of her first
volume, *Different Ways to Pray*, suggests, Nye grounds selfhood upon the
recognition and articulation of differences. Of note is her depiction of
a sense of individual wholeness articulated through internal as well as
external complexity. Thus, in the poem "The Whole Self" Nye writes of
"the long history of the self / on its journey to becoming the whole self,"
a journey of perpetual process that acknowledges and makes space for
self-division as well as continuity: "*Dance!* The whole self was a current,
a fragile cargo / a raft someone was paddling through the jungle, / and I
was there, waving, and I would be there at the other end" (*Different
Ways*, 13).

This complexity of identification both within and across cultural
boundaries informs the concerns that intersect in Nye's writing and
translation work,[9] and in her own positioning as a Palestinian American
of mixed heritage. In the poem "Blood," Nye offers a nuanced meditation on the notion of cultural "blood inheritance," moving from a
lightly humorous consideration of the possibilities of being a "true
Arab" offered by her father's folk tales to a deeply troubled questioning

of the implications and responsibilities of this identity. The poem deconstructs the naturalization of an Arab cultural "essence," while simultaneously foregrounding the politicized overdetermination of Palestinian identity. "Years before, a girl knocked, / wanted to see the Arab," Nye writes. "I said we didn't have one. / After that, my father told me who he was, 'Shihab'—'shooting star'— / a good name, borrowed from the sky." But such affirmation is neither simple nor unburdened; the poem continues, "Today the headlines clot in my blood. /. . ./ Homeless fig, this tragedy with a terrible root / is too big for us." Nye's ability to take her father's "true Arab" identity and "change [it] . . . to fit the occasion" is juxtaposed with the starkness of inscription into the exigencies of Palestinian history. Written in the context of Israeli and Lebanese Phalangist massacres of Palestinians during the 1982 Israeli invasion of Lebanon and its aftermath, "Blood" forces a hard look at the destructively exclusionary agendas frequently implicit in concepts of "true" identity, while insisting on the inescapable reality of the tragedies that burden Palestinian identity. The poem's concluding plea, imbued with a deep awareness of the ways in which memory informs present action, is at once urgent and despairing: "What does a true Arab do now?" (*Yellow Glove*, 31).

Less painfully, but with no less awareness of the complex processes through which identities are negotiated, the prose poem "Trouble with Spanish" delineates the interpenetration of lives and cultures on which all of Nye's writing insists. In this poem, the familiarity of language that nonetheless spills out beyond the boundaries of comprehension becomes

> the optimist's happy raft floating crazily on these wild waves. It may not save me. But I'm hanging onto it, with my deceptively confident rolling R and my threadbare Arabic, that likes to sneak into Spanish sentences whenever it can, as if, as if, it all went together, these fragments of language, these piecemeal lives. (*Mint*, 15)

Like the familiarity of an almost-known language, memory serves as a raft throughout Nye's work—buoying her up, offering fragments of knowledge that intersect "as if, as if, it all went together"—the hesitation of the repeated "as if" marking the gaps that language and memory must cross to forge meaning and narration in the "piecemeal lives" of those who move between diverse languages and cultures.

In David Williams's collection *Traveling Mercies* (1993), exploration of the movement across boundaries of culture and experience comes together with an unwavering acknowledgment of dislocation and loss, voiced through poetry that insists on the redemptive possibilities of memory and community. Informed by an understanding of memory that situates the individual within contexts of history and responsibility, Williams posits the past as a legacy to be both claimed and transformed. Ethnic identification here makes possible an exploration of individual relationship to history and to community, facilitating a deep sense of solidarity across, as well as rootedness within, cultural borders. Memory functions not as nostalgia, nor even simply as documentation (though the narration of untold stories is undertaken as a crucial task), but as a transformative exploration of the relevance of the past to present and future action.

Williams brings to his work a keen consciousness of the fluidity of borders, a passionate awareness of the ways in which his experiences—as a Lebanese American, an activist on Central American issues, a teacher of Pueblo children and refugees, and a citizen of his local community—offer points of connection across what might seem to be disparate facets of experience. True to its title, the collection is informed by a sense of compassion, of mercy, not bounded in a particular location but traveling across and beyond specific definitions of heritage and identity, in a motion that expands the boundaries of the familiar notions of family and community. The book's structure echoes this recognition of interconnection; instead of being divided into predictable sections on Lebanon, Central America, and North America, *Traveling Mercies* unfolds into a complex negotiation between the tonalities of memory and the imperatives of history. Thus, poems of personal memory become meditations on communal history, firmly situated in the natural world, while poems of historical testimony are distilled through an acute consciousness of individual experience.

Although actively claiming connection to elements of Lebanese culture—its ancient history, its community and family ties, its capacity for "ecstatic" expression (Interview)—Williams demonstrates a clear acknowledgment of the oppressive as well as enriching cultural elements of this culture. In "My Grandmother and the *Dirbakeh*" (6–7), a man plays the *dirbakeh*—a traditionally male activity—whereas the grandmother's creative energies are confined to domestic labor. But the poem concludes with a gesture toward the transforming potential of memory. The speaker imagines his grandmother playing the drum in private, inspired by the memory of another woman who opposed tradition by preparing a water pipe (usually smoked by men) for herself "like a tower from which to praise God, / balance the coals, draw the smoke through the well, / taste it, blow it out, and laugh" (7). Although Williams can only imagine his grandmother playing the *dirbakeh* when alone, such poems demonstrate a consistent faith in the possibility of a progressive future grounded in transformed legacies of the past. "Only the spirit never tires," he insists. "Try to feed off its blood / and your jaws lock, bone against bone. / But surrender it your pulse / and generations link hands / in the dance and stamp the earth / to wake the dead" (6).

Throughout *Traveling Mercies,* memory offers what "In Memory," a poem mourning the civil war in Lebanon, terms "a crazy faith" (43). Though seemingly ineffectual against the enormity of suffering, memory reaches back across the radical disjunction of war with a desperate potency, reflecting a faith as sure as that of people who tie bits of sick people's clothing to trees at mountain shrines in hopes of a cure.

> But this is a strip of story
> tied to a tree. I'm telling you someone
> still remembers where the old springs are
> and can lay down stones to guide a runnel
> that will link the terraced crops.
>
> No, listen, this is a crazy faith
> in the way rain slips between paving stones
> and finds crevices in rocks,
> and reaches a grotto as clear, cool drops
> a woman with steady eyes
> touches for a blessing to her breasts.

"Crazy" or not, this belief in the tenacity of the human spirit and memory offers sustenance through the recurring confrontations with "the chaos of grief" (66) that *Traveling Mercies* documents.

Memory emerges not as a master narrative, however, but as fragments to be connected and understood through moments of clarity and vision. In "A Tree by the Water/Saltatory Process," the speaker "work[s] to learn" his father's history (13), memory's saltatory process—a movement proceeding by leaps, like dancing—leading not to a straightforward transcription of history, but to a transforming engagement with the past. The facts on which history relies tell only part of the story, and not always the most important part; rather, it is the personal engagement of memory that articulates the connections that yield meaning. Invoked as a kind of inheritance—though with none of the determinism such metaphors are capable of—memory offers the possibility of continuity despite historical and personal devastations: "The body keeps faith with something / even stripping its own nerves. / A gesture, a glance, is passed on. / Blue shadows of Lebanese cedars / still move us over here, / currents of a distant sea / that take up what nerves / can no longer bear" (15). Generating moments of coalescence, memory brings into focus the difficult histories within which subjectivity is embedded. "So much goes along with us / on the border of vision," the poem concludes, " 'street arabs,' / orphans when we have no names / to bring them before our eyes" (16).

Despite the difficulty of naming and remembering suggested here, confrontation with the legacy of grief and silencing is presented as facilitating both community and agency. Indeed, the capacity for memory, like the "breath" (a word whose Arabic translation also means "spirit" or "soul") that reverberates throughout these poems, situates people in relationship to communal and intercultural contexts as well as to individual agency. Thus, in the collection's opening poem, "Breath," Williams writes:

> The people I come from were thrown away
> as if they were nothing . . .
> The stunned drone of grief becomes the fierce,
> tender undertone that bears up the world. . . .
> I'm thirsty for words to join that song—
> cupped hands at the spring, a cup of
> rain passed hand to hand, rain pooled
> on stone, a living jewel, a clear
> lens trembling with our breath.
> (5)

Although "the people I come from" are Williams's Lebanese forebears, described in other poems as surviving blockade, Ottoman rule, famine, emigration, poverty, and civil war, the "undertone" of transformed grief extends in *Traveling Mercies* to include other people "thrown away" by history as well: Central American refugees, Native Americans, poor people everywhere. Ethnicity is thus situated in a global context, voiced through affiliation, activism, and cultural interconnections.

Contemporary Arab American writing in general suggests that the future articulation of Arab American identity lies in precisely this kind of engagement across borders. The intercultural connections that emerge in the work of Williams, Nye, and others suggest that ethnicity cannot be understood as a singular cultural essence invoked through nostalgia but must be explored at sites of multiple border crossings, where exclusionary divisions between Arab and American, Old World and New World, male and female roles, give way to a far more fluid, tentative, and potentially transformative interaction. If, as Lisa Lowe argues, "the articulation of differences dialectically depends upon a socially constructed and practiced notion of identity" (39), Arab Americans, who are only now sedimenting a "constructed and practiced . . . identity," may need to continue the process of cultural validation and consolidation reflected in projects such as the *Grapeleaves* anthology. Recent literature, however, suggests that this consolidation may occur simultaneously with the articulation of heterogeneity and the interrogation of difference, establishing diverse and complex connections across borders. As Williams suggests, "There are different ways to tell the story" (Interview). Or as Nye writes in the poem "Telling the Story," which explores the gestures through which people interpret their lives,

> There should be an answer,
> and it should
> change.
> (*Yellow Glove*, 44)

Notes

1. I am grateful to a number of people who read and commented on drafts of this paper: Nabeel Abraham, Azizah al-Hibri, Anita Norich, Julie Olin-Ammentorp, Warren Olin-Ammentorp, Laura Porter, Ranu Samantrai, Michael Suleiman, and Iris Marian Young. But responsibility for shortcomings remains my own.

2. Following general scholarly example, I take "Arab American" to refer to North Americans of Arabic-speaking background. Most of the texts I examine here were originally written in English; although there are, in addition, Arab American texts in Arabic, I do not discuss them here.

3. I take this definition of panethnicity from Laurie Kay Sommers's "Inventing Latinismo," 35.

4. The various ways in which Arab Americans have been identified during this century offer a useful example of the instabilities of identification. Arabic-speaking immigrants, predominantly Christians from the province of Greater Syria under Ottoman rule, were termed "Turks from Asia" or "Other Asians" on official records until 1920, after which the term "Syrian" was officially adopted. The creation of the independent state of Lebanon in 1945 provoked a debate about nomenclature among immigrants, and "Lebanese" identity gained currency. The panethnic term "Arab American" is relatively recent, and has gained particular force with the emergence of national Arab American organizations in the last two decades. The racial identification of Arab Americans throughout this century reflects similar contestation: at various junctures Arab immigrants have been defined and have defined themselves as white and nonwhite, Asian and Caucasian.

5. In a discussion of Kalil Bishara's bilingual study *The Origin of the Modern*

Syrian—written in response to a 1914 court case excluding Syrians, as Asians, from American citizenship—Michael Suleiman notes the omission of the prophet Muhammad in Bishara's English list of notable Semites, despite his inclusion in the corresponding Arabic section of the text. Suleiman argues that the omission reflects Bishara's wariness of American anti-Muslim prejudice (44–45). Clearly, prejudice against Muslims could have significant consequences: a Yemeni immigrant denied citizenship in 1942 was rejected in part on the grounds that as a Muslim he could not be assimilated into American culture. See Massad's discussion of this case in "Palestinians and the Limits of Racialized Discourse," 108–109.

6. See Evelyn Shakir, "Starting Anew," 27. With the publication of more recent Arab American texts, such as Joseph Geha's *Through and Through: Toledo Stories,* this description is arguably outdated.

7. Shakir discusses the ways in which Arab American literature refutes Orientalist stereotypes while mythologizing Arab women in the process. See her "Mother's Milk: Women in Arab-American Autobiography."

8. Louise Cainkar's sociological discussion of the intertwining of memory, gender, and ethnicity in Palestinian American communities substantiates the concrete ways in which Palestinian women in the United States live out the symbolism and labor of cultural maintenance. Cainkar notes that the inscription of Palestinian women in the United States within traditional roles is usually challenged only through political activity on behalf of Palestine. Her study provides a useful context within which to read texts such as Palestinian American Hala Jabbour's novel *A Woman of Nazareth,* which situates its critique of Arab gender roles within a didactic explication of the Palestinian struggle, embedding the possibilities for feminist action within the crucial necessity of political action.

9. Nye has served as second translator for a number of publications put out by Project of Translation from Arabic (PROTA), directed by Salma Khadra Jayyusi. In addition, she has edited *This Same Sky,* a collection of international poems in translation.

Works Cited

Abinader, Elmaz. *Children of the* Roojme: *A Family's Journey.* New York: Norton, 1991.

———. "Letters from Home: Stories of Fathers and Sons." Ph.D. diss. University of Michigan, 1989.

Anderson, Benedict. *Imagined Communities: Reflections on the Origin and Spread of Nationalism.* London: Verso, 1983.

Bourjaily, Vance Nye. *Confessions of a Spent Youth.* New York: Dial, 1960.

Cainkar, Louise. "Palestinian Women in the United States: Coping with Tradition, Change, and Alienation." Ph.D. diss. University of Michigan, 1990.

———. "Palestinian Women in the United States: Who Are They and What Kind of Lives Do They Lead?" In *Images and Reality: Palestinian Women under*

Occupation and in the Diaspora, edited by Suha Sabbagh and Ghada Talhami, 55–66. Washington, D.C.: Institute for Arab Women's Studies, 1990.

Di Leonardo, Micaela. *The Varieties of Ethnic Experience: Kinship, Class, and Gender among California Italian-Americans.* Ithaca: Cornell University Press, 1984.

Doane, Janice, and Devon Hodges. *Nostalgia and Sexual Difference: The Resistance to Contemporary Feminism.* New York: Methuen, 1987.

Farhoud, Abla. "The Girls from the Five and Ten," translated by Jill MacDougall. In *Plays by Women: An International Anthology,* edited by Catherine Temerson and Francoise Kourilsky, 103–159. N.p.: Ubu Repertory Theater, 1988.

Geha, Joseph. *Through and Through: Toledo Stories.* St. Paul: Graywolf, 1990.

Gibran, Gibran Kahlil. *Mirrors of the Soul.* Translated by Joseph Sheban. New York: Philosophical Library, 1965.

———. "To Young Americans of Syrian Origin." *The Syrian World* 1, no. 1 (1926): 4–5.

Hamod, Sam. "After the Funeral of Asam Hamady." In *Grapeleaves: A Century of Arab American Poetry,* 165–69. Salt Lake City: University of Utah Press, 1988.

———. "Dying with the Wrong Name: Three Parts of an Unfinished Poem." In *Grapeleaves: A Century of Arab American Poetry,* 169–72. Salt Lake City: University of Utah Press, 1988.

———. "Leaves." In *Grapeleaves: A Century of Arab American Poetry.* Salt Lake City: University of Utah Press, 1988.

Hazo, Samuel. "A Poet Is a Tree Whose Leaves Blow Everywhere." *Arab Perspectives* 1, no. 2 (1980): 49–55.

Joseph, Lawrence. *Before Our Eyes.* New York: Farrar, Straus and Giroux, 1993.

———. *Curriculum Vitae.* Pittsburgh: University of Pittsburgh Press, 1988.

———. "Lawrence Joseph: Poet/Lawyer." Interview by Richard Tillinghast. *Michigan Today* 21, no. 5 (Dec. 1989): 1–3.

———. *Shouting at No One.* Pittsburgh: University of Pittsburgh Press, 1983.

Layoun, Mary N. "Fictional Formations and Deformations of National Culture." *South Atlantic Quarterly* 87, no. 1 (1988): 53–73.

Lowe, Lisa. "Heterogeneity, Hybridity, Multiplicity: Marking Asian American Differences." *Diaspora* 1, no. 1 (1991): 24–44.

Massad, Joseph. "Palestinians and the Limits of Racialized Discourse." *Social Text* 34 (1993): 94–114.

Melhem, D. H. *Rest in Love.* 2d ed. New York: Dovetail, 1978.

Nassar, Eugene Paul. "Cultural Discontinuity in the Works of Kahlil Gibran." *MELUS* 7, no. 2 (1980): 21–36.

———. *Wind of the Land: Two Prose Poems.* AAUG Monograph Series 11. N.p.: Association of Arab American University Graduates, 1979.

Nye, Naomi Shihab. *Different Ways to Pray.* Portland, Ore.: Breitenbush Publications, 1980.

———. *Mint.* Brockport, N.Y.: State Street Press Chapbooks, 1992.

———. *Yellow Glove.* Portland, Ore.: Breitenbush Publications, 1986.

———, ed. *This Same Sky: A Selection of Poems from Around the World.* New York: Four Winds Press, 1992.

Orfalea, Gregory. *Before the Flames: A Quest for the History of Arab Americans.* Austin: University of Texas Press, 1988.

————, and Sharif Elmusa, ed. *Grapeleaves: A Century of Arab American Poetry.* Salt Lake City: University of Utah Press, 1988.

Rich, Adrienne. "Notes toward a Politics of Location." In *Blood, Bread, and Poetry: Selected Prose, 1979–1985,* 210–31. New York: Norton, 1986.

Rihbany, Abraham Mitrie. *A Far Journey.* Boston: Houghton Mifflin, 1914.

Rizk, Salom. *Syrian Yankee.* Garden City, N.Y.: Doubleday, 1943.

Shakir, Evelyn. "Mother's Milk: Women in Arab-American Autobiography." *MELUS* 15, no. 4 (1988): 39–50.

————. "Pretending to Be Arab: Role-Playing in Vance Bourjaily's 'The Fractional Man.'" *MELUS* 9, no. 1 (1982): 7–21.

————. "Starting Anew: Arab-American Poetry." *Ethnic Forum* 3, nos. 1–2 (Fall 1983): 23–36.

Sommers, Laurie Kay. "Inventing Latinismo: The Creation of 'Hispanic' Panethnicity in the United States." *Journal of American Folklore* 104, no. 411 (1991): 32–53.

Suleiman, Michael W. "Early Arab-Americans: The Search for Identity." In *Crossing the Waters: Arabic-Speaking Immigrants to the United States before 1940,* edited by Eric J. Hooglund, 37-54. Washington, D.C.: Smithsonian Institution Press, 1987.

Williams, David. Interview by author, tape recording, Worcester, Mass., 21 April 1991.

————. *Traveling Mercies.* Cambridge: Alice James Books, 1993.

Zogby, John. "The Role of Tradition." In *Taking Root, Bearing Fruit: The Arab-American Experience.* Special issue of *ADC Reports,* edited by James Zogby, 9–11. Washington, D.C.: ADC Research Institute, 1984.

Zoghby, Mary. Review of *Grapeleaves: A Century of Arab American Poetry,* edited by Gregory Orfalea and Sharif Elmusa. *MELUS* 15, no. 4 (1988): 91–101.

Feathering the Serpent:

Chicano Mythic "Memory"

RAFAEL PÉREZ-TORRES

As long as the world will endure,
the fame and glory of Mexico-Tenochtitlán
will never perish.
—Domingo Chimalpahín Cuauhtlehuanitzin

In Delano, California, in 1965, a procession of campesinos walked away from the heat and dust of nonunionized grape fields into the stark sun of historical scrutiny. The group, organized and led by César Chávez, demanded the right to fair wages, legal protection, decent working conditions, and "basic, God-given rights as human beings." These demands were outlined in "The Plan of Delano" issued by the National Farm Workers Association (NFWA). On 16 September 1965, the NFWA voted to join Filipino grape pickers in their strike against union-busting landowners. As one of its first actions, the group undertook a 250-mile pilgrimage to Sacramento during which "The Plan of Delano" was issued. The plan states: "Our sweat and our blood have fallen on this land to make other men rich. This Pilgrimage is a witness to the suffering we have seen for generations" (198).

"Land" once again in the history of the poor and dispossessed sparked demands for reform and change. "Land" again incited the sense of right-ness and passion for justice necessary in engendering political action. The strike in Delano triggered the varied events known as *el Movimiento* and incited calls for justice and empowerment that, thankfully, are still sounded today. The call for reform and recognition in Delano was prem-ised upon a prior claim: the history of Mexican laborers migrating up and down the Valley of San Joaquín. This claim, in turn, became linked to an even earlier one: Aztlán. The invocation of indigenous ancestry valorized Chicanos' claim to a land that was home prior to invasion and dispossession. Although the skin tone and physiognomy of many Chicanos make this link evident, the significance of pre-European connections to the Americas is not circumscribed simply by genetic encoding. Nor is it bound by territorial claims. The significance, ultimately, is constructed and reconstructed by each emerging cultural group.[1]

Finding the Center

Like a persistent dream that returns vaguely during daytime, the notion of an ancestral memory has haunted contemporary Chicano cultural production. The claim for rights and land, intensified during the political activism of the 1960s, brought with it a re-collection and revaluation of indigenous cultures both contemporary and pre-Cortesian. The procession of campesinos in Delano in 1965 marched—just as their ancestors had since *el Grito de Dolores* in 1810—behind both a firm sense of justice and the outstretched banner of Our Lady of Guadalupe. This connection to a Mexican political past resonates with a spirituality invoked by the beneficent presence of the Virgin. The Virgin of Guadalupe also evokes a more distant spirituality, since the image of the Virgin represents a postconquest confluence of pre-Cortesian and European religious imagery.[2] Ancestral memory thus merges with mythic memory, and a central trope in the articulation of Chicana culture emerges.

Whereas folk legend and indigenous cultural practices form a living memory for many Chicano writers—one thinks immediately of Rudolfo Anaya and Jimmy Santiago Baca, to name but two—the recollection of Nahua and (less commonly) Mayan myths and images by Chicano poets employs pre-Cortesian cultures and values as a foil, as a rejection of the most pernicious influences of the Enlightenment and capitalism, as a source of alternative and empowering forms of social organization, as a dream for contemporary Chicana life. This mythic memory with its resultant storehouse of imagery and symbolism has helped shape the discourse of Chicano poetry over the last twenty-five years.

Cordelia Candelaria, in her excellent study *Chicano Poetry: A Critical Introduction,* divides symbolism in Chicana poetry into four areas: the pre-American, *mestizaje, el Movimiento,* and *non-raza* Other (74). Although I am often loath to think in terms of categorization when encountering something that seems as resistant to teasing out of patterns as Chicano poetry, the grouping of these symbolic images is—especially for the poetry produced in the 1960s and 1970s—very useful. For the purposes of this discussion, I am most interested in the focus on pre-American imagery, which functions, according to Candelaria, on two levels. It conveys specific information about pre-Cortesian cultures before European influences became pervasive, and it conveys "a sense of the uninterrupted continuum of human experience from the earliest legends about Aztlán to the Chicana adaptations of the meaning of Aztlán for contemporary purposes—a millennium's span in time, a continent's span in space" (74–75). From this perspective, the deployment of pre-Cortesian symbology invokes a mythic memory that implies an unproblematic and uninterrupted recuperation and "remembering" of devalued knowledge made manifest through myths and legends. Chicana literature thus seems to "reveal" connections between the troubled and fruitless present of Chicana disempowerment and a richer, fuller, and more holistic but lost past. This connection and contrast helps identify and articulate the "unique" and "authentic" qualities of Chicana identity.

Although I am in complete sympathy with Candelaria's project and agree with much of her analysis, it can prove productive to problematize the idea of a pre-American heritage from which Chicano poetry draws its symbology. This heritage proves central to the idea of a mythic memory forming and informing "authentic" Chicano poetic practices. The pre-Cortesian elements that populate Chicano literary production—Aztlán, *flor y canto*, eagles, serpents, cactus fruits, the fifth world—are appropriations of an indigenous culture that in its pre-European context has ceased to exist for more than four centuries. The fragments and shards of this culture remain in the form of archaeological and historical evidence that scholars have taken great pains to reconstruct. This heritage, then, as with all heritages, is discursively constructed. The constructed quality of a Chicano heritage proves doubly apparent, since its symbolic system does not form a part of the residual culture of the Mexica: there are no more warrior clans, there is no reverence for Huitzilopochtli, the god of war, and there is no Nahua *flor y canto*. For the most part, the symbology associated with the Aztec Empire must be garnered from museums and books.[3]

The notion Candelaria proposes, that pre-Cortesian symbology lends "a sense of the uninterrupted continuum of human experience from the earliest legends about Aztlán to the Chicana adaptations of the meaning of Aztlán" (74–75), seems a little overstated. What emerges from the history of Mexico and the Southwest United States is narratives full of discontinuities: imperial devastation, economic exploitation, racist vituperation, and an incessant devaluation of indigenous cultures by European-identified settlers. In order to construct a literary critique premised on resistance and historical re-presentation, the Chicana critic might want to focus on the pressing issue of discontinuity. In the end, the disruption between past and present—marked by military attacks, invasions, and conquests—forms one primary theme of Chicana poetry. Pre-Cortesian symbology, therefore, does not represent "an uninterrupted continuum of human experience." On the contrary, it represents a resistant response to discontinuity and violence, to cultural imperialism and discursive erasure. One of its strategies of resistance, the formation of a counterdiscourse, resides in the idea of mythic memory. The disrupted, the discontinuous, the devalued—these qualities become foregrounded as Chicana poetry invokes indigenous cultural practices that have been made marginal. This invocation helps to focus the privileged critical lens of a Chicana counterdiscourse.[4]

In addition to the recuperation of pre-Cortesian symbology, the ethnopoetic tradition of which Chicano poetry is a continuation forms a locus where the trajectories of history, politics, and aesthetics converge. Within the context of Euro-American literature, interest in ethnopoetics dates to the 1950s and 1960s with the work of Gary Snyder and Jerome Rothenberg. Their influence, as well as poetic performances such as the *corrido* and other forms of public poetic expression, form a confluence that shapes the ethnopoetics of contemporary Chicano poetry. Chicano poetic expression problematizes this connection to "tradition" as it works with and through ethnopoetic forms. A good deal of Chicano poetry has been performed as event: Corky Gonzales's *I am Joaquín* was written for and recited at numerous rallies before it found its way into book form, and, as Tomás Ybarra-Frausto has pointed out about Alurista, a significant dimension of Chicano poetry is that it is meant to be spoken rather than read (118). However, more recent poetic expression forms a dialogue rather than an antagonism between ethnopoetic performativity and other traditions: Bernice Zamora's "And All Flows Past" influenced by Theodore Roethke (himself interested in Native American cultures), Gary Soto influenced by Philip Levine's use of narrative poetry, Jimmy Santiago Baca's debt to John Donne and Ezra Pound.

If we are willing to take into account a dialogic relationship between Chicana poetry and "tradition" (indigenous, pre-Cortesian, European,

Euro-American), the object of Chicana poetry becomes much more dynamic than the recuperation of lost or noncanonical poetic practices. By looking at the works of three poets—Alurista, Ana Castillo, and Gloria Anzaldúa—the movements of interpretation and reinterpretation involved in the construction of an empowering Chicana mythic memory become evident. Their poetry assumes a culturally resistant stance by which claims for agency and empowerment, scrutiny of subject positions and interpellation, examination of devalued knowledges and histories, all come into play within the aesthetic field. As exemplified by their work, the idea of a Chicana mythic memory manifested in ethnopoetic expression represents less an unproblematic recuperation of indigenous culture than a complex cultural construction of self-identity. From this view, the myths and legends that tend to infuse Chicana literary products cease to be collectible fragments of a non-European Other and become instead part of a larger cultural palette from which Chicana artists draw as they scrutinize the complex and contentious identities comprising the subject positions "Chicano" and "Chicana."

Closing the Circle: Alurista

The attempt to demarcate the "space" of Chicano culture, the move to note its distinct and unique qualities, and the desire to define its formal and thematic concerns drive one trajectory of Chicano literary critical thought in the 1960s and 1970s. Often working from an ethnopoetic point of view, this trajectory seeks to create a Chicano cultural identity based on a reconnection with a world of spirituality, linked to a pre-Cortesian world infused with indigenous myths and legends. The move is an empowering one, one that allows for the imaginative reconceptualization of human activity. As Arnold Krupat observes, "The reverential stance toward 'ordinary' life, the sense of human responsibility to nature, the commitment to a relationship of 'participant maintenance' (in Robert Redfield's phrase) toward the universe: these are all attitudes familiar to the Native tradition" (125). The indigenous dynamic of Chicano poetry certainly seeks to connect with this tradition, and it does so often through the invocation of a mythic memory as a remembrance/expression of pre-Cortesian power and might.

   What is sometimes overlooked in the articulation of Chicana mythic memory is its status as cultural product. The desire to articulate what is Chicana, the need to define and delimit its cultural space, often leads to an essentialist notion of the culture. It is easy to fall into an essentializing trap when seeking to articulate the peculiar values of Chicana or any other multicultural literature. Many times, Chicano literary critics have become snared in an essentialist fallacy while—as a political response to the academic and cultural marginalization of their culture—trying to define the space of Chicana literature.

Francisco Lomelí, for example, articulates a position where the "universality" of Chicano literary production becomes a standard by which the critic must judge its worth: "Our literature needs to be judged according to universal literary criteria, but its own particular modes of expression and motifs should not be sacrificed in the process. Its origin already implies distinctive features, such as the motif of the barrio, codes of meaning through interlingualism, and the relationship between Anglo and Mexican histories" ("Overview," 106–107). Although Chicana literature is distinct in the particularities of expression, culture codifications, and the history it evokes, Lomelí posits a situation in which the deep structures of all literatures somehow signify in similar ways. In the same vein, Salvador Rodríguez del Pino defines postmovement Chicano poets as members of "the New Trajectory" who "consciously search, within traditional poetic forms, new models, new personal metaphors using a chicano expression to create images within a chicano artistic realty that locates our sensibility within the universal artistic mosaic" (79).[5] These poets "attempt a universality without leaving their roots" (79).[6] And Sylvia Gonzáles writes that "the artist must be true to her own soul and her own personal experiences, and in so doing, the message will be universal and eternal" (15). Lomelí, Rodríguez del Pino, and Gonzáles attempt to valorize Chicano literature by claiming for it the status of the "universal," insisting for it a place in the pantheon of timeless literature.[7]

In a similar vein, the production of early Chicana poetry, especially that associated with the second phase of poetic production, worked toward the articulation of a cultural identity distinct and disengaged from dominant Euro-American traditions.[8] This poetry—whose influence resonates throughout the field of Chicano literary production—seeks to empower through the invocation of spiritual strength and of cultural origins that are non-European, antirational, and historically devalued. The early poetry is often meant to represent the angry outcry of the pueblo. Constructed through *indigenismos* interwoven with *chicanismos*—pre-Cortesian stories, myths, and phrases intermixed with the *caló* and the phraseology of the barrio—early poetry like that by Alurista articulates an unproblematized voice of "the Chicano" blithely posited upon an essentialized identity. This production of a community and community voice—interesting as a strategy of resistance and a tool for political activism—ultimately delimits the "space" of Chicana experiences.

In his poem "libertad sin lágrimas," Alurista demonstrates the processes of poetic recuperation favored by early Chicano poets.[9] The poem calls for a "freedom without tears," without pain, "and with pride / la Raza / nosotros / we won't let it / freedom shall not escape us." The *nosotros* who form the locus of agency in the poem are represented as though speaking through the poetic voice. This communal voice proclaims in the declamatory style of Chicano protest poetry.[10] The call for liberation—from what or toward what specifically is left unclear—concludes with an affirmation of "our will / to be men / caballeros / clanes tigres / proud guerrero plumaje / free like the eagle / y la serpiente." The poem, characteristic of most of Alurista's work during this period, makes a claim for the idealized dual identity of Chicano *mestizaje*. The *caballero* refers to the Spanish horseman of the conquest, a term that also signifies nobleman. Part of the Chicano *mestizaje* that Alurista's poem invokes suggests connection to the formality and courtly manners of Old World conduct. In addition to this European aristocracy, the *clanes tigres* invokes one of the aristocratic Mexica warrior clans, the jaguar warriors, wearing their "proud warrior plumage." The poem thus alludes to two worlds of order—the courtly society of Spain and the warrior society of the Mexica—as immediately available loci of cultural pride.

The cultural roots defining Chicanismo are immanently accessible. These merge with the power of "our will / to be men" to construct an unmediated bridge between cultural origin and its unproblematic access through personal agency. As the poem states that "we won't let it / freedom shall not escape us," the poetic voice oscillates between registers at once declamatory and imperative. The speaking voice asserts an agency that erases its contradictory position in relation to the community for which and to which it ostensibly speaks. Does it articulate a community position, or does it stand beyond, exhorting it? How the power to "will" and to "be" manifests itself, just as whether the speaker assumes the role of voice or conscience of the community, remains in the poem an unspoken issue.[11]

Implicit in the declamatory style of the poem is that the poetry itself will enact agency, will provide the impetus, will will itself into becoming reality. "Part of what literature can do, or at least what I'm trying to do,"

Alurista asserts, "is make it a healing art, not only a reflective art. It is also a surgical tool. . . . By now I'm convinced that, given the power to describe reality, we can construct a more human reality beginning with a more human description" (Bruce-Novoa, *Authors*, 279–80). Certainly this is a function of the ethnopoetic in which the literary plays a part within processes of ritualistic transformation and shamanism. Alurista's poem does not function within social, economic, or political spaces where shamanism forms a valued type of knowledge. The poem thus finds itself in a position where its expression is discontinuous with its modes of reception. The poem works within a cultural system of exchange that helps reveal the silences and absences within the social, economic, and political systems of exchange, implicitly broaching a counterdiscursive move. Still and all, the poem speaks outside these socioeconomic systems of exchange as an Other. Its shamanistic invocations, its declamations of will, and its affirmation of agency are in essence expressions that function at the level of wish fulfillment. Implicit to the poem is the assumption that by simply stating agency and liberation, these conditions will be so. The invocation of a mythic memory centering on the cultural clash and pride to be found in *mestizaje* thus serves a performative function that closes the circle between word and world.

As part of a contemporary symbolic system, however, "libertad sin lágrimas" reveals its own discontinuous position not only in relation to the contemporary systems of exploitative exchange outside of which it ostensibly stands, but also in relation to the originary culture that stands as emblem and catalyst of agency. The phrase "proud warrior plumage" leads a bit too obviously into the final allusive lines of the poem—"free like the eagle / y la serpiente." Within pre-Cortesian thought, the eagle, as representative of flight, and the snake, associated with the earthbound, represent the central tension in Nahua thought between the spiritual and the physical. These images are united in the image of Quetzalcóatl, whose name means "Precious-Feather Snake." This god was, for the Mexica, the personification of wisdom. According to Nahua myth, Quetzalcóatl engaged in a quest for a beyond where, unlike on earth, there would be no sin and people would not age. Through penance and meditation he discovered that the dual divinity, Ometéotl—emblematic of masculine and feminine principles, of earth and sky, of day and night—maintains and gives order to the universe and makes itself apparent in the red light of day and black darkness of night. Hence within Nahua symbology, the colors red and black come to represent writing and wisdom. Quetzalcóatl, who according to legend was light-skinned and fair-haired, was tricked by the god of war Huitzilopochtli into committing incest by lying with his sister. Shamed, he felt compelled to wander toward the east, eventually crossing the ocean, promising to return to his people one day.[12] It is this god with whom the Mexica confused Hernán Cortés at the beginning of his advance into Mexico.

Beyond the immediate instrumentality of instilling cultural pride in the Chicana reader, the purpose of Alurista's symbology in this poem remains vague. The poem represents a type of fetishization of pre-Cortesian themes and icons that Jorge Klor de Alva critiques in his essay "California Chicano Literature and Pre-Columbian Motifs: Foil and Fetish." Chicanas, he notes, "have consistently emphasized the form over the content of native ideology and symbolism by oversimplifying both to the point of caricaturing the intricate and enigmatic codes that veil the meanings of the original texts" (24). Alurista's poem represents a historical and cultural decontextualization of pre-Cortesian symbology that disrupts the hermeneutics of his text. The invocation of pre-Cortesian symbols and images in "libertad sin lágrimas" neither undermines the relationship between signifier and signified as a way of achieving a modernist "undecidability" nor functions within a coherent system of symbolic exchange. What does the evocation of the eagle and the snake suggest? An allusion to a newfound wisdom to be had as the result of political struggle? A meditation on the incommensurable tensions evident in human existence as part physical, part spiritual? A reference to the idea that an emergent Chicana populace will represent the second coming of a new spirituality? A simple nationalist allusion to the figures portrayed on the Mexican flag? Or does the allusion serve as a convenient and recognizable—though decontextualized—image that, like a bell, rings when struck but proves hollow?

Alurista's poem constructs a dehistoricized and essentialized identity meant to instill a sense of pride. Its untenable position ultimately sends it, however, crashing back into history. While the poem proclaims agency and celebrates alterity, it reveals itself as an instrument working toward articulating a sense of identity it does not suspect. The poem invokes but does not possess shamanistic qualities. It does, however, present the impossibility of its claims, and at this level functions counterdiscursively. In its silence on the issue, the poetic voice speaks of the disempowered position of Chicanos. In its inability to achieve the transformative incantation its words imply, the poem deconstructs both the silence imposed by dominant cultural discourses and the ethnopoetic heritage from which its symbology ostensibly emerges.

Obviously, the culture of Chicanos does not derive directly or literally from this Nahua past. There were hundreds of tribes throughout Central America at the time of the conquest, and the cultural identity of Chicanos is as complex and diverse as the identity of any other people tracing their ancestry to the original inhabitants of the Americas. Alurista's poetry attempts to activate and articulate a Chicano identity through an appeal to the glories of a common indigenous civilization. He looks toward the Aztec Empire as a cultural icon that can form a locus of pride. Nahuatl symbology helps form a cultural nexus about which members of disparate Chicano communities can find common cause. As Alurista has noted,

> There has been an antagonistic relationship between [Chicano communities], specifically [in] California and Texas, that I think in order to wage and to forge a national consciousness, we must overcome. Our unity is not bound to, let us say, homogeneity. I mean we aren't all the same, and because we recognize that, we looked for something older than us and that had more future than us, that was based on the present. (Monleón, 442).

His articulation of that something older, although motivated by historical political demands and essentialist in practice, nevertheless serves to strike a cultural chord that has resonated throughout the entire range of Chicano cultural production.

Although influential in the movements of Chicana poetry, Alurista's construction of a poetics that relies on mythic memory ultimately falters. In its attempt to unite disparate communities, this type of poetics ultimately results in "the glorification of a remote past [that tends] to obscure the historical contradictions of Indio-Chicano relationships within the United States" and to "make barrio vatos think of themselves as descendants of Aztec nobility without focusing on the basic realities of pre-Hispanic life" (Ybarra-Frausto, 130). Furthermore, this valorization of mythic memory in its imaginative leaps into the past constructs a cultural identity blind and mute to the important distinctions between and among the different cultural communities supposedly served by the invocation of that memory. Immigrant or long-term resident, New Mexican or Californian, feminine or masculine, gay or straight, young or old, poor or affluent, rural or urban, the needs and peculiar perspectives afforded through difference within a community become—in the facile identification of the pre-Cortesian with the contemporary Chicana— elided. Only an essentialist vision of identity remains. Finally one is left with a notion of memory that unproblematically links past and present without foregrounding the contradictions and discontinuities inherent in the history that connects that past to this present. The "re-membering" of fragmented pre-Cortesian and indigenous cultural icons—myths, legends, tales, and figures—becomes coterminous with the "recuperation" of those icons.

Opening the Circle: Ana Castillo

This discussion has focused so incessantly on Alurista because his literary production has been terribly influential in the construction of a Chicano poetics. Moreover, his work marks a turning point in the history of contemporary Chicano literature, as its interests broaden the strict political instrumentality and strident didacticism of *Movimiento* poetry. Since the passing of the *Movimiento* and its influence on poetic production, Chicano poetry makes two moves in terms of its ethnopoetic practices. One move, exemplified by poetic texts from Gloria Anzaldúa to Bernice Zamora, reworks the idea of ethnopoetics in order to make of it anew a resistant practice. The other move, while not negating the importance of ethnopoetic form, downplays the quest for an originary or authentic voice and opens a wider poetic field by which to articulate the subject positions Chicano/Chicana. Consequently, one can discern in Chicano poetic production a greater concern with notions of appropriation than those of recuperation.[13] The construction of a mythic memory through the appropriation of such cultural artifacts as Nahuatl symbology is no longer treated as a connection between the multiplicitous term *Chicano* and some clearly definable cultural identity. Rather, *the Chicano* is constantly under construction and revision. Not a return to Aztlán, to a homeland, to be a Chicano becomes more and more a journey toward a becoming across the multiplicitous borderlands that make up North American contemporary cultural landscapes. The transformation in the idea of mythic memory serves to mark this significant transformation in the changing terrain of Chicano cultural production.

As is evident in the poetry of Alurista, the mythic memory imagined by a Chicana poetics turns on the construction of heritage, a move that forms a part of a larger counterdiscourse of cultural self-identification. It need not require those of us who—for better or for worse—are critically suspicious of carte blanche mysticism to embrace the mythicoreligious practices this mythic memory invokes. This embrace, after all, would rely on a rather straightforward mimetic model whereby the invocation of the Quetzalcóatl myth somehow makes present the "universal truths," "deep structures," or "archetypal models" that myth represents. This crystalline connection between signifier and signified represents a tyrannical regimen of meaning that—in mediated but pertinent ways— functions out of the same rationale that has historically delimited the meaning of the words *race* and *heritage, tradition* and *history.*

Rather than reinscribe this ideology, one might want to look at the relationship between the signifier and signified of Chicana mythic memory, look at how the conventions of meaning are employed in specific cultural acts of empowerment, how symbolic exchange functions within and against social and political economies. I would argue that the crossing of communal, archetypal, spiritual, and ancient forms of communication with isolated, creative, alienated, and modern forms of expression presents a point where genres, cultures, histories, and epistemes cross. The literature becomes a sundial of history.[14] A criticism that seeks to articulate the historically resistant tendencies of Chicana literature might best abjure the quest for the universal within Chicana literary practices and focus more sharply on the ruptures implicit in the construction of mythic memory, which is to say, it is no longer necessary to shed light on the universality behind the myth of the plumed serpent; but it is productive to examine how that serpent is feathered.

The poetry of Ana Castillo—spanning the period from the late 1970s to the present—provides us with an opportunity to contrast how notions of mythic memory have changed as they are constructed and reinscribed within a changing Chicano cultural space.[15] Her 1976 poem "Our Tongue Was Nahuatl" represents an exemplary attitude toward ideas of Chicano identity clearly incorporating the type of mythic memory worked by Alurista. In both its almost mechanical invocation of Nahuatl culture and its simplistic view of oppression, the poem becomes a near parody of ethnic outrage.[16]

"Our Tongue Was Nahuatl" takes the form of a dramatized first-person account told by a Chicana as she encounters a Chicano: "You. / We have never met / yet / we know each other / well." An immediate recognition occurs, and a bond is forged in that fleeting moment. The speaker's connection with the young man is based on physiognomy as she recognizes his "high / set / cheekbones" and his "slightly rounded / nose." A communal bond is activated by the physical presence, a connection founded on genetic encoding. The Chicano's "near-slanted eyes / follow me— / sending flashback memories / to your so-called / primitive mind. / And I know / you remember." This spark of supposed recognition marks a mythic, nearly genetic memory of a pre-Cortesian past. The racial and the cultural thus conflate, a quintessential image of an essentialized identity.

The spark of memory serves to connect Chicano to Chicana, present to past, the discontent of contemporary life with a near-Edenic time "of turquoise blue-greenness, / sky-topped mountains, / god-suns / wind-swept rains; / oceanic deities / naked children running / in the humid air." The evocation of "turquoise" as an indigenous stone symbolic of (among other things) life and water in Nahuatl symbology mimics the moves made by earlier examples of Chicano ethnopoetic form. This move is undercut somewhat by odd terms like "god-suns" and "oceanic deities." The poem creates a generic vision of pantheistic pre-Cortesian life evocative more of Greek than of Nahua myth.

The poem presents a utopian image of fecundity and harmony, posits a "remembered" time of plenitude and sacred worship of "our / rich golden / Earth" when "our tongue was Nahuatl" and "we were content— / With the generosity / of our gods / and our kins." This remembrance is marked by a domestic tranquillity and gendered division of labor that relies more on post–World War II ideology than it does on Nahua social organization: "I ground corn / upon a slab of stone, / while you bargained / at the market / dried skins." The woman, the good mother watching "our small sons / chase behind your bare legs / when you came home those days," prepares the evening meal and basks in the glow of domestic and social tranquillity.

The utopia of pre-Cortesian life abruptly ends when the Spaniards cross "the bitter waters" and enact a process of racial, political, and economic denigration. The "white foreign strangers / riding high / on four-legged / creatures" force the natives to bow before them in submission and defeat, to bow in "our ignorance to the / unknown /. . . / until our skin became / the color of caramel / and nothing anymore / was our own." This miscegenation and erasing of "color" marks on a genetic level the fall into a postlapsarian world. The erasure of color also signifies a lack made present on a material level in which all possessions, all indigenous religious worship, and all forms of integrity are lost: "Raped of ourselves— / Our civilization— / Even our gods turned away / from us in shame." The speaker incorporates the trope of rape in order to highlight the sense of cultural alienation inscribed by a metaphorical as well as a literal rape. The trope, suggesting violence and violation, activates the sense of domination inherent in the Spaniards' forcing the natives to bow before them and triggering as well the forced process of *mestizaje*.[17] This domination and violation, the speaker indicates, is yet evident in the present helpless economic position in which Chicanas find themselves: "Yet we bowed, / as we do now— / On buses / going to factories / where 'No-Help Wanted' signs / laugh at our faces, / stare at our hungry eyes. / / Yet we bow . . . / WE BOW!" An economic submission returns in the present as a repetition of the originary moment of conquest. Against this continual conquest, the mythic memory of a utopian other, a prelapsarian age, stands as an icon of empowerment ostensibly resisting the present condition of humiliation and violation. The poetic voice concludes: "But I remember you / still— / It was a time / much different / than now. . . ."

Castillo's poem exemplifies the contradictory comfort inherent in this construction of mythic memory. That time which was "much different than now" represents a time irrevocably in the past. Ruptured by conquest, it is made more distant as the first moment of conquest returns in the disempowering present. Mexica forced to submit are now Chicanos forced into submission. The speaker's moment of recognition opening the poem represents an imagined nostalgia for a time and culture with which the speaker of the poem is obviously not terribly familiar. That time, for the speaker, represents a praxis impossible to recuperate. Even the imaginative powers of literature can leave us only with the impotent realization that "it was a time / much different / than now. . . ." The ellipses underscore the dissociation between the mythic memory of pre-Cortesian life and contemporary reality.

Although speaking of connection and cohesion, the poem throughout serves only to fix alienation. The Edenic qualities the poem associates with the pre-Cortesian world remain inexorably disconnected in a time and space separated by a double conquest. The potentially liberating qualities of mythic memory (liberating within the logic of the poem's discourse)—the integrated relationship with nature and the gods, the clearly defined gender roles, the fecundity and productivity of the Mexican past—are undercut by the hopelessness of ever connecting that mythic memory in any transformative way to the present. Just as the idealized vision of the past is dissociated from the historical reality of the present, the poem sunders its mythic memory from a historic one. It evokes a hazy but ideal portrait of a native past, which the title—"Our Tongue Was Nahuatl"—ties to a historically specific and socially complex group, the imperialistic warrior tribe the Mexica. The invocation of harmonious economic and familial relations does little to make present the historical specificity of those people it ostensibly evokes.[18]

This vision is further complicated by the evocation of sexuality and economics in the poem. The speaker's mythic memory is activated, it would appear, through an action implicated in sexual desire. While subjected to the power of the male gaze ("Your near-slanted eyes / follow me"), the Chicana speaker evokes an image of harmony between male and female within the fecund confines of pre-Cortesian family and home.[19] Sexuality—safely domesticated within a strictly heterosexual reproductive role—is contained and controlled. Similarly, economic exchange is controlled through a system of use-value implied in the bartering of "dried skins / and other things / that were our own." Ownership and domesticity go hand in hand, a vision not too dissimilar to the dominant ideology of the American Dream.[20] The male gazer, whom the speaker has never met yet "recognizes," follows her with his near-slanted eyes in an act of possession and, ultimately, domination.

Although from the speaker's perspective this look might imply a spark of recognition, the gaze—most reasonably sparked by desire—serves a highly objectifying and containing function. We might think of Luce Irigaray's discussion of the repressive power of the masculine gaze: "The predominance of the visual, and of the discrimination and individualization of form, is particularly foreign to female eroticism. Woman takes pleasure more from touching than from looking, and her entry into a dominant scopic economy signifies, again, her consignment to passivity: she is to be the beautiful object of contemplation" (25–26).[21] The speaker so reifies the dramatic situation that prompts her reveries that the reality of gender relations in the present fade from sight. The speaker enters into a scopic economy in which she becomes the possessed, the consumed, the passive object.

Castillo's poem projects onto the male gaze a function not of containment but of liberation: the mythic memory of a harmonious and empowered time. This projection is at odds both with the presumable reality of the gaze within the poem and with the historical realities from which the poem arises. Masculine power manifests itself through the gaze. Rape forms another more violent, more violating means of masculine power. Thus the trope of rape employed by the poem to describe the alienation of one's (lost) self from one's (lost) civilization remains blind to the asymmetrical power dynamic inherent in the "near-slanted eyes" following the woman speaker. Obviously this is not to say that the poem evokes and misreads a rape in the making. But it does suggest that the poem—essentializing the condition and identity of the Chicano—blindly asserts a sameness about the discontinuous subject position Chicano/a.

Twelve years later, Castillo returns to an evocation of pre-Cortesian iconography in the title of her collection *My Father Was a Toltec* (1988). This collection does not fully reject the idea of connection and mythic memory. It does, however, serve to mark the tenor with which more recent Chicana poetry problematizes the construction of cultural identity. Instead of positing an essential ethnic self that derives directly from a by now mythologized past, Chicana poetry articulates the mediated processes of desire and representation. The use of pre-Cortesian cultural artifacts becomes a way of scrutinizing the discontinuities erupting around class and gender identity in contemporary Chicana society. Taking the idea of a reified ethnic identity a step further, the poems here foreground the fact of reification, focusing on configurations of race, ethnicity, and gender through the use of indigenous myth. The mythic memory developed in early Chicana poetry as an unproblematic locus of cultural pride and political action is transformed into a cultural icon, employed in scrutinizing an antiheroic world of street fights and difficult families. Unlike her earlier work, Castillo's poem does not rely upon a romanticized memory to serve as a foil against which the problems of the socioeconomic present become more visible. Instead, an indigenous cultural past is used as an icon, quoted in order to construct a commentary on the problems, conflicts, and inadequacies of the Chicana present. Rather than locate the defining content of a Chicana mythic memory, Castillo's collection explores what the cultural construction of a mythic memory does.

"Ixtacihuatl Died in Vain," a complex and enigmatic poem in Castillo's collection, serves to expand the significance of cultural memory and its function as an articulation of Chicana identity. In Mexican legend, Ixtacihuatl is a princess who falls in love with Popocatépetl, a warrior from a rival tribe. Upon hearing of his death in battle, reported to her erroneously, Ixtacihuatl kills herself out of sorrow. Popocatépetl returns safely victorious from his military exploits only to find his beloved dead. He takes her up in his arms and carries her to the mountains, where he stretches her out and hunches beside her, guarding her body by the fires he burns eternally for her. Thus are explained the twin volcanoes Ixtacihuatl and Popocatépetl, which loom above the Valley of Mexico.

In an explanatory footnote, Castillo's poem evokes the legend to serve as a foil for the poem's main topic: the subject position of women in the speaker's family. In the first of its three sections, the poem articulates the difficult position of Chicanas who are "hard on the mothers who've died on us / and the daughters born to us."

> Hard are the women of my family,
> hard on the mothers who've died on us
> and the daughters born to us,
> hard on all except sacred husbands
> and the blessings of sons.
> We are Ixtacihuatls,
> sleeping, snowcapped volcanoes
> buried alive in myths
> princesses with the name of a warrior
> on our lips.
> (34)

The women of her family—described by that most unfeminine adjective *hard*—interiorize and manifest a schizophrenic subjectivity. They are hard to and on each other, mother and daughter, hard on all except "sacred husbands" and "the blessings of sons." The antagonism and tension beneath a patriarchal order causes the women to turn hard against each other. Thus the first section concludes: "We are Ixtacihuatls, / sleeping, snowcapped volcanoes / buried alive in myths / princesses with the name of a warrior / on our lips." Myths and legends, frozen in the stillness of some reified and unchanging realm of tradition, bury the speaker and the women of her family (and by extension Chicanas generally) beneath the weight of a subject position meant to be self-sacrificing and reverent. The legend of Ixtacihuatl serves to instruct the Chicana in the great Mexican truth about women: she must be willing to sacrifice herself for her warrior, to die with his name on her lips as a proper tribute to his stature and to her devotion. She should be prepared either to live through her man or to die.

The second section shifts its point of view, speaking from a male perspective addressing his "impossible bride" and evoking a number of myths that can bury women beneath the heavy weight of expectation.

> You, my impossible bride,
> at the wedding where our mothers were not invited,
> our fathers, the fourteen
> stations of the cross—
>
> You, who are not my bride,
> have loved too vast, too wide.
> Yet I dare to steal you
> from your mother's house.

It is you
I share my son with
to whom I offer up
his palpitating heart
so that you may breathe,
and replenish yourself,
you alone, whom I forgive.

Opening with a reference to "the wedding where our mothers / were not invited, / our fathers, the fourteen / stations of the cross," this section conflates the exclusion of female antecedents with a patriarchal evocation of pain, suffering, and sacrifice—Christ's passion. The marriage serves to sever the bride from "our mothers" only to wed her to the suffering of the fourteen stations leading to Calvary. Beyond the allusion to Christ's crucifixion and consequent marriage to his bride, the church, these lines suggest that the marriage is a terrible culmination of sacrifice—a death that gives rebirth. The progeny of this renascence, however, is left unclear.

This "impossible bride," the would-be husband notes, is "not my bride" for having "loved too vast, too wide." The refusal by the prospective fiancée to limit her devotion to a single object, a single love, does not inhibit the suitor from stealing her from her mother's house. The taking of the bride exemplifies a male aggression and possessiveness counteracted by the giving evoked in the subsequent lines. For the marriage that is not a marriage leads to the male speaker's sharing of his son with his would-be bride. It is to her whom he offers his son's "palpitating heart / so that you may breathe, / and replenish yourself." From the male point of view, it is not the bride who becomes the sacrifice, but rather the son who—in a conflation of Christian and Nahua ritual—is offered in order to enact a rebirth. The section thus closes with the male figure, speaking as deity, as godhead, indicating that it is the woman alone "whom I forgive." The process of redemption (and by implication, blame) shifts from the first section, where the woman is an object of sacrifice, to the second section, where she becomes instead—from the male perspective—the beneficiary of salvation within the domestic sphere of marriage.

The tension evoked by this twin production of sacrifices seeks some synthesis in the third and final section of the poem.

Life is long enough
to carry all things
to their necessary end. So

if i am with you
only this while,
or until our hair goes white,
our mothers have died,
children grown,
their children been born,
or when you spy someone
who is me
but with fresh eyes that see
you as Coatlicue once did—
and my heart
shrivels with vanity;
or a man takes me out to dance
and i leave you at the table
ice melting in your glass;
or all the jasmine in the world
has lost its scent,
let us place this born of us
at Ixtacihuatl's grave:
a footnote in the book of myths
sum of our existence—
"Even the greatest truths
contain the tremor of a lie."

The female speaker of the first section returns, in a tumble of images strung together by conjunctions and prepositions, to note that "life is long enough / to carry all things / to their necessary end." The process of rebirth implied in the first section begins in the rush of the third section to make itself manifest. If, the speaker notes, "i am with you / only this while, / or until our hair goes white," the lovers will leave something behind as a tribute to the history of sacrifice inscribed in the pre-Cortesian/Christian myths evoked by the rest of the poem. It is worth noting that the personal pronoun "I" in the male section of the poem gives way to the "i" of this last section, a diminution that speaks of a sense of identity overwhelmed and dwarfed by the myths against and through which it is forged. For the "i" suggests that someday the addressee may spy "someone / who is me / but with fresh eyes that see / you as Coatlicue once did." Coatlicue, the Mexica god who gave birth to the powerful and destructive god of war Huitzilopochtli, is an androgynous figure represented with shrunken breasts wearing a skirt of snakes and a necklace of human hearts. Decapitated, from her neck twin snakes sprout, signifying the blood and sacrifice necessary to the perpetuation of life and abundance. Coatlicue thus sees all as a process of death and rebirth, as a tension between the reciprocal action of destruction and fruition.

Just as the male speaker in the second section ambiguously portrayed the woman as an "impossible bride / . . . / You, who are not my bride," here the speaker maintains a sense of ambiguity and denial. She identifies and does not identify herself with Coatlicue. She imagines that she will "with fresh eyes" see the man "as Coatlicue once did," and yet she immediately imagines a time when her "heart / shrivels with vanity." This last image suggests both the sin of pride and the hopelessness of futility. Her identification with the god that is also not an identification causes the speaker to recoil from such weighty subjects, to realize the futility and hopelessness of such a project. This position recalls the title of the poem, as the sense of uselessness infuses the signifying process of the poem. The speaker goes on to evoke the more mundane image of her going off with a man who "takes me out to dance / and i leave you at the table / ice melting in your glass." Does this suggest that the tensions in the relationship signal necessary forms of destruction to engender a more powerful union? Or could the sense of necessary sacrifice suggested by the image of Coatlicue stand in juxtaposition with the petty jealousies evoked by the deserted dance partner, watery drink in hand? Does the poem suggest a heroic or ironic posture? From either perspective, the pre-Cortesian symbology becomes a cultural icon employed to scrutinize the difficult and contradictory position of the contemporary Chicana.

This last section of "Ixtacihuatl Died in Vain" is constructed around a conditional framework: "So / if i am with you / only this while, / or until our hair goes white, / . . . / or when you spy someone / who is me . . . / or a man takes me out to dance / . . . / or all the jasmine in the world / has lost its scent." If any or all of these things—mundane and cosmic, immediate and eternal—occur, the speaker has one last request. She urges that they place at Ixtacihuatl's grave "this born of us." The process of creation activated in the first section reaches its conclusion. What is born is a simple "footnote in the book of myths / sum of our existence— / 'Even the greatest truths / contain the tremor of a lie.' " The evocation of myth serves less to suggest a connection and active memory of an alternative and better world existing sometime in the past than to help construct an ambiguous and complex portrait of the present. This present is infused with the demands of mythic memories that help make up the complex subject positions of Chicanas. The image the poem creates is one of victimization and victimizing, one that reveals the tension between models of identity—the "greatest truth"—and the failure of those models—"the tremor of a lie." Against this tension, the speaker negotiates the treacherous terrain that serves to comprise the space of Chicana subjectivity.

"Ixtacihuatl Died in Vain" forms a striking departure from the use of mythic memory in Castillo's "Our Tongue Was Nahuatl." The evocation of myth in this later work does not serve to glorify myth or to signal a lack that the myth seeks to fill. Instead it becomes an icon employed in the revision and scrutiny of Chicano cultural and personal identity. The desire is not to return to some holistic and wholesome past evoked by mythic memory. There is no yearning that seeks to transcend the present. The present serves as a dynamic moment inscribed by a frozen mythic past that, because frozen, delimits the positions Chicanas can rightfully assume. The poem invokes mythic memory not to admire it or ironize it, but to scrutinize its power and to speak a countertruth: that which is "born of us" and which forms the "sum of our existence" is but a "footnote in the book of myths." The diminution (marked by the use of the personal pronoun "i") can be read as a small, wry commentary on the vanity of grandiose "mythic" visions propounded by earlier Chicano poetry.

Other Memories: Gloria Anzaldúa

This is not to suggest that the desire for a spiritual connection represented by myth and its evocation is no longer an influential force within Chicana culture. A spiritual longing, even mysticism and recollection of lost gods, persists throughout Chicana literature and culture. More recently, however, the sense of stridency, insistence, and advocacy of an alternative space gives way to a more modulated and complicated evocation that crosses alternative cultural expressions like *curanderismo* and indigenous forms of worship with politically charged and historically inscribed discourses. The evocation of mythic memory suggests a distinct and unique but nevertheless constructed cultural identity. The employment of myth becomes a strategy by which to present a critique of all too present forms of repressively interpellated subject positions.

Gloria Anzaldúa's *Borderlands/La frontera*, a collection of essays and poetry, constructs an ethnopoetic strategy that may at times seem as much an expression of wish fulfillment as Alurista's "libertad sin lágrimas." In the essay *"Tlilli, Tlapalli:* The Path of the Red and Black Ink," Anzaldúa articulates the purposes of her artistic practice.

In the ethno-poetics and performance of the shaman, my people, the Indians, did not split the artistic from the functional, the sacred from the secular, art from everyday life. The religious, the social and aesthetic purposes of art were all intertwined. Before the Conquest, poets gathered to play music, dance, sing and read poetry in open-air places. . . . The ability of story (prose and poetry) to transform the storyteller and the listener into something or someone else is shamanistic. The writer, as shape-changer, is a *nahual*, a shaman. (66)

But these are not preconquest times, and an image of art as functioning integrally within social and religious as well as aesthetic and cultural systems represents an image that stands in contradistinction to what actually is the condition of art in contemporary society. Anzaldúa's writing evinces an awareness and discontent with these realities. As a result, mythic memory plays a counterdiscursive practice within contemporary symbolic economies. She goes on to insist that we "stop importing Greek myths and the Western Cartesian split point of view and root ourselves in the mythological soil of this continent" (68). Her writing speaks against specific (Eurocentric) systems of appropriation and exchange.

For Anzaldúa, mythic figures allow for a vision of connection associated with but not inexorably tied to some distant, more authentic past. These figures provide an image, a cultural icon that can be employed in numerous divergent, even self-contradictory ways. As Anzaldúa explains in *"La conciencia de la mestiza,"* the *"new" mestizaje* of Chicano culture implies a radical pluralism where "nothing is thrust out, the good the bad and the ugly, nothing rejected, nothing abandoned. Not only does [the new mestiza] sustain contradictions, she turns the ambivalence into something else" (79). The "good the bad and the ugly"—a phrase evocative not only of Clint Eastwood but also of Oliver North—includes the clichéd, the tired, the worn, which flickers again with a form of life in a process of reconsideration and reconfiguration. Whereas early Chicano poetry would invoke myth as a primary strategy in locating cultural identity, Anzaldúa's work evokes mythic elements as part of a cultural pastiche that moves toward but never ultimately fixes Chicano identity. Her work exemplifies a complex position in which the "local, discontinuous, disqualified, illegitimate knowledges" of a society or culture are entertained.[22] The presence of this disqualified knowledge within her poetry suggests a tenuous condition marked not so much by a faith in pre-Cortesian religious icons as by a need for spirituality.

Anzaldúa's poem *"Antigua, mi diosa"* provides an example of this use of icons. The poem, written in Spanish, forms a plea to the poet's ancient and dark goddess. The speaker, "barefoot, blindly crawling" like a new-born animal, follows the faint footprints and ancient lineage of the goddess as she recalls previous visitations.[23] Amid the screeching trains of Brooklyn, the goddess came and "filled the hollowness of my body with light." The poem discusses these visitations as having planted seeds of light whose harvest is "this restlessness / that grows into agony" as the speaker searches for the vanished goddess. The speaker begs for another sign, another ray of light, another chance to be reborn "in your darkest skin." The poem signals a dissatisfaction with the fact that the goddess has abandoned the speaker and evokes a spiritual yearning that informs the poetic meditation on the lost goddess, whose burning light has fled. The poem crosses this spiritual disaffection with images of the dark and unnamed goddess suggestive of Coatlicue.

As with Castillo, Anzaldúa's evocation of the goddess serves to mark a tension between creation and destruction. At one level, this tension can be read as that which characterizes the longing the speaker feels for her lost but driving goddess. Coatlicue both creates and destroys the spiritual life of the speaker. At another level, the tension reflects the process by which the poem itself is created. Although the poem marks the simultaneous presence and absence of Coatlicue, the actuality of the goddess herself is not at issue. Rather than suggest that spiritual need is *caused* by the loss of pre-Cortesian myth and actual Nahua gods, the poem indicates that the absent goddess *signals* a spiritual need.

The discursive practices characteristic of Chicana poetry over the last quarter-century—the evocation of mythic religion, the memory of lost cultures, the yearning for a glorious past—are employed by Anzaldúa to convey a sense of a present spiritual longing rather than a nostalgic social or cultural one. Indeed, the goddess with whom the speaker pleads has already made herself present in the speaker's life. Instead of invoking a long-lost culture or religious system—as the early poetry of Castillo and Alurista does—Anzaldúa's poem employs the image of the dark goddess juxtaposed with the screaming trains and urban decay of Brooklyn. By contrasting the spiritual power embodied in the ancient Coatlicue with the disintegration and emptiness of the modern city, the poem makes manifest the pressing need for a spirituality lost within the logic of dominant social practices. Moreover, it evokes the types of devalued knowledge that have been repressed by a history of disempowerment, oppression, and cultural genocide. *"Antigua, mi diosa"* thus functions counterdiscursively, creating—through the invocation of knowledge and poetic practices relegated to the margins of contemporary culture—an expression of spiritual need within and against the cultural practices of dominant North American society.

The cultural icons Anzaldúa employs to form this spiritual counterdiscourse are those which have been accumulated through the various movements of Chicano poetry. Her poem dwells on some of the images and icons that evoke a memory of pre-Cortesian religion but does so to mark the thematic concerns of the poem. Norma Alarcón has noted: "For many writers the point is not so much to recover a lost 'utopia' nor the 'true' essence of our being. . . . The most relevant point in the present is to understand how a pivotal indigenous portion of the mestiza past may represent a collective female experience as well as 'the mark of the Beast' within us—the maligned and abused indigenous woman" ("Chicana Feminism," 251). The evocation of myth in Anzaldúa does not exclusively signal a longing for a return to purity or essence. It represents a strategy that allows for the expression of a longing integrally linked to the imperialist, racist, and sexist practices that have served to silence the disqualified knowledges her poetry evokes. Her work does not recuperate the iconography of a lost past in order to recover that past. Rather it appropriates that iconography to signal the distress of a culture attempting to articulate the significance of its multiplicitous and devalued historical presence.

From the first, Chicana art and literature have used an aesthetic of appropriation and pastiche. Only recently, however, has Chicano poetry begun to foreground this process of continuing cultural *mestizaje* and the abjuring of a lost native past. Chicano culture no longer seems to fixate on the articulation of an "authentic" Chicana identity or culture. Instead, it demonstrates a cultural identity constantly being transformed and shaped, perpetually finding itself in new positions, new locations. The terrain has shifted, and its ruptures and discontinuities become apparent. In this landscape, the migratory nature of Chicano culture and the multiplicity and diversity of Chicana experiences find voice. Here the uses of mythic memory no longer form strategies by which the connection to an originary moment of identity is forged. Rather, the evocation of myth becomes a strategy that helps map additional realms through which Chicano culture and Chicana identity can move.[24]

Notes

1. One attempt to draw attention to the linguistic privileging of gender within the term *Chicano* is to inscribe the dichotomy of exclusion/inclusion into

the very phrase: "Chicano/a" or "Chicanas/os." This phrasing works in some types of writing but not in others. Throughout this essay, *Chicano* and *Chicana* will appear interchangeably as a way of avoiding erasure. Where either term is appropriate for specific gender identification, the context in which the term is used should make clear its significance.

2. See Jacques Lafay's *Quetzalcóatl and Guadalupe* and Eric R. Wolf's "The Virgen de Guadalupe" for discussions of the conflation of the Virgin Mary and the Aztec goddess Tonantzin.

3. In keeping with practices by Inga Clindennen and Miguel León-Portilla, I use the term *Aztec* to refer only to the empire formed by the alliance between Tenóchtitlan and Tlatelolco. Nahua refers to the culture, Nahuatl to the language. The people themselves who migrated from Aztlán and settled in the twin cities Tenóchtitlan and Tlatelolco called themselves Mexica.

4. By *counterdiscourse* I mean the writing against dominant and dominating discourses. This does not imply simply finding an "authentic" or "original" voice of complete alterity. Counter-discursive practices incorporate and deconstruct dominant discourses, incorporating "marginal" or devalued forms of knowledge and discourse in the process. Thus some third form of knowledge is produced. This is the condition of postcoloniality. For a clear overview of these issues, see Helen Tiffin's "Post-Colonial Literatures and Counter-Discourse."

5. "Llamo poetas de 'La Nueva Trayectoria' a aquellos que conscientemente buscan, dentro de las formas poéticas tradicionales, nuevos modelos, nuevas creaciones de metáforas personales usando la expresión chicana para crear imágenes dentro de una realidad artísticamente chicana que fije nuestra sensibilidad dentro del mosaico artistico universal." These poets, Rodríguez del Pino goes on to note, are not the spontaneous expression of political movement or the popular sentiment of the moment. Instead, they are poets who have read and studied international poetry, from classical poets like Homer to the Beat poets like Allen Ginsberg.

6. "Los que tratan de alcanzar universalidad sin dejar de pisar sus raíces."

7. Other articles that seemingly essentialize notions of Chicano cultural identity include "Mexican American Authors and the American Dream," by Raymund Paredes, "The Problem of Identifying Chicano Literature," by Luís Leal, and "The Space of Chicano Literature," by Juan Bruce-Novoa.

8. Candelaria divides Chicano poetry through the early 1980s into three phases: the first produced the polemical poetry of *el Movimiento,* the second moved toward defining a Chicano poetics, the third saw a flowering of Chicano poetry in "a sophistication of style and technique, an individuality in treatment of subject and theme, and a mature skill and control that signal an inevitably developed form" (137).

9. Alurista's poem is printed in *Floricanto en Aztlán,* published in 1971. Poets whose products resemble Alurista's work in these respects include Sergio Elizondo, José Montoya, and Leo Romero, among others.

10. Candelaria's study provides a useful description of Movement or Phase 1 poetry and its stylistic peculiarities. See especially pp. 39–42.

11. Of his role as poet, Alurista states: "I'm convinced that my poetry reflects, or at least I try deliberately to reflect the experience of our people. I am not the

author of my poetry. . . . The people are the authors of the language; the people are the authors of the imagery, of the symbols" (Bruce-Novoa, *Authors*, 273). His position as a "mirror" of reality seems a little disingenuous, especially since Alurista of his own accord introduced the idea of Aztlán into Chicano discourse. The "people" in this case were consumers, not producers, of "their" symbols. See Luís Leal, "In Search of Aztlán," and Elyette Labarthe, "The Vicissitudes of Aztlán," for a discussion of Alurista's role in "discovering" Aztlán.

12. See Miguel León-Portilla's classic *Aztec Thought and Culture* for discussions of the various manifestations of Quetzalcóatl. See also Inga Clendinnen's study *Aztecs*. For a concise sketch of the significance of Quetzalcóatl and his legends, see the introduction by David Johnson to *The Lord of the Dawn*, Rudolfo Anaya's fictional re-creation of the Quetzalcóatl myth.

13. Rosa Linda Fregoso and Angie Chabram discuss the complexity of Chicano cultural identification in "Chicana/o Cultural Representations: Reframing Alternative Critical Discourses." Their article is premised on Stuart Hall's observation that "cultural identity is neither continuous nor constantly interrupted but constantly framed between the simultaneous operation of the vectors of similarity, continuity, and difference" (206).

14. The image is from Theodor Adorno's "Lyric Poetry and Society." Adorno argues that the aesthetic work marks the contradictions inherent in social order in history and is the manifestation of an anticipated time beyond history. This transcendent function of art resides, Adorno suggests, in the hermetic and resistant aesthetics associated with a complex and ambiguous modernism or in the authentically longing voice of folk literature. Chicano literature, speaking from a position that crosses these matrices of cultural production, stands outside Adorno's conceptualization of negative critique.

15. Castillo has published two chapbooks—*Otro Canto* (1977) and *The Invitation* (1979)—and two collections of poetry—*Women Are not Roses* (1984), which includes some of her earlier as well as new work, and *My Father Was a Toltec* (1988).

16. The poem appeared originally in *Revista Chicano-Riqueña* 4, no. 4 (Autumn 1976). It is reprinted in Dexter Fisher's *Third Woman*, 390–92.

17. Octavio Paz discusses the sense of violation inherent in Mexican self-identity in *The Labyrinth of Solitude*. He writes: "The *Chingada* is the Mother forcibly opened, violated or deceived. The *hijo de la Chingada* is the offspring of violation, of abduction or deceit. If we compare this expression with the Spanish *hijo de puta* (son of a whore), the difference is immediately obvious. To the Spaniard, dishonor consists in being the son of a woman who voluntarily surrenders herself: a prostitute. To the Mexican it consists in being the fruit of violation" (79–80). See as well María Herrera-Sobek's "The Politics of Rape" and Norma Alarcón's "Traddutora, Traditora" for a discussion of rape as a trope in the articulation of Chicano (and particularly Chicana) cultural identity.

18. The Mexica formed a highly stratified and class-bound society. It also formed a dynamic society, transforming itself over the course of its imperial expansion between A.D. 1248, when it first arrived in the central plateau of Mexico, and 1440, when Montezuma I ruled the empire. In addition, Nahuatl was a

language spoken by many tribes—Texcocans, Cholulans, Chalcans, and Tlaxcal-tecas—in addition to the Mexica. See in particular the introduction to Miguel León-Portilla's *Aztec Thought and Culture.*

19. Inga Clendinnen notes that women could achieve "fair independence and substantial mobility in Mexica society, despite their exclusion from the spectacular careers open to males" (*Aztecs,* 157–58), and that although women had no public role, they functioned within their society exercising a degree of individual autonomy perhaps denied even men (*Aztecs,* 206). These small liberties for women were, previous to the establishment of empire, more expansive and central to social organization. As June Nash notes in "The Aztecs and the Ideology of Male Dominance," the transformation from "a kinship-based society with a minimum of status differentiation to a class-structured empire" led steadily to the exclusion of lines of authority that included women. Women possessed at one time equal rights in the law and in the economy. Moreover, Toltec and early Aztec societies most likely passed on power and property matrilineally (350–53).

20. In this respect I take exception to the arguments by Raymund Paredes in "Mexican American Authors and the American Dream." Paredes claims that Chicano writers invariably resist the ideology of possession that consumes American society. Chicano authors—speaking for and about the labor pool necessary to capitalism—often scrutinize economic relations in the United States. However, their work seems to function more within and against than outside the false consciousness represented by the American Dream.

21. Although we might remain suspicious of Irigaray's essentialized version of the sexuality of "Woman," her analysis of the male gaze is particularly compelling.

22. As we have seen Michel Foucault articulate it, these forms of "micro-knowledge" work against the claims of "a unitary body of theory which would filter, hierarchise and order them in the name of some true knowledge and some arbitrary idea of what constitutes a science and its objects" (83). Thus micro-knowledge, working toward a resistance of dominant modes of thought, forms an alternative body of knowledge that—in the case of Chicano culture—derives from a variety of sources, including the mythic and the folkloric.

23. For convenience, I have translated the quotes into English.

24. I wish to acknowledge the University of Wisconsin System Institute on Race and Ethnicity, which provided funding for the period during which I wrote this essay.

Works Cited

Adorno, Theodor W. "Lyric Poetry and Society." Translated by Bruce Mayo. *Telos* 20 (Summer 1974): 56–71.

Alarcón, Norma. "Chicana Feminism: In the Tracks of 'the' Native Woman." *Cultural Studies* 4, no. 3 (1990): 248–56.

———. "Traddutora, Traditora: A Paradigmatic Figure of Chicana Feminism." *Cultural Critique* 13 (Fall 1989): 57–87.

Alurista. "libertad sin lágrimas." In *Florícanto en Aztlán*. 2d ed. Los Angeles: Chicano Studies Center, 1976 (1971).

Anaya, Rudolfo A. *The Lord of the Dawn: The Legend of Quetzalcóatl*. Introduction by David Johnson. Albuquerque: University of New Mexico Press, 1987.

Anzaldúa, Gloria. "Tlilli, Tlapalli." In *Borderlands: the New Mestiza = La frontera*. San Francisco: Aunt Lute, 1987.

Bruce-Novoa, Juan. *Chicano Authors: Inquiry by Interview*. Austin: University of Texas Press, 1980.

———. "The Space of Chicano Literature." *De Colores* 1, no. 4 (1975): 22–42.

Candelaria, Cordelia. *Chicano Poetry: A Critical Introduction*. Westport, Conn.: Greenwood Press, 1986.

Castillo, Ana. "Ixtacihuatl Died in Vain." In *My Father Was a Toltec*, 34–35. Novato, Calif.: West End Press, 1988.

———. "Our Tongue Was Nahuatl." *Revista Chicano-Riqueña* 4, no. 4 (Autumn 1976). Reprinted in *The Third Woman: Minority Women Writers of the United States*. Edited by Dexter Fisher. Boston: Houghton Mifflin: 1980. 390–92.

Clendinnen, Inga. *Aztecs*. New York: Cambridge University Press, 1991.

Foucault, Michel. *Power/Knowledge: Selected Interviews and Other Writings, 1972–1977*. Edited by Colin Gordon. New York: Pantheon Press, 1980.

Fregoso, Rosa Linda, and Angie Chabram. "Chicana/o Cultural Representations: Reframing Alternative Critical Discourses." *Cultural Studies* 4, no. 3 (1990): 203–12.

Gonzáles, Sylvia. "National Character vs. Universality in Chicano Poetry." *De Colores* 1, no. 4 (1975): 15–18.

Herrera-Sobek, María. "The Politics of Rape: Sexual Transgression in Chicana Fiction." In *Chicana Creativity and Criticism: Charting New Frontiers in American Literature*, edited by María Herrera-Sobek and Helena Viramontes, 171–81. Houston: Arte Público Press, 1988.

Irigaray, Luce. *This Sex which Is Not One*. Ithaca: Cornell University Press, 1985.

Klor de Alva, J. Jorge. "California Chicano Literature and Pre-Columbian Motifs: Foil and Fetish." *Confluencia* 1, no. 2 (Spring 1986): 18–26.

Krupat, Arnold. *The Voice in the Margin: Native American Literature and the Canon*. Berkeley: University of California Press, 1989.

Labarthe, Elyette Andouard. "The Vicissitudes of Aztlán." *Confluencia* 5, no. 2 (Spring 1990): 79–84.

Lafaye, Jacques. *Quetzalcóatl and Guadalupe: The Formation of Mexican National Consciousness, 1531–1813*. Translated by Benjamin Keen. Chicago: University of Chicago Press, 1976.

Leal, Luís. "The Problem of Identifying Chicano Literature." In *The Identification and Analysis of Chicano Literature*, edited by Francisco Jiménez. New York, Bilingual Press, 1979.

———. "In Search of Aztlán." Translated by Gladys Leal. *Denver Quarterly* 16, no. 3 (Fall 1981): 16–22.

León-Portilla, Miguel. *Aztec Thought and Culture*. Translated by Jack Emory Davis. Norman, Okla.: University of Oklahoma Press, 1963.

Lomelí, Francisco A. "Internal Exile in the Chicano Novel: Structure and Paradigms." In *European Perspectives on Hispanic Literature of the United States*. Edited by Genviève Fabre. Houston: Arte Público Press, 1988.

————. "An Overview of Chicano Letters: From Origins to Resurgence." In *Chicano Studies: A Multidisciplinary Approach,* edited by Eugene E. García, Francisco A. Lomelí, and Isidro D. Ortiz, 103–19. New York: Teachers College Press, 1984.

Monleón, José. "Mesa redonda con Alurista, R. Anaya, M. Herrera-Sobek. A. Morales y H. Viramontes." *Maize: Xicano Art and Literature Notebooks* 4, nos. 3–4 (1981): 6–23. Reprinted in *Rudolfo A. Anaya: Focus on Criticism.* Edited by César A. González-T. La Jolla, Calif.: Lalo Press, 1990, 439–58.

Nash, June. "The Aztecs and the Ideology of Male Dominance." *Signs* 4, no. 2 (Winter 1978): 349–62.

Paredes, Raymund. "Mexican American Authors and the American Dream." *MELUS* 8, no. 4 (Winter 1981): 71–80.

Paz, Octavio. *Labyrinth of Solitude.* Translated by Lysander Kemp, Yara Milos, and Rachel Phillips Belash. 1961. Reprint, New York: Grove Press, 1985.

"Plan of Delano." *Aztlan: An Anthology of Mexican American Literature.* Edited by Luís Valdez and Stan Steiner. New York: Alfred A. Knopf, 1973.

Rodríguez del Pino, Salvador. "La poesía chicana: una nueva trayectoria." In *The Identification and Analysis of Chicano Literature,* edited by Francisco Jiménez, 68–89. New York: Bilingual Press/Editorial Bilingüe, 1979.

Tiffin, Helen. "Post-Colonial Literatures and Counter-Discourse." *Kunapipi* 9, no. 3 (1987): 17–34.

Wolf, Eric R. "The Virgen de Quadalupe: A Mexican National Symbol." *Journal of American Folklore* 71, no. 279 (January–March 1958).

Ybarra-Frausto, Tomás. "Alurista's Poetics: The Oral, the Bilingual, the Pre-Columbian." In *Modern Chicano Writers: A Collection of Critical Essays,* edited by Joseph Sommers and Tomás Ybarra-Frausto, 117–32. Englewood Cliffs, N.J.: Prentice-Hall, 1979.

Chicanismo as Memory:

The Fictions of Rudolfo Anaya,

Nash Candelaria, Sandra Cisneros,

and Ron Arias

A. ROBERT LEE

To John J. Halcón and María de la Luz Reyes

For those of us who listen to the Earth, and to the old
legends and myths of the people, the whispers of the
blood draw us to our past.
—Rudolfo A. Anaya, *A Chicano in China*

Mexican, the voice in his deep dream kept whispering.
Mejicano. Chicano.
—Nash Candelaria, *Memories of the Alhambra*

I'm a story that never ends. Pull one string and the whole
cloth unravels.
—Sandra Cisneros, "Eyes of Zapata"

I might say that I studied Spanish and Hispanic literature
. . . because I had to know more about my past, my
historical past.
—Ron Arias in Bruce-Novoa, *Chicano Authors*

 $\mathbf{F}$our Chicano storytellers, four calls to legacy. No less than
other American cultural formations, *chicanismo* invites a play of memory

coevally personal and collective. If one begins with the historical sediment, the substrata that have made up Chicano culture, it is first to underscore the human passage involved, those transitions from past to present that its novelists, poets, and dramatists have so remembered when making imagined worlds out of actual ones.

The Olmecs and Mayans provide a founding repository, passed-down legends, belief systems, alphabets, and an architecture. *Los aztecas* and the European intrusion of Hernán Cortés in turn bequeath the very memory of *mestizaje*, a first joining to be endlessly repeated through time. Mexican Independence in 1821, the Texas-Mexican War of 1836, the Mexican-American War of 1846–1848, and above all the Mexican Revolution of 1910–1917 again make for history as iconography, fact as also inward memory. Villa and Zapata, for their parts, supply the epic names, substance, and yet, as always, shadow. Seen from the 1960s and beyond, and to a population burgeoning by both birth rate and immigration, it comes as no surprise that *Aztlán* has found new currency, a term of rally and consciousness, yet always a remembrance, a reference back to *chicanismo*'s first homeland.[1]

Memory, thus, for virtually every Chicano/a, has meant a dramatic crossply, Nezahualicóyotl and Moctezuma invoked alongside *Los Reyes Católicos*, or La Malinche, La Llorona, and La Virgen de Guadalupe alongside Cortés, Coronado, and Cabeza de Vaca. It has meant overlapping *cuentos* of war and peace, from the *aztecas* to the conquistadores, or from the Alamo of the Mexican-American conflict to the Los Alamos of the atomic bomb. It looks to the transition whereby *Alto México* became the "American" Southwest of New Mexico, Arizona, Colorado, California, and Texas. *Brujería* and *curanderismo*, likewise, carry a folk pastness into a later Catholicism of First Communions and Mass. So rich a human "text" has increasingly found its literary equivalent, memory as the pathway into a renaissance of Chicano word and narrative.

In the same way as a Chicano legacy invokes the rural, a *campesino* life of crops and herding and festival, so does it invoke the urban. Barrios from East Los Angeles to Houston, Albuquerque to Denver, bear witness to the history of an estimated 60 percent of Chicanos who have now moved into the cities. If Harlem for African Americans carries the residues of both Dixie and Manhattan, then an East Los Angeles or Houston for Chicanos looks back to both el *campo* and the exhilarations and losses of inner-city life.

One refraction lies in popular culture, whether mariachi bands or Los Lobos, mural art or low-rider cars, work songs or "Latin" rap. Memory, at times nostalgia, it can be admitted, runs right through the cultural rebirth of the 1960s, from the music of Ritchie Valens to the *actos* of Luis Valdez's Teatro Campesino, with, in train, the singing of Linda Ronstadt, the comedy of Cheech Marin, and the screenwork and directing of Edward James Olmos. In this latter respect, films like *La Bamba, Zoot Suit, The Milagro Beanfield War, Stand and Deliver, American Me, Blood In, Blood Out* (coscripted by Jimmy Santiago Baca), and even television's once mooted *El Pueblo/L.A.,* for all their resemblance to the contemporary, could not have been more permeated by pastness, the appeal to shared recollection.

In like manner there has been the view of Chicano community, even in poverty, as in and of itself a kind of memorial art form, an inherited pageant of culture and custom. In this, Chicano foodways bear an especially ancestral insignia—a now familiar menu of *chile, frijoles, enchiladas, mole, chimichangas,* or *tamales.* If, however, a single token of legacy were needed, it would surely be found in the *ristras* hanging in almost every Chicano home.

In common with its *nuyorriqueño* and *cubano-americano* counterparts, *chicanismo* also involves a past held inside two seemingly parallel but actually deeply unparallel languages.[2] For under American auspices English has long emerged as the language of power, leaving Spanish as the assumed lesser idiom, a signifier of illiteracy or migrant outsiderness. Even so, this is anything but to suggest that the two languages have not been historically symbiotic. Chicano Spanish, for its part, may resort to the street or vernacular *caló* of *pachucos, vatos,* and *chulas,* but it also abounds with borrowed anglicisms like *watchar la tele* or *kikear* (the drug habit). American English has in mirror fashion long made its own borrowings, like *barrio* and the all-serving *gringo,* as well as farm or ranch borrowings, like *lasso, adobe, bronco, cinch,* or *sombrero.* Endless repetition on television and other commercials of food terms like *taco, tortilla,* and *nacho* has made quite as marked an impact, one language's "history" remembered (or more aptly misremembered) inside another.

In the case of anglicization, Chicano memory has been stirred in another way as well. In categories like Hispanic or, depending on the user, even the more generally favored Hispano or Latino, many have heard the carryover of a note of condescension. "Ethnic" likewise arouses suspicion, a WASP hegemony's self-appointed rubric for patronage of minority culture. The English Only campaigns, now under way in more than twenty states, recapitulate the same discriminatory process. Here, in all its historic loading, is but the latest effort to make the language as well as the general sway of Anglo culture the presumed standard for America at large. Does not, then, an accusing politics of memory lie behind a reaction like "English Yes, But Only, No"?

A *corrido*, or folk song, like "The Ballad of Gregorio Cortez," adapted for the screen by PBS in 1982 from Américo Paredes's version with Edward James Olmos in the title role, nicely points up the discrepancy.[3] The tale of a "Mexican" smallholder in the Texas of 1901 falsely accused of horse theft, it turns on how the word *horse* in English can translate into Spanish as both masculine and feminine, namely *caballo* and *yegua*. At issue, however, is infinitely more than a quirk of philology. The ballad speaks on the one hand to Gregorio Cortez's Mexican Chicano ancestry, and on the other, to the Anglo hegemony that lies behind the Texas Rangers who pursue him and the Yankee judge and court that try him for the murder of the sheriff. What is involved here is the remembrance of two value systems, two misreadings across the cultural divide. Much as English and Spanish might seem to have been saying the same thing, the gap has been symptomatic, and in this case, fatal.

Similar discrepancies in fact underlie a whole array of "popular" versions of American history. No better instance offers itself than the Siege of the Alamo (1836), and in its wake, the defeat of Santa Anna at San Jacinto. Told one way, the Siege has come to signify Anglo triumphalism. Where more so than in John Wayne's 1960 Hollywood version with its "Lone Star State" hurrahs and featuring James Bowie and William B. Travis as the truest of patriot martyrs? Told in another way, did not Santa Anna's attack on the Alamo represent a timely resistance, a counterforce to Yankee expansionism? Such a perspective, going against the grain, appears in Jesús Salvador Trevino's television film of 1982, *Seguín*.

These splits and divergences in memory extend more generally to the American Southwest and West, not least when they double as *el norte*. From a mainstream viewpoint, the link is to Manifest Destiny, an *indigenista*, tribal-Chicano world preordained to be won and settled. A Mexican or tribal viewpoint, however, speaks of colonized land, stolen *tierra* or *patria*. Counterversions of the Mexican Revolution similarly arise, on the one hand the Red plot, the Bolshevism so warningly reported (and then not reported) by, say, the Hearst press, and on the other hand the heroizing popular revolution of the Institutional Revolutionary Party (known as the PRI) and leftist recollection in general.

Sleepy Lagoon and the Zoot-Suit riots of 1942–1943 also yield their twofold interpretations. Were the assaults of a largely white Southern navy in wartime Los Angeles "straight" racism or, more obliquely, the fascination of one uniformed group (Anglo, English-speaking, Bible-Protestant, military) with its also uniformed opposite (Latin, Spanish-speaking, sexually knowing, baroque)?[4] How, subsequently, should one remember 1960s movements like César Chávez's United Farm Workers, especially the 1968 grape boycott, José Angel Gutiérrez's La Raza Unida in Texas, and "Corky" Gonzales's Crusade for Justice in Denver? Do they best refer back to mainstream labor politics (in Chávez's case, on account of the alliances with Filipino and other Asian workers) or, when linked back into the wartime *bracero* programs, to a wholly more discrete Chicano politics?

Nor, however collective the memory, does *chicanismo* yield some unconflicted view of itself. The class hierarchy, for instance, created by the conquistadores who devastated Moctezuma's Aztecs, has had its modern footfalls, still based on blood, skin color, landedness, and, as often, family name. Old *chicanismo* plays against new, especially between certain New Mexico dynasties and those of a supposedly inferior birthright. Does this also not call up the disdain of Spanish-born *gachupines* for colonial-born *criollos* or Creoles, and theirs, in turn, for *los indios* (especially *genízaros*—Indians forced to lose their tribal language and to speak only Spanish), for mestizos, and for *negros* (a distinct but Spanish-speaking black population)?[5]

Just as a missionary-begun Catholicism largely took over from Aztec and other cosmologies (though obliged to coexist with vernacular practices like *curanderismo*), so did evangelical Protestantism increasingly make inroads into that same Catholicism.[6] This, and the impact of Latin American liberation theology, has led to increasing doubts about the church's attitude to family, women, birth control, divorce, and authority in general. How are Chicanas, especially, to "remember" Catholicism? As spiritual sanctuary or as yet another patriarchy able to oppress with its gendered rules of conduct?

Another major contradiction lies in the continuing pull of California. It has, undoubtedly, promised betterment, the dream of *abundancia*, whatever the risk of repeated deportations by *la migra*. Somewhere in this persists the remembered myth of *el dorado*, the continuing lure of *Las Siete Ciudades de Cíbola*. But California has notoriously also flattered to deceive. Chicano unemployment has soared, as have high school dropout rates, *barrio* poverty and crime, and the wars of attrition with the police and courts. Yet as the continuing surge of cross-border migration bears out, and despite each amnesty over residence papers, California remains history both made and still in the making.[7]

Imagining and reimagining the past may well be, in L. P. Hartley's apt and rightly celebrated phrase, to visit a "foreign country"—especially in an America notoriously obsessed with the future. Yet Chicanos, no doubt having known the flavors of defeat as well as those of triumph, have had good reason to dwell there. Whether it was the conquistador regime, a border as redolent of human flight as *El Río Grande*, the history by which *Tejas* was reconstituted as Texas, or the duality of California as promise and yet denial, the prompt to memory has been always ongoing. For it is the memory that serves as solvent for each generation's telling of *la raza*, and nowhere more so than in the ongoing body of fiction of what rightly has become known as *chicanismo*'s literary renaissance.[8]

Certainly that has been the case for Anaya, Candelaria, Cisneros, and Arias, however differently they have styled their uses of memory. Indeed, the Chicano tradition can virtually be said to have thrived on the shaping energies of remembrance, a present told and reinvented in the mirrors of the past. This is true especially for one of the seminal novels of *chicanismo*. José Antonio Villarreal's *Pocho* (1959) not only offers the life of its writer-protagonist, Richard Rubio, as a portrait of the artist, it also locates that life within the history of migration from Mexico to southern California—thus memory as collective in scope yet specific, a single trajectory.[9]

In a story cycle as delicately imagistic as Tomás Rivera's "*. . . Y no se lo tragó la tierra*"/*And the Earth Did not Part* (1971),[10] another kind of memory holds sway, that of a single migrant-labor year of a Chicano dynasty headed for "Iuta" (Utah) in which all other similar years and journeys are to be discerned. Raymond Barrio's *The Plum Plum Pickers* (1971) makes for a linking memorialization,[11] this time set in the Santa Clara Valley during the Reagan governorship. Its very accusations of labor exploitation and racism lie in remembrance. In *Peregrinos de Aztlán* (1974),[12] Miguel Méndez takes a more vernacular direction—the memories of Loreto Maldona, car washer in Tijuana—as an anatomy of border life, of poverty and dreams, nationality and *mestizaje*. For his part, Alejandro Morales in *Caras viejas y vino nuevo* (1975),[13] translated as *Old Faces and New Wine* in 1981, transposes *barrio* Los Angeles into a kind of working archive, a city of inheritances and the present-day told in its own imaginative right as at once then and now.

In *Klail City y sus alrededores* (1976),[14] as in the rest of the "Klail" series, Rolando Hinojosa subjects Belken County to Faulknerian rules, a south

Texas Chicano and white "mythical kingdom" invoked as through a lattice of multicultural (and bilingual) recollection. Daniel Cano's *Pepe Rios* (1991) attempts historical fiction of an older kind,[15] the Mexican Revolution as an epilogue to colonialism and yet a prologue to *chicanismo*. Arturo Islas looks to memory as myth in *The Rain God* (1984),[16] the portrait of a Tex-Mex dynasty descended in the aftermath of the Mexican Revolution from the escaping but always imperturbable matriarch Mama Chona. In all these different modes of using *chicanismo* as memory, fiction lays claim to a special kind of authority, a heritage of time and voice given its own dialogic measure.

Memory has equally shaped an increasingly emergent Chicana fiction, in whose ranks Sandra Cisneros has been little short of a luminary. Isabella Ríos's *Victuum* (1976),[17] through the psychism of its narrator, Valentina Ballesternos, renders womanist history as a kind of ongoing dream script. Ana Castillo's *The Mixquiahuala Letters* (1986) creates an epistolatory,[18] and teasingly self-aware, feminist novel of women's friendship that also explores the pasts of America and Mexico, a historic *mestizaje* again taken up in her fantasia, *Sapogonia* (1990), and in her New Mexico almanac-memoir, *So Far from God* (1993).[19] Cherrié Moraga's storytelling (and essay work), of which the anthology she co-edited with Gloria Anzaldúa, *This Bridge Called My Back: Writings by Radical Women of Color* (1981), and her *Loving in the War Years* (1983) and *The Last Generation* (1993) can be thought symptomatic, yields another remembrance, that of the "silence" that, by historic writ, has surrounded lesbian life in a culture so given to patriarchy.[20]

Literatura chicanesca, non-Chicano writing about Chicano life and culture, affords another styling of memory in John Nichols's *The Milagro Beanfield War* (1974).[21] However specifically set in the 1970s or local the story, its drama of contested water rights again calls up an inlaid older history of Indian, Mexican, and Anglo conflict that, across four centuries, took New Mexico from a Spanish colony to a territory to America's forty-seventh state. Joe Mondragón finds himself fighting Ladd Devine and his Miracle Valley Recreation Area Development for the right to irrigate his land. In fact, what Nichols portrays tacitly is the fight for the Chicano heritage in which the bean field acts as a trope for the very soil, the nurturing medium, of a whole people's history. Nichols's novel and the Redford-Esparza movie of 1988 (with its appropriately multiethnic cast of Ruben Blades, Carlos Riquelme, Sonia Braga, and Christopher Walken) can so play "fact" against *el mundo de los espíritus,* the historicity of the past as open to a figural or any other kind of access.

Chicano autobiography as a related kind of "fiction" has been wholly as various in its uses of memory, whether Oscar Zeta Acosta's rambunctious, Beatnik-influenced narratives of the 1960s, *The Autobiography of a Brown Buffalo* (1972) and *The Revolt of the Cockroach People* (1973), or Richard Rodriguez's elegiac, if controversially assimilationist, *Hunger of Memory* (1981) and *Days of Obligation* (1992), or Linda Chavez's radically conservative manifesto, *Out of the Barrio* (1991), or Ray Gonzalez's El Paso "border" history, the lyric and pertinently titled *Memory Fever* (1993).[22]

For as these texts, too, "remember" (even those of an assimilationist bent) so, like the novels and stories they accompany, they inevitably contest and dissolve mainstream decreation of *chicanismo*. Perhaps, overall, Frances A. Yates's notion of "memory theatre" applies best—the forms of the past, however obliquely, always to be remembered and re-remembered in the forms of the present.[23]

"Some time in the future I would have to build my own dream of those things which were so much a part of my childhood." So does the narrator of Rudolfo Anaya's *Bless Me, Ultima* (1972) reflexively look back to the pending *cuentista* or authorial self who will write that childhood, that past, into being.[24] The note, for Anaya, is typical, one of retrospect, pastness, and memory as a textualized weave of events actual and imaginary, which, if less persuasively, also runs through his subsequent novels, *Heart of Aztlán* (1976), *Tortuga* (1979), and *Alburquerque* (1992).[25]

The novel typically begins in remembrance. "The magical time of childhood stood still," says Antonio Márez at the outset. He repositions himself as the seven-year-old raised in the 1940s Spanish-speaking New Mexico who finds himself pulled between the *vaquero*, herdsman, Márez clan on his father's side and the farmer-cultivator Luna clan on his mother's. But he also acknowledges the writer-in-waiting who will learn to appropriate as his own the shamanism, the *brujería*, of Ultima, the *anciana* and *curandera* invited by his parents to spend her last days with the family.

Anaya enravels each inside the other, a Chicano childhood as literal event, in Antonio's case often the most traumatic kind, and a drama of inner fantasy and imagining. "Experience" and "dream," he rightly recollects, "strangely mixed in me." This blend makes the imagined landscape of *Bless Me, Ultima* not a little Proustian, a New Mexico there on the map and yet personalized and sacralized by personal remembrance.

One contour, thus, has the adult Antonio recalling his ill-matched parents, his sisters, Deborah and Theresa, and the three absentee brothers with their eventual disruptive return from the wars in Europe and Japan. It looks back to the Spanish of the home, the English of school, the latter having anglicized him from Antonio to Tony. It summons back his parents' competing hopes for him: his father's dream of a new beginning in California and his mother's hope that he will enter the priesthood. He sees, too, as he could not have done in childhood, the irony of a horseman father now asphalting the highways as if to seal in, to inhume, the very *tierra* his family once proudly herded.

Yet another contour remembers the dreamer child within, drawn to the *indio* myths of earth, mountain, and river and to the legend of the Golden Carp—a creation myth of a god-protector of the village—in which he comes to believe under the tutelage of his friends Samson and Cisco. The center of all these memories, however, has to be Ultima— ancient, as her name implies, midwife at his birth, explainer of his *pesa-dillas*, or nightmares, teacher of herbs and flora, and martyr who at the cost of her own death has brought down the murderer Tenorio Trementina. Her grave, whose secret celebrant he becomes, serves the novel in two ways: as a figuration of both his past and his future, his legacy and at the same time his destiny.

Antonio thus finds himself irresistibly drawn in memory to her bag of potions, her nostrums, her deific owl with its links to a Christly dove or an Aztec eagle, and her very aroma. But if she signifies for him as at once guardian angel, muse, and the very anima of *chicanismo,* he, for his part, plays the perfect apprentice, the word maker with his own eventual kind of *brujería.*

This double weave, the memory of the "facts" of his history and of his first prompts to imagination, determines the whole novel. He thinks back to the deaths he has witnessed: Lupito, who, unhinged by his Asian war experiences, shoots at the sheriff only to invite his own destruction; Narciso, the harmless drunk who, all too true to his name, is killed by Trementina; Florence, the drowned boyhood friend who first guided him to the Golden Carp; and Ultima herself. Each death "happens," or "happened," but each, equally, goes on "happening" in his own chambers of memory, to await transcription by the memoirist he will become.

The back-and-forth movement of memory also encloses Jason's Indian, the unspeaking sentinel to a pre-conquistador past; like the carp and the owl, he embodies the tribal and vernacular folk past as against the Holy Weeks, Communions, and Masses of Father Byrne's parish church. There is a sheen, a membrane, that also settles over the novel's place-names, notably Los Alamos, as indeed the Poplars, but also, the irony of which is anything but lost on Anaya, as the atomic test site. More domestically, for Antonio, "El Puerto" ("refuge," "harbor") as the home of the Lunas and "Las Pasturas" ("pasture") as that of the Márez family resonate with equal effect—even as they pass into time past. Memory, in other words, in all its overlapping and coalescing kinds, also yields mixed emotional fare for the narrator-memoirist, pain and warmth, breakage as well as love.

But "build my own dream" *Bless Me, Ultima* does, a landmark portrait of childhood's dream itself told as a dream. The spirit of the dream derives, overwhelmingly, from Ultima, her creativity carried by the narrator from childhood to adulthood, from first associations to written word. For the memory of her, as of his family, of his land, and of all the voices and myths that have made up his legacy of *chicanismo*, cannot be thought other (such is Anaya's triumph) than Antonio Márez's memory—and memorialization—of himself.

"His thoughts carried him farther. Across the ocean to the source, the beginnings." Jose Rafa's pondering of his New Mexico dynasty and of the past to which it belongs can serve as a gloss for all three parts of Nash Candelaria's trilogy, *Memories of the Alhambra* (1977), *Not by the Sword* (1982), and *Inheritance of Strangers* (1985).[26] Each invokes a distinct phase in the evolution of Chicano history while at the same time building into the larger, more encompassing memory. One reverberation is made to play against another, from as early as 1492 and *Los Reyes Católicos* and the enraveled heritage of conquistador and *azteca*, through *Nueva España* and the emergence of the American Southwest, and out of the nineteenth century into a wholly contemporary California and New Mexico.

If, at times, Candelaria has been felt to go too slowly, to risk a certain inertness, he cannot be faulted for ambition. His fiction seeks nothing less than to remember a whole multicultural ebb and flow in the making of *chicanismo*, a history, but also in William Styron's celebrated phrase, "a meditation on history." *Memories of the Alhambra,* too, as a title consciously taken over from the composer Albéniz, gives added resonance, *hispanidad* as both a European and an American past and to be so echoed in sound and memory.

For Jose himself memory begins specifically with the family move from Albuquerque to California in the 1920s, a move into the barrio even as he dreams his dynast's dream of "pure" Castilianism. When,

years later, after his father's funeral and at the behest of the fake genealogist Señor de Sintierra ("Without Land"), he takes off for Mexico in the
hope of discovering high-born roots, no paradox can disabuse him of
the fantasy. The Virgen de Guadalupe may be a Catholic saint, but her
indigenista originals are to be seen in everyday streets and byways. If Mexico for him calls up conquistador heroism, what price the *cantina* murder
he witnesses or his flashback to the time when he himself was detained
at the border as a suspected "illegal"? His, in other words, is selective
memory, the wished-for over the actual.

Pushing on for a past of ideality, he crosses to Spain, his hope of conquistador patrimony secreted as he believes in yet another genealogy,
The Archives of the Indies. But the Spain he finds is anything but impe-
rium, more village poverty than a world of court and *hidalgo*. In his encounter with Señor Benator, a *morisco* businessman, however, a memory
of still deeper paradox is brought to bear.

Spanish racial purity, quite as much as its Hispano-American off-
shoots, has been an illusion from the start, its genealogies variously Visi-
goth, Andalusian, Catalan, Galician, Basque, Gypsy, Jewish, and Moor-
ish. Thus the "Recuerdos de la Alhambra" Jose hears in Sevilla with
Benator (harking back to an Islamic emirate of no less than eight centuries) again points to the blurs and overlap of even the original *hispanidad*.
Rafa's heart attack could not be more emblematic, the deadly price of
memory as idealization.

His son Joe, decried by his cousins as "an anglicized Chicano—which
was almost nothing at all"—and yet a multiculturalist in the making, is
left to understand his family's competing skeins of memory. "Words.
Feelings. Wheels inside of wheels," he ponders, "with the need for different words. Accurate words." The best memory for him, and by implication for the Rafa inheritance and all *chicanismo*, points to a sense of history, a language, able to recognize and then accept cross-culture, and
within it "winners and losers both."

Not by the Sword takes as its present the Mexican-American War of
1846–1848, unraveling through its principal figure, Father Jose Antonio
Rafa III ("Tercero," as he is known to the family), a fierce, mid-nine-
teenth-century bid for ascendancy between the Spanish and the Anglos,
with the Indian population a muted third presence. Yet another novel
itself a memory, it draws on a sequence of incremental other memories:
"the old Spanish" land grants; the intrigue centered on Santa Fe's *palacio
de gobernadores*; the Albuquerque militias formed to combat the Yankees;

the saga of Tercero's adventurist twin brother which involves the Comanches, Utes, and Navajos; and the eventual Treaty of Guadalupe, which Hidalgo signed in February 1848. Even the interpolated story of Michael Dalton, *El Gaélico*, involves a memory within a memory of the Mexican-American War. In telling, too, of his own abandonment of priesthood in favor of marriage and his accession to the Rafa patrimony, Tercero blends the personal into a wider history, two kinds of memory interwoven into one.

By *Inheritance of Strangers*, Tercero has become the *abuelo*, an elder and oral archivist, the time and place now "Los Rafas, U.S. Territory of New Mexico, 1890." The story he tells, of dark, internecine land wars with Yankee buccaneers on one side and the vigilante *Hijos de Libertad* on the other, has a listener in fourteen-year-old Leonardo Rafa, the grandson most bewitched by (as Candelaria has Tercero call these memories) his "recitations." The arc of memory once more is wide—the Taos Rebellion and the death of his brother Carlos, the saga of Don Pedro Bacas unhinged by the Yankee murder of his family. But if memory exhilarates Leonardo, it also leads directly to his death as the boy embroils himself in a misconceived honor code. Yet by the novel's end, Tercero is to be heard telling another grandson, another Carlos Rafa, "Once upon a time . . . there was a land called New Mexico." Memory, as throughout the Rafa trilogy, so embarks on a latest version of the past, one—Candelaria leaves little doubt of this—still not finally told, still not free of self-circling and the necessary behest of its tellers.

"Estos cuentitos." Sandra Cisneros's inviting, homespun diminutive could not better underwrite the Tex-Mex *chicanismo* of *Woman Hollering Creek* (1992). The note is one of the cultural memory as intimacy, a *Dubliners*-like *latina* cycle of childhood, family, religion, and love affairs told through the two overlapping vernaculars of English and *español*. "You must remember to keep writing," says a dying aunt to Esperanza Cordero, child fabulist of *The House on Mango Street* (1989). "It will keep you free." The twenty-some stories that comprise *Woman Hollering Creek* might be thought of as a further making good, a bouquet, a *ristra*, of yet another kind of Chicano remembrance.[27]

The characteristic accent is set in opening stories like "My Lucy Friend Who Smells like Corn," with its childlike word inversion and remembered fidgets of little girlhood; or "Eleven," which beautifully calls back from memory a girl's mortification at being thought by her teacher, Mrs. Price, to be the owner of a tatty, left-behind sweater "that smells like cottage cheese"; or "Mericans," set in the context of Mexican Chicano churchgoing ("Why do churches smell like the inside of an ear?" asks the girl narrator), a shrewdly pitched vignette about Anglo patronage in which a picture-taking tourist observes, "But you speak English!" and the girl's brother replies as if in memory of all such condescension, "Yeah . . . we're Mericans."

Another memory lies behind the reflexivity of "Tepeyac," in which the storyteller—who thinks back to "Abuelito," to the family store, and to a particular *cinco de mayo* on the Mexican side of the border—confides: "It is me who will remember when everything else is forgotten." The observation implies a whole freight of remembrance, a *chicanismo* in which time is place, family is self.

Such is to be heard in "One Holy Night," the story of a sexual first encounter, pregnancy, and birth, but told also as the echo of a Mayan fertility legend. In "My *Tocaya*," a black comedy of mistaken identity, the doubling assumes an unexpected form—that of a schoolgirl fantasy, the missing child as the storyteller's own martyr "other." "Never Marry a Mexican" tells of remembered love, in particular one she has shared with a father and son, to be looked back to in the "amphibious" teacher-artist-narrator's mind as an emissary of some parallel universe of gender. "Little Miracles, Kept Promises" offers a fond harking back to the often imploring *milagritos* safety-pinned to effigies of the Virgin and name saints. As each message builds into a mosaic, an even "further back" memory takes shape—that of a first, dark, Aztec cosmos, the source of *chicanismo*.

"Woman Hollering Creek" as the title story depends on yet other forms of intertwined memory: one of a failed, abusive, and cross-border marriage, another of the legend of *la Llorona,* actuality and myth as joint testimony to the rage against patriarchy. "*Bien* Pretty," on a lighter note, acts as its narrator's self-watchful recollection of her affair with Flavio Michoacán ("I've never made love in Spanish before"): love itself as a style of *mestizaje* which can cause the world to seem a field of chattering *urracas* or magpies. The story, however, yields another dimension. Thinking of the time Flavio hit his thumb with a hammer, she observes, "He never yelled 'Ouch!' he said '¡Ay!' The true test of a native Spanish speaker." In that "Ay," surely, lies also the larger memory, the intimacy indeed of a culture at large called back by Cisneros with quite daunting idiosyncrasy.

Chicanismo *as Memory*

In Ron Arias's *The Road to Tamazunchale* (1975),[28] Chicano fiction reaches, unashamedly, the shores of magic realism. Although a novella, it nevertheless suggests Cervantean expansiveness, with an increment of Latin *fantasía* in its echo of Carlos Fuentes's *Cambio de Piel/Change of Skin* (1967).[29] Memory thus becomes a source of metamorphosis in which Fausto Tejada, ex-salesman of encyclopedias and an East Los Angeles *anciano* and widower, can face the imminence of his own death with his remembrances of life.

"Suddenly the monstrous dread of dying seized his mind. . . . No! he shouted. . . . As long as I breathe, it won't happen." His memories can be literal enough, of his put-upon and accusing dead wife, Evangelina, and their choruslike parakeet, Tico-Tico. But they are just as likely to take on Ovidian invention, an imagined flight into the Peruvian jungles, or a sailor-smuggling scam across the border at Tijuana. He can leave one time period for another, that of the Nahua-Aztecs and Incas, the Lima of the sixteenth century, the early-twentieth-century Tamazunchale (a literal Moctezuma River Valley town but again fantasy, as the wordplay in "Thomas and Charlie" implies), and, finally, barrio Los Angeles networked by the modernity of its street life and everyday *caló*.

Don Fausto, who finds his Sancho Panza in the *pachuco* Mario, true to his maguslike name revels in these magical powers of memory, acts of imaginative life whereby death is held in abeyance. The anachronistic shepherd Marcelino Huanca, thus, can direct his sheep through rush-hour traffic as if to silhouette an earlier time zone of herdsmanship within the era of the freeway. Equally he can advise Tejada on how to ensure his own futurity by an ancestral act of stone-upon-stone ritual. Tejada can both literally disrobe and, in imagination, peel off his own dying skin in a replay of the Aztec immortality rite of Xipe Topec.

Other memories add further transformative meaning: the body of a *mojado*, a wetback, brought back to life in a tribal revival ceremony; a community theater group performing a play called "The Road to Tamazunchale," which then disappears into the night sky; a *puta* who guides the old man into a jungle clearing where, sexually exhilarated, he joins in a tribal mourning. If these, too, are memories, they speak to the myths and arcana of *chicanismo*, remembrance as its own form of wizardry.

Tejada travels through an actual continuum of bookshops, a restaurant echoingly called the Cuatro Milpas (Four Cornfields), a picnic in the equally well named Elysian Fields, and a film set in which he and Mario are taken for Hollywood extras. Yet always there is the other continuum, that of surrealized recall, which supplies the life-giving memory of the larger *azteca*-Chicano history. On the one hand, beset with kleenex, meals prepared by his niece, his old man's clothes and knickknacks, he lies dying of heart failure in his room. But in imagination he is clad not in a dressing gown but in a conquistador cloak, grasps not a hoe but a regal crook, and feels himself, a latter-day Orpheus, called not to a void but to Elysium.

It is this cumulative memory that allows him to defeat death even as death defeats him. Tamazunchale, in turn, acts as the sign, the index of all such metamorphosis, at once endemically familiar (at least as reflected through Los Angeles) and endemically other. *The Road to Tamazunchale*, in other words, brings Chicano memory full circle. It offers a memory not only of the past, nor even of the present, but, in Arias's novel as playfield, of nothing other than the future.

Notes

1. The following usefully address Chicano history and politics: George I. Sánchez, *Forgotten People: A Study of New Mexicans* (Albuquerque, N.M.: C. Horn, 1940); Carey McWilliams, *North from Mexico: The Spanish-Speaking People of the United States* (New York: Greenwood Press, 1948); Matt S. Meier and Feliciano Rivera, *The Chicanos: A History of Mexican-Americans* (New York: Hill and Wang, 1972); Rodolfo Acuña, *Occupied America: The Chicano's Struggle Towards Liberation* (San Francisco: Canfield Press, 1972); Richard Griswold de Castillo, *The Los Angeles Barrio, 1850–1890: A Social History* (Berkeley: University of California Press, 1979); Marcia T. García et al., eds., *History, Culture and Society: Chicano Studies in the 1980s* (Ypsilanti, Mich.: Bilingual Press/Editorial Bilingüe, National Assocation of Chicano Studies, 1984); Alfredo Mirandé, *The Chicano Experience: An Alternative Perspective* (Notre Dame, Ind.: University of Notre Dame Press, 1985); Rodolfo O. de la Garza et al., eds., *The Mexican American Experience* (Austin, Tex.: University of Texas Press, 1985); and Renate von Bardeleben, Dietrich Briesemeister, and Juan Bruce-Novoa, eds., *Missions in Conflict: Essays on US-Mexican Relations and Chicano Culture* (Tübingen: Gunter Verlag, 1986).

2. See Andrew D. Cohen and Anthony F. Beltramo, eds., *El Lenguaje de los Chicanos: Regional and Social Characteristics Used by Mexican-Americans* (Arlington, Va.: Center for Applied Linguistics, 1975); also Dogoberto Fuentes and José A. López, *Barrio Language Dictionary: First Dictionary of Caló* (Los Angeles, Calif.: Southland Press, 1974).

3. Américo Paredes, *"With His Pistol in His Hand": A Border Ballad and Its Hero* (Austin, Tex.: University of Texas Press, 1979).

4. A persuasive interpretation of these events is found in Mauricio Mazón, *The Zoot-Suit Riots: The Psychology of Symbolic Annihilation* (Austin, Tex.: University of Texas Press, 1984).

5. For the implications of this nomenclature, see Alfred Yankauer, "Hispanic/

Latino—What's in a Name?" and David E. Hayes-Bautista and Jorge Chapa, "Latino Terminology: Conceptual Bases for Standardized Terminology," both in *American Journal of Public Health* 77, no. 1 (1987): 61–68. I am grateful to Dr. Arthur Campa of the School of Education, University of Colorado at Boulder, for directing me to these references.

6. A symptomatic publication would be Freddie and Ninfa García, *Outcry in the Barrio* (San Antonio, Tex.: Freddie García Ministries, 1988).

7. Perhaps the most provocative history remains Acuña, *Occupied America*.

8. For bearings on this achievement, see Joseph Sommers and Tomás Ybarra-Frausto, *Modern Chicano Writers: A Collection of Critical Essays* (Englewood Cliffs, N.J.: Prentice-Hall, 1979); Juan Bruce-Novoa, *Chicano Authors: Inquiry by Interview* (Austin, Tex.: University of Texas Press, 1980); Juan Bruce-Novoa, *Chicano Authors: A Response to Chaos* (Austin, Tex.: University of Texas Press, 1982); Salvador Rodríguez del Pino, *La Novela Chicana Escrita en Español: Cinco Autores Comprometidos* (Ypsilanti, Mich.: Bilingual Press/Editorial Bilingüe, National Association of Chicano Studies, 1982); Charles M. Tatum, *Chicano Literature* (Boston: Twayne, 1982); Robert G. Trujillo and Andrés Rodríguez, *Literatura Chicana: Creative and Critical Writings through 1984* (Oakland, Calif.: Floricanto Press, 1985); Luis Leal et al., eds., *A Decade of Chicano Literature, 1970–1979: Critical Essays and Bibliography* (Santa Barbara, Calif.: Editorial La Causa, 1982); Houston Baker, ed., *Three American Literatures: Essays in Chicano, Native American, and Asian-American Literatures for Teachers of American Literature* (New York: Modern Language Association, 1982); Luis Leal, *Aztlán y México: Perfiles Literarios e Históricos* (Binghamton, N.Y.: Bilingual Press/Editorial Bilingüe, National Association of Chicano Studies, 1985); Marta Ester Sánchez, *Contemporary Chicana Poetry* (Berkeley, Calif., University of California Press, 1985); María Herrera-Sobek, ed., *Beyond Stereotypes: The Critical Analysis of Chicana Literature* (Binghamton, N.Y.: Bilingual Press/Editorial Bilingüe, 1985); Julio A. Martínez and Francisco A. Lomelí, eds., *Chicano Literature: A Reference Guide* (Westport, Conn.: Greenwood Press, 1986); Cordelia Candelaria, *Chicano Poetry: A Critical Introduction* (Westport, Conn.: Greenwood Press, 1985); Vernon E. Lattin, ed., *Contemporary Chicano Fiction: A Critical Survey* (Binghamton, N.Y.: Bilingual Press/Editorial Bilingüe, 1986); Carl R. Shirley and Paula W. Shirley, *Understanding Chicano Literature* (Columbia, S.C.: University of South Carolina Press, 1988); Francisco A. Lomelí and Carl R. Shirley, eds., *Chicano Writers First Series, Dictionary of Literary Biography*, vol. 82 (Detroit, Mich.: Bruccoli Clark Layman, 1989); Asunción Horno-Delgado et al., eds., *Breaking Boundaries: Latina Writing and Critical Readings* (Amherst, Mass.: University of Massachusetts Press, 1989); Ramón Saldívar, *Chicano Narrative: The Dialectics of Difference* (Madison, Wis.: University of Wisconsin Press, 1990); and Héctor Calderón and José David Saldívar, eds., *Criticism in the Borderlands: Studies in Chicano Literature, Culture, and Ideology* (Durham: Duke University Press, 1991).

9. José Antonio Villarreal, *Pocho* (New York: Doubleday, 1959).

10. Tomás Rivera: *". . . Y no se lo tragó la tierra"/And the Earth Did Not Part* (Berkeley, Calif.: Quinto Sol Publications, 1971).

11. Raymond Barrio, *The Plum Plum Pickers* (Sunnyvale, Calif.: Ventura Press, 1969; rpr., with introduction and bibliography, Binghamton, N.Y.: Bilingual Press/Editorial Bilingüe, 1984).

12. Miguel Méndez, *Peregrinos de Aztlán* (Tucson, Ariz.: Editorial Peregrinos, 1974).

13. Alejandro Morales, *Caras viejas y vino nuevo* (México: J. Mortiz, 1975).

14. Rolando Hinojosa, *Klail City y sus alrededores* (La Habana: Casa de las Américas, 1976); *Generaciones y semblazas*, trans. Rosaura Sánchez (Berkeley, Calif.: Justa Publications, 1978). Author's English version: *Klail City* (Houston, Tex.: Arte Público Press, 1987).

15. Daniel Cano, *Pepe Rios* (Houston, Tex.: Arte Público Press, 1991).

16. Arturo Islas, *The Rain God* (New York: Avon Books, 1984, 1991).

17. Isabella Ríos, *Victuum* (Ventura, Calif.: Diana-Etna, 1976).

18. Ana Castillo, *The Mixquiahuala Letters* (Binghamton, N.Y.: Bilingual Press/ Editorial Bilingüe, 1986).

19. Ana Castillo, *Sapogonia* (Houston, Tex.: Bilingual Press/Editorial Bilingüe, 1990) and *So Far From God* (New York: W. W. Norton, 1993).

20. Cherrié Moraga et al., eds., *Cuentos: Stories by Latinas* (New York: Kitchen Table/Women of Color Press, 1983); Cherrié Moraga and Gloria Anzaldúa, eds., *This Bridge Called My Back: Writings by Radical Women of Color* (Watertown, Mass.: Persephone Press, 1981); Cherrié Moraga, *Loving in the War Years: lo que nunca pasó por los labios* (Boston: South End Press, 1983); Cherrié Moraga, *The Last Generation* (Boston: South End Press, 1993).

21. John Nichols, *The Milagro Beanfield War* (New York: Holt, Rinehart, 1974). The rest of the trilogy comprises *The Magic Journey* (New York: Holt, Rinehart, 1978) and *The Nirvana Blues* (New York: Holt, Rinehart, 1981).

22. Oscar Zeta Acosta, *The Autobiography of a Brown Buffalo* (San Francisco: Straight Arrow, 1972) and *The Revolt of the Cockroach People* (San Francisco: Straight Arrow, 1973); Richard Rodriguez, *Hunger of Memory* (Boston: Godine, 1981) and *Days of Obligation: An Argument with My Mexican Father* (New York: Viking Penguin, 1992); Linda Chavez: *Out of the Barrio* (New York: Basic Books, 1991); and Ray Gonzalez, *Memory Fever* (Seattle, Wash.: Broken Moon Press, 1993).

23. Frances A. Yates, *The Art of Memory* (Chicago: University of Chicago Press, 1966). Some of these implications of "memory" I have explored elsewhere. See A. Robert Lee, "*The Mill on the Floss:* 'Memory' and the Reading Experience," in Ian Gregor, ed., *Reading the Victorian Novel: Detail into Form* (London: Vision Press, 1980).

24. Rudolfo Anaya, *Bless Me, Ultima* (Berkeley, Calif.: Quinto Sol Publications, 1972).

25. Rudolfo Anaya, *Heart of Aztlán* (Berkeley, Calif.: Editorial Justa Publications, 1976); *Tortuga* (Berkeley, Calif.: Editorial Justa Publications, 1979); and *Alburquerque* (Albuquerque, N.M.: University of New Mexico Press, 1992).

26. Nash Candelaria, *Memories of the Alhambra; Not by the Sword* (Ypsilanti, Mich.: Bilingual Press/Editorial Bilingüe, 1982); and *Inheritance of Strangers* (Binghamton, N.Y.: Bilingual Press/Editorial Bilingüe, 1985).

27. Sandra Cisneros, *The House on Mango Street* (Houston: Arte Público, 1983; rev. ed., New York: Vintage Books, 1989); *Woman Hollering Creek and Other Stories.*

28. Ron Arias, *The Road to Tamazunchale* (Reno, Nev.: West Coast Poetry Review, 1975; rpr. Albuquerque: Pajarito Publications, 1978).

29. Carlos Fuentes, *Cambio de Piel* (México: Joaquín Mortiz, 1967).

Works Cited

Acosta, Oscar Zeta. *The Autobiography of a Brown Buffalo*. San Francisco: Straight Arrow, 1972.

———. *The Revolt of the Cockroach People*. San Francisco: Straight Arrow, 1973.

Acuña, Rodolfo. *Occupied America: The Chicano's Struggle Towards Liberation*. San Francisco: Canfield Press, 1972.

Anaya, Rudolfo A. *Alburquerque*. Albuquerque, N.M.: University of New Mexico Press, 1992.

———. *Bless Me, Ultima*. Berkeley, Calif.: Quinto Sol Publications, 1972.

———. *A Chicano in China*. Albuquerque, N.M.: University of New Mexico Press, 1986.

———. *Heart of Aztlán*. Berkeley, Calif.: Editorial Justa Publications, 1976.

———. *Tortuga*. Berkeley, Calif.: Editorial Justa Publications, 1979.

Arias, Ron. *The Road to Tamazunchale*. Reno, Nev.: West Coast Poetry Review, 1975. Reprint, Albuquerque, N.M.: Pajarito Publications, 1978.

Baker, Houston, ed. *Three American Literatures: Essays in Chicano, Native American, and Asian-American Literatures for Teachers of American Literature*. New York: Modern Language Association, 1982.

Barrio, Raymond. *The Plum Plum Pickers*. Sunnyvale, Calif.: Ventura Press, 1969. Reprint, with introduction and bibliography, Binghamton, N.Y.: Bilingual Press/Editorial Bilingüe, 1984.

Bruce-Novoa, Juan. *Chicano Authors: Inquiry by Interview*. Austin, Tex.: University of Texas Press, 1980.

———. *Chicano Authors: A Response to Chaos*. Austin, Tex.: University of Texas Press, 1982.

Calderón, Héctor, and José David Saldívar, eds. *Criticism in the Borderlands: Studies in Chicano Literature, Culture, and Ideology*. Durham: Duke University Press, 1991.

Candelaria, Cordelia. *Chicano Poetry: A Critical Introduction*. Westport, Conn.: Greenwood Press, 1985.

Candelaria, Nash. *Inheritance of Strangers*. Binghamton, N.Y.: Bilingual Press/Editorial Bilingüe, 1985.

———. *Memories of the Alhambra*. Palo Alto, Calif.: Cibola Press, 1977. Reprint, Ypsilanti, Mich.: Bilingual Press/Editorial Bilingüe, 1977.

Cano, Daniel. *Pepe Rios*. Houston, Tex.: Arte Público Press, 1991.

Castillo, Ana. *The Mixquiahuala Letters*. Binghamton, N.Y.: Bilingual Press/Editorial Bilingüe, 1986.

———. *Sapogonia*. Houston, Tex.: Bilingual Press/Editorial Bilingüe, 1990.

———. *So Far From God*. New York: W. W. Norton, 1993.

Chavez, Linda. *Out of the Barrio*. New York: Basic Books, 1991.

Cisneros, Sandra. *The House on Mango Street*. Houston, Tex.: Arte Público, 1983. Revised edition, New York: Vintage Books, 1989.

———. *Woman Hollering Creek and Other Stories*. New York: Random House, 1991.

Cohen, Andrew D., and Anthony F. Beltramo, eds. *El Lenguaje de los Chicanos:*

Regional and Social Characteristics Used by Mexican-Americans. Arlington, Va.: Center for Applied Linguistics, 1975.

de la Garza, Rodolfo O., et al., eds. *The Mexican American Experience.* Austin, Tex.: University of Texas Press, 1985.

Fuentes, Carlos. *Cambio de Piel.* México: Joaquín Mortiz, 1967.

Fuentes, Dogoberto, and José A. López. *Barrio Language Dictionary: First Dictionary of Caló.* Los Angeles, Calif.: Southland Press, 1974.

García, Freddie, and Nina García. *Outcry in the Barrio.* San Antonio, Tex.: Freddie García Ministries, 1988.

García, Marcia T., et al., eds. *History, Culture, and Society: Chicano Studies in the 1980s.* Ypsilanti, Mich.: Bilingual Press/Editorial Bilingüe, National Association of Chicano Studies, 1984.

Gonzalez, Ray. *Memory Fever.* Seattle, Wash.: Broken Moon Press, 1993.

Griswold de Castillo, Richard. *The Los Angeles Barrio, 1850–1890: A Social History.* Berkeley: University of California Press, 1979.

Hayes-Bautista, and Jorge Chapa. "Latino Terminology: Conceptual Bases for Standardized Terminology." *American Journal of Public Health* 77, no. 1 (1987): 61–68.

Herrera-Sobek, María, ed. *Beyond Stereotypes: The Critical Analysis of Chicana Literature.* Binghamton, N.Y.: Bilingual Press/Editorial Bilingüe, 1985.

Hinojosa, Rolando. *Generaciones y semblazas.* Translated by Rosaura Sánchez. Berkeley, Calif.: Justa Publications, 1978.

———. *Klail City y sus alrededores.* La Habana: Casa de las Américas, 1976. Translated by Rolando Hinojosa as *Klail City.* Houston, Tex.: Arte Público Press, 1987.

Horno-Delgado, Asunción, et al., eds. *Breaking Boundaries: Latina Writing and Critical Readings.* Amherst, Mass.: University of Massachusetts Press, 1989.

Islas, Arturo. *The Rain God.* New York: Avon Books, 1984, 1991.

Lattin, Vernon E., ed. *Contemporary Chicano Fiction: A Critical Survey.* Binghamton, N.Y.: Bilingual Press/Editorial Bilingüe, 1986.

Leal, Luis. *Aztlán y México: Perfiles Literarios e Históricos.* Binghamton, N.Y.: Bilingual Press/Editorial Bilingüe, National Association of Chicano Studies, 1985.

Leal, Luis, et al, eds. *A Decade of Chicano Literature, 1970–1979: Critical Essays and Bibliography.* Santa Barbara, Calif.: Editorial La Causa, 1982.

Lee, A. Robert. "*The Mill on the Floss:* 'Memory' and the Reading Experience." In *Reading the Victorian Novel: Detail into Form,* edited by Ian Gregor. London: Vision Press, 1980.

Lomelí, Francisco A., and Carl R. Shirley, eds. *Chicano Writers, First Series,* vol. 82. Detroit, Mich.: Bruccoli Clark Layman, 1989.

Martínez, Julio A., and Francisco A. Lomelí, eds. *Chicano Literature: A Reference Guide.* Westport, Conn.: Greenwood Press, 1986.

Mazón, Mauricio. *The Zoot-Suit Riots: The Psychology of Symbolic Annihilation.* Austin, Tex.: University of Texas Press, 1984.

McWilliams, Carey. *North from Mexico: The Spanish-Speaking People of the United States.* New York: Greenwood Press, 1948.

Meier, Matt S., and Feliciano Rivera. *The Chicanos: A History of Mexican-Americans.* New York: Hill and Wang, 1972.

Mendez, Miguel. *Peregrinos de Aztlán*. Tucson, Ariz.: Editorial Peregrinos, 1974.

Mirandé, Alfredo. *The Chicano Experience: An Alternative Perspective*. Notre Dame, Ind.: University of Notre Dame Press, 1985.

Moraga, Cherríe. *The Last Generation*. Boston: South End Press, 1993.

————. *Loving in the War Years: lo que nunca pasó por los labios*. Boston: South End Press, 1983.

Moraga, Cherríe, and Gloria Anzaldúa, eds. *This Bridge Called My Back: Writings by Radical Women of Color*. Watertown, Mass.: Persephone Press, 1981.

Moraga, Cherríe, et al., eds. *Cuentos: Stories by Latinas*. New York: Kitchen Table Women of Color Press, 1983.

Morales, Alejandro. *Caras viejas y vino nuevo*. México: J. Mortiz, 1975.

Nichols, John. *The Magic Journey*. New York: Holt, Rinehart, 1978.

————. *The Milagro Beanfield War*. New York: Holt, Rinehart, 1974.

————. *The Nirvana Blues*. New York: Holt, Rinehart, 1981.

Paredes, Américo. *"With His Pistol in His Hand": A Border Ballad and Its Hero*. Austin, Tex.: University of Texas Press, 1979.

Ríos, Isabella. *Victuum*. Ventura, Calif.: Diana-Etna, 1976.

Rivera, Tómas. *". . . Y no se lo tragó la tierra"/And the Earth Did Not Part*. Berkeley, Calif.: Quinto Sol Publications, 1971.

Rodriguez, Richard. *Days of Obligation: An Argument with My Mexican Father*. New York: Viking Penguin, 1992.

————. *Hunger of Memory*. Boston: Godine, 1981.

Rodríguez del Pino, Salvador. *La Novela Chicana Escrita en Español: Cinco Autores Comprometidos*. Ypsilanti, Mich.: Bilingual Press/Editorial Bilingüe, National Association of Chicano Studies, 1982.

Saldívar, Ramón. *Chicano Narrative: The Dialectics of Difference*. Madison, Wis.: University of Wisconsin Press, 1990.

Sánchez, George I. *Forgotten People: A Study of New Mexicans*. Albuquerque, N.M.: C. Horn, 1940.

Sánchez, Marta Ester. *Contemporary Chicana Poetry*. Berkeley, Calif.: University of California Press, 1985.

Shirley, Carl R., and Paula W. Shirley. *Understanding Chicano Literature*. Columbia, S.C.: University of South Carolina Press, 1988.

Sommers, Joseph, and Tomás Ybarra-Frausto. *Modern Chicano Writers: A Collection of Critical Essays*. Englewood Cliffs, N.J.: Prentice-Hall, 1979.

Tatum, Charles M. *Chicano Literature*. Boston: Twayne, 1982.

Trujillo, Robert G., and Andrés Rodriguez. *Literature Chicana: Creative and Critical Writings through 1984*. Oakland, Calif.: Floricanto Press, 1985.

Villarreal, José Antonio. *Pocho*. New York: Doubleday, 1959.

von Bardeleben, Renate, Dietrich Briesemeister, and Juan Bruce-Novoa, eds. *Missions in Conflict: Essays on US-Mexican Relations and Chicano Culture*. Tübingen: Gunter Narr Verlag, 1986.

Yankauer, Alfred. *"Hispanic/Latino—What's in a Name?" American Journal of Public Health 77*, no. 1 (1987): 15–17.

Yates, Frances A. *The Art of Memory*. Chicago: University of Chicago Press, 1966.

Select Bibliography

This list supplements entries in *Memory, Narrative, and Identity* (1994) and in the works cited following individual essays in this volume.

Ahmad, Aijaz. *In Theory: Classes, Nations, Literatures.* London: Verso, 1992.

Almaguer, Tomás. *Racial Fault Lines: The Historical Origins of White Supremacy in California.* Berkeley: University of California Press, 1994.

Appiah, Kwame Anthony. *In My Father's House: Africa in the Philosophy of Culture.* New York: Oxford University Press, 1992.

Aronowitz, Stanley. *Dead Artists, Live Theories and Other Cultural Problems.* New York: Routledge, 1994.

Bell-Scott, Patricia, ed. *Double Stitch: Black Women Write about Mothers and Daughters.* Boston: Beacon Press, 1991.

Bhabha, Homi, ed. *Nation and Narration.* London: Routledge, 1990.

Bodnar, John E. *Remaking America: Public Memory, Commemoration and Patriotism in the Twentieth Century.* Princeton: Princeton University Press, 1992.

Bremer, Sidney H. *Urban Intersections: Meetings of Life and Literature in the United States.* Urbana: University of Illinois Press, 1992.

Bruce-Novoa. *RetroSpace: Collected Essays on Chicano Literature, Theory, and History.* Houston: Arte Público Press, 1990.

Burch, Betty Ann. *The Assimilation Experience of Five American White Ethnic Novelists in the Twentieth Century.* New York: Garland, 1990.

Calderon, Hector, and Jose David Saldívar, eds. *Criticism in the Borderlands: Studies in Chicano Literature, Culture and Ideology.* Durham: Duke University Press, 1991.

Carby, Hazel. *Reconstructing Womanhood: The Emergence of the Afro-American Woman Novelist.* New York: Oxford University Press, 1987.

Casey, F. S. *Remembering: A Phenomenological Study.* Bloomington: Indiana University Press, 1987.

Clifford, James, and George E. Marcus, eds. *Writing Culture.* Berkeley: University of California Press, 1986.

Dathorne, O. R. *In Europe's Image: The Need for American Multiculturalism.* Westport, Conn.: Bergin & Garvey, 1994.

Davis, Charles T. *Black Is the Color of the Cosmos: Essays on Black Literature and Culture, 1942–1981.* New York: Garland, 1982.

Fabre, Geneviève, and Robert O'Meally, eds. *History and Memory in African American Culture.* New York: Oxford University Press, 1994.

Fischer, Michael M. J. "Ethnicity and the Post-Modern Arts of Memory." In *Writing Culture: The Poetics and Politics of Ethnography,* edited by James Clifford and George E. Marcus, 194–233. Berkeley: University of California Press, 1986.

Florescano, Enrico. *Memory, Myth, and Time in Mexico: From the Aztecs to Independence.* Translated by Albert G. Bork with the assistance of Kathryn R. Bork. Austin: University of Texas Press, 1994.

Friedlander, Saul, Geulie Arad, and Dan Diner, eds. *History and Memory: Studies in Representation of the Past.* Bloomington: Indiana University Press, 1994.

Gates, Henry Louis, Jr. "Critical Fanonism." *Critical Inquiry* 17 (1992): 457–70.

Gattuso, John. "Seeing, Knowing, Remembering." In *A Circle of Nations: Voices and Visions of American Indians/North American Native Writers and Photographers.* Hillsboro, Ore.: Beyond Words Publications, 1993.

Grossberg, Lawrence, and Cary Nelson, eds. *Marxism and the Interpretation of Culture.* Urbana: University of Illinois Press, 1988.

Halbwachs, Maurice. *The Collective Memory.* 1950. Reprint, New York: Harper & Row, 1980.

Hedges, Elaine, and Shelley Fisher Fishkin. *Listening to Silences: New Essays in Feminist Criticism.* New York: Oxford University Press, 1994.

Hord, Fred L. *Reconstructing Memory: Black Literary Criticism.* Chicago: Third World Press, 1991.

Hutcheon, Linda. "Colonialism and the Postcolonial Condition: Complexities Abounding." *PMLA* 110, no. 1 (January 1995): 7–16.

Jeffrey, Jaclyn, and Glenace Edwall, eds. *Memory and History.* Lanham: University Press of America, 1994.

Kruger, Barbara, and Phil Mariani, eds. *Remaking History.* Seattle: Bay, 1989.

Krupat, Arnold. *Ethnocriticism: Ethnography, History, Literature.* Berkeley: University of California Press, 1992.

LaCapra, Dominick. *History, Politics and the Novel.* Ithaca, N.Y.: Cornell University Press, 1987.

Lee, A. Robert. "Acts of Remembrance: America as Multicultural Past in Ralph Ellison, Nicholasa Mohr, James Welch and Monica Sone." In *Multiculturalism and the Canon of American Culture,* edited by Hans Bak, 81–103. Amsterdam: VU University Press, 1993.

Marchetti, Gina. *Romance and the "Yellow Peril": Race, Sex and Discursive Strategies in Hollywood Fiction.* Berkeley: University of California Press, 1993.

Marotti, Arthur F., et al., eds. *Reading with a Difference: Gender, Race and Cultural Identity.* Detroit: Wayne State University Press, 1993.

Marshall, Brenda. "Resisting Closure and Toni Morrison's *Beloved.*" In *Teaching the Postmodern: Fiction and Theory.* New York: Routledge, 1992.

Mead, Margaret. "We Are All Third Generation." In *And Keep Your Powder Dry: An Anthropologist Looks at America,* 27–53. New York: Morrow, 1942.

Michaels, Walter Benn. "Race into Culture: A Critical Genealogy of Cultural Identity." *Critical Inquiry* 18 (1992): 655–85.

Mohanty, Chandra Tolpade, Ann Russo, and Lourdes Torres, eds. *Third World Women and the Politics of Feminism.* Bloomington: Indiana University Press, 1991.

Select Bibliography

Mohanty, Satya. "The Epistemic Status of Cultural Identity: On *Beloved* and the Postcolonial Condition." *Cultural Critique* 24 (1993): 41–80.

Morrison, Toni. "The Site of Memory." In *Inventing the Truth: The Art and Craft of Memoir*, edited by William Zinsser, 102–24. Boston: Houghton Mifflin, 1987.

Nelson, Cary. *Repression and Recovery: Modern American Poetry and the Politics of Cultural Memory, 1910–1945*. Madison: University of Wisconsin Press, 1989.

Nora, Pierre. *Les Lieux de mémoire: La République*. Paris: Gallimard, 1984.

North, Michael. *The Dialect of Modernism: Race, Language, and Twentieth-Century American Literature*. New York: Oxford University Press, 1994.

Olney, James, ed. *Studies in Autobiography*. New York: Oxford University Press, 1988.

Otis, Laura. *Organic Memory: History and the Body in the Late Nineteenth and Early Twentieth Centuries*. Lincoln: University of Nebraska Press, 1994.

Pacernick, Gary. *Memory and Fire: Ten American Jewish Poets*. New York: Peter Lang, 1989.

Padilla, Genaro. *My History, Not Yours: The Formation of Mexican American Autobiography*. Madison: University of Wisconsin Press, 1993.

Painter, Nell. "Of Lily, Linda Brent and Freud: A Non-Exceptionalist Approach to Race, Class and Gender in the Slave South." *Georgia Historical Quarterly* 76 (Summer 1992): 241–59.

Pearlman, Mickey, ed. *American Women Writing Fiction: Memory, Identity, Family, Space*. Lexington: University Press of Kentucky, 1989.

Powell, Richard, ed. *The Blues Aesthetic: Black Culture and Modernism*. Washington, D.C.: Washington Project for the Arts, 1989.

Rich, Adrienne. "Resisting Amnesia: History and Personal Life." In *Blood, Bread, and Poetry*. New York: W. W. Norton, 1986.

Ross, Bruce M. *Remembering the Personal Past: Descriptions of Autobiographical Memory*. New York: Oxford University Press, 1991.

Rubenstein, Roberta. *Boundaries of the Self: Gender, Culture, Fiction*. Urbana: University of Illinois Press, 1987.

Ruoff, LaVonne Brown, and Jerry W. Ward, Jr. *Redefining American Literary History*. New York: Modern Language Association of America, 1990.

Said, Edward. *Culture and Imperialism*. New York: Knopf, 1993.

Schafer, R. *Narrative Actions in Psychoanalysis*. Worcester: Clark University Press, 1981.

Sellers, Susan, ed. "History, Memory and Language in Toni Morrison's *Beloved*." In *Feminist Criticism: Theory and Practice*. Toronto: University of Toronto Press, 1991.

Sollors, Werner, ed. *The Invention of Ethnicity*. New York: Oxford University Press, 1989.

Spivak, Gayatri Chakravorty. *In Other Worlds: Essays in Cultural Politics*. New York: Methuen, 1987.

Staub, Michael E. *Voices of Persuasion: Politics of Representation in 1930s America*. New York: Cambridge University Press, 1994.

Swann, Brian, and Arnold Krupat, eds. *I Tell You Now: Autobiographical Essays by Native American Writers*. Lincoln: University of Nebraska Press, 1987.

Tomlinson, John. *Cultural Imperialism: A Critical Introduction.* Baltimore: Johns Hopkins University Press, 1991.

Trinh, T. Minh-ha. *Woman, Native, Other: Writing Postcoloniality and Feminism.* Bloomington: Indiana University Press, 1989.

Urgo, Joseph R. *Novel Frames: Literature as a Guide to Race, Sex and History in American Culture.* Jackson: University Press of Mississippi, 1991.

Wall, Cheryl A., ed. *Changing Our Own Words: Essays on Criticism, Theory, and Writing by Black Women.* New Brunswick: Rutgers University Press, 1990.

Washington, Mary Helen, ed. *Invented Lives: Narratives of Black Women, 1860–1960.* Garden City, N.Y.: Anchor, 1987.

Wong, Hertha D. *Sending My Heart Back Across the Years: Tradition and Innovation in Native American Autobiography.* New York: Oxford University Press, 1992.

Young, Mary E. *Mules and Dragons: Popular Culture Images in the Selected Writings of African-American and Chinese-American Women Writers.* Westport, Conn.: Greenwood, 1993.

Zandy, Janet, ed. *Liberating Memory: Our Work and Our Working-Class Consciousness.* New Brunswick: Rutgers University Press, 1994.

Editors and Contributors

Robert E. Hogan is Professor of English and Chair of the Department of English at Rhode Island College. He has published articles on Herman Melville, Edward Bellamy, and John Updike in journals such as *Studies in American Fiction* and *Ball State University Forum*.

Amritjit Singh, Professor of English at Rhode Island College, is currently at work on an intellectual biography of Richard Wright's final phase, for which he has received fellowships from ACLS, NEH, the Rockefeller Foundation, and the W. E. B. Du Bois Institute for Afro-American Research at Harvard University. Books written and edited by him include *The Novels of the Harlem Renaissance* (1976), *India: An Anthology of Contemporary Writing* (1983), *The Magic Circle of Henry James* (1989), *The Harlem Renaissance: Revaluations* (1989), and *American Studies Today* (1995). He was recently involved in preparing two reprint editions of Richard Wright's books: *The Color Curtain* with an afterword, and *Black Power* with a new introduction.

Joseph T. Skerrett, Jr., Professor of English at the University of Massachusetts, Amherst, has written extensively on African American writers, including James Weldon Johnson, Richard Wright, Toni Morrison, and Paule Marshall for journals such as *Callaloo, American Quarterly*, and *Twentieth-Century Literature*. Skerrett is the editor of *MELUS*, the journal of the Society for the Study of the Multi-Ethnic Literature of the United States.

Victoria Aarons, Professor of English at Trinity University, has published extensively in the area of Jewish American writers, particularly the works of Grace Paley and other contemporary Jewish American women writers. She is currently completing a book manuscript, *A Measure of Memory: Storytelling and Identity in American Jewish Fiction*, forthcoming from the University of Georgia Press.

Herman Beavers, Assistant Professor of English at the University of Pennsylvania, is the author of a chapbook of poems entitled *A Neighborhood of*

Feeling (1986). He has also completed *Wrestling Angels into Song: The Fictions of Ernest J. Gaines and James Alan McPherson,* to be published by the University of Pennsylvania Press. His current research focuses on the construction of African American masculinity in literature and popular culture.

William Boelhower, Associate Professor of American Literature at the University of Trieste, Italy, is the author of *Immigrant Autobiography in the United States, Through a Glass Darkly: Ethnic Semiosis in American Literature,* and *Autobiographical Transactions in Modernist America.* He is the editor of *The Future of American Modernism: Ethnic Writing Between the Wars,* editor and translator of Lucien Goldmann, *Method in the Sociology of Literature,* and translator of Antonio Gramsci, *Selections from Cultural Writing.* Besides publishing essays on the work of Gramsci and Goldmann, he has also published on American literature and culture in such journals as *American Literary History, Journal of American Studies, Contemporary Literature, Early American Literature, Word & Image,* and *MELUS.*

Jennifer Browdy de Hernandez teaches in the English Department at Simon's Rock College of Bard, specializing in multicultural North American, Latin American, and Caribbean literature. Her essay on the politics of ethnic autobiography in Leslie Marmon Silko's *Storyteller* appeared recently in *a/b: Auto/Biography Studies* (Spring 1994), and an article on the postcolonial politics of Rigoberta Menchu's testimonial is forthcoming in the volume *Interventions: Gender, Ideology and Third World Feminisms,* edited by Bishnupriya Ghosh and Brinda Bose.

G. Thomas Couser is Professor of English and Co-chair of American Studies at Hofstra University. He is the author of *American Autobiography: The Prophetic Mode* (1979) and *Altered Egos: Authority in American Autobiography* (1989). With the support of an NEH grant, he is working on a book on illness, disability, and contemporary American life-writing.

Gurleen Grewal is Assistant Professor in Women's Studies at the University of South Florida. She is currently completing a book on Toni Morrison.

Yiorgos Kalogeras teaches American studies at Aristotle University Thessaloniki, Greece. His articles include a study of the immigration stories of Theano Papazoglou-Margaris in *Journal of Modern Greek Studies* (May 1990) and a study of magic realism and the carnivalesque in Greek-American narrative appearing in *International Fiction Review* (Winter 1989). He has also published in *MELUS* and *Ethnic Forum.*

346

Editors and Contributors

Toby C. S. Langen works for the Tulalip Tribes Snohomish Language Program at the Tulalip Reservation in western Washington. She is writing a book on the work of Tulalip storyteller Martha Lamont.

A. Robert Lee teaches American literature/studies at the University of Kent at Canterbury and in 1994 was a Visiting Professor of Ethnic Studies at the University of California at Berkeley. His publications include eleven volumes in the Vision Critical Series, *Black American Fiction Since Richard Wright* (1983), *A Permanent Etcetera: Cross-Cultural Perspectives on Post-War America* (1993), *Shadow Distance: a Gerald Vizenor Reader* (1994), and a wide range of essays on American multicultural writing.

Lisa Suhair Majaj is completing a dissertation entitled "Arab American Literature and the Politics of Identity" for the University of Michigan. She has taught courses on American ethnic literature and Arabic literature at Amherst and Holy Cross Colleges, and is currently co-editing with Paula Sunderman a collection of critical essays on contemporary Arab women's writing. A personal essay, "Boundaries, Borders, Horizons," appears in the collection *Food for our Grandmothers: Writings by Arab-American and Arab-Canadian Feminists*, published by South End Press. Her poetry and reviews have appeared in various journals and anthologies, including *The Worcester Review, Woman of Power, The Hungry Mind Review, Middle East Insight,* and *Unsettling America.*

David Palumbo-Liu is Associate Professor of Comparative Literature at Stanford University. He is editor of *The Ethnic Canon: History, Institutions, Interventions* (1995). He has published in the areas of cultural studies and ethnic literature in journals such as *Cultural Critique, differences,* and *Public Culture.* He is currently completing a book on Asian American cultural studies and the production of social subjectivities.

Sandra Pouchet Paquet is Associate Professor of English and Director of the Caribbean Writers Summer Institute at the University of Miami, where she teaches Caribbean literature and African American literature. She is the author of *The Novels of George Lamming* and numerous articles on Caribbean and African American literature. She is currently completing a book on Caribbean autobiography.

Rafael Pérez-Torres teaches Chicano studies at the University of California, Santa Barbara. His interests include theories of the postmodern and their intersection with postcolonial and multicultural literary production. His essays include "Nomads and Migrants—Negotiating a Multicultural Postmodernism" in *Cultural Critique* and "The Ambiguous Outlaw: John

Rechy and Complicitous Homotextuality" in *The Fiction of Masculinity: Crossing Cultures, Crossing Sexualities*. A book on contemporary Chicano poetry entitled *Movements in Chicano Poetry—Against Myths, Against Margins* is forthcoming from Cambridge University Press.

Sandra G. Shannon is Associate Professor of English at Howard University and a published August Wilson scholar. Her work on Wilson has appeared in the collections *May All Your Fences Have Gates: Essays on the Drama of August Wilson* (1994) and *August Wilson: A Casebook* (1994). She has also published material on Wilson in *African American Review, Callaloo, Obsidian II, Emerge,* and *MELUS.* She has just completed the forthcoming study *The Dramatic Vision of August Wilson* (Howard University Press), funded by a grant from the National Endowment for the Humanities.

Stan Yogi is a program officer with the California Council for the Humanities. He compiled, with King-Kok Cheung, *Asian American Literature: An Annotated Bibliography* (MLA, 1988). His articles and reviews have appeared in *Amerasia Journal, French Review of American Studies, MELUS, Reading the Literatures of Asian America,* and *Studies in American Fiction.*

Index

Index

Index

Index